Pre-Raphaelite

and Other Masters

THE ANDREW LLOYD WEBBER COLLECTION

Pre-Raphaelite
and Other Masters

THE ANDREW LLOYD WEBBER COLLECTION

ROYAL ACADEMY OF ARTS

First published on the occasion of the exhibition

Pre-Raphaelite and Other Masters

THE ANDREW LLOYD WEBBER COLLECTION

Royal Academy of Arts, London
20 September – 12 December 2003

in association with

CHRISTIE'S

Supported by UBS Wealth Management

The Royal Academy of Arts is grateful to Her Majesty's Government for agreeing to indemnify this exhibition under the National Heritage Act 1980, and to Resource, The Council for Museums, Archives and Libraries, for its help in arranging the indemnity.

EXHIBITION CURATORS

Norman Rosenthal
MaryAnne Stevens

EXHIBITION ORGANISATION

Emeline Max
Marjorie Shiers
Anne Starkey

PHOTOGRAPHIC AND COPYRIGHT CO-ORDINATION

Miranda Bennion
Roberta Stansfield

CATALOGUE

Royal Academy Publications
David Breuer
Harry Burden
Carola Krueger
Fiona McHardy
Peter Sawbridge
Nick Tite

Copy-editing: Michael Foster
Design: Philip Lewis
Colour origination: DawkinsColour

Printed in Italy by Graphicom

British Library Cataloguing-in-Publication Data

A catalogue record for this book is available from the British Library

ISBN 1-903973-40-6 (paperback)
ISBN 1-903973-39-2 (hardback)

Distributed outside the United States and Canada by Thames & Hudson Ltd, London

Distributed in the United States and Canada by Harry N. Abrams, Inc., New York

ACKNOWLEDGEMENTS

The Royal Academy would like to thank the following for their invaluable assistance during the preparation of this catalogue:

Naomi Allen
Martin Beisly
Judith Bronkhurst
John Christian
Sandra Coley
Mary Cowling
Alan Crawford
James Davidson
Colleen Denney
David Elliott
Sue Graves
John Hardy
Heather Haskins
Marilyn McCully
Maria Luisa Pacelli
Elizabeth Prettejohn
Robert Rosenblum
Jason Rosenfeld
Nicholas Savage
Douglas Schoenherr
Libby Sheldon
Peyton Skipwith
Alison Smith
Reena Suleman
Virginia Surtees
Malcolm Warner
Peter White
Andrew Wilton
Christopher Wood

THE ANDREW LLOYD WEBBER ART FOUNDATION

Four pictures in this exhibition are owned by the Andrew Lloyd Webber Art Foundation: Pablo Picasso's *Angel Fernández de Soto* (cat. 282), Giovanni Antonio Canaletto's *The Old Horse Guards, London, from St James's Park* (cat. 283), Stanley Spencer's *The Garage* (cat. 279) and John William Waterhouse's *St Cecilia* (cat. 95).

The Foundation is a charity funded by Andrew Lloyd Webber. Its remit is widely drawn to cover all areas of the arts, although its activities are currently restricted to the ownership of these four pictures. Two would otherwise have left Britain. The Picasso has been brought to this country from the USA. Andrew Lloyd Webber's other charitable activities, such as his sponsorship of the National Youth Music Theatre and the Open Churches Trust, have to date been funded by him outside the Foundation.

The Foundation regularly loans its pictures to appropriate galleries and exhibitions.

EDITORIAL NOTE

All works in the exhibition have been lent by Lord Lloyd-Webber, with the exception of the four that belong to the Andrew Lloyd Webber Art Foundation.

Measurements are given in centimetres, height before width before depth.

Illustration on page 2: detail of cat. 100.

Contents

Foreword

'I will not have Victorian junk in my flat.' Thus uttered my grandmother in response to my request to borrow £50 to buy Frederic, Lord Leighton's *Flaming June* from a Fulham Road shop in the early 1960s.

Her refusal was irritating. I had just bought a set of beautifully illustrated tomes by Dugdale about English monasteries entitled *Monasticon Anglicanum* with the proceeds of selling a best-forgotten tune to a music publisher, and the chances of repeating such a sale were slim. Granny had been tolerant about allowing the huge set of books into her flat but was emphatically not prepared to finance the purchase of a large, dirty and unframed canvas that a West London dealer had described to an art-obsessed schoolboy as the work of a former President of the Royal Academy.

Today *Flaming June* hangs in the Museo de Arte de Ponce in Puerto Rico, having been confirmed as the real thing by the great pioneer dealer in Victorian art Jeremy Maas. But much as I frequently still curse my grandmother for denying me the chance to buy a painting that is today billed as 'the *Mona Lisa* of the southern hemisphere', I can't really blame her. How could she have been expected to take *Flaming June* seriously? Born in 1898, she had seen the young men of her generation decimated in the First World War and had lived through another. Leighton's sensuous image must have seemed appallingly irrelevant to her.

Granny was something of a rebel, albeit with a strange cause. She claimed to be a founder of one of life's greater contradictions, the shortlived Christian Communist Party. To her, even more than to some of her contemporaries, Victorian art and architecture represented the apotheosis of a set of values she detested. Tractarian architecture was the world of bells, smells and mumbo jumbo. She was all for Dr Leslie Weatherhead and the free church. She idolised Viscount Stansgate, who was eventually to reinvent himself as Tony Benn. It must have been deeply distressing that her grandson should wax passionate about the artistic fruits of the Victorian era.

Most of her generation distrusted Victorian art, even going so far as to nickname Waterhouse's masterpiece *The Lady of Shalott* 'After the May Ball'. The consequence was that in my grandmother's lifetime his paintings could scarcely be given away. There is a famous story that a certain Alma-Tadema painting was found chucked in a builder's skip. Its owner had kept the frame, thinking it more valuable. In the early 1960s it seemed to me that only the 'sentimental schlocky musicals of Rodgers and Hammerstein' (as my school music-master described them) were considered by the politically correct tastemakers of the day to be of such dire artistic merit.

Needless to say, I loved both Rodgers and Hammerstein and Victoriana. Of course, I was partly egged on by the vehemence of my peers' abuse of my various *causes célèbres*, for in truth my interests in music, art and architecture were far broader. But youthful *causes célèbres* are passions that never truly leave you. As I began to have the good fortune to succeed in musical theatre, I inevitably wanted to form an art collection. The area of art that I knew something about was Victorian and, importantly for me, it was affordable. If I had wanted to spread my collector's wings wider it would have been difficult: in the early 1970s the Marlborough Gallery offered me Francis Bacon's *Van Gogh in a Landscape* for about fifteen times what a well-known colleague of mine had paid another West End dealer for a superb Waterhouse.

A few years ago I decided that I had almost 'done' the Victorians. My collecting today has taken me into fields as diverse as 20th-century American and Second World War Jewish art. These are for another exhibition, but I have been lucky enough recently to be able to add three wonderful Victorian pictures to the collection. My Victorian heart still beats.

It is a joy for me to be able to share the fruits of my years as a collector so far. But as Sir Nikolaus Pevsner said on finishing the final volume of his monumental series *The Buildings of England*, 'It is, dear reader, the second edition that counts.'

I hope that after my death my family will be able to find a way to exhibit the best of my collection on a more permanent basis. It is unlikely, however, that it will ever be seen in a setting as stunning as the lofty galleries of the Royal Academy.

Finally, I must thank my friend the wonderfully colourful art-dealer David Mason. Without him this exhibition would have been impossible.

ANDREW LLOYD WEBBER

President's Foreword

Rossetti and Burne-Jones; Leighton and Millais; Tissot and Atkinson Grimshaw; Dadd and Stanley Spencer; William Morris and William De Morgan; Canaletto and Picasso: such is the collection of paintings, works on paper, tapestries, carpets, furniture, books and ceramics that Andrew Lloyd Webber has assembled with commitment and determination over the past four decades.

He began at a time when regard for Victorian art and architecture was at its lowest. With a sure eye and a keen understanding, he has created one of the finest collections of its kind in private hands. Like any private collection, his does not purport to be comprehensive; instead it reflects specific enthusiasms, especially a fascination with scenes from contemporary life, and the persistence in British art of an engagement with 'dream-reality'. Although a small number of works have been lent to temporary exhibitions in the recent past, this presentation at the Royal Academy is the first public showing of the greater part of his collection.

Many of these works have associations with the Royal Academy. A significant number were created by Royal Academicians – from Sir Joshua Reynolds, our first President, to Stanley Spencer – and many have appeared in past Summer Exhibitions. Although the Academy was later to reflect the early 20th-century reticence towards Victorian art, it nevertheless celebrated all the major Victorian Royal Academicians with memorial exhibitions immediately after their deaths; Landseer (1874), Leighton (1897), Millais (1898), Poynter (1919) and Alma-Tadema (1913) were so honoured, as also was Rossetti (1883), despite his determination to avoid any engagement with the Academy during his lifetime. More recently, retrospective exhibitions of the work of Millais (1967), Rossetti (1973), Stanley Spencer (1980) and Leighton (1995) have been held here, and in 1999–2000 the Academy's holdings of Victorian painting and sculpture toured five American venues. Given this record, it is fitting that so many distinguished examples of Victorian art once again line the walls of our galleries.

We have many reasons to thank Andrew Lloyd Webber. At short notice, he kindly agreed to bring this exhibition forward in order to fill a gap that had suddenly and unavoidably appeared in the Academy's programme. Equally importantly, he has accepted with great equanimity the upheaval that the exhibition has caused and the denuding of the walls of his homes for four months. We are enormously grateful to Andrew Lloyd Webber and to his wife, Madeleine, for their understanding and forbearance.

Andrew Lloyd Webber's involvement in the planning of the exhibition has been consistent throughout. He has assisted two members of the Royal Academy's staff, Norman Rosenthal and MaryAnne Stevens, in the selection of the exhibits, and contributed to the presentation, guided by the exhibition designer Ivor Heal. Invaluable advice has been generously given by the Victorian art specialist John Christian and, for the decorative arts, by Peter Cormack, acting keeper of the William Morris Art Gallery in Walthamstow. David Mason of MacConnal-Mason Fine Paintings has been a great support, from initial exploratory discussions about the possibility of presenting the exhibition to the detailed planning stages. Despite the need to produce a catalogue in a very short period of time, we have been wonderfully served by the knowledge and enthusiasm of a team of leading British and American scholars whom we thank most warmly.

On the organisational front, Andrew Lloyd Webber's staff, in particular Jonathan Webster, Sarah Miller and Jan Eade, together with Hamish Dewar, have been unstinting in their efficiency. Their collaboration with an organisational team from the Royal Academy, expertly led by Emeline Max and Anne Starkey, has ensured the safe and smooth realisation of the exhibition. We extend our gratitude to them all.

No exhibition can be undertaken without the support of sponsors. Christie's has most generously given support in kind for the major photographic project necessary to create the exhibition catalogue. UBS Wealth Management have given additional sponsorship, and we thank them in particular for their support of the opening week.

This exhibition is a manifestation of one collector's commitment to the quality and rich variety of 19th- and early 20th-century British art. Andrew Lloyd Webber stands within the tradition of those who kept faith with a group of artists who had been sidelined by the followers of Modernism. We hope that our visitors will enjoy and learn from this rich array of works that he and his wife have so generously permitted the Academy to present to the public.

PROFESSOR PHILLIP KING CBE PRA

Realists and Romantics, Storytellers and Symbolists: Changing Attitudes towards Victorian Art

RICHARD DORMENT

INDIFFERENCE OVERCOME: THE RISE OF
VICTORIAN ART CONNOISSEURSHIP

Seventy years ago, to mark the centenary of the birth in June 1833 of Edward Burne-Jones (cat. 30–62, 176, 191), the Tate Gallery mounted an exhibition devoted to his art. At the private view, Burne-Jones's nephew Stanley Baldwin made a short speech, and the novelist Angela Thirkell, a granddaughter, served tea to selected guests in the refreshment room. To the collector W. Graham Robertson, who had known the artist well, the scene was 'rather sad – a little crowd of forlorn old survivals paying their last homage to the beauty and poetry now utterly scorned and rejected'.[1] For a superannuated Victorian aesthete like Robertson, the art of his revered Burne-Jones had no place in a gallery hung with the excesses of Walter Sickert and Stanley Spencer. For the 1933 exhibition marked not the beginning of a Burne-Jones revival, but the nadir of his critical reputation.

If the high noon of Victorian art lasted roughly from the 1850s to the 1890s, we can date its sunset precisely – to 1895, when the trial of Oscar Wilde cut short the late flowering of British romantic painting. In the wake of Wilde's imprisonment, a whole generation of aesthetes and Symbolist and Decadent artists sought the more tolerant atmospheres of Dieppe, Menton, Paris and Venice. For one reason or another Sickert, Aubrey Beardsley, Charles Conder, Alfred Gilbert and James McNeill Whistler all lived abroad. Their exodus, followed by Beardsley's death in 1898, left a vacuum to be filled by beer-drinking, bicycle-riding members of the New English Art Club, and later by the Camden Town Group, Bloomsbury and the Euston Road School, who all looked for stylistic inspiration not to the visual traditions of their own country but to France. The triumph of Post-Impressionism all but snuffed out the long line of Symbolist art that had passed from William Blake (1757–1827) and Dante Gabriel Rossetti (cat. 1–18) to

Burne-Jones and Beardsley. For a time, the British tradition of the poet–painter ceased to exist. Those qualities were lost that make British art British in the first place: a proud insularity; an ecstatic, visionary love for Britain's history and landscape; the intermingling of art, literature and narration; and a profound Symbolist orientation.

As with painting, so with design and architecture. As early as 1911 H. G. Wells could write: 'Will anyone consent to live in the houses the Victorians built . . . value the furnishings they made . . . or esteem . . . their art?'[2] Then came the catastrophe of the First World War. In its aftermath, modern young men and women rejected cultural values they associated with their parents' generation. Exhilarated by their discovery of Cézanne, Picasso and Matisse, the Bloomsbury circle of painters and writers could not understand what their parents had seen in the pictures of William Powell Frith (cat. 155), William Holman Hunt (cat. 64, 67, 70, 103, 108, 109), Frederic Leighton (cat. 138, 141, 150) and Lawrence Alma-Tadema (cat. 143–5). And Bloomsbury was not the only, nor even the most deadly, enemy of Pre-Raphaelite and other Victorian art. In the first decades of the century a gentle pall of Georgian good taste settled over British art and literature. Admirers of Ambrose McEvoy, William Nicholson, Glyn Philpot and Rex Whistler turned aside from the brutal intensity of Rossetti's *Found* (fig. 1) and the *horror vacuii* of Holman Hunt's *Lady of Shalott* (fig. 2). Paintings that had been worth a fortune in the 1880s were relegated to attics, salerooms, junk shops and museum storerooms.

The indifference shown by British museums and galleries towards Victorian art for most of the 20th century can hardly be exaggerated. A glance at the National Art Collections Fund's list of acquisitions from 1928 to 1956 reveals that only a handful of paintings – two by G. F. Watts, one each by Burne-Jones, William Etty and Edwin Landseer – were acquired for the nation during those three decades.[3] The first exhibition devoted

Fig. 1 **Dante Gabriel Rossetti**, *Found*, 1854 (unfinished). Oil on canvas, 91.4 × 80 cm. Delaware Art Museum: Samuel and Mary R. Bancroft Memorial, 1935

Fig. 2 **William Holman Hunt OM**, *The Lady of Shalott*, c. 1886–1905. Oil on canvas, 44.4 × 34.1 cm. Manchester City Art Gallery

to a major Victorian painter after the Second World War was the pioneering Landseer exhibition at the Royal Academy, organised by John Woodward, a champion of early Victorian painters, and Derek Hill in 1961. But this was a one-off. By 1960 the art of Watts and Leighton had disappeared almost entirely from the Tate Gallery. Later in the decade, during Lawrence Gowing's tenure as curator (1965–67), the Tate consigned work by Holman Hunt, Rossetti and John Everett Millais (cat. 19–29) to a basement gallery near the Gents. At least no one at Millbank tried to de-accession the paintings. In June 1958, Christie's held a notorious sale of Victorian pictures from the Lady Lever Art Gallery at Port Sunlight. Burne-Jones's *Love and the Pilgrim*, a large study in coloured chalks (see cat. 176), sold for 45 guineas. Of the twenty drawings by Burne-Jones in the sale, most sold for between 9 and 38 guineas each. An oil by Alma-Tadema went for 230 guineas.[4] No British institution was among the bidders.

Although the flame burned low from the 1930s to the 1960s the candle never quite guttered out. In each of those decades a few enthusiasts nurtured the reputations of long-neglected artists, and so passed on their love for Victorian art. Even as family and friends raised their sherry glasses to 'A Dream of Fair Women' at that Burne-Jones private view in 1933, a band of young aesthetes at Eton and Oxford had already begun to look again at the unfashionable art of the Victorian period. In his novel *Brideshead Revisited* (1945) Evelyn Waugh described the Oxford rooms of just such a 1920s aesthete, Lord Sebastian Flyte, who lived surrounded by 'a harmonium in a gothic case, an elephant foot waste-paper basket, a dome of waxed fruit'. This exactly characterises the taste of Harold Acton, Robert Byron, Sacheverell Sitwell and Waugh himself (fig. 4), the dandies of the 1920s who collected Victorian bric-à-brac both for their own amusement and to cock a snook at the earnestness of the Omega Workshops, founded by Roger Fry in 1913.

Some, of course, were simply striking a pose. What singles out Acton, Waugh and John Betjeman is the total lack of irony in their appreciation of Victorian art. While at Oxford, Acton lectured on the paintings of Etty, Frith, Augustus Egg, John Martin and David Wilkie.[5] Waugh, stimulated by a family connection with Holman Hunt, privately published a study of the Pre-Raphaelite Brotherhood in 1926. His short book on Rossetti

Fig. 3 **Sir John Everett Millais Bt PRA**, *The Blind Girl*, 1854–56.
Oil on canvas, 81.2 × 62.3 cm.
Birmingham Museum and Art Gallery

appeared as early as 1928, the same year as Kenneth Clark's *The Gothic Revival*. And in his novel *A Handful of Dust* (1934) Waugh describes the ecclesiastical gloom of Tony Last's Neo-Gothic stately home, Hetton Abbey, in wholly sympathetic terms.[6]

With regard to the dissemination of knowledge and understanding of this art, none of these early champions was as effective as Sacheverell Sitwell, whose *Narrative Pictures: A Survey of English Genre and Its Painters* appeared in 1937. Though it encompassed 18th- and early 19th-century painting as well as Victorian, Sitwell's book was for many readers the first time they had seen high-quality reproductions of pictures as significant as Millais's *The Blind Girl* (fig. 3), Arthur Hughes's *April Love* (fig. 2, p. 99; see also cat. 72) and John Brett's *Val d'Aosta* (cat. 107). If Sitwell's judgements on individual works of art might be questioned today – he described Frith's *Derby Day* (Tate

Britain, London) as 'a panorama on an immense scale, but not a work of art' – Michael Sevier's notes on the illustrations represent the first scholarly attempt to catalogue art of this kind in the 20th century.

As these examples indicate, Victorian art was written about long before dealers sold it or collectors bought it. James Laver's *Tissot* (1936), Peter Quennell's *Victorian Panorama* (1937), William Gaunt's *The Pre-Raphaelite Tragedy* (1942) and *Victorian Olympus* (1952), John Steegman's *Consort of Taste* (1950), Graham Reynolds's *Painters of the Victorian Scene* (1953): all were published in the decades when it was almost impossible to see more than a smattering of Victorian pictures in British galleries, and all helped to pave the way for the revival that was to come.

In the early 1940s an eloquent polemicist for Victorian art found both his voice and his platform when he published superbly crafted essays on Burne-Jones and Beardsley in *Horizon*.[7] This was Robin Ironside, who baulked at the formalist notion of 'significant form'. For him the poetic content of a picture was at least as important as the composition and handling of paint. 'It would be quite useless to approach the study . . . of Burne-Jones with the notion that "formal relationships", "pattern", "structure", etc. have any absolute value in a picture. . . . The interpretation of the subject matter, the beauty of the conception, must be the basis for appreciation or criticism of [his] work.'[8] A practising artist and set designer, Ironside's appreciation of painting was direct, deep and extravagantly personal. His introduction to Phaidon Press's 1948 survey *Pre-Raphaelite Painters* (the first illustrated study of the movement since Percy Bate's *The English Pre-Raphaelite Painters: Their Associates and Successors* of 1899) therefore perfectly complemented the scholarly notes on the plates by John Gere, a young keeper in the Department of Prints and Drawings at the British Museum. Even today the poetic intensity of Ironside's lushly descriptive prose is spellbinding. Noting, for example, that Hughes painted *April Love* in an age of repressed sexual feeling and rigid social constraint, he imaginatively draws the reader into the heart and soul of the picture. 'The broken pledge, in such a moral order, inflicted an incurable wound; the long engagement was a corroding interval of anxiety and frustration; and all April loves were tended and guarded in the fear that they might die before the harvesting.'[9]

Ironside belonged to the Neo-Romantic generation of artists, writers and critics, who included Geoffrey Grigson, David Jones, John Minton, the young Graham Sutherland, Keith Vaughan and Denton Welch. All in their different ways attempted to recover the intensely subjective vision of Blake and Samuel Palmer, of the Ancients and the Pre-Raphaelites. Like Holman Hunt in *Fairlight Downs (Sunlight on the Sea)* (cat. 109) or Ford Madox Brown in *Southend, Essex, Looking Towards Sheerness* (cat. 104), the Neo-Romantics loved the British landscape with an almost mystical intensity. Or, like Hughes in his *Knight of the Sun* (cat. 74), they looked to the origins of British history for themes taken from Celtic or Arthurian legend. Ironside's particular insight was to see Pre-Raphaelite and other Victorian art in its European context, comparing Burne-Jones to Gustave Moreau, for example, or showing the links between the British Symbolists and Paul Gauguin,

Ferdinand Hodler, Gustav Klimt and Giovanni Segantini.[10]

Even by the 1940s serious collectors of Victorian painting were few and far between. An American, Grenville L. Winthrop, had been buying significant Pre-Raphaelite pictures and drawings both before the First World War and in the 1920s and '30s. But Winthrop was born in 1864, and was therefore a Victorian who essentially continued to collect artists who had been popular in his youth.[11] One of the earliest of the new generation of collectors was Evelyn Waugh. Soon after his marriage to Laura Herbert in 1937, Waugh bought his first important Pre-Raphaelite drawing, Rossetti's *The Spirit of the Rainbow* (cat. 16; see fig. 4). Waugh also acquired a version of Hughes's *The Woodman's Child* (*c.* 1860; now in the Andrew Lloyd Webber collection) and Holman Hunt's portrait of his mother-in-law, Mrs George Waugh (1868; Cleveland Museum of Art). In general, however, Waugh tended to

Fig. 4 Evelyn Waugh's dining room at Piers Court, Dursley, showing W. A. Atkinson's *The Upset Flower Cart* (cat. 160) and Dante Gabriel Rossetti's *The Spirit of the Rainbow* (cat. 16)

Fig. 5 **William Holman Hunt OM**, *The Awakening Conscience*, 1853. Oil on canvas, 76.2 × 55.9 cm. Tate Britain, London

favour narrative pictures, such as George Smith's *The Rightful Heir* and *Into the Cold World* (1874, 1876; both private collections), George Elgar Hicks's *The General Post Office at One Minute to Six* (Museum of London), W. A. Atkinson's *The Upset Flower Cart* (cat. 160; see also fig. 4) and Michael Frederick Halliday's *The Measure for the Wedding Ring* (cat. 79).[12] In this respect, his collection reflected a taste prevalent among British collectors from after the Second World War until the 1990s. At the same time as Waugh, Sir David Montagu-Douglas-Scott was assembling his superb collection of Victorian narrative and genre paintings – including Frith's *The Lovers' Seat* (1877; private collection), Sophie Anderson's *No Walk Today* (1856; private collection) and R. W. Chapman's *The First Letter* (1857; private collection). Scott's is, incredibly, the only extensive postwar collection of Victorian art that survives virtually intact.[13]

Waugh and Scott were not quite alone in their affection for Victorian painting. An important, but hardly representative, collector in the 1950s and '60s was the painter L.S. Lowry (cat. 270), who concentrated on the

work of a single artist, Rossetti. J. Kerrison Preston, W. Graham Robertson's heir, owned works by Watts and drawings by Burne-Jones. Sir Colin Anderson's collection included work by Arthur Boyd Houghton, Simeon Solomon (cat. 80) and James Tissot (cat. 128–35), and it was he who bequeathed to the Tate Gallery that supreme example of the Victorian 'modern moral subject', Holman Hunt's *The Awakening Conscience* (fig. 5). Roger Makins, later Lord Sherfield, acquired pictures to add to a group of Pre-Raphaelite paintings that had been in his family since the 19th century. Thomas Laughton, brother of the film star Charles Laughton, kept his collection of Victorian paintings in his hotel in Scarborough. They included Richard Dadd's *Contradiction: Oberon and Titania* (cat. 115). John Betjeman's friend John Bryson acquired no less than 82 works on paper by the Pre-Raphaelites and their associates, many of the highest quality and of historical importance. He bequeathed his collection to the Ashmolean Museum, Oxford, in 1977.

Even taking into account these collectors, the taste for Victorian painting lagged behind the burgeoning interest in the architecture and design of the period. This essay is not primarily concerned with the appreciation and collecting of works of decorative art, but it is worth noting that in 1952 the Victoria and Albert Museum's Circulation Department, run by Peter Floud and staffed by Elizabeth Aslin, Shirley Bury and Barbara Morris, mounted the first scholarly art-historical survey of 19th-century British textiles, furniture and ceramics, choosing only known designers and fully documented works with secure provenances. That show marked the beginning of serious study and conservation of such material.[14] Yet if the founding of the Victorian Society in 1958 shows that attitudes towards all things Victorian had begun to change, it must still be noted that the V&A did not complete its primary gallery devoted to Victorian decorative arts until 1966.

The 1952 V&A show was important for another reason: it inspired the young scholar Charles Handley-Read, working in partnership with his wife, Lavinia, to form the most important private collection of Victorian and Edwardian decorative arts ever assembled. Although it contained works by Walter Crane, William Dyce and Albert Moore, the strength of the collection lay not in painting, but in superb examples of tiles, furniture, glass,

Fig. 6 The exhibition of Charles and Lavinia Handley-Read's collection of Victorian decorative arts at the Royal Academy of Arts, London, 1971

metalwork, sculpture, architectural drawing, books, textiles and jewellery.[15] After the Handley-Reads' untimely deaths in 1971, an exhibition of the collection was held at the Royal Academy (fig. 6). Though the collection was dispersed, Charles and Lavinia Handley-Read's enthusiasm and dedication had helped to focus the careers of many young scholars, curators and dealers.

After the war, the role that dealers began to play in the dawning revival of interest in Victorian art was far more important than that of museums and galleries. The Leicester Gallery in Leicester Square held two exhibitions devoted to Tissot in the late 1940s. Charlotte and Robert Frank, refugees from Nazi Germany, had arrived in England in 1939. Robert Frank (uncle of the diarist Anne Frank) specialised in the work of the visionary painter John Martin. After her husband's death,

Charlotte ran the gallery in St James's Street, relying on her own extensive knowledge and superb eye to find under-appreciated paintings by artists such as Crane and William Bell Scott. Also active at an early date was the Ferrers Gallery in the Piccadilly Arcade, owned by Sir Robert Abdy and his wife, Jane, well known for promoting the then-undervalued work of Tissot and John Atkinson Grimshaw (cat. 110, 111, 116–26). In 1961 Jeremy Maas opened his gallery in Clifford Street with the first of a succession of legendary shows of High Victorian art. Maas was to remain the most respected dealer in the field until his death in 1997. Venerable firms such as M. Newman, Leggett, and Thomas Agnew continued to deal in Victorian art. The Fine Art Society, a firm of dealers founded in 1876, mounted important exhibitions of Victorian sculpture and decorative arts in 1968 and

1969, with catalogues by Lavinia Handley-Read and Charlotte Gere respectively. Paralleling all this activity in London in the 1960s and '70s, the firm of Durlacher Brothers in New York sold paintings by Alma-Tadema, Moore and Simeon Solomon.[16]

Yet it was not until 1968 that Christopher Wood of Christie's picture department began to hold specialised Victorian sales. In 1971 Peter Nahum of Sotheby's opened the picture department at new premises in Belgravia, the first auction room dedicated to the Victorian era. At the start of what was to become the great revival of interest in Victorian art, prices were not high. Holman Hunt's *Lady of Shalott* sold at Christie's for 9,500 guineas in 1959, a price comparable to the 10,500 guineas paid for Millais's *Christ in the House of His Parents (The Carpenter's Shop)* (Tate Britain, London) in 1921. In 1963 Jeremy Maas sold Leighton's *Flaming June* (fig. 7) to Governor Luis A. Ferré of Puerto Rico for £2,000. Prices began to move upwards when Millais's great portrait of Ruskin at Glenfinlas (fig. 1, p. 139) fetched 25,000 guineas at auction in 1965. In 1970 the American A&P supermarkets heir Huntington Hartford sold Millais's *Huguenot* (fig. 1, p. 46) to Agnew's for £30,000 guineas.[17]

Saleroom prices are seldom discussed in exhibition catalogues, but what better way is there to chart the rising esteem in which Victorian art was held than by following the fortunes of a single picture? Edward Poynter's exercise in Edwardian kitsch *The Cave of the Storm Nymphs* (cat. 142) has been sold four times since 1969, first for £3,500, in 1981 for $180,000, in 1988 for £400,000 and in 1994 (to Andrew Lloyd Webber) for £500,000. Similar trajectories could be traced for Luke Fildes's *Village Wedding* (cat. 161) and Tissot's *Le Banc de jardin* (cat. 134), but it hardly seems necessary to labour the point.[18]

Once again, the single most important factor in accelerating interest in Victorian and Pre-Raphaelite art was the publication of copiously illustrated books, including Graham Reynolds's *Victorian Painting* (1966) and Quentin Bell's *Victorian Artists* (1967). By this time, art dealers were as likely to be engaged in researching and publishing

Fig. 7 **Frederic, Lord Leighton PRA**, *Flaming June*, 1895. Oil on canvas, 120.6 × 120.6 cm. Museo de Arte de Ponce (The Luis A. Ferré Foundation), Puerto Rico

articles and books about these artists as their museum colleagues. The *Urtext* for the revival of interest in Victorian painting was Jeremy Maas's magisterial survey *Victorian Painters* (1969). When Christopher Wood left Christie's in 1976 to open his own gallery in Motcomb Street, he had already published his *Dictionary of Victorian Painters* (1971) and *Victorian Panorama: Paintings of Victorian Life* (1976). He was to write studies of Tissot, the Pre-Raphaelites and Burne-Jones. In 1969 Diana Holman-Hunt raised public awareness of the Pre-Raphaelite Brotherhood with the publication of her entertaining bestseller *My Grandfather, His Wives and Loves*.

All these were popular books for the general public. Of a different order were the closely researched exhibitions organised by Mary Bennett at the Walker Art Gallery in Liverpool of the work of Madox Brown (1964), Millais (1967) and Holman Hunt (1969). Simultaneously in the United States and Canada, survey exhibitions of Victorian art in Indianapolis (1964), Ottawa (1965) and Detroit and Philadelphia (1968) testified to the increasing interest taken in this art by museums.[19]

Allen Staley's *Pre-Raphaelite Landscape* (1973), William Fredeman's *Pre-Raphaelitism: A Bibliocritical Study* (1965) and Virginia Surtees's two-volume *catalogue raisonné* of the works of Rossetti (1971) all signalled a new level of serious scholarship in Pre-Raphaelite painting. Richard Ormond's monograph on the still unfashionable John Singer Sargent appeared in 1970. His equally forward-looking Daniel Maclise exhibition in 1972 for the Arts Council, and the monograph he wrote with Leonée Ormond on Leighton (1975), added to a growing sense that this was an area ripe for academic research. Meanwhile, the formidable Rosalie, Lady Mander, worked tirelessly to promote the National Trust's Wightwick Manor in Wolverhampton, a Victorian house with original Morris & Co. interiors filled with Pre-Raphaelite pictures and furniture. The later 1970s saw shows such as John Christian's magisterial Burne-Jones retrospective at the Hayward Gallery, London (1975), and Manchester City Art Gallery's *Victorian High Renaissance* (1977). The Tate Gallery finally mounted a Pre-Raphaelite show in 1984.

The modern era of collecting Victorian pictures began not in London but in New York. The most important single collection formed anywhere in the 20th century was that put together by Huntington Hartford in the 1960s. Its rapid dispersal and the eccentricities of its owner have tended to obscure the quality of its pictures, which included Burne-Jones's *Perseus* series (1875–85; Staatsgalerie Stuttgart) and *Laus Veneris* (fig. 8). In 1970 another American, the twenty-year-old Christopher Forbes, began to amass what was to become a holding of more than 360 works of Victorian art. At first Forbes confined himself to works of art that had been shown at the Royal Academy during the reign of Queen Victoria, but by 1975 that constraint had been abandoned and the collection eventually included paintings by artists who rarely if ever showed at the Academy, such as Burne-Jones, Hunt, Moore, Rossetti and Watts. When it came up for auction in February 2003, the collection fetched £18 million. At that sale, Lord Lloyd-Webber acquired a late masterpiece by Moore, *Lightning and Light* (cat. 148), Edith Hayllar's enchanting genre scene *A Summer Shower* (cat. 170) and Kate Hayllar's watercolour '*A thing of beauty is a joy forever*' (cat. 169).

In his early collecting days Forbes had few serious competitors. One, the American television personality (and former assistant to Cecil Beaton) Allen Funt, assembled a group of works by Alma-Tadema, but this was dispersed in 1973, soon after being shown at the Metropolitan Museum of Art, New York, in an exhibition entitled *Victorians in Togas*. Later came another American, Frederick Koch, who in the 1980s brought exceptional flair to his collecting, acquiring distinguished canvases by Alma-Tadema, Leighton, Moore and others. This collection, too, has been largely dispersed.

One of the strengths of the Forbes collection lay in narrative and genre pictures. In this it could be said to have epitomised a quintessentially British taste, as encapsulated in the Waugh and Scott collections. A very different kind of collector had also emerged by the 1970s, represented by Joe Setton and Robert Walker, who both carried American passports but lived in Paris. Setton started his collection with the purchase in the late 1960s of Burne-Jones's *Pygmalion and the Image* (cat. 49). Working through the London dealer Julian Hartnoll, he went on to form the Pre-Raphaelite Trust with pictures of remarkable quality, such as Hughes's *Silver and Gold*, J. M. Strudwick's *Gentle Music of a Byegone Day* and Moore's *Red Berries*. After Setton's untimely death, Andrew Lloyd

Fig. 8 **Sir Edward Coley Burne-Jones Bt ARA**, *Laus Veneris*, 1873–75. Oil on canvas, 122 × 183 cm. Laing Art Gallery, Newcastle-upon-Tyne

Webber acquired all three pictures (cat. 77, 88, 147). Walker was a dealer in Pre-Raphaelite pictures as well as a collector. He owned the supreme example of late Pre-Raphaelite visionary art in Lord Lloyd-Webber's collection, Burne-Jones's *Fall of Lucifer* (cat. 62). The significant point about Setton and Walker, and about the curators in German and French museums who bought from Hartnoll in the 1970s, is that their interest arose from a profound understanding of European design and Symbolist painting.

In general, continental European collectors have been a less significant factor in the market for Victorian art than their Canadian, Australian and Japanese counterparts, all of whom, to a greater or lesser extent, were Andrew Lloyd Webber's rivals for important pictures in the 1980s and '90s. Not one has yet shown the absolute commitment to Victorian art that he has. Even after the National Gallery of Art in Washington staged its magnificent survey of Victorian art in 1997, American collectors and major American museums have failed to manifest a serious interest in Victorian painting. A Francophile tendency in the American cultural establishment has effectively perpetuated British attitudes of the pre-Robin Ironside era. In Britain the situation is only a little better. Though there are more Victorian pictures on view at the Tate than ever before, the Pre-Raphaelites were seen to better advantage there in 1960 than they are now. Shows like *Exposed: The Victorian Nude*, seen at Tate Britain in 2001, have concentrated more on sociological concerns than on artistic quality.

ENTHUSIASM AND COMMITMENT: THE ANDREW LLOYD WEBBER COLLECTION

Andrew Lloyd Webber first became interested in Victorian art at the age of eight, unaware, of course, that he was part of a pattern of changing attitudes in the 1950s towards the Victorian era. It all started through his childhood passion for historic buildings. Family holidays meant visits to castles, abbeys and churches – where he began to notice rood screens, carvings and stained glass. As a schoolboy in the early 1960s, he spent his spare time wandering through London's inner-city churches, Pevsner in hand, taking in the medieval splendours of Westminster Abbey, the Baroque grandeur of St Paul's and the High Victorian Gothic of William Butterfield's All Saints, Margaret Street. Other early encounters with Victorian art included Burne-Jones's stained-glass windows in St Martin's-on-the-Hill, Scarborough, and

St Martin's, Brampton, and, aged nine or ten, a precocious difference of opinion with a Shell Guide that told him he should be admiring the ruins of Cardiff Castle when what really bowled him over were the Victorian additions to the castle by William Burges, and the same architect's reconstruction of Castell Coch nearby.

If there is one artist in the collection who is closer to Lord Lloyd-Webber's heart than any other it is clearly Burne-Jones. Once again, this appreciation goes back to his schooldays when, at the age of thirteen, he peeled off from a school trip to Rome and discovered for himself that little-known architectural gem, St Paul's Within-the-Walls, a Romanesque Revival American Episcopal church built by George Street from 1872 to 1876, its interior shimmering with golden mosaics designed by Burne-Jones in the 1880s and '90s. Since the church was almost unvisited by tourists in 1961, we can only imagine the dismay of Andrew Lloyd Webber's teachers when he announced that it was the 'best thing' he had seen in the Eternal City. As though in homage to that early epiphany, he today owns two of the artist's studies for the mosaics, *Christ Enthroned* and *The Archangel Zophiel* (cat. 58, 59), as well as a masterwork that evolved from an unexecuted project for the west wall, *The Fall of Lucifer* (cat. 62). Later, as a teenager, when he discovered Stanley Spencer's visionary murals for the Sandham Memorial Chapel at Burghclere in Hampshire, he at once recognised the link between Spencer's work and that of Burne-Jones.

Like the Oxford aesthetes before him, Andrew Lloyd Webber and his friends at Westminster School admired Victorian art precisely because a whiff of controversy surrounded it. When the art master fulminated against the Pre-Raphaelites, Lloyd Webber wondered why, if the art was so bad, the galleries in which their pictures hung were so full. The story has passed into legend of how, in his early teens, he spotted Leighton's *Flaming June* out of its frame and covered in grime in a Fulham Road shop. The good news is that the price was £50. The bad news is that he had already spent the £50 he possessed on William Dugdale's three-volume *Monasticon Anglicanum* (1655–73). He could be said to have spent a lifetime of passionate collecting in an attempt to rectify this lost opportunity.

When Andrew Lloyd Webber first began to make a living by writing music (*Joseph and His Amazing Technicolor Dreamcoat* was first performed at Colet Court, London, in 1968, *Jesus Christ Superstar* was released as an album in the USA two years later), among his first purchases were Burne-Jones's enchanting illustrations in pen and ink for the *The Fairy Family* (cat. 30), microscopic visions of a world crowded with impudent elves that in many ways resemble one of the jewels he later added to his collection, Richard Dadd's *Contradiction: Oberon and Titania* (cat. 115). Other early buys included drawings by Rossetti (cat. 12, 17) and Millais's magical design for a Gothic-style window (cat. 19), a fluent, witty image drawn during the rainy August of 1853 while the artist was staying with John and Effie Ruskin at Glenfinlas in Scotland. The design is drawn on grocery paper, a fact that conjures up the spontaneous, improvisational nature of a work teeming with youthful invention and high spirits. Landscapes and cityscapes by Atkinson Grimshaw, Burne-Jones's *Sleeping Princess* from the *Briar Rose* series (cat. 46) and John William Waterhouse's *Danaïdes* (cat. 96) were all early acquisitions, in part because such pictures were affordable.

In his early years as a collector, Lord Lloyd-Webber was not in a position to buy major Pre-Raphaelite paintings. When Huntington Hartford sold Millais's *Huguenot* in 1970 for £30,000, and Burne-Jones's great canvas *Laus Veneris* went for £33,000 a few years later, these prices were double what Andrew Lloyd Webber had just paid for his first home, and thus far beyond the grasp of a young man starting out on a precarious theatrical career. By the time the huge successes of *Evita* (1976), *Cats* (1981), *Phantom of the Opera* (1986) and *Sunset Boulevard* (1993) had placed art of this importance within his reach, early works by members of the original Pre-Raphaelite Brotherhood rarely came up for sale. When they did, he bought astutely.

It would be hard to find in a private collection a more winning portrait by Millais than *James Wyatt and His Granddaughter Mary Wyatt* (cat. 20) or a more romantic subject picture than that of *The Proscribed Royalist, 1651* (cat. 24). Millais's later work has nothing to do with Pre-Raphaelitism, yet that did not stop our collector acquiring *Chill October* (cat. 28), a melancholy view of a wintry lake under leaden skies, birds flying against the wind. Likewise, '*Yes*' (cat. 27) is a Trollopian genre scene so blatantly theatrical in its inspiration that it could easily record the moment when soprano and tenor move centre stage to pledge their love in Act II of a Lloyd Webber musical.

Another member of the original Brotherhood whose work Lord Lloyd-Webber has avidly collected is Holman Hunt. His acquisitions include a rarity painted before Hunt met Millais or Rossetti, the lovely *Old Church at Ewell* (cat. 103). A decade later, burning with the fever of high Ruskinian naturalism, the artist created one of the gems of the collection, *Fairlight Downs (Sunlight on the Sea)* (cat. 109), a little oil painting on panel that captures for all eternity the soft glow of a late summer afternoon on the English coast. Unlike either Millais or Rossetti, Hunt continued throughout his career to paint in accordance with the 'pure' Pre-Raphaelite principle of absolute fidelity to nature. Andrew Lloyd Webber has three superb examples of these later works. *Morning Prayer* (cat. 67) glows with the clarity and gravity of a Van Eyck. *The Shadow of Death* (cat. 64) is a quarter-sized autograph replica of the 1873 painting in Manchester City Art Gallery and, if anything, the smaller scale intensifies the picture's visual power. In front of Hunt's portrait of his son *Master Hilary — The Tracer* (cat. 70) it takes a few minutes to realise that the child is seen on the far side of a *trompe l'œil* window pane, with leaves, branches and butterfly on 'our' side of the glass.

Very different from Holman Hunt's uncompromising realism is the poetic and transcendental art of Rossetti. From the artist's Pre-Raphaelite years, Lord Lloyd-Webber owns the superb early watercolour *Giotto Painting the Portrait of Dante* (cat. 1), the near-expressionist pen and ink drawing *How They Met Themselves* (cat. 3) and the severely linear pencil drawing *The Virgin Mary Being Comforted* (cat. 2). The collection is also distinguished by its commitment to Rossetti's later work, such as the blissfully sensual *A Vision of Fiammetta* (cat. 6), a rare portrait in oil of Marie Stillman in a flame-red shift posed against pink-tinged apple blossoms, illustrating lines from one of Rossetti's own poems. Despite the picture's high finish and voluptuous Venetian colour, stepping up to it is like entering a chamber in which the doors have been sealed and curtains drawn. Though a true likeness of the sitter (as is indicated by Rossetti's red chalk drawing of her [cat. 5]), the painting is as sinuously artificial as a portrait by the 16th-century Mannerist Agnolo Bronzino. When he chose, Rossetti could also evoke a sitter's character, as in

the portrait in coloured chalks of his sister Christina (cat. 4), her head heavy, her thoughts far away and her body, which is rendered with the freedom of a hasty sketch, as massive as Gertrude Stein's in Picasso's famous portrait.

Andrew Lloyd Webber has also bought masterpieces by artists closely associated with the Brotherhood but not part of it. An example is Brett's *Val d'Aosta* (cat. 107), a *tour de force* inspired by Ruskin and shown at the Royal Academy in 1859, painted with the painstaking attention to naturalistic detail familiar from the early work of Millais or Hunt. The collection is rich in the work of that most loveable of near-Pre-Raphaelites, Arthur Hughes, including the small replica (cat. 72) of the Tate's *April Love* (fig. 2, p. 99), a version of *Ophelia* (cat. 71) and the quintessential romantic image of medieval chivalry, *The Knight of the Sun* (cat. 74). Slightly later in date and more freely painted, but still exuding Hughes's inimitable sweetness, is *Silver and Gold* (cat. 77).

In a category of its own is Dadd's *Contradiction: Oberon and Titania* (cat. 115), in which the obsessive detail reflects not what Dadd saw, but what he knew. The Victorian genre of fairy painting foreshadows the relationship of writer and reader in science fiction by requiring of both the artist and the viewer not only imagination, but also belief. That is why Dadd, a schizophrenic confined to Bedlam for murdering his father, was the greatest fairy painter of all. *Contradiction* is so mesmerising because at some profound level Dadd 'saw' the beings he was painting. The clarity and detail with which the tiny (and unexpectedly scary) figures are realised in paint underlines the reality of their existence for the artist. The viewer stands in spellbound silence before Dadd's picture — 'fairy-struck', like all mortals who stumble upon the elfin folk.

Andrew Lloyd Webber's holdings of Burne-Jones's work are the core strength of the collection and constitute a virtual retrospective of the artist's long career. They trace his development from the dreamy amateur, his head swimming with the ideals of the Oxford Movement (cat. 30), via the successful designer of ecclesiastical stained glass for Morris & Co. (cat. 47), to the elder statesman of Victorian art and idol of the French Symbolists (cat. 57). We move from touchingly naïve early watercolours such as the *Annunciation (The Flower of God)* (cat. 39), redolent of 15th-century Florentine art,

to a mature work like *The Mirror of Venus* (cat. 48), in which Burne-Jones impresses with his virtuoso draughtsmanship and feel for the cadences of a complex figure composition. Different again is the rarefied poetical world he reveals in the *Holy Grail* tapestries (cat. 191), a visionary tableau in which absolute stillness reigns. As we pass though the dark forest where the story is set, it is as though heroic actions are performed in time to slow music. Burne-Jones himself saw these works as equivalent to the radiantly uplifting music of Wagner's *Parsifal*.

Burne-Jones is not generally known as a portrait painter, and yet looking at his depictions of Amy Gaskell and Cicely Horner (cat. 50, 53) we realise that he was one of the supreme portraitists of his age. These two pictures are both responses to the aestheticism of Whistler (an artist not represented in the Andrew Lloyd Webber Collection; see fig. 2, p. 143) — what might be called Burne-Jones's 'Symphonies in White and Black'. And yet, with his curious mixture of urgency and innocence, he comes closer than any other Victorian painter to the expression of the inarticulate yearnings of adolescence. As his portraits of Dorothy Mattersdorf and Philip Comyns Carr (cat. 51, 52) indicate, among British painters only Sir Joshua Reynolds (1723–1792) so completely captured the innocence of childhood.

As early as the 1860s, Burne-Jones was among the generation of young British painters who were beginning to abandon Pre-Raphaelitism in order to explore its antithesis, classicism. Look, for example, at *The Lament* (cat. 43), in which, instead of the narrative subject that Victorian audiences expected, he used pose and gesture to establish a mood of reverie. From here it was but a step to the full-blown Symbolism of *Evening Star* and *Night* (cat. 40, 41), with their figures floating over darkened seas and in front of star-speckled skies.

The Aesthetic Movement, unfairly caricatured in George du Maurier's cartoons of silly maidens swooning over blue-and-white china, was in fact a serious attempt by later Victorians to establish new standards by which to live their lives in an age of gross materialism and empty spiritual values. The credo of 'art for art's sake' raised aesthetic creation and perception to the forefront of human experience. Victorian pictures simply do not come any lovelier than the three works by Moore in the collection, *Companions*, *Red Berries* and *Lightning and Light*

(cat. 146–8), each of which reveals the importance of the Elgin Marbles for artists of this period. Such pictures confirm, too, that Moore was the greatest colourist in British art after Turner. It becomes readily understandable that it was aestheticism — or rather, Burne-Jones's position as the leading aesthete of the British school — that prompted the young Picasso to set off for London to see his work before being waylaid by the attractions of Paris.[20]

The possible influence of Burne-Jones on Picasso's Blue Period is of particular fascination to Andrew Lloyd Webber. In an article published in the *Daily Telegraph* on 14 October 1997, he notes the predominance of the colour blue in the late pictures of Burne-Jones and points to the similarity between Burne-Jones's languidly drooping heads (see cat. 34) and those of Picasso's sickly beggars and bohemians. Both stylistic strains are present in the Spaniard's magnificent portrait of Angel Fernández de Soto (cat. 282). Citing Anthony Blunt's and Phoebe Pool's observation that the 'fluid, wavy shapes of Burne-Jones are detectable in many of Picasso's early drawings and paintings', Lord Lloyd-Webber suggests that in *The Fall of Lucifer* (cat. 62) Burne-Jones plays with a 'sort of two-dimensional cubism' and that the interplay of cracked and broken folds in the drapery of *The Challenge in the Wilderness* (cat. 32) verges on cubist abstraction.

As his collection of more than 40 works by Burne-Jones attests, Andrew Lloyd Webber is not afraid to buy in depth when he likes an artist. Another case in point is the variety of the paintings by Atkinson Grimshaw he owns. They range from the almost Pre-Raphaelite detail of *Ghyll Beck, Barden, Yorkshire, Early Spring* (cat. 111) to that strange Symbolist image of a dead woman floating down a river at night, *The Lady of Shalott* (cat. 125), before changing direction again with a Whistlerian evocation of twilight, *Lights on the Mersey* (cat. 116). Yet none of these pictures is typical. In most works by Grimshaw the month is November, the time dusk. Mists are rising and the silver moon rides high over black, scudding clouds. Orange lights glow from within shop windows and suburban mansions, emphasising the loneliness of the unfortunate few still out in the chill night air (cat. 122–4, 126, 127). With their rain-swept pavements and their lights from houses glinting through the bare branches of wintry trees, such images bring with them a pang of

Cat. 34
Sir Edward Coley Burne-Jones Bt ARA (1833–1898)
The Judgement of Paris, early 1870s
Oil on canvas, 107.2 × 69.2 cm

Cat. 32
Sir Edward Coley Burne-Jones Bt ARA (1833–1898)
The Challenge in the Wilderness, c. 1894/98
Oil on canvas, 129.5 × 96.5 cm

melancholy, a stabbing longing for home. They make us feel at once sad and safe.

Grimshaw became a rich man selling his paintings to northern industrialists who might well have lived in the suburbs he painted. When he turned his attention to the depiction of his own magnificent house and garden, he let the common light of day fall into richly appointed interiors. If both *Dulce Domum* and *Il Penseroso* (cat. 117, 118) call to mind Tissot's *Quiet* or *Le Banc de jardin* (cat. 130, 134) that is because in all these pictures well-dressed, soulful young women inhabit lovingly described Aesthetic homes and gardens. Not only do the two artists share a meticulous painting technique, but each also presents a small psychological study, the opening chapter in a story that is never quite told. Tissot develops this tendency towards narration further than Grimshaw, as can be seen in the wonderful *L'Orpheline* (cat. 135), in which the sad-eyed young woman

and her charge appear to the viewer among the autumnal foliage like an accidental encounter on a country walk with Proust's Madame Swann and little Gilberte.

The individuality of Andrew Lloyd Webber's choice of artists and works of art underscores the deeply private nature of the collection. Thus, it contains only three works by Alma-Tadema, an artist one might have expected to be far better represented in a collection of Victorian art, though it would be difficult to name a finer painting by Alma-Tadema than *The Baths of Caracalla* (cat. 143). Neither does Lord Lloyd-Webber feel constrained by date or school if he falls in love with a picture. Canaletto's snapshot of a London morning *c.* 1749, *The Old Horse Guards, London, from St James's Park* (cat. 283); Reynolds's swagger portrait of the Prince of Wales (cat. 284); Alfred Munnings's lush, freely painted and colour-drenched sketches of gypsy encampments (cat. 269);

Stanley Spencer's endearing self-portrait (cat. 278); Giovanni Boldini's self-dramatising *Marchesa Luisa Casati* (cat. 136) with her superbly accessorised greyhound: all found their way into the collection simply because the way each artist applied pigment to canvas raises the hairs on the back of the neck.

Instinct tells me that Andrew Lloyd Webber is not interested in looking at Victorian paintings for what they may or may not tell us about Victorian morals or customs. The finest among the handful of purely narrative pictures in the collection – the sort favoured by such early collectors as Waugh and Scott – is Abraham Solomon's *First Class – The Meeting* (cat. 156). Its inconsequential charm seems miles away from the social realism of Adrien-Emmanuel Marie's powerful *Feeding the Hungry after the Lord Mayor's Banquet* (cat. 167) and John Henry Henshall's *Behind the Bar* (cat. 168), in which the artist pulls no punches in his scrutiny of the lives of the poor. In Fildes's *Village Wedding* (cat. 161) much of the pleasure lies in studying the wonderful range of expressions – all of them happy and excited – as our eyes move from the wedding party to the onlookers. In a different category again is Joseph Noel Paton's scene from the Indian Mutiny (then a very recent occurrence), *In Memoriam* (cat. 157), a mesmerising study of the expression of extreme emotion that, to my mind, ranks with the work of such 17th-century masters as Guido Reni and Nicolas Poussin. All these paintings are superb examples of an important strand in the history of 19th-century British art, and yet, in the context of Lord Lloyd-Webber's holdings as a whole, they appear isolated. The backbone of the collection lies in a British tradition of painting that stretches back to the Renaissance and is the precise opposite of realism. Burne-Jones himself summed up what this art was about when he said: 'I don't want to copy *objects*, I want to tell people something.'

Towards the end of the collection's chronological span appears the mature work of John William Waterhouse. His ravishing *St Cecilia* (cat. 95) and *Pandora* (cat. 97), as well as E. Reginald Frampton's *Passage of the Holy Grail to Sarras* (cat. 84), show how the followers of Burne-Jones closed their eyes to the world they lived in to cultivate their own idiosyncratic inner visions. Looking at these pictures reveals the deep sincerity of British art, its touching lack of cynicism, its batty belief that this island is a Never-Never Land peopled with saints and squires and damsels in need of rescue. Suddenly, Stanley Spencer no longer looks like a lone eccentric, but registers as part of a long-established tradition of visionary painters stretching back through Rossetti and Burne-Jones to Blake. It is the sheer madness and innocence of this art that catches the viewer by the throat.

My thanks to Charlotte Gere, Julian Hartnoll, Richard Ormond, Christopher Riopelle, Allen Staley, Virginia Surtees and Christopher Wood.

1 J. Kerrison Preston (ed.), *Letters from W. Graham Robertson*, London, 1953, p. 290.
2 Jonathan Penny, 'Towards the Victorian Society', *The Victorian Society Annual*, 1994, p. 23.
3 National Art Collections Fund Acquisitions Lists 1928–56, Tate Britain Research Centre, London.
4 *Catalogue of Modern Pictures and Drawings mainly of the British School of the Nineteenth Century, the Property of the Trustees of the Lady Lever Art Gallery, Port Sunlight*, sale catalogue, Christie's, London, 6 June 1958.
5 Martin Green, *Children of the Sun: A Narrative of 'Decadence' in England after 1918*, London, 1977, p. 190.
6 See John Summerson, 'A Victorian Exhibition in Aid of St Bartholomew's Hospital', *Country Life*, 20 June 1931, pp. 25–6.
7 Denys Sutton, 'A Champion of Romantic Painting', *Apollo*, March 1975, pp. 158–62.
8 Robin Ironside, 'Gustave Moreau and Burne-Jones', *Apollo*, March 1975, p. 180 (first published in *Horizon*, June 1940).
9 Robin Ironside and John Gere, *Pre-Raphaelite Painters*, London, 1948, p. 13.
10 Sutton (note 7), p. 161.
11 Miriam Stewart, 'Beauty, Austerity, Idealism: Grenville L. Winthrop and British Art', in *Between Reality and Dreams: Nineteenth Century British and French Art from the Winthrop Collection of the Fogg Art Museum*, exh. cat., National Museum of Western Art, Tokyo, 2002, pp. 252–60.
12 Christopher Wood, 'Evelyn Waugh: A Pioneer Collector', *The Connoisseur*, September 1981, pp. 30–4.
13 See *Sunshine and Shadow: The David Scott Collection of Victorian Paintings*, exh. cat., National Gallery of Scotland, Edinburgh, 1991.
14 Anthony Burton, *Vision and Accident: The Story of the Victoria and Albert Museum*, London, 1999, pp. 204–5.
15 Mark Girouard, 'Two Collectors Extraordinary: Charles and Lavinia Handley-Read', *Country Life*, 16 March 1972, pp. 614–15, and Halina Grubert, 'The Passionate Pursuit of Charles and Lavinia Handley-Read', *The Antique Collector*, April 1985, pp. 64–8.
16 Allen Staley, 'Preparing the Ground', in *The Forbes Collection of Victorian Pictures and Works of Art*, sale catalogue, Christie's, London, 19–20 February 2003, vol. 2, pp. 15–19.
17 Christopher Wood, 'An Amazing Revival', The Annual British Antique Dealers Association Lecture, Victoria and Albert Museum, London, 28 May 2003.
18 Ibid.
19 Staley (note 16), p. 19.
20 See Roland Penrose, *Picasso: His Life and Work*, London, 1958, p. 62: 'Picasso assured me, when he was staying in London in 1950, that for him [his 1900 trip to] Paris was merely to be a halt on a journey which would take him further north, to London . . . he had conceived a great admiration for England . . . and . . . some English painters, especially Burne-Jones.'

Dante Gabriel Rossetti

JULIAN TREUHERZ

Dante Gabriel Rossetti (1828–1882) was one of the most unusual and original of all Victorian artists. He reacted against the prevailing tendency towards realism and created a new kind of art, painting in his maturity powerful and mysterious dreamlike images of women that convey, through poetic suggestiveness and allusive detail, ideas of sensuality, beauty, love, death and destiny. For Rossetti, women embodied the mystery of life, and this belief ran through his diverse subject matter from his early pictures of the Virgin Mary, typifying female virtue, to the *femmes fatales* of his later work, representing the power of women over men. A distinguished poet as well as a painter, he was able to enrich his work through his familiarity with European literature, especially with his namesake Dante (1265–1321). Rossetti gained his love of the Italian poet's work from his father, a Dante scholar who had come to London as a political exile.[1] Dante's intense vision of Beatrice, his ideal love for her that transcended death, was one of the wellsprings of Rosssetti's art, and at times his own life seemed to run in parallel. The visionary world he constructed in his art was imaginary, but it was built on personal experience; his ideals of female beauty were inspired by the delicate features of Elizabeth Siddal, his early muse, who died tragically soon after their marriage,[2] and then by the statuesque Jane Morris, the wife of his friend William Morris. But he also frequently used professional models.

The young Rossetti, impatient with discipline, did not complete his art education and this encouraged him to value meaning and expression above academically correct drawing.[3] Along with William Holman Hunt (cat. 64, 67, 70, 103, 108, 109) and John Everett Millais (cat. 19–29), he played a crucial role in the formation of the Pre-Raphaelite Brotherhood in 1848, but then rejected the minutely naturalistic style adopted by the other Pre-Raphaelites. In the 1850s Rossetti worked on a small scale, making meticulously detailed drawings and jewel-like watercolours in an original technique influenced by medieval manuscripts.[4] He returned to oil painting in the 1860s with a series of decorative portrayals of women, celebrating their beauty and desirability.[5] In his later work he made extensive use of coloured chalks as well as oils, and turned to more sombre and melancholic themes. He laid great stress on the formal qualities of his work, even designing his own frames.[6]

Rossetti was a largely invisible presence in Victorian art for, after creating a sensation in 1849 and 1850 with his first two exhibited paintings in the Pre-Raphaelite style, *The Girlhood of Mary Virgin* and *Ecce Ancilla Domini!*,[7] he then hardly showed in public, preferring to sell his work directly to a circle of initiates. His paintings were much written about, however, and from the late 1850s a number of friends and followers, chief among them Edward Burne-Jones (cat. 30–62, 176, 191), disseminated the values seen in his work. Yet it was not until after his death in 1882 and the two memorial exhibitions held in London the following year that the full force of his originality could be appreciated.[8]

The earliest Rossetti drawing in the Andrew Lloyd Webber Collection is *The Virgin Mary Being Comforted* (cat. 2), dated May 1852. This was one of a number of scenes from the life of the Virgin[9] that Rossetti was planning in the late 1840s and early '50s. Mary's youth was the subject of the first two paintings, *The Girlhood of Mary Virgin* depicting her as a young girl and *Ecce Ancilla Domini!* showing her on the brink of adulthood. These have become famous as definitive images of the early Pre-Raphaelite style, but they were only part of his project to show different episodes from the life of Mary. *Ecce Ancilla Domini!*, for example, was intended to be one half of a diptych, the other half showing the death of the Virgin, and he also planned a triptych about her. Neither of these was completed: Rossetti's career is littered with ideas for paintings that were never realised, but exist only as studies and sketches.

Rossetti shows the Virgin Mary flanked by Mary Magdalen, on the left, and Mary, wife of Cleophas, on the right, with St John the Evangelist in anguish to the left of Mary Magdalen. According to St John's Gospel (19:25) the three Maries stood at the foot of the cross, but Rossetti places them against a background of earlier episodes in the story leading up to the crucifixion. The scene on the left probably represents the freeing of Barrabas; on the right is Pilate washing his hands, with the mocking of Christ below. The drawing shows marked similarities to the three Maries in the mural *The Procession to Calvary* by the contemporary French painter Hippolyte Flandrin in the church of St Germain des Près, Paris,[10] which Rossetti described as 'Wonderful! Wonderful!! Wonderful!!!' in a letter of 1849 from Paris.[11] This shows that the Pre-Raphaelites did not take inspiration exclusively from early Italian painting, as their name suggests.

Giotto Painting the Portrait of Dante (1852; cat. 1) was also ultimately intended as part of a triptych, *The Youth of Dante*, with companion scenes entitled *Dante Condemning Guido Cavalcanti to Exile* and *Dante in Exile* (a subject also painted by Lord Leighton; cat. 138). Only the present watercolour was completed. Its vivid colour and detail, together with the complex meaning it expresses, typify Rossetti's watercolours of the 1850s. His idea for the picture was prompted by the discovery in Florence of what purported to be an original portrait of Dante by Giotto (*c.* 1266–1337), a copy of which was sent to Rossetti's father. This portrait was the basis of the likeness in his picture, which shows the young Giotto seated on a platform painting Dante's portrait in fresco. Behind Giotto is his master, Cimabue, and to the left of Dante is his friend the poet Guido Cavalcanti, reading from a book of verse by the older poet Guido Guinizelli. Below, a procession of beautiful young women passes by. Rossetti took as his starting point two quotations from Dante. The first is a famous passage from the *Purgatorio*[12] about the transience of artistic fame; just as Cimabue's fame was eclipsed by Giotto's, so Guinizelli's was by Cavalcanti's, and by implication Dante's outshines both: in the painting he therefore holds a pomegranate, a symbol of immortality. Rossetti may also have had in mind his own role in reviving the fame of his artistic forbears through his paintings and his translations of Italian poetry. The second quotation, from the *Vita Nuova*,[13] concerns the sight of Beatrice as a vision of perfection; thus Rossetti shows Dante gazing intently at Beatrice, whose red hair and delicate features resemble

those of Elizabeth Siddal. The subject, wrote Rossetti, combined 'all the influence of Dante's youth – Art, Friendship and Love – with a real incident embodying them'.[14] These key ideas – youth, art, friendship and love – are written in Latin in Gothic lettering on the frame, probably designed by the architect J. P. Seddon.[15]

From the late 1850s Rossetti abandoned narrative subjects for a series of half-length portrayals of women arrayed in luxurious clothes and surrounded by beautiful objects, jewels and flowers. One of the most spectacular of these celebrations of female beauty and sexual allure is *The Blue Bower* (fig. 1),[16] which shows a woman with flaming red hair wearing a vivid green robe unbuttoned to reveal a fur undergarment and a hint of pink cleavage. Fanny Cornforth, one of Rossetti's favourite models, sat for this painting, and cat. 12 is a study of her for the oil. Rossetti's half-lengths of beautiful women in close-up seem to push the sitters forward into a close relationship with the viewer, and this is also the case in the drawing. Cornforth is said to have been the mistress of both Rossetti and his friend the painter George Price Boyce (1826–1897), who bought this drawing from Rossetti in 1865.

Cornforth may also have sat for the study for *My Lady Greensleeves* (cat. 13),[17] which relates to a painting of 1863, another half-length female beauty, showing a medieval lady winding her sleeve around a helmet, also the subject of a poem by Rossetti. A different model, the wife of Rossetti's studio assistant W. J. Knewstub, sat for the oil, where she appears in a slightly altered pose.

Another work set in the Middle Ages is *How They Met Themselves* (cat. 3), inspired by the notion of the *Doppelgänger*. Rossetti pictures two lovers walking in a wood who are suddenly confronted by their exact doubles. The real woman faints in shock and the man draws his sword at the sight of the ghosts. The drawing shows Rossetti's fascination with the visual rhythms set up by images of pairs and opposites (see also cat. 2, 7).

Medieval themes were a feature of Rossetti's work up to the 1860s, but in the middle and late '60s he increasingly adopted classical subjects, part of a general trend among British painters. Also in the late '60s coloured chalks became one of his favourite materials. He used this soft, delicate medium for a number of highly finished drawings that are among his most beautiful works. Reds and browns predominate, making the images almost

Fig. 1 **Dante Gabriel Rossetti**,
The Blue Bower, 1865.
Oil on canvas, 61 × 51 cm.
Barber Institute of Fine Arts,
University of Birmingham

monochromatic. *Penelope* (cat. 18), a drawing of the model Ellen Smith, shows the wife of the Greek hero Odysseus, who waited faithfully for him to come back from his epic journey. Many sought her hand in marriage, assuming he would never return. Vowing she would not marry until she had finished her tapestry, she unravelled her weaving each night to keep her suitors at bay. Rossetti shows her dreamily holding her shuttle; as in other drawings of this period, with titles such as *Reverie* and *Silence*,[18] the melancholic, abstracted expression of the sitter initiates a similar mood of contemplation in the viewer.[19]

Rossetti also used coloured chalks for straightforward portraits. Some were of family members, such as that of his sister the poet Christina (cat. 4), dated September 1866, which shows that Rossetti could create a sympathetic but accurate likeness, quite different from the idealised style of his subject pictures. He also drew many coloured chalk heads similar to cat. 14 and 15. The first of these shows Marie Spartali, the daughter of a wealthy Greek merchant and a member of the cultured Greek community in London. The other sitter may also be from this circle, which included the collectors Luke and Constantine Ionides, and Marie Zambaco, model and lover of Burne-Jones. Marie Spartali was a painter (see

cat. 83), trained under Ford Madox Brown (cat. 104), who exhibited at the Dudley and later the Grosvenor Gallery.[20] In 1871 she married the American journalist W. J. Stillman and spent much of her married life in Florence and Rome, where he was a newspaper correspondent. She frequently modelled for Rossetti; a contemporary described her as 'Mrs. Morris for beginners. The two marvels had many points in common . . . yet Mrs. Stillman's loveliness conformed to the standard of ancient Greece and could at once be appreciated, while study of her trained the eye to understand the more esoteric beauty of Mrs Morris'.[21]

Jane Morris married William Morris in 1859 and they went to live at Red House, Bexleyheath, Kent, designed by Philip Webb. In 1865 they returned to London and she was able to sit more frequently for Rossetti, who was increasingly drawn towards her. Cat. 9 is one of many informal portrait drawings of her, but she also became Rossetti's principal inspiration for a series of paintings and drawings that are at once portraits, representations of Rossetti's innermost ideas and expressions of love. One of his favourite paintings of her depicted her as Proserpine, the goddess who was captured by Pluto and forced to spend most of her life in the underworld, being

Cat. 1
Dante Gabriel Rossetti (1828–1882)
Giotto Painting the Portrait of Dante, 1852
Watercolour over pencil, heightened
with gum arabic, on paper,
36.8 × 47 cm

released for only a few months each spring. The subject
of a woman locked into an unhappy relationship must
have had special resonance as it echoed the situation of
Rossetti with Jane and William Morris. The painting
gave Rossetti great difficulty, and of the eight oil versions
and replicas only three survive. One of the unsuccessful
ones was cut down and turned into *Blanzifiore* (cat. 11),
a head of Jane Morris with primroses in her hair and
holding a bunch of snowdrops, perhaps a reference to
the association of Proserpine with spring.

Rossetti also depicted Morris as *La Donna della Finestra*
(cat. 10), the woman from the *Vita Nuova* who looked
down from her window with compassion for Dante as
he wept over the death of Beatrice: the subject, which
exists in several versions and was the theme of a sonnet
by Rossetti, was also known as *The Lady of Pity*. Rossetti

identified her as Gemma Donati, the woman whom
Dante eventually married; with Dante and Gemma
Donati, as with Rossetti and Jane Morris, there is again
an overlapping of a real portrait, based on a deeply felt
relationship, with a symbolic representation.

Owing to its association with love, music was often
a feature of Rossetti's paintings of women. *Desdemona*
(cat. 17) is a drawing for a painting conceived in the early
1870s showing the tragic heroine of Shakespeare's *Othello*
singing the willow song while her maid Emilia combs her
long, flowing hair. In *La Ghirlandata* (cat. 7) the beautiful
but impassive Alexa Wilding is depicted plucking at the
strings of a harp, garlanded with lushly blooming roses
and honeysuckle, flowers that Rossetti associated with
sexual attraction. Her hair is again loose and her draperies
flutter about her neck in decorative flowing lines. The

chalk drawing is more muted than the richly glowing oil in the Guildhall Art Gallery, London, for which this is the finished study, but, like the oil, the drawing is a carefully controlled decorative composition that creates an enclosed world of art, beauty and love.[22] Fluttering draperies are likewise a feature of Rossetti's only representation of a full-length female nude, *The Spirit of the Rainbow* (cat. 16), which illustrates a sonnet by the artist's friend Theodore Watts-Dunton (1832–1914).

Alexa Wilding modelled for *The Damsel of the Sanct Grael* (cat. 5). Rossetti first painted this subject, taken from *Le Morte d'Arthur*, a collection of tales by Sir Thomas Malory (c. 1408–1471), in 1857 when he was immersed in Arthurian themes. The Holy Grail, the object of the knights' quest, was the cup used by Christ at the Last Supper in which Joseph of Arimathea supposedly received the Saviour's blood at the Cross. Malory describes it as being carried by a pure young woman;[23] the combination of Alexa Wilding's flaming red hair and red lips with the dove of the Holy Spirit and the gesture of benediction makes for a slightly uneasy blend of sacred and secular.

With *The Blessed Damozel* and *A Vision of Fiammetta* Rossetti created images of great beauty that express his deeply held beliefs about love and death. His poem *The Blessed Damozel*, originally published in 1850, describes lovers separated by death: the Damozel, in heaven, yearns to be reunited with her lover, who is imprisoned on earth.[24]

The chalk drawing (cat. 8) is the finished study for the oil painting,[25] which is in two parts, the upper panel showing the Damozel (modelled by Alexa Wilding) looking down from heaven at her lover, the lower one depicting him gazing up at her. In the oil she is shown with white lilies and red roses, symbolising love that is both pure and physical, but in the chalk drawing she bears only lilies. *A Vision of Fiammetta* (cat. 6) was inspired by a sonnet by the Italian poet Giovanni Boccaccio (1313–1375) about his last sight of Fiammetta, the object of his love. The original sonnet, Rossetti's translation of it and a further sonnet written by Rossetti about Fiammetta are all inscribed on the frame.[26] Fiammetta, modelled by Marie Spartali, wears a flame-coloured dress in allusion to her name. Her figure stands glowing against a dark background: a vision of the brief moment between life and death. The short-lived apple blossom signifies the transience of beauty: Fiammetta stands entwined in the branches of an apple tree surrounded by emblems of the departing soul a shower of falling red and white blossom, a blood-red bird (the messenger of death), butterflies (symbols of the soul) and an angel in the aureole around her head.[27] The painting has an extraordinary power and presence. With its frame designed by the artist, it is a beautiful object in itself and a representation of female allure; at the same time it is an image of death and of love that lasts beyond the grave.

1 Jan Marsh, *Dante Gabriel Rossetti: Painter and Poet*, London, 1999, pp. 1–3.

2 Jan Marsh, *The Legend of Elizabeth Siddal*, London, 1989; *Rossetti's Portraits of Elizabeth Siddal*, Virginia Surtees, exh. cat., Ashmolean Museum, Oxford, 1991.

3 William Michael Rossetti (ed.), *Dante Gabriel Rossetti: His Family Letters, With a Memoir*, 2 vols, London, 1895, vol. 1, p. 159.

4 Julian Treuherz, 'The Pre-Raphaelites and Medieval Manuscripts', in Leslie Parris (ed.), *Pre-Raphaelite Papers*, London, 1984, pp. 158, 163–7.

5 *The Blue Bower: Rossetti in the 1860s*, Paul Spencer-Longhurst, exh. cat., Barber Institute of Fine Arts, University of Birmingham, 2000.

6 Alastair Grieve, 'The Applied Art of D. G. Rossetti – 1. His Picture Frames', *Burlington Magazine* 115, 1973, pp. 16–24.

7 Both pictures are in the Tate collection; Alastair Grieve, in *The Pre-Raphaelites*, exh. cat., Tate Gallery, London, 1984, pp. 64, 73, nos. 15, 22.

8 *Works by the Old Masters, including a Special Selection from the Works of John Linnell and Dante Gabriel Rossetti*, exh. cat., Royal Academy of Arts, London, 1883; *Pictures, Drawings, Designs and Studies by the late Dante Gabriel Rossetti*, exh. cat., Burlington Fine Arts Club, London, 1883.

9 Alastair Grieve, *The Art of Dante Gabriel Rossetti: The Watercolours and Drawings of 1850–1855*, Norwich, 1978, pp. 32–40.

10 Ibid., p. 41, fig. 32.

11 William E. Fredeman (ed.), *The Correspondence of Dante Gabriel Rossetti: The Formative Years 1835–1862*, 2 vols, Cambridge, 2002, vol. 1, p. 109.

12 Canto XI, translated by William

Michael Rossetti in idem (ed.), *The Works of Dante Gabriel Rossetti*, London, 1911, p. 300.

13 Ibid., p. 334.

14 Fredeman (note 11), vol. 1, p. 224.

15 I owe this suggestion to Virginia Surtees. J. P. Seddon was the brother of the first owner of the work, the artist Thomas Seddon.

16 *The Blue Bower* (note 5), p. 50, no. 8.

17 The model has also been identified as Ellen Smith.

18 Virginia Surtees, *The Paintings and Drawings of Dante Gabriel Rossetti (1821–1882): A Catalogue Raisonné*, 2 vols, Oxford, 1971, vol. 1, p. 118, no. 206, and p. 122, no. 214.

19 Helen E. Roberts, 'The Dream World of Dante Gabriel Rossetti', *Victorian Studies* 17, 1973–74, pp. 373–4.

20 *Pre-Raphaelite Women Artists*, Jan Marsh and Pamela Gerrish Nunn, exh. cat., Manchester City Art Gallery, 1998, pp. 131–5.

21 W. Graham Robertson, *Time Was*, London, 1931, p. 95.

22 Grieve, in *The Pre-Raphaelites* (note 7), p. 223, no. 144.

23 *William Morris and the Middle Ages*, Joanna Banham and Jennifer Harris (eds), exh. cat., Whitworth Art Gallery, Manchester, 1984, p. 166.

24 Rossetti (note 12), pp. 3–5.

25 The principal oil is in the Fogg Art Museum; a slightly different version is in the Lady Lever Art Gallery, Port Sunlight.

26 Rossetti (note 12), pp. 413, 229.

27 Frederic George Stephens, 'Mr. Rossetti's New Picture, "A Vision of Fiammetta"', *Athenaeum*, 5 October 1878, p. 440.

Cat. 2
Dante Gabriel Rossetti (1828–1882)
The Virgin Mary Being Comforted, 1852
Pencil on paper, 22.2 × 27.3 cm

Cat. 3
Dante Gabriel Rossetti (1828–1882)
How They Met Themselves, 1864
Watercolour with gum arabic on paper,
27.9 × 24.1 cm

Cat. 4
Dante Gabriel Rossetti (1828–1882)
Christina Rossetti, 1866
Coloured chalks on pale blue paper,
79 × 63.5 cm

Cat. 5
Dante Gabriel Rossetti (1828–1882)
The Damsel of the Sanct Grael, 1874
Oil on canvas, 92 × 57.7 cm

Cat. 6
Dante Gabriel Rossetti (1828–1882)
A Vision of Fiammetta, 1878
Oil on canvas, 146 × 88.9 cm

Cat. 7
Dante Gabriel Rossetti (1828–1882)
La Ghirlandata, 1873
Coloured chalks on paper,
90.1 × 76.2 cm

Cat. 8
Dante Gabriel Rossetti (1828–1882)
Study for 'The Blessed Damozel', 1873
Coloured chalks on paper,
78.7 × 89 cm

Cat. 9
Dante Gabriel Rossetti (1828–1882)
Jane Morris, c. 1869/70
Black crayon on paper, 33 × 25.4 cm

Cat. 10
Dante Gabriel Rossetti (1828–1882)
La Donna della Finestra (Jane Morris), 1880
Coloured chalks on two sheets of buff paper,
83.8 × 71.1 cm

Cat. 11
Dante Gabriel Rossetti (1828–1882)
Blanzifiore (Snowdrops), 1873
Oil on canvas, 41.5 × 34 cm

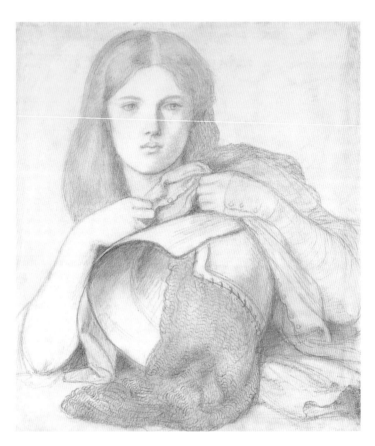

Cat. 12
Dante Gabriel Rossetti (1828–1882)
Fanny Cornforth, c. 1865
Pencil on paper, 39.3 × 26.6 cm

Cat. 13
Dante Gabriel Rossetti (1828–1882)
My Lady Greensleeves, c. 1860/63
Pencil on paper, 36.8 × 31.7 cm

Cat. 14
Dante Gabriel Rossetti (1828–1882)
Portrait of a Lady, 1870
Coloured chalks on paper,
48.9 × 39.4 cm

Cat. 15
Dante Gabriel Rossetti (1828–1882)
Marie Stillman (née Spartali), 1869
Coloured chalks on two pieces of
grey-green paper, 62.2 × 47 cm

Cat. 16
Dante Gabriel Rossetti (1828–1882)
The Spirit of the Rainbow, 1876
Black chalk on paper, 105.4 × 72.4 cm

Cat. 17
Dante Gabriel Rossetti (1828–1882)
Desdemona, c. 1878/81
Black chalk on paper, 69.8 × 50.8 cm

Cat. 18
Dante Gabriel Rossetti (1828–1882)
Penelope, 1869
Coloured chalks on paper, 89 × 67 cm

John Everett Millais

JASON ROSENFELD

The career of Sir John Everett Millais Bt (1829–1896) revolved around the Royal Academy of Arts. He entered its Schools as a Probationer at the age of ten and died while serving as its tenth President. He was born in 1829 in Southampton to John William Millais (1800–1870), a minor official and military officer from a distinguished Jersey family, and Mary Emily Hodgkinson, née Evamy (1789–1864), whose family were saddlers. His brother William Henry Millais (1828–1899) also became an artist. After living in Southampton, St Helier in Jersey and Dinan in Brittany the family settled in London in 1838 so that Millais could pursue art studies.

Millais first exhibited at the Royal Academy in 1846, when he showed *Pizarro Seizing the Inca of Peru* (Victoria and Albert Museum, London), and was a founding member of the Pre-Raphaelite Brotherhood, whose initial meeting was held in September 1848 in his family home at 83 Gower Street.[1] Early works, such as *Isabella* (1848–49; Walker Art Gallery, Liverpool) and *Christ in the House of His Parents* (1849–50; Tate Britain, London), brought him both notoriety and praise. Millais's Pre-Raphaelitism culminated in the meticulous realism of *John Ruskin* (fig. 1, p. 139), followed in 1856 by two major symbolic pictures marking a shift in his subject matter: *The Blind Girl* (fig. 3, p. 13) and *Autumn Leaves* (Manchester City Art Gallery). Subsequently, in *The Vale of Rest* (1858; Tate Britain) and *The Black Brunswicker* (1859–60; Lady Lever Art Gallery, Port Sunlight), Millais experimented with subtle evocations of complex moods or romantic imagery endowed with historical resonance.

On 7 November 1853 Millais was elected an Associate of the Royal Academy, and on 3 July 1855 he married Effie Gray of Perth, formerly the wife of the critic John Ruskin. They were to have eight children. Elected a full Academician on 18 December 1863, and with a growing family and increased social and business obligations, Millais pursued a line of production that revealed him to have one eye trained on modern painting in Britain and abroad, and the other on the popular market. 'Fancy pictures', often of child subjects, such as *My First Sermon* (1863; Guildhall Art Gallery, London) and the double portrait *'Leisure Hours'* (1864; Detroit Institute of Arts), endeared him to a newly rich middle-class clientele and were ideal for Academy exhibitions and for sales of the prints that might be made after them. He also produced many innovative designs for engraved illustrations to Tennyson's poems, Trollope's novels and other literary works. Poetic pictures, including *The Eve of St Agnes* (1862–63; Her Majesty Queen Elizabeth The Queen Mother Collection, Clarence House, London), and portraits, such as his masterpiece of ascendant Aestheticism, *Sisters* (1868; private collection), drew acclaim at the Exposition Universelle in Paris in 1867 and again in 1878, when he won a gold medal and was named an officer of the *Légion d'honneur*. These works reflected an ability to deal with complexities of unifying colour, abstract surface and formal design that anticipated and challenged works by his contemporaries James McNeill Whistler (fig. 2, p. 143), John Singer Sargent and Albert Moore (cat. 146–8).

In the 1870s Millais reinvented himself as a landscapist and carried over the surface design characteristic of these works into such portraits as *Twins* (1875–76; private collection) and *Hearts Are Trumps: Portraits of Elizabeth, Diana and Mary, Daughters of Walter Armstrong, Esq.* (1872; Tate Britain). By this decade only Frederic Leighton could claim to rival Millais as the most important artist in Britain. Success was validated by his unceasing flow of commissions, his magnificent Italianate house at 2 Palace Gate, Kensington,[2] and his becoming the first British artist to be given a hereditary title when he was made a Baronet on 16 July 1885. In the 1880s and '90s Millais's portraits, original and expressive landscapes, ruminative subject pictures, including *The Ruling Passion* (1885; Glasgow Museums, Art Gallery and Museum, Kelvingrove), and 'fancy pictures', such as

Bubbles (1886; private collection), continued themes from his early works, reflecting contemporary meditations on mortality and loss, while also reworking Old Master and 18th-century British paintings in a modern idiom. When he began his brief Presidency of the Academy 1896, there was no more lauded artist in Britain. He died aged 67 on 13 August of that year and was buried in Painters' Corner in the Crypt of St Paul's Cathedral.

Millais's pictures in the Andrew Lloyd Webber Collection form a representative survey of a half-century of vital and innovative art. *Four Children of the Wyatt Family* (cat. 21) and *James Wyatt and His Granddaughter Mary Wyatt* (cat. 20) of 1849 reveal both Millais's early Pre-Raphaelite manner and his swift progress to artistic maturity. They were among several portraits commissioned by James Wyatt, the Duke of Marlborough's curator at Blenheim, a collector, art dealer, frame-maker, carver, gilder, print-seller and former mayor of Oxford who lived above his shop at 115 High Street.[3] Mary Wyatt figures in both pictures: as a beaming, cross-legged tot, and then as a dreamy-looking girl leaning on her grandfather. In the formal portrait the finely attired children pose in a corner of a room in Wyatt's house, a sample of his art collection hanging in the background. The more accomplished and casual picture of James and Mary Wyatt is responsive to the private life of someone quite important to Millais. Wyatt had bought the artist's *Cymon and Iphigenia* (1848; private collection) and Millais was living in his house. Wyatt sits in an easy-chair, leaning forward from the lace antimacassar to embrace Mary. He has been reading a book; his eyeglasses lie folded on its pages. The right background is filled with objects redolent of Wyatt's profession and lineage – fine china in a cabinet and framed paintings of his family and ancestors. The left side presents a wealth of Pre-Raphaelite natural detail – a bouquet and potted plants inside, Wyatt's sun-splashed garden outside.

Preoccupation with nature was characteristic of early Pre-Raphaelitism, when artists such as Millais, William Holman Hunt (cat. 108, 109) and Ford Madox Brown (cat. 104), along with the later adherents John Brett (cat. 105–7, 114), Arthur Hughes (cat. 68, 69, 71, 72, 74, 77) and John Atkinson Grimshaw (cat. 110), seemed to follow Ruskin's injunction to work directly from nature in order to capture an ethical and visual truth in paint.

This involved long hours labouring outdoors in all manner of weather and resulted in the extraordinary backgrounds of Millais's subject pictures of the early 1850s: *A Huguenot, on St Bartholomew's day, refusing to shield himself from danger by wearing the Roman Catholic badge* (fig. 1) and *Ophelia* (fig. 2), seen here in smaller versions, and *The Proscribed Royalist, 1651*. *Ophelia* and *A Huguenot* were painted in the environs of Ewell in Surrey during the summer and autumn of 1851, when Millais and Holman Hunt were working in tandem and perfecting their brilliant outdoor manner. In early December, Millais returned to London with canvases completed but for blank areas in the centre for the figures, which he painted from models and lay-figures in his studio over the winter. Lord Lloyd-Webber's *Ophelia* (cat. 22) is a far freer treatment in watercolour that was commissioned in 1865 by Agnew's, one of Millais's many dealers. Such replicas were much sought after by collectors and provided Millais with a welcome supplementary income. *A Huguenot* (cat. 25) is a quarter-

Fig. 1 **Sir John Everett Millais Bt PRA**, *A Huguenot, on St Bartholomew's day, refusing to shield himself from danger by wearing the Roman Catholic badge*, 1851–52. Oil on canvas, 92.7 × 62.2 cm. The Makins Collection

Fig. 2 **Sir John Everett Millais Bt PRA**, *Ophelia*, 1851–52. Oil on canvas, 76.2 × 111.8 cm. Tate Britain, London

sized oil version of the original, formerly owned by the artist's contemporary Thomas E. Plint, a Leeds connoisseur, and the American J. Pierpont Morgan. In contrast to the tightly controlled, painstaking application of paint in the original, the more broadly brushed surface testifies to Millais's stylistic evolution since the early 1850s, although each flower bud and all details of the figures' glowing clothing are depicted perfectly. *A Dream of the Past: Sir Isumbras at the Ford* (cat. 23) is a smaller variant of an oil painting exhibited at the Academy in 1857 and now in the Lady Lever Art Gallery, Port Sunlight.

Most spectacular is *The Proscribed Royalist, 1651* (cat. 24), one of only a handful of important Pre-Raphaelite Brotherhood pictures in private hands. It was painted at Hayes, near Bromley in Kent, in the summer of 1852, finished in London and exhibited at the Academy in 1853. In the chaos of the Civil War, a Roundhead wearing a splendid orange/copper-coloured satin garment desperately hides her Cavalier lover, posed for by Arthur Hughes, in a massive oak.[4] Most remarkable is the rendering of the moss at the base of the tree in a variety of green pigments highly diluted so as to produce a glassy, moist and translucent appearance. Building on the success of *A Huguenot*, Millais painted many such images of star-crossed romances in turbulent historical circum-

stances. *The Proscribed Royalist* was transformed into a steel engraving to take advantage of the burgeoning market for prints, and it spawned a tourist site – the 'Millais Oak' on West Wickham Common, a place of pilgrimage for Millais admirers throughout the late 19th century.

The depiction of the natural world, nurtured by Ruskin's *Modern Painters*, was a Pre-Raphaelite preoccupation, as was the predilection for the Gothic style as an antidote to the perceived decadence of the Renaissance. This was recognised by both critic and artist, and when Millais accompanied the older man to Scotland to paint his portrait while he prepared his first public lectures, he drew some designs for Gothic-style architecture.[5] The finest (cat. 19) is a charcoal and wash drawing of a window incorporating lip-locked angels whose bodies and appendages form the decorative arches. The design relates to works shown during one of Ruskin's lectures, but was never carried out. Millais was assisted in some of the drawings by Effie Ruskin, whom he was tutoring in art at the time and whose face provided the model for those of the angels in the design included here. Her relationship with Millais in Scotland was platonic, but passions had been aroused and a short time later she sought, and received, an annulment of her marriage to Ruskin so as to be free to marry Millais.

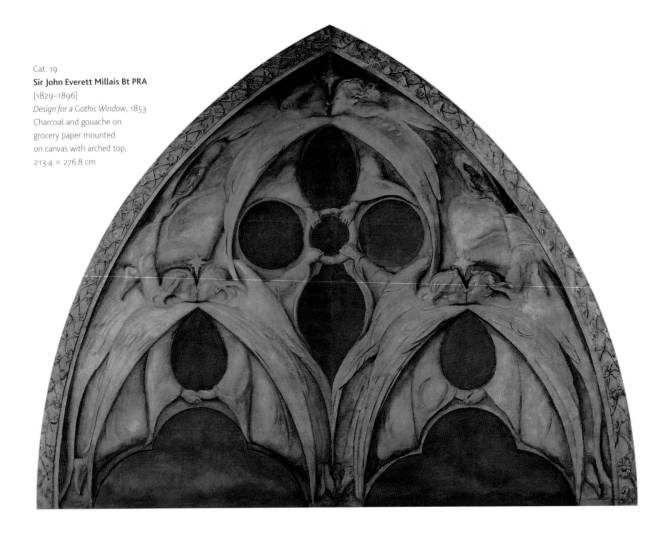

Cat. 19
Sir John Everett Millais Bt PRA
(1829–1896)
Design for a Gothic Window, 1853
Charcoal and gouache on
grocery paper mounted
on canvas with arched top,
213.4 × 276.8 cm

Millais established himself as the dominant interpreter of nature in British painting in 1871 with *Chill October* (cat. 28), his first large-scale pure landscape. Twenty pictures of Scottish scenery followed. Dramatic and melancholic, full of striking effects and atmosphere, these late landscapes are the great dark horses of his career. They attracted fulsome praise from contemporary critics and artists, notably the young Vincent van Gogh.[6] *Chill October* was a challenge to post-Pre-Raphaelite notions of nature in British art and a personal response to Millais's beloved Scottish scenery, specifically that of Perthshire, his wife's home county. The artist spent the autumn and winter months there, renting a series of extravagant houses, painting and engaging in sporting activities. *Chill October*, which he painted on the spot, shows a backwater of the River Tay downstream from Perth. The surface of the canvas is marvellously alive, ranging from the lowering steel-grey cloud bank at the top, against which are etched the shapes of fourteen darting

swallows, via the densely rendered whiter sky beyond, consisting of a number of impasto horizontal strokes above the trees, to the reeds in the lower right foreground, executed in a series of bravura strokes applied over the other paint layers so that the flecked forms of their leaves are slightly raised. This grand work was the result of Millais's ambition, as revealed in a letter of 1868: 'I am very anxious to come out particularly strong next year in our new Exhibition rooms and I must try & paint an outdoor picture if I can.'[7] Millais did not get round to painting this picture until two years later and showed it at the Academy in 1871, the third Summer Exhibition to be held at that institution's new home, Burlington House.

The Old Garden (cat. 29), painted seventeen years later, superbly captures the grounds of Murthly Castle, seat of Sir Archibald Douglas Stewart. In contrast to the wild nature in *Chill October*, here all is manicured and manipulated, the shovel and smock evidence of a gardener's presence, a bubbling fountain providing a sonorous complement to the still Scottish air, the broad dusk sky and the purple-tinted hills. At the time, Millais was living at Birnam Hall, often called Dalpowie, a hunting lodge in the garden that Stewart rented out in season. Such pictures particularly appealed to those of Millais's fellow Englishmen who fancied themselves lairds when visiting Scotland for recreational purposes.

Finally, two works reveal Millais's technical bravura in a manner far removed from the detailed brushwork of early Pre-Raphaelitism. 'Yes' (cat. 27) of 1877 is a scene of contemporary life related to Millais's book illustrations, yet its brilliant brushwork transforms the small-scale black-and-white of those woodblock prints and bears witness to an assimilation of English and Continental Old Masters. It completed a trilogy of works begun in 1871 with *Yes or No?* (Yale Center for British Art, New Haven), which shows a widow holding a photograph of her deceased and mulling over the written proposal of a new suitor, and continued four years later with *No!* (unlocated), in which a woman reads over her rejection of a proposal. 'Yes' depicts an elegantly attired woman, sporting a double-strand pearl and gold chocker, responding positively to her suitor's offer, and just in the nick of time, as he is packed and dressed for a journey, wearing a finely striated Ulster overcoat and holding a deerstalker hat. All emotion centres on the highlighted face of the woman, while he, still on tenterhooks, stands

largely in shade. Marble architecture frames the figure of the man, who is about to return to the city and 'civilisation', while leaves appear behind the head of the woman, emblematic of nature submitting to his will. Intensely popular with the general public both when exhibited and in the form of a mezzotint published by Agnew's, this picture reprises the romantic couples of Millais's earlier works (cat. 24, 25), using three-quarter-length figures like those in the portraits that were the artist's bread and butter at this time.[8]

Cinderella (cat. 26) of 1881 is both literary and sentimental.[9] It is related to Millais's popular images of children, such as *Bubbles* and *Cherry Ripe* (1879; private collection). In emphasising states of melancholy, and Aestheticist style in the dress, these paintings employed contemporary ideas to reinterpret 'fancy pictures' à la Thomas Gainsborough and Sir Joshua Reynolds. In *Cinderella* a peacock feather introduces a touch of beauty and hope into the girl's drab existence; two carefully depicted mice in the lower right corner allude to the fact that, later in the story, they will be transformed into Cinderella's coach horses. The image recalls the wistful uncertainty prevalent in Millais's earlier pictures,[10] while the far-off stare of the young princess-to-be runs counter to the 18th-century tradition of fancy pictures by presenting, as in all the artist's paintings of children,[11] a vivid sense of a surprisingly mature inner life.

1 Now no. 7 and marked by a Blue Plaque.

2 Designed by Philip Hardwick and completed in 1876–77. Jeremy Musson, 'Has a Pot of Paint Done All This? The Studio-House of Sir John Everett Millais, Bt.', in *John Everett Millais: Beyond the Pre-Raphaelite Brotherhood*, Debra N. Mancoff (ed.), Studies in British Art 7, New Haven and London, 2001, pp. 95–118.

3 Malcolm Warner, in *The Pre-Raphaelites*, exh. cat., Tate Gallery, London, 1984, pp. 80–2; *Millais: Portraits*, exh. cat., National Portrait Gallery, London, 1999, pp. 67–72.

4 Malcolm Warner, in *The Pre-Raphaelites* (note 3), pp. 104–5.

5 The lectures were given at the Edinburgh Philosophical Institution in November. Ruskin was also indexing *The Stones of Venice* for publication.

6 Van Gogh was working in London in 1875 when he saw *Chill October* at Christie's and referred to it frequently in his letters. He also sent a photograph of *A Huguenot* (fig. 1) to his brother Theo. *English Influences on Vincent van Gogh*, exh. cat., University of Nottingham and The Arts Council of Great Britain, 1974, p. 19; *Van Gogh in England: Portrait of the Artist as a Young Man*, Martin Bailey, exh. cat., Barbican Art Gallery, London, 1992, pp. 36–43, 136.

7 Pierpont Morgan Library, Millais Papers, MA.1485.A: Millais to Effie Millais, dated 5 August 1868.

8 Often Millais painted formal portraits of those who modelled for the figures in these pictorial dramas.

9 The model, Beatrice Buckstone, sat for two other pictures that year, 'Sweetest Eyes Were Ever Seen' (National Gallery of Scotland, Edinburgh) and *Caller Herrin'* (Armand Hammer Collection, Los Angeles).

10 For example, *Waiting* of 1854 (Birmingham Museum and Art Gallery).

11 Such as *Autumn Leaves* and 'The Little Speedwell's Darling Blue' (1891–92; Lady Lever Art Gallery).

Cat. 20
Sir John Everett Millais Bt PRA
(1829–1896)
James Wyatt and His Granddaughter
Mary Wyatt, 1849
Oil on panel, 35.5 × 45 cm

Cat. 21
Sir John Everett Millais Bt PRA
(1829–1896)
Four Children of the Wyatt Family, 1849
Oil on panel, 45.7 × 30.5 cm

Cat. 22
Sir John Everett Millais Bt PRA
(1829–1896)
Ophelia, 1865–66
Watercolour with gouache,
17.8 × 25.4 cm

Cat. 23
Sir John Everett Millais Bt PRA
(1829–1896)
A Dream of the Past: Sir Isumbras
at the Ford, c. 1857
Oil on panel, 27.3 × 36.5 cm

Cat. 24
Sir John Everett Millais Bt PRA
(1829–1896)
The Proscribed Royalist, 1651, 1852–53
Oil on canvas framed with arched
top, 102.8 × 73.6 cm

Cat. 25
Sir John Everett Millais Bt PRA
(1829–1896)
A Huguenot, c. 1852/55
Oil on board with arched top,
24.7 × 17.7 cm

Cat. 26
Sir John Everett Millais Bt PRA
(1829–1896)
Cinderella, 1881
Oil on canvas, 125.7 × 88.9 cm

Cat. 27
Sir John Everett Millais Bt PRA
(1829–1896)
'Yes', 1877
Oil on canvas, 152.4 × 116.8 cm

Cat. 28
Sir John Everett Millais Bt PRA
(1829–1896)
Chill October, 1870
Oil on canvas, 141 × 186.7 cm

PREVIOUS PAGES Detail of cat. 28

Cat. 29
Sir John Everett Millais Bt PRA
(1829–1896)
The Old Garden, 1888
Oil on canvas, 114.5 × 174 cm

'Too beautiful not to be true': Edward Burne-Jones

DEBRA N. MANCOFF

In 1890 Sir Edward Coley Burne-Jones Bt (1833–1898) received a young visitor in his studio. She watched as he worked on *The Star of Bethlehem*, a watercolour on a plane of paper so vast that the artist employed a mobile ladder to reach its upper sections (fig. 1). The figures were as tall as Burne-Jones himself, and the sumptuous raiment of the Magi and the presiding angel revealed his mastery of rich colour and complex pattern. *The Star of Bethlehem* (fig. 3) evoked a still and reverent world, distant from mundane reality, where wealthy kings bowed in deference to a Holy Child. When the little girl boldly asked if the artist believed the story, Burne-Jones's reply was as telling as it was sincere: 'It is too beautiful not to be true.'[1]

Throughout his career Burne-Jones pursued an elusive vision. Then as now, his work was often misunderstood as escapist, rooted in his imagination rather than in his experience. As a dreamer and a romantic in a pragmatic and materialistic time, Burne-Jones fully acknowledged the artifice of his endeavour: 'I don't want to pretend that this isn't a picture'.[2] Rather than as an escape from reality, Burne-Jones conceived his art as an alternative, a vision of the boundless potential of the human body and spirit. He unleashed the transcending power of an imagination that released both the artist and the viewer from prosaic concerns of known existence, and he claimed that when beauty was allied with the imagination 'we are close to the secret of all things'.[3] Burne-Jones was aware that to be close to the mystery was not the same thing as possessing it, but he remained dedicated to the pursuit of beauty in art that bore witness to what could not be explained but would always be true.

Born in Birmingham on 28 August 1833, Burne-Jones experienced little in childhood that would nurture the imagination. His mother died a week after his birth, and his father, Edward Jones, a gilder and frame-maker, hired Ann Sampson, a pious but unschooled woman, to keep house and care for his son.[4] Although shy and physically fragile, Burne-Jones was precocious, and as he grew up he expanded the limited horizons of his modest circumstances through reading and drawing. From 1844 to 1853 he attended the King Edward VI Grammar School, where he covered his exercise books with caricatures and cartoons of devils, and his passion for reading led to academic distinction. Upon completion of the Classics course, he left for Oxford to study at Exeter College and prepare for a clerical career.

In his first days at Oxford, Burne-Jones met his life-long friend William Morris. Disenchanted with the curriculum, they devised their own course of reading that reflected their fascination with the medieval revival, including the works of Alfred Tennyson, Thomas Carlyle and John Ruskin. Through Ruskin's writings they became

Fig. 1 Burne-Jones in front of his *Star of Bethlehem*, 1890. Photograph by Barbara Leighton. National Portrait Gallery, London

acquainted with Pre-Raphaelite art, and soon both young men identified with its quest for authentic sources and sincere expression. In the summer of 1855, after a walking tour with Morris through northern France, Burne-Jones discarded his clerical aspirations, vowing instead to seek his destiny as an artist. In the autumn he travelled to London to hear Dante Gabriel Rossetti (cat. 1–18) lecture at the Working Men's College. Swayed by Rossetti's enthusiasm, Burne-Jones decided to leave Oxford the following year without completing his degree.

Aside from rudimentary lessons with Rossetti and irregular attendance at the life drawing classes at J.M. Leigh's Academy, Burne-Jones relied upon intense independent practice to develop his skill. His ready facility for drawing had already brought him a commission to design illustrations for *The Fairy Family* (1854/56; cat. 30), a collection of fantastic tales for children compiled by Archibald Maclaren. Burne-Jones produced at least 88 images in pencil and ink for the book in a tight, meticulously detailed style influenced by Rossetti's angular

aesthetic. In 1856 Burne-Jones secured his first commission to design stained glass, and in 1857 he tried his hand at mural painting, joining Rossetti, Morris and others in decorating the interior of the Oxford Union's new Debating Hall with images from *Le Morte d'Arthur* by Sir Thomas Malory (*c.* 1408–1471). When Ruskin saw his drawings in 1859 he declared: 'Jones, you are gigantic.'[5]

On 9 June 1860 Burne-Jones married Georgiana Macdonald and moved to Bloomsbury. They were to have two surviving children, Philip, born in 1861, and Margaret, born in 1866. His friends had also been wed, Morris to Jane Burden in 1859 and Rossetti to Elizabeth Siddal in 1860. Morris had a home built for his bride at Bexleyheath in Kent, and Red House, designed by Philip Webb, became the centre of their artistic activity. Morris recruited his friends to cover the interior walls with murals and to design all the furnishings, including painted furniture, tiles, stained glass and textiles. The decoration of Red House inspired Morris to found the artists' cooperative Morris, Marshall, Faulkner & Co.,

Cat. 30a–g
Sir Edward Coley Burne-Jones Bt ARA
(1833–1898)
Seven Illustrations for 'The Fairy Family',
1854/56
Pen and ink on paper: two rectangular
(14.5 × 9.8 cm), one oval (7.4 × 5.8 cm),
four circular (left to right, diam. 6.1 cm,
7.2 cm, 6.1 cm, 5.9 cm)

'Fine Art Workmen in Painting Carving, Furniture and the Metals' (known as 'The Firm'). Burne-Jones painted furniture and designed stained glass, tapestries and tiles for The Firm, and in 1875, when Morris reorganised the cooperative as Morris & Co., only Burne-Jones remained associated with it.

Burne-Jones received his first major commission at the recommendation of the architect G.F. Bodley. This was for an altarpiece for St Paul's in West Street, Brighton, which the artist painted in 1861. Dissatisfied with the crowded appearance of the central panel of this triptych, he completed a second version (cat. 36), which was installed in the church and remained on the high altar until 1975. Both feature the Adoration of the Magi in the centre flanked by panels depicting the Annunciation, but the aesthetic choices that distinguish them reveal how Burne-Jones had begun to develop his own distinctive style. In the second version he reduced the number of figures from eleven to no more than the Magi and the Holy Family, and in place of recognisable portraits – a practice associated with Pre-Raphaelite art and with the Red House murals – Burne-Jones gener- alised his figures' features. In replacing complexity with simple grandeur, he shed the salient characteristics of his early technique, the tight line and closed composition that reflected Rossetti's formative influence.

Other factors contributed to this change. Burne-Jones took his first trip to Italy in 1859, and the composition of his second triptych recalls the atmospheric aesthetic governing the work of such quattrocento painters as Botticelli, Ghirlandaio and Mantegna, which he saw in Florence, Siena and Milan. He returned to Italy in 1862 with his wife. Ruskin accompanied them to Parma and Milan and gave Burne-Jones lists of works to see and copy as the couple proceeded to Verona, Padua and Venice. Burne-Jones disliked the assignment, producing only what he called 'rotten little sketches', but he was grateful for Ruskin's attention.[6] The artist's new-found appreciation of the luminous works of the High Renais- sance painters Carpaccio, Correggio and Giorgione awakened his sensitivity to the lyrical potential of colour. *The Annunciation (The Flower of God)* (cat. 39), painted the following summer, displays an unprecedented tonal harmony in shades of rose tempered by ochre and green. Details of the composition – the raked floorboards, the

long plane of the bed and the little pair of shoes in the foreground – reveal another influence: Jan van Eyck's *Giovanni Arnolfini and His Wife Giovanna Cenami* (1434) in the National Gallery, London.[7] Upon election to membership of the Old Water-Colour Society in 1864, Burne-Jones exhibited this Annunciation with three other watercolours, including *The Merciful Knight* (Birmingham Museum and Art Gallery), marking his public debut in the London art world.

Critical opinion of Burne-Jones's unorthodox watercolour compositions was mixed, but the exhibition introduced the artist's work to his most significant patrons, William Graham, a former merchant with a trading branch in India, and Frederick Leyland, a Liverpool ship magnate. With increased financial security, Burne-Jones moved his family to Kensington in 1865. His circle of friends widened to include the artists James McNeill Whistler, Albert Moore (cat. 146–8) and Frederic Leighton (cat. 138, 141, 150), the rising star of the Royal Academy of Arts. Although Rossetti had advised him against the influence of classical antiquity, Burne-Jones now spent long hours in the British Museum and the South Kensington Museum sketching the Elgin Marbles and Marcantonio Raimondi's reproductive engravings of High Renaissance masterworks. The artist's wife, Georgiana, described it as a time of transition and self-absorption 'to make up for lack of earlier training'.[8] As seen in the poignant composition *The Lament* (cat. 43), with its direct reference to the seated figure of Ares on the Parthenon frieze, his figures took on solidity and dignity, as well as an air of serenity.

Burne-Jones's new-found classical lyricism did not diminish his passion for the Middle Ages. Rather, he merged his sources, creating an aesthetic synthesis that John Christian has compared to that of Chaucer.[9] Whether medieval or antique in origin, Burne-Jones's subjects taken from legend existed in a domain of tranquil beauty, undisturbed by dramatic expression or archaeological detail. His approach to the legend of St George, in a series of seven canvases commissioned in 1865 by fellow painter Myles Birket Foster to decorate the dining room of his home The Hill at Witley in Surrey, reveals this balance. The artist's source was Jacobus da Voragine's 13th-century compendium *The Golden Legend*, which sets the tale in the Roman era. But in *The Princess*

Cat. 31
Sir Edward Coley Burne-Jones Bt ARA
(1833–1898)
Love and Beauty, 1874
Chalks on paper, 89 × 118 cm

Sabra Led to the Dragon (cat. 38), the fourth canvas in the series, Burne-Jones has generalised details of architecture and costume, creating a realm that is remote yet timeless and striking a poignant mood in a grim narrative.

Morris struck a similar synthesis in his poetic epic *The Earthly Paradise*. Inspired by Chaucer's *Canterbury Tales* (*c.* 1387–1400), Morris here described an encounter of Norse mariners and Greek islanders who exchanged a cycle of 24 tales. In 1865 he proposed that Burne-Jones illustrate a folio edition of the work and, although the project was never realised, the tales became part of the painter's repertoire.[10] The watercolour *Zephyrus and Psyche* (cat. 37), painted in 1865, closely resembles his woodcut design, but the subtle harmonies of Psyche's pale rose gown and Zephyrus' steel-grey robe against the sweep of ice-blue sky and the greens of the landscape heighten the lyricism of the composition. Burne-Jones turned to the subject again in 1872, when he collaborated with Morris on a sequence of twelve paintings for the dining room in the Kensington house of George Howard, Earl of Carlisle. Burne-Jones lost interest in the commission – it was completed by Walter Crane – but the subject continued to intrigue him. Although an entry in his studio log indicates that he designed a procession of trumpeters for Psyche's wedding, it appears that he did not begin the

stark and noble oil *The Challenge in the Wilderness* (cat. 32) until the 1890s. It remained unfinished at his death and, while the heroic proportions of the musicians and the sculpted folds of their robes typify his late style, the composition originated in his 1865 pencil studies.

Burne-Jones's fascination with the legend of Pygmalion and the Image – the story of the ancient Cypriot sculptor who created a statue so beautiful that it won his heart – can also be traced to his *Earthly Paradise* designs. In 1868 he condensed the story into four oil paintings, which he completed in 1870. The titles provide a narrative quatrain. In 'The heart desires' (cat. 49a) Pygmalion reflects upon female beauty represented by the cold ideal of sculpture and the vital energy of the townswomen who pass the door of his studio. The sculpted image of Galatea in 'The hand refrains' (cat. 49b) fills him with desire, and Venus rewards his restraint by transforming the marble statue into flesh in 'The godhead fires' (cat. 49c). In 'The soul attains' (cat. 49d) the sculptor kneels before his now mortal love. Burne-Jones painted the series a second time, in 1875–78, on a larger scale and in a pale, icy palette. He had produced the first set on a commission from Euphrosyne Cassavetti, a member of the sophisticated Greek cultural enclave in London. The artist entered into a brief but tempestuous affair with Cassavetti's daughter Marie Zambaco, a sculptor whose exotic beauty shaped Burne-Jones's female ideal for nearly a decade. Her image appeared in the 1869 watercolour *Phyllis and Demophoön* (Birmingham Museum and Art Gallery), which bore a Latin legend that raised suspicions among the gossips of the art world when it was shown at the Old Water-Colour Society in 1870: 'Tell me what I have done, except to love unwisely'. Patrons took offence to the male nudity in the work, and Burne-Jones was asked to remove it from the exhibition. He readily complied, but resigned from the Society when the exhibition closed.

In the years that followed, Burne-Jones retreated from public judgement. He later recalled the time as 'the seven most blissfullest years of work that I ever had; no fuss, no publicity, no teasing about exhibiting, no getting pictures done against times'.[11] Now living in The Grange, an 18th-century house in Fulham which he had purchased

in 1867, he found contentment in the studio working with his assistants on projects for Morris and a few select patrons. He travelled to Italy in 1871, spending hours in the Sistine Chapel studying the frescoes of Michelangelo. This new-found inspiration strained his friendship with Ruskin, but study of the Italian master's style transformed Burne-Jones's approach to the figure, prompting him to add weight and gravity to his forms without diminishing their characteristic grace and ethereality. This extraordinary balance is seen in the allegory *Music* (cat. 42); the positioning of the seated figure echoes that of the Sistine prophets and sibyls, but the figure itself is languid and sweet, untouched by Michelangelo's fierce energy. Burne-Jones went to Italy for the last time in 1873. Accompanied as far as Florence by Morris, he continued alone to Ravenna, where he became ill and was forced to return home. Never robust, his bout of 'Ravenna fever' discouraged future visits, but he

Cat. 32
Sir Edward Coley Burne-Jones Bt ARA
(1833–1898)
The Challenge in the Wilderness, c. 1894/98
Oil on canvas, 129.5 × 96.5 cm

cultivated his memories as an imaginative ideal: 'I may say quite literally that I walk about here and live in Italy.'[12]

In 1877 Burne-Jones broke his self-imposed ban on public scrutiny by sending eight works for display to the new Grosvenor Gallery.[13] Hung as an ensemble in the main gallery, the selection revealed his wide-ranging mastery, from the sensual *Beguiling of Merlin* (1874–76; Lady Lever Art Gallery, Port Sunlight) to the reverent *Days of Creation* (1870–76; Fogg Art Museum, Harvard University, Cambridge, MA). In *The Mirror of Venus* (Calouste Gulbenkian Foundation, Lisbon) the sole subject was beauty. Inspired by 'The Hill of Venus' in Morris's *Earthly Paradise*, Burne-Jones portrayed Venus joining a group of comely women who are contemplating their reflections in a glassy pond. He completed a smaller version of this work in 1877 (cat. 48), and the finely drawn figures, poised with infinite grace, embody a meditation on the nature of beauty that is as poignant as it is sweet. The novelist Henry James expressed the critical consensus when he dubbed Burne-Jones 'the lion of the exhibition'.[14]

The unprecedented recognition that greeted Burne-Jones's return prompted Georgiana to declare: 'From that day he belonged to the world in a sense that he had never done before, for his existence became widely known and his name famous.'[15] Over the next decade, with the exception of 1881, he exhibited annually at the Grosvenor Gallery. Critical accolades were often tempered with bewilderment at the melancholic languor of his figures, leading some observers, James among them, to sense an unhealthy – and even unmanly – element in his art. Writing in 1898, the French critic Robert de La Sizeranne explained this quality as a conflict between Burne-Jones's Italianate passion for physical beauty and the legacy of romantic Northern fatalism. According to La Sizeranne, Burne-Jones's heroes, although magnificent in their proportions, were 'weary of their strength, embarrassed by their height, and almost ashamed of their good looks'.[16] This enigmatic balance of brittleness and strength can be seen in the artist's treatment of King Cophetua and the Beggar Maid. Based on Tennyson's poem 'The Beggar Maid' (1842), this is the tale of an African king who values romantic love over power and wealth. In a gouache rendition (cat. 35), the maid rewards the king with a subtle smile, but the grand version in oil (fig. 2), exhibited at the Grosvenor Gallery in 1884, is

drained of emotion and unnervingly still. Burne-Jones employed surface richness – bright, jewel-like tonalities and sumptuous detail – rather than narrative action to convey his message. Hailed by the conservative critic of *The Times* as 'not only the finest work Mr. Burne-Jones has ever painted, but one of the finest ever painted by an Englishman', *King Cophetua and the Beggar Maid* established the artist's international reputation when it was shown at the 1889 Exposition Universelle in Paris.[17] The enigmatic characteristics that often troubled British critics thrilled an audience drawn more to suggestion than explicitness, and the artists allied with the Symbolist movement recognised a kindred spirit in Burne-Jones and the exquisite, fragile world of his imagery.

The wistful beauty that ennobled Burne-Jones's figures idealised his portraits. He had little interest in the precise rendering of likeness and explained his approach as 'the perpetual hunt to find in a face what I like, and leave out what mislikes me'.[18] His favourite sitter was his daughter Margaret, whose wide expressive eyes and chiselled features appeared to have been forged in accordance with her father's aesthetic; in addition to painting her portrait in 1886, he had her model for *The Sleeping Princess*

Cat. 33
Sir Edward Coley Burne-Jones Bt ARA
(1833–1898)
Manuscript volume of illustrated letters and humorous drawings sent to Helen Mary Gaskell, 1897–98
Size of binding 18 × 12.5 × 2 cm

Cat. 34
Sir Edward Coley Burne-Jones Bt ARA
(1833–1898)
The Judgement of Paris, early 1870s
Oil on canvas, 107.2 ×69.2 cm

Fig. 2 **Sir Edward Coley Burne-Jones Bt ARA,**
King Cophetua and the Beggar Maid, 1884. Oil on
canvas, 293.5 × 136 cm. Tate Britain, London

Cat. 35
Sir Edward Coley Burne-Jones Bt ARA
(1833–1898)
King Cophetua and the Beggar Maid, 1883
Gouache and gum arabic on paper,
72.3 × 37 cm

(cat. 46, 54) in his *Briar Rose Series* and as a Roman vestal
in *Flamma Vestalis* (cat. 44). His portraits of children have a
pensive and fragile air that is remarkably evocative of the
evanescence of youth and innocence. Burne-Jones liked
children and enjoyed painting the portraits of the sons
and daughters of friends, such as Cicely Horner (cat. 53),
the daughter of his close confidant Frances Horner and
the granddaughter of his patron William Graham. Philip
Comyns Carr (cat. 52), the son of the director of the
Grosvenor Gallery, was a fidgety sitter who tried the
artist's patience. The books held by Katie Lewis (cat. 55)
and Dorothy Mattersdorf (cat. 51) may have provided the

needed distraction, but possibly also reflect the painter's
boyhood joy in reading. His most haunting portrait is of
Amy Gaskell (cat. 50), the daughter of one of his dearest
friends. The contrast of her dark brown hair and black
garments is stark against her pale, luminous skin. No
longer a girl, but not yet a woman, Gaskell possesses
a wraithlike beauty that expresses the enigma of this
moment of transition.

Burne-Jones designed stained glass throughout his
career.[19] Drawing had always come easily to him and,
after a day's work in the studio, he liked to design his
cartoons in the evening, often in the company of his

Fig. 3 **Sir Edward Coley Burne-Jones Bt ARA**,
The Star of Bethlehem, 1888–91.
Watercolour on paper, 256.5 × 386 cm.
Birmingham Museum and Art Gallery

family and guests. He worked in black and white, most often in charcoal; colour selection was left to Morris when the designs were translated into glass. Many cartoons had an extended life. When they were returned to his studio, Burne-Jones often added watercolour or transposed the designs into paintings. The monumental figure of St Luke (cat. 60) had its origin in the design for the central panel of a window in the chapel of Jesus College, Cambridge (1873). Worked in charcoal and gouache, the painting's limited palette recalls the Northern Renaissance practice of grisaille, or 'stone painting', and the firm lines of the drapery folds testify to Burne-Jones's virtuosity as a draughtsman. He also favoured the tall, vertical format dictated by the window light in his single-figure compositions, as seen in *Caritas* (cat. 47), a personification of Charity, the principal Christian virtue.

In 1881 the architect G. E. Street invited Burne-Jones to design mosaics for the recently completed American Episcopal Church in Rome. The commission was a source of great pleasure, fulfilling the artist's long-standing desire to execute a public work on a grand scale, but it was also a source of intense frustration. He created designs to cover the walls of the apse and the inside of the dome with a vision of the New Jerusalem crowned by an image of Christ Enthroned in Majesty and surrounded by angels (cat. 58, 59). With Morris's help, he selected colours for the tesserae, but without leaving England he could not monitor their production in Venice or the installation in Rome. Work progressed slowly and, although the first mosaic was unveiled in 1885, other projects, as well as sporadic illness, drew his attention elsewhere. The designs were eventually completed by his assistant Thomas Matthew Rooke after the artist's death. The steel-toned gouache *The Fall of Lucifer* (cat. 62), developed from a discarded design for this ensemble, indicates the spectacular complexity he envisioned.

In contrast to the Roman project, Morris's commission to design a tapestry featuring the Adoration of the Magi for the chapel of Exeter College in 1886 offered Burne-Jones an opportunity for the close collaboration and control he preferred. Even before completing the design in 1888, he agreed to repeat the composition in watercolour on a vast scale for the Corporation of Birmingham for inclusion in the new municipal art gallery. The studies of the Magi for *The Star of Bethlehem* (cat. 56), executed in chalk on coloured paper, and the full watercolour study (cat. 57) have highlights of gold and anticipate the awe-struck mood and grandeur of the final work (fig. 3). Burne-Jones believed that his finest designs revealed the realms inhabited by his imagination and thus transcended the limits of any one artistic medium, whether chalk drawing, tapestry or large-scale watercolour.

Sarras, the mystical city where Galahad had a vision of the Holy Grail that ended his quest for that mystic vessel, was among Burne-Jones's favourite imagined realms. He became acquainted with the saga of the Grail in 1855, when he and Morris discovered a copy of Malory's *Morte d'Arthur* in a Birmingham bookshop. From his earliest drawings to his last designs, Burne-Jones turned for inspiration to the Grail story, and remarked to Georgiana near the end of his life: 'Lord, how that San Graal story is ever in my mind and thoughts continually. Was ever anything in the world as beautiful as that is beautiful?'[20] In 1890 he began a set of tapestry designs, commissioned from Morris & Co. by William D'Arcy, an Australian mine owner, that traced the pursuit of the Grail by King Arthur's knights. Every loom at Morris's Merton Abbey Tapestry Works was used to execute the tapestries and, after their completion in 1895, a second set was made for D'Arcy's partner George McCulloch (cat. 191). Burne-Jones narrated the quest in five scenes, the most striking of which is *The Attainment* (cat. 191d), in which Galahad kneels in a garden of lilies and daisies at the door of a chapel where angels with multi-coloured wings are guarding the Grail. The artist depicted the attainment as the moment of Galahad's recognition of the Grail, rather than as his later receipt of spiritual nourishment from it. By leaving the story open-ended in this way, he ensured that it remained timeless and encouraged further imaginings and dreamings on the part of the viewer. In any case, Burne-Jones believed that recognition of the sacred and beautiful was more important than any subsequent reward.

Burne-Jones had slight regard for the honours that came his way late in life. Although elected an Associate of the Royal Academy in 1885, he resigned in 1893, and hesitated before accepting a baronetcy in 1894. He derived most satisfaction from his continued collaboration with Morris, notably on *The Works of Geoffrey Chaucer* (cat. 267). Morris's death in 1896 dealt Burne-Jones a severe blow. He turned to working on the unfinished paintings in his studio. In 1897 he completed a painted version of a subject he had conceived for a tapestry 30 years earlier. *Love Leading the Pilgrim* was initially designed for a set of hangings based on the 13th-century poem *Romaunt of the Rose* for Isaac Lowthian Bell's North Yorkshire home, Routon Grange (cat. 176). In pursuit of perfect love, symbolised by a vision of an exquisite rose, the pilgrim follows his guide over a stony path overgrown with brambles. A quest for something rare, elusive and beautiful – Galahad seeking the Grail, the Magi journeying from the east to find the Holy Child – proved more than a favourite source of motifs for Burne-Jones; it became his motive as an artist. He once defined his art as 'a beautiful romantic dream of something that never was, never will be – in a light better than any light ever shone, in a land no one can define or remember – only desire'.[21] He never ceased striving to reach that land, continuing to paint until his death on 17 June 1898. His conviction that beauty illuminated life had shaped his work and, at its finest, his work confirmed that conviction. In a materialistic world that often fell short of his expectations and desires Burne-Jones explored alternative realms, where it was possible to recognise ideals 'too beautiful not to be true'.

1 G[eorgiana] B[urne]-J[ones], *Memorials of Edward Burne-Jones*, 2 vols, London, 1904, vol. 2, p. 209.
2 Ibid., p. 261.
3 Letter to Helen Gaskell, n.d.; Burne-Jones Papers, Cambridge University Department of Manuscripts, Fitzwilliam Museum, XXVII: 30.
4 Until the end of his student days, the artist was known by his father's surname, Jones. He added Burne, his godmother's married name, sometime in the late 1850s.
5 Burne-Jones (note 1), vol. 1, p. 182.
6 Ibid., vol. 1, p. 246.
7 Burne-Jones's admiration of Van Eyck's painting was enduring: on 19 February 1897 he described it to his assistant Thomas Rooke as 'the

finest picture in the world'. Mary Lago (ed.), *Burne-Jones Talking*, London, 1982, p. 136.
8 Burne-Jones (note 1), vol. 1, p. 286.
9 *Edward Burne-Jones: Victorian Artist–Dreamer*, John Christian and Stephen Wildman (eds), exh. cat., Metropolitan Museum of Art, New York, 1998, p. 117.
10 Morris was dissatisfied with the quality of type available for the publication, believing that it did not stand up to the rich impressions of the woodcut prints. Before the project was abandoned Burne-Jones produced 70 sketches for 'Cupid and Psyche', twenty for 'The Hill of Venus' and twelve for 'Pygmalion and the Image'. *The Earthly Paradise* was

published in three volumes by Chiswick Press in 1868–70 with a single Burne-Jones illustration, on the title page.
11 Burne-Jones (note 1), vol. 2, p. 13.
12 Ibid., vol. 2, p. 38.
13 He had exhibited once during this period, showing *Love Among the Ruins* (1872; destroyed) and *The Hesperides* (1872; Kunsthalle, Hamburg) at the Dudley Gallery in February 1873. The paintings received little attention. His disappearance from the art world after the scandal surrounding *Phyllis and Demophoön* at the Old Water-Colour Society prompted one woman to write to Georgiana that she 'had thought the painter must be dead'. Burne-Jones (note 1), vol. 2, p. 75.

14 'The Picture Season in London' (1877), in Henry James, *The Painter's Eye*, Cambridge, MA, 1956, p. 144.
15 Burne-Jones (note 1), vol. 2, p. 75.
16 Robert de La Sizeranne, *English Contemporary Art* (1898); quoted in *Masters of Art 2*, July 1901, p. 31, an issue devoted to Burne-Jones.
17 *The Times*, 1 May 1884, p. 4.
18 Burne-Jones (note 1), vol. 1, p. 299.
19 Alan Crawford notes that the artist produced more than 650 designs for stained glass. 'Burne-Jones as Decorative Artist', in *Edward Burne-Jones* (note 9), p. 21.
20 Burne-Jones (note 1), vol. 2, p. 333.
21 *Exhibition of Drawings and Studies by Sir Edward Burne-Jones*, Burlington Fine Arts Club, London, 1899, p. vii.

Cat. 36
Sir Edward Coley Burne-Jones Bt ARA
(1833–1898)
*Triptych: The Adoration of the Kings
and the Annunciation*, 1860–61
Oil on three canvases:
108 × 156.5 cm (central panel),
108 × 77.3 cm (side panels)

Cat. 37
Sir Edward Coley Burne-Jones Bt ARA
(1833–1898)
Zephyrus and Psyche, 1865
Watercolour and gouache with
gum arabic, 37 × 25.5 cm

Cat. 38
Sir Edward Coley Burne-Jones Bt ARA
(1833–1898)
The Princess Sabra Led to the Dragon,
1865–66, reworked 1895
Oil on canvas, 108 × 96.6 cm

Cat. 39
Sir Edward Coley Burne-Jones Bt ARA
(1833–1898)
The Annunciation (The Flower of God), 1863
Watercolour and gouache on paper,
61 × 53.3 cm

Cat. 40
Sir Edward Coley Burne-Jones Bt ARA
(1833–1898)
Night, 1870
Watercolour and gouache on paper,
79 × 56 cm

Cat. 41
Sir Edward Coley Burne-Jones Bt ARA
(1833–1898)
Vesper (The Evening Star), 1872–73
Watercolour, gouache and gold paint
on paper, 79 × 56 cm

Cat. 42
Sir Edward Coley Burne-Jones Bt ARA
(1833–1898)
Music, 1876
Oil on canvas, 68.9 × 45.1 cm

Cat. 43
Sir Edward Coley Burne-Jones Bt ARA
(1833–1898)
The Lament, after 1866
Oil on canvas, 27.9 × 38.7 cm

Cat. 45a, b
Sir Edward Coley Burne-Jones Bt ARA
(1833–1898)
Two Studies of a Woman's Head,
date unknown
Pencil on paper, each 22.5 × 16.5 cm

Cat. 44
Sir Edward Coley Burne-Jones Bt ARA
(1833–1898)
Flamma Vestalis, 1886
Oil on canvas, 107.9 × 37.4 cm

Cat. 46
Sir Edward Coley Burne-Jones Bt ARA
(1833–1898)
The Sleeping Princess, 1886/88
Gouache with gold paint on paper,
96.5 × 147.5 cm

Cat. 47
Sir Edward Coley Burne-Jones Bt ARA
(1833–1898)
Caritas, 1867/71, 1885
Watercolour and gouache,
heightened with gold paint,
on paper, 152 × 68.5 cm

Cat. 48
Sir Edward Coley Burne-Jones Bt ARA
(1833–1898)
The Mirror of Venus, 1867–77
Oil on canvas, 79 × 122 cm

a 'The heart desires'

b 'The hand refrains'

Cat. 49a–d
Sir Edward Coley Burne-Jones Bt ARA
(1833–1898)
Pygmalion and the Image, 1868/70
Oil on four canvases, each 66 × 51 cm

c 'The godhead fires'

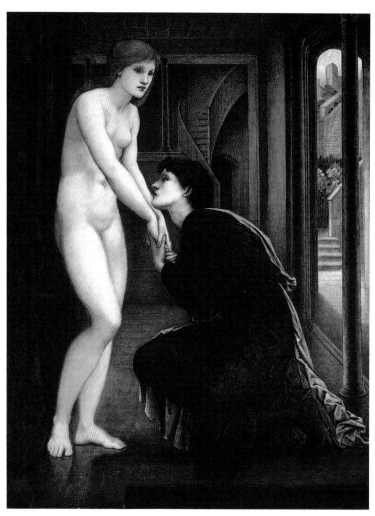

d 'The soul attains'

Cat. 50
Sir Edward Coley Burne-Jones Bt ARA
(1833–1898)
Amy Gaskell, 1893
Oil on canvas, 96.5 × 52 cm

Cat. 51
Sir Edward Coley Burne-Jones Bt ARA
(1833–1898)
Dorothy Mattersdorf, 1893
Oil on canvas, 64 × 42.5 cm

Cat. 52
Sir Edward Coley Burne-Jones Bt ARA
(1833–1898)
Philip Comyns Carr, 1882
Oil on canvas, 71 × 48.5 cm

Cat. 53
Sir Edward Coley Burne-Jones Bt ARA
(1833–1898)
*Cicely Horner (later Mrs George
Lambton),* 1895
Oil on canvas, 73.3 × 45.2 cm

Cat. 54
Sir Edward Coley Burne-Jones Bt ARA
(1833–1898)
Study for 'The Sleeping Princess', 1894
Red chalk heightened with white on
pink paper, 26 × 31.7 cm

Cat. 55
Sir Edward Coley Burne-Jones Bt ARA
(1833–1898)
Study for 'Katie Lewis', c. 1886
Black chalk on buff paper,
52 × 120.5 cm

a The Virgin

b Melchior

c Gaspar

Cat. 56a–f

Sir Edward Coley Burne-Jones Bt ARA
(1833–1898)
*Six Studies for 'The Adoration of the Magi
(The Star of Bethlehem)'*, 1887
Chalks with gold paint on buff paper
a 30.8 × 18.7 cm
b 33.7 × 16.5 cm
c 32.3 × 23.2 cm
d 33.7 × 16.5 cm
e 33.7 × 16.5 cm
f 33.7 × 16.5 cm

d Joseph

e Gaspar

f Balthazar

Cat. 57
Sir Edward Coley Burne-Jones Bt ARA
(1833–1898)
The Adoration of the Magi
(The Star of Bethlehem), 1887/88
Watercolour, gouache and gold paint
on paper, 64.5 × 98.5 cm

Cat. 58
Sir Edward Coley Burne-Jones Bt ARA
(1833–1898)
Christ Enthroned, 1883/84
Pastel, gouache and gold paint on paper,
68.6 × 42.5 cm

Cat. 59
Sir Edward Coley Burne-Jones Bt ARA
(1833–1898)
The Archangel Zophiel, 1883/84
Gouache on board, 51.5 × 26.5 cm

Cat. 60
Sir Edward Coley Burne-Jones Bt ARA
(1833–1898)
St Luke, 1890s (?)
Gouache and charcoal on canvas,
141 × 68.6 cm

Cat. 61a
Sir Edward Coley Burne-Jones Bt ARA
(1833–1898)
The Vision of St Catherine, c. 1878
Grey and brown wash with gouache
on buff paper, 90 × 61.7 cm

Cat. 61b
Sir Edward Coley Burne-Jones Bt ARA
(1833–1898)
The Entombment of St Catherine, c. 1878
Grey and brown wash with gouache
on buff paper, 89.7 × 61.3 cm

Cat. 62
Sir Edward Coley Burne-Jones Bt ARA
(1833–1898)
The Fall of Lucifer, 1894
Gouache and gold paint on paper
laid down on canvas and stretched
over board, 245 × 118 cm

The Persistence of Pre-Raphaelitism:
From Hughes to Frampton

STEPHEN WILDMAN

An important group of paintings in the Andrew Lloyd Webber Collection perfectly illustrates the later history of the Pre-Raphaelite movement. Separately treated in this catalogue is the work of Edward Burne-Jones (cat. 30–62, 176, 191), arguably its true spiritual heir, and J. W. Waterhouse (cat. 89–100), whose more limited range of work maintained its popular appeal.

That the pictures of the Pre-Raphaelite Brotherhood and its close associates – especially those by Walter Deverell (1827–1854), William Holman Hunt (1827–1910; cat. 64, 67, 70, 103, 108, 109) and John Everett Millais (1829–1896; cat. 19–29) shown at the Royal Academy in the early 1850s – had a dramatic impact on British painting is confirmed by the strength of controversy in the contemporary art press. At first resisted by the art establishment as a dangerous subordination of traditional values, the influence of Pre-Raphaelitism, chiefly focusing on precision of detail, archaic subject matter and brilliant colour, is evident in the slow but unstoppable capitulation of the press, in such magazines as the *Art Journal*, the *Spectator* and the *Athenaeum* (which in 1861 took on as its art critic F. G. Stephens, a founding member of the Brotherhood).

Michael Frederick Halliday (1822–1869) was close to the Brotherhood itself. He shared a studio with Holman Hunt and a close friendship with Millais and, as *The Measure for the Wedding Ring* (1855; cat. 79) shows, he equalled his friend in devising simple but telling two-figure compositions.[1] This canvas also recalls the work of William Mulready (1786–1863), whereas the crisp detail underlying the poignancy of *The Blind Basket-maker with His First Child* (1856; cat. 78) shows its impeccable Pre-Raphaelite credentials; that it was shown at the Academy only two years after Millais's *The Blind Girl* (fig. 3, p. 13) is unlikely to be coincidental. Never a full-time painter – he earned a living as a clerk to the House of Lords – the genial 'Mike' Halliday features regularly in Pre-Raphaelite journals, and his early death in 1869 was greatly mourned, coming soon after that of another in the circle, Robert Braithwaite Martineau (1826–1869).

William Gale (1823–1909) and George Adolphus Storey (1834–1919) were two among the many young painters exhibiting at the Royal Academy in the 1850s who fell under the influence of Pre-Raphaelitism. Both were students in the Academy Schools, but soon broadened their horizons: Gale spent time in Italy from 1851 and, like Holman Hunt later, made extended trips to the Holy Land in the 1860s, while Storey travelled to Madrid in 1862 to study the work of Velázquez. These artists' two early works are among the finest from this area of the Pre-Raphaelite fringe, both typically intense in their almost obsessive detail. While they follow others' examples, there are also interesting pre-echoes – of W. S. Burton's celebrated *Wounded Cavalier* (1856; Guildhall Art Gallery, London) in the case of Gale's *The Wounded Knight* (1853; cat. 73) and of *The Knight of the Sun* by Arthur Hughes (cat. 74), begun in the autumn of 1859, in Storey's *The Bride's Burial* (1859; cat. 75). Dressed in Van Dyck costume, Gale was photographed by David Wilkie Wynfield (1837–1887) in the 1860s (fig. 1) as part of a series entitled *Photographic Portraits of Living Artists, Taken in the Style of the Old Masters*, which featured many other Pre-Raphaelite and genre painters, among them Millais dressed as Dante, Storey as a medieval monk and Simeon Solomon in oriental garb.[2]

Similar overlaps occurred between Pre-Raphaelite and other painters, including those of the so-called St John's Wood Clique, although there could be strong differences of opinion. Jeanie Adams-Acton recalled the irritation of some artists that leading dealers, such as Ernest Gambart, favoured one party over another: 'St. John's Wood did not agree with him; but the successful man runs with the hare and hunts with the hounds. Pre-Raphaelitism, for the time being, like the poor, was always with us. It became the one absorbing topic of conversation, artists talked of nothing else, and never

Fig. 1 **David Wilkie Wynfield**, *William Gale*, 1860s.
Albumen print, 21.2 × 16.1 cm. Royal Academy of Arts, London

Cat. 63
Sir John Everett Millais Bt PRA (1829–1896) and
Michael Frederick Halliday (1822–1869)
Scrapbook of Painting Tours, 1850–55
Sketches and inscriptions cut from a notebook or notebooks and
mounted in a scrapbook of 61 leaves, 44.9 × 32 cm

was anything so abused by them, while their wives vied with each other in similar fashion – each with a tale of some new picture and its atrocities, over which they expatiated till they and the topic were exhausted.'[3] There was a leaven of humour, however, as in this response to the avowed distaste of Henry Stacy Marks (1829–1898) for the Pre-Raphaelite manner:

Of that School Marks his horror discloses;
Yet paints, we are all well aware,
Mediaeval old cocks with red noses,
But objects to young girls with red hair.[4]

Another who passed through an early Pre-Raphaelite phase was George Dunlop Leslie (1835–1921), whose important early painting *Matilda* (1860), a Dante subject, has recently reappeared.[5] A member of the St John's Wood Clique, he was hugely impressed on a visit to Burne-Jones's lodgings, and hoped to emulate the casual

but highly advanced Aesthetic interior that formed the backgrounds of many later Pre-Raphaelite paintings: 'A stunning medieval sideboard, all beautifully painted, as fine as Chinese in colour. The curtains of delicate indigo blue, embroidered by hand by his wife. There is a dark wainscot half-way up the wall, dull green paper, and lots of Chinese and Japanese ornaments; one, a little looking-glass, with folding doors of blue silk.'[6] Leslie bemoaned the fact that the approval of John Ruskin, the most influential critic of the 1850s and a strong supporter of the Pre-Raphaelite cause, did not necessarily bring automatic success (as John Brett also discovered, after painting *The Val d'Aosta* [cat. 107]). 'Ruskin was at the Academy the other day', he wrote to Storey in 1863, 'and looked at nothing else but my pictures, and praised them tremendously, and said I would be a greater man than my father [the painter C. R. Leslie]; but why didn't he buy them? damn him.'[7]

Ruskin's praise was certainly important for Arthur

Hughes (1832–1915) who, as the most consistent exhibitor at the Academy within the Pre-Raphaelite circle, increasingly bore the brunt of controversial criticism. *April Love* (1856; fig. 2) Ruskin found 'exquisite' – though he could not quite persuade his father to buy it, leaving the field free for William Morris – and in his *Academy Notes* enthused over 'the sweetness of the tender face, shaken, like a leaf by winds upon its dew, and hesitating back into peace'.[8] Like many of his contemporaries, Hughes painted versions and replicas, often concurrently. The smaller *April Love* (cat. 72) and the reduction (cat. 71) of his earlier *Ophelia* (1852; Manchester City Art Gallery) are hardly less significant than the originals. Both were included in the seminal exhibition held at Russell Place in the summer of 1857, effectively of Pre-Raphaelite painting and largely the work of members of the Pre-

Raphaelite-saturated Hogarth Club, which travelled to three cities in America during the following winter as an *Exhibition of British Art*. Lacking the social or intellectual background of the Brotherhood, and not quite a member of its inner sanctum, Hughes had to work hard for success, but achieved it by dint of perseverance. *The King's Orchard* (1858; cat. 69) and *Silver and Gold* (1863; cat. 77), now accepted as classics of second-phase Pre-Raphaelitism, were not uniformly well received, critics noting the slightly awkward figure drawing and the unnaturally vivid colour. While in one sense shortcomings, these are also integral to Hughes's highly individual style, which could accommodate an exceptional range of subjects, from the romantic medievalism of *The Knight of the Sun* of c. 1859/60 (cat. 74, which recalls his contributions to the Oxford Union murals) to the domestic interior and child portrait (combined in *Bed-Time* [c. 1861; cat. 68]), at which it was generally agreed that he excelled. 'Mr. Hughes's children', wrote William Michael Rossetti in 1870, 'are always delightful creations. To begin with, they are lovely in point of mere beauty; and they are so replete with harmless sweetness, and happy yet not unthoughtful innocence, that the work rises immediately beyond the "bread-and-butter" level of domesticity.'[9]

Holman Hunt's arduous work in the Holy Land in 1854–56 was finally rewarded in 1860, when the exhibition of *The Finding of the Saviour in the Temple* (Birmingham Museum and Art Gallery) brought him not only fame but financial security. Through engravings, this and *The Light of the World* (1854; Keble College, Oxford) became universally known images. As the most religious-minded of the original Brotherhood, he continued to apply its principles to ever more ambitious subjects, culminating in the extraordinary *Triumph of the Innocents* (1876–87; Walker Art Gallery, Liverpool), a painting that revived Ruskin's interest in the movement. Equally important was *The Shadow of Death*, one of the most memorable religious images of the 19th century; again, this was engraved (by Frederick Stacpoole in 1877), the version in Lord Lloyd-Webber's collection (cat. 64) being painted for the engraver in 1873 and showing some differences from the oil begun in Palestine in 1869 (fig. 3), although it is virtually identical with the larger canvas of 1870–73 (Manchester City Art Gallery). In total contrast are *Morning Prayer* (1866; cat. 67), a jewel-like 'cabinet' work

Fig. 2 **Arthur Hughes**, *April Love*, 1856. Oil on canvas, 91.5 × 51 cm. Tate Britain, London

Fig. 3 **William Holman Hunt OM**, *The Shadow of Death*, 1869–73. Oil on canvas, 92.7 × 73 cm. Leeds City Art Gallery

related to an illustration for Isaac Watts's *Divine and Moral Songs*, and *Master Hilary – The Tracer* (1886; cat. 70). A depiction of the artist's seven-year-old son, the latter ranks among the finest of all Pre-Raphaelite portraits and is one of the most original of the century.

Together with portraits of his two other children, *Master Hilary* was shown at the Grosvenor Gallery in 1887. Relaunching Burne-Jones's career on its opening in 1877, the Grosvenor became the focus for an eclectic mix of paintings no longer entirely welcome within the walls of the Academy, which had come to be increasingly dominated by classicists such as Lord Leighton (1830–1896, President from 1878; cat. 138, 141, 150), Sir Edward Poynter (1836–1919; cat. 142) and Sir Lawrence Alma-Tadema (1836–1912; cat. 143–5). Ever more elaborate variations of the Pre-Raphaelite idiom could be seen alongside the refined bucolic idylls of Frederick Walker (1840–1875), the Greek abstractions of Albert Moore (cat. 146–8)and the ground-breaking nocturnes by James McNeill Whistler (1834–1903; fig. 2, p. 143). It could thus encompass Frederick Sandys's *Perdita* (c. 1866; cat. 81) as well as Spencer Stanhope's *Charon and Psyche* (first exhibited 1833; cat. 85).

The iconic image of female beauty, drawing inspiration from the example of Dante Gabriel Rossetti's Titianesque half-lengths of the 1860s (few of which, however, were ever put on public display), increasingly became associated with independent galleries. A major scandal erupted over the exclusion from the Royal Academy exhibition of Sandys's *Medea* (Birmingham Museum and Art Gallery) in 1868, and although it was accepted the following year, the artist's confidence was undermined and thereafter he turned almost exclusively to large chalk drawings. *Perdita* just predates this sea change, and has the riveting intensity of all Sandys's oils, combined with a brilliant technique few of his peers could match. Rossetti's claim that the younger man was plagiarising his work may also have been born of frustration at Sandys's effortless skill: one need only compare the background blossom with Rossetti's in *A Vision of Fiammetta* (cat. 6).

Less wholly original are romantic personifications of womanhood by three very different artists. The bluff Val Prinsep (1838–1904), nephew of the photographer Julia Margaret Cameron, did well to rise from the comfort of life at Little Holland House to become a Royal Academician.

Cat. 64
William Holman Hunt OM
(1827–1910)
The Shadow of Death, 1873
Oil on panel, 104.5 × 82 cm

Cat. 65
Charles Fairfax Murray (1849–1919)
The Concert, first exhibited 1890
Oil on canvas, 63.5 × 243.8 cm

A member of several aesthetic coteries, he was a painter of some individual distinction, as *Il Barbagianni (The Owl)* (first exhibited 1863; cat. 82) demonstrates. Marie Stillman, née Spartali (1843–1927), was the daughter of the Greek Consul-General in London and a notable model (chiefly for Ford Madox Brown and Rossetti [see cat. 15]) as well as an artist. *'The Lady Prays-desire'* (cat. 83), taking its title from Edmund Spenser's epic poem *The Faerie Queene* (1590–96), is an early self-portrait in the Rossetti manner, shown at the third exhibition of the Dudley Gallery in 1867. Also in watercolour is a favourite Rossettian subject, *Beatrice* (1860; cat. 80), by Simeon Solomon (1840–1905), whose homoerotic tendencies and fall from grace in 1873 overshadowed an exceptional if erratic talent.

Like Solomon, John Roddam Spencer Stanhope (1829–1908) was part of the Pre-Raphaelite circle from the late 1850s. His work appeared alongside Burne-Jones's at the first Grosvenor exhibition in 1877, and attracted almost equal attention, being universally admired for its depth of colour and strength of drawing. *Orpheus and Eurydice on the Banks of the Styx* (cat. 86) was shown at the Paris Exposition Universelle of 1878, and typifies a personal style that some reviewers found strange, while holding that it had 'both a decorative beauty and an imaginative delight'.[10] Burne-Jones called Stanhope 'the greatest colourist of the century. If he had but studied drawing more, what a great artist he would have been'.[11] As powerful in its way was the work of Arthur Hughes's nephew, Edward Robert Hughes

(1851–1914), whose best pictures – including his master-piece, *Night with Her Train of Stars* (1912; Birmingham Museum and Art Gallery) – were in watercolour, often on a large scale. *Bertuccio's Bride* (1895; cat. 76) shows his fondness for recondite literature, richly illustrating a dramatic moment from a story by the 16th-century Italian writer Gianfrancesco Straparola: 'Edward Hughes has done another of those Italian story books', noted Burne-Jones in 1898, 'and has had more fun. But as for the stories I don't care for them.'[12]

Narrative is less important than the evocation of mood in two paintings both shown at the third New Gallery exhibition in 1890. *The Concert* (cat. 65) is one of the most important works by Charles Fairfax Murray (1849–1919), friend and assistant of Burne-Jones and a significant figure in the world of art commerce. 'My long picture', as he called it, was bought by the architect Thomas Collcutt for Richard D'Oyly Carte as decoration for the foyer of his new Palace Theatre at Cambridge Circus.[13] With this musical connection, the painting has found a singularly appropriate place in Lord Lloyd-Webber's collection. *The Gentle Music of a Byegone Day* (cat. 88) by John Melhuish Strudwick (1849–1937) also suggests the sound of music – that most evanescent yet inspiring of the arts – as both a complement to and an equivalent of visual art. Strudwick worked as an assistant to Stanhope and to Burne-Jones, and although it is impossible not to see their strong influence in his painting, he devised an immediately recognisable style, incorporating Italian Renaissance echoes and decorative details even richer than those of his masters into canvases that George Bernard Shaw found 'full of subdued but glowing light'.[14]

Evelyn De Morgan, née Pickering (1855–1919), was Stanhope's niece, and had to battle against parental dis-approval to succeed as a painter, achieving her first success at the Grosvenor in 1877. A superb draughtswoman, she produced an astonishing body of work, including many large-scale paintings on literary and allegorical themes. *The World's Wealth* (1896; cat. 87) was one of eight paintings acquired by her foremost patron, William Imrie. A summation of continuing Pre-Raphaelite inspiration, her work was described in those terms by the critic E. V. Lucas: 'In style she is more precise and less wilful than Burne-Jones; more simple and more direct than Rossetti; more colourful than Holman Hunt. . . . I cannot remember any collection of pictures from one hand conveying such an impression of creative zest and delight. . . . My eyes are filled with their glow.'[15]

Phoebe Traquair's *Love's Testament* (1898; cat. 66) has little of De Morgan's detail but much intense mystery, and a concentration on symbolism shared with the work of E. R. Frampton (1872–1923) – like Traquair, also a muralist. Frampton's images generally reflect the flat, linear manner of a decorator and designer who was also a member of the Tempera Society. In *The Passage of the Holy Grail to Sarras* (1907; cat. 84) he revisits Arthurian legend, one of the earliest inspirations of the Pre-Raphaelite movement, in a painting replete with what Aymer Vallance called 'a restful and dignified serenity, no less satisfying than transcendental'.[16] 'The ripples of the agitation started by the formation of the Pre-Raphaelite Brotherhood', wrote Percy Bate in 1899, 'are still sweeping on, and widening as they go.'[17]

Cat. 66
Phoebe Anna Traquair (1852–1936)
Love's Testament, 1898
Oil on canvas, 53.3 × 35.5 cm

1 Some of these were created in collaboration, as is indicated by the Millais/Halliday notebook in the Andrew Lloyd Webber Collection (cat. 63).

2 *Princes of Victorian Bohemia: Photographs by David Wilkie Wynfield*, Juliet Hacking, exh. cat., National Portrait Gallery, London, 2000.

3 A. M. W. Stirling, *Victorian Sidelights from the Papers of the late Mrs. Adams-Acton*, London, 1954, p. 73.

4 Ibid.

5 Christie's, London, 10 June 2003, lot 103; like Hughes's *Silver and Gold* (cat. 77), the painting belonged to the collector John Hamilton Trist.

6 Gladys Storey, *All Sorts of People*, London, 1929, p. 59.

7 Ibid., p. 58.

8 John Ruskin, *Notes on some of the Principal Pictures exhibited in the Rooms of the Royal Academy, and the Society of Painters in Water Colours:*

No. II – 1856, London, 1856, p. 34.

9 W[illiam] M[ichael] Rossetti, 'English Painters of the Present Day', *Portfolio*, August 1870, p. 114.

10 *The Times*, 1 May 1877, p. 10.

11 A. M. W. Stirling, *A Painter of Dreams and other Biographical Studies*, London, 1916, p. 334.

12 Mary Lago (ed.), *Burne-Jones Talking*, London, 1982, p.172.

13 Information kindly supplied by David Elliott.

14 George Bernard Shaw, 'J.M. Strudwick', *Art Journal*, April 1891, p. 101.

15 A. M. W. Stirling, *The Merry Wives of Battersea*, London, 1956, pp. 216–17.

16 Aymer Vallance, 'The Paintings of Reginald Frampton, R.O.I.', *Studio*, December 1918, p. 68.

17 Percy Bate, *The English Pre-Raphaelite Painters, Their Associates and Successors*, London, 1899; 4th edn, London, 1910, p. 113.

Cat. 67
William Holman Hunt OM
(1827–1910)
Morning Prayer, 1866
Oil on panel, 25.5 × 18.5 cm

Cat. 68
Arthur Hughes (1832–1915)
Bed-Time, c. 1861
Oil on canvas laid down on panel,
71.1 × 58 cm

Cat. 69
Arthur Hughes (1832–1915)
The King's Orchard, 1858
Oil on canvas, 66 × 50.8 cm

Cat. 70
William Holman Hunt OM
(1827–1910)
Master Hilary – The Tracer, 1886
Oil on canvas, 122.2 × 66 cm

Cat. 71
Arthur Hughes (1832–1915)
Ophelia, 1852/57
Oil on lunette-shaped panel,
50.8 × 91.4 cm

Cat. 72
Arthur Hughes (1832–1915)
April Love, c. 1855/56
Oil on panel, 45.5 × 26 cm

Cat. 73
William Gale (1823–1909)
The Wounded Knight, 1853
Oil on panel, 50.2 × 67.2 cm

Cat. 74
Arthur Hughes (1832–1915)
The Knight of the Sun, c. 1859/60
Oil on canvas, 101.6 × 132 cm

Cat. 75
George Adolphus Storey RA
(1834–1919)
The Bride's Burial, 1859
Oil on canvas, 104.2 × 86.3 cm

Cat. 76
Edward Robert Hughes (1851–1914)
Bertuccio's Bride, 1895
Pencil and watercolour on paper,
100.3 × 76.1 cm

Cat. 77
Arthur Hughes (1832–1915)
Silver and Gold, 1863
Oil on canvas, 99 × 67.3 cm

Cat. 78
Michael Frederick Halliday
(1822–1869)
The Blind Basket-maker
with His First Child, 1856
Oil on canvas, 94 × 56 cm

Cat. 79
Michael Frederick Halliday
(1822–1869)
The Measure for the Wedding Ring, 1855
Oil on canvas, 90.1 × 67.3 cm

Cat. 80
Simeon Solomon (1840–1905)
Beatrice, 1860
Watercolour heightened with white and
gum arabic on paper, 40.6 × 29.2 cm

Cat. 81
Frederick Sandys (1829–1904)
Perdita, c. 1866
Oil on panel, 33 × 27.9 cm

Cat. 82
Valentine Cameron Prinsep
(1836–1904)
Il Barbagianni (The Owl),
first exhibited 1863
Oil on canvas, 77.5 × 54 cm

Cat. 83
Marie Stillman (née Spartali)
(1844–1927)
The Lady Prays-desire,
first exhibited 1867
Watercolour with gold paint on paper,
41.9 × 30.5 cm

Cat. 84
Edward Reginald Frampton
(1872–1923)
The Passage of the Holy Grail to Sarras,
1907
Oil on canvas, 122 × 152.5 cm

Cat. 85
John Roddam Spencer Stanhope
(1829–1908)
Charon and Psyche, first exhibited 1883
Oil on canvas, 95.2 × 138.4 cm

Cat. 86
John Roddam Spencer Stanhope
(1829–1908)
*Orpheus and Eurydice on the Banks
of the Styx*, first exhibited 1878
Oil on panel, 100 × 140 cm

Cat. 87
Evelyn De Morgan (1855–1919)
The World's Wealth (The Crown of Glory),
1896
Oil on canvas, 104.7 × 53.7 cm

Cat. 88
John Melhuish Strudwick
(1849–1937)
The Gentle Music of a Byegone Day,
first exhibited 1890
Oil on canvas, 80.2 × 63.8 cm

John William Waterhouse

PETER TRIPPI

It seems appropriate that Andrew Lloyd Webber's collection of paintings by John William Waterhouse (1849–1917) – the largest of its kind – be exhibited at the Royal Academy of Arts, the institution that lay at the centre of this painter's life. Waterhouse created most of his major pictures for display at Burlington House, where he intended their glowing colours and lively brushwork to delight collectors, reviewers and the public. Although he served on the Academy's governing Council and won admission to the fashionable Athenaeum Club, contemporaries rarely mentioned Waterhouse in their correspondence; his scarce surviving letters suggest a man of few words, so it is only his pictures which remain to speak for him.

It was perhaps inevitable that Waterhouse's career should focus on the Academy, as both his parents exhibited there and may even have met in its galleries. He was born and baptised in Rome, the first child of the Yorkshire-born painter William Waterhouse (1816–1890) and his second wife, Isabella Mackenzie (c. 1821–1857). The boy was given an Italian nickname (Nino) that stayed with him all his life. In 1854 the family settled in Kensington, but by 1861 Waterhouse was at school in Leeds, where he relished Roman history and contemplated engineering as a career. Back in London, he assisted his father with portraits and entered the Academy Schools as a Probationer in sculpture in 1870. Six months later he was admitted as a Student, but soon began to exhibit paintings, not sculpture, at the Dudley Gallery and the Society of British Artists. The pictures ranged from *Undine* (private collection), which showed the eponymous water nymph pining by a fountain and was the first of many female figures associated with water, to an exotic beauty in *The Unwelcome Companion: A Street Scene in Cairo* (Towneley Hall).

In 1874 an allegory with Roman setting, *Sleep and His Half Brother Death* (private collection), became Waterhouse's first submission to the Academy's Summer Exhibition, where he showed regularly until 1917. Three years later *A Sick Child Brought into the Temple of Aesculapius* (private collection) hung 'on the line' there, the second of his entries accorded this honour. These classicised pictures echo Lawrence Alma-Tadema (cat. 143–5) in their pseudo-archaeological accuracy, yet their scale is larger and their mood more melancholy. Waterhouse produced genre scenes in 1877 while visiting Italy, where he was enthralled by Pompeii.

Acquisitions by municipal galleries began in 1883, when the Art Gallery of South Australia purchased *The Favourites of the Emperor Honorius*, which typically emphasises the physical and psychological distance between a single figure and a group. In 1883 Waterhouse married the Ealing flower painter Esther Kenworthy (1857–1944). Although he was married in the Church of England, Waterhouse's ongoing depictions of ritual magic suggest that he was interested in occultism. The childless couple rented rooms near 3 Primrose Hill Studios, which Waterhouse had leased in 1878.

Waterhouse's dramatic pictures of supernatural women in antiquity found buyers and plaudits at the Academy. *Consulting the Oracle* (1884) and *St Eulalia* (1885) were acquired by Henry Tate, and *The Magic Circle* (1886) for the nation through the Chantrey Bequest (all now Tate Britain, London). Waterhouse sent smaller genre pictures to the Grosvenor Gallery; he joined the Institutes of Oil Painters and Painters in Water Colours, as well as the Art-Workers' Guild and Arts Club. His much-noticed depiction of Eulalia's martyrdom ensured his election in 1885 as an Associate of the Royal Academy, where he taught in the Life and Painting Schools regularly from 1887 to 1908.

Waterhouse's prestige grew after his enormous canvas of the Hebrew martyr Mariamne (1887; private collection) earned medals in Paris, Chicago and Brussels. Like the other women he painted in the 1880s, Mariamne is dramatic in her presence; even George Bernard Shaw perceived Waterhouse's fascination with the stage during this, the heyday of Sarah Bernhardt and Ellen Terry. Coursing throughout Waterhouse's oeuvre are narratives of extreme passion, most famously the rapturous self-destruction in *The Lady of Shalott* (1888; Tate Britain). The Lady's haunted expression and broadly painted surroundings were borrowed from Jules Bastien-Lepage (1848–1884), whose Impressionist-influenced style Waterhouse probably discovered through the Belgian-trained Englishmen William Logsdail and Frank Bramley.

The Lady of Shalott constituted Waterhouse's first foray into Pre-Raphaelitism not only because its subject was Tennysonian, but also because it demonstrated the impact that John Everett Millais's *Ophelia* (fig. 2, p. 47, and cat. 22) made when it was shown again in 1886. Victorians inter-associated water, women and drowning, and in 1889 Waterhouse sent to the Academy his own *Ophelia* (cat. 90), a Pre-Raphaelite subject even more popular than the Lady of Shalott (see cat. 125). He presented this Shakespearean martyr with dishevelled hair and unladylike pose, before she nears the stream in which she will drown singing. Waterhouse again focused on an intense gaze derived from Bastien-Lepage and repeated the form of the reclining virgin in Millais's 1859 canvas *Spring (Apple Blossoms)* (Lady Lever Art Gallery, Port Sunlight), which Waterhouse probably saw when it was sold in 1886. Ophelia is on the verge of sexual awakening, posing provocatively among symbols of natural fecundity that will also fade.

Shaw felt that this *Ophelia* succeeded where *The Lady of Shalott* had failed – 'in the relation between the landscape and the face'.[1] Unfortunately for Waterhouse, most reviewers resented this blend of imaginative subject and realistic setting, or were weary of Bastien's influence. Thus Waterhouse never sold this *Ophelia*, which he later loaned to the Academy while completing his Diploma Picture, *A Mermaid* (1900; Royal Academy). A period photograph suggests that he later made Ophelia's gaze less haunting, though her stare still rivets the viewer's attention. The artist kept this painting all his life, and it is significant that only two subjects inspired him to three separate treatments: Ophelia and the Lady of Shalott. His final *Ophelia* (cat. 100) appeared at the Academy in 1910: a full-breasted woman moves toward the viewer, at whom she gazes, her cheeks flushed and eyes hysterical, her

Cat. 89
John William Waterhouse RA (1849–1917)
Spring (The Flower Picker), c. 1900
Watercolour heightened with white on paper, 46.2 × 29.2 cm

elegant gown out of place near the stream. Her gaze constitutes a thrilling anomaly in Waterhouse's late production, which is otherwise quite calm. Although set outdoors, the scene might almost be on stage, and Waterhouse heightened his powerfully dramatic effect with two figures watching from the bridge.

In 1890 Waterhouse's father died, and he did not exhibit at the Academy for the first time in sixteen years. Like so much of the artist's life, this hiatus is undocumented, but it seems to have encompassed a self-reinvention, for he returned in 1891 with a new fascination for classical enchantresses and a new aesthetic strategy. Particularly characteristic are the masterworks *St Cecilia* (first exhibited 1895; cat. 95) and *Pandora* (1896;

cat. 97). Here Waterhouse offers wistful, mildly eroticised maidens – their singular beauty both natural and unattainable – posed in timeless settings that evoke a vaguely melancholy languor. Waterhouse's best works bypass vigorous action for a decorative stillness that conveys the narrative's pivotal moment and meaning. The *Times* critic saw them as 'pre-Raphaelite pictures in a more modern manner', painted by 'a kind of academic Burne-Jones, like him in his types and his moods, but with less insistence on design and more on atmosphere'.[2] Indeed *St Cecilia* is Waterhouse's response to Edward Burne-Jones's popular *Briar Rose* cycle (1890; Faringdon Collection, Buscot Park, Oxon – see cat. 46, 54), which told Tennyson's Sleeping Beauty story in a similarly hypnotic atmosphere.

Painted over two years, *St Cecilia* was hailed as a milestone and prompted Waterhouse's election to the rank of full Academician after unsuccessful nominations since 1892. In the exhibition catalogue the artist condensed a relevant stanza from Tennyson's 'The Palace of Art', but his audience knew already that the patron saint of musicians – a subject eminently suited to Andrew Lloyd Webber – had envisioned an angel and heard celestial music. *St Cecilia* is Pre-Raphaelite because it shows an awareness of how Burne-Jones and Dante Gabriel Rossetti handled this subject, and because it looks back to art before the time of Raphael, especially to scenes of the Annunciation to the Virgin Mary. Like Tennyson, Waterhouse drew upon the medieval motif of the Virgin in her bower, and he may have shared alchemists' association of roses blooming in gardens with the attainment of inner knowledge.

The warmest praise for *St Cecilia* appeared in *The Studio*. Its editor, Gleeson White, argued that Waterhouse's paintings were 'decorative panels of colour, less conventional than tapestry, less flat than if they were mural decoration, but all the same, not openings through a wall looking into the real world or the world of fancy, but panels self-complete with beauty of line, beauty of mass, and beauty of colour'.[3] Like William Morris, White encouraged painters to study tapestries, and indeed *St Cecilia* features dark masses against which Waterhouse

Cat. 90
John William Waterhouse RA
(1849–1917)
Ophelia, first exhibited 1889
Oil on canvas, 98 × 158 cm

– like an Impressionist seated at a loom – set brilliant pigments recurring harmoniously across the surface. Many observers saw decoration as the latest phase of Pre-Raphaelitism and were spurred by the passing of Morris, Millais and Burne-Jones to identify the movement's inheritors. Most rejected the work of Burne-Jones's disciples as insufficiently virile, and encouraged instead Waterhouse, Frank Dicksee (cat. 149, 151) and other young Academicians who, as the critic Claude Phillips put it, embraced 'the modern French standpoint' without disregarding 'the face of English art'.[4] Not everyone approved: D. S. MacColl attacked St Cecilia as 'illustration by way of "decorative painting"' and another Waterhouse painting as 'half-realism, which is convincing neither as dream nor as daylight'.[5]

Because Waterhouse found beauty and emotional power both in classical literature and in writing admired by the Pre-Raphaelites, he celebrated Psyche and Ariadne, but also Keats's La Belle Dame Sans Merci (1819), the tale of 'Tristram and Isolde' from Thomas Malory's Morte d'Arthur (c. 1469) and episodes from the works of Giovanni Boccaccio (1313–1375). Indeed Pandora appeared just a year after St Cecilia. Claude Phillips offered an insight into Pandora which pertains to Waterhouse generally: 'For a cold pseudo-classicism, which to-day convinces neither the painter nor his public, Mr. J. W. Waterhouse substitutes a romanticism with which his own artistic temperament, as well as that of his race, is thoroughly in accord.'[6] Despite their enthusiasm for the classical scenes of Alma-Tadema and Edward Poynter (cat. 142), Englishmen of the 1890s perceived their national art as fundamentally romantic. Waterhouse did not always use a bright palette to communicate romantic warmth, however: the sober colouring of Pandora provides an ideally decorative background for touches of hot colour, especially in the lips and cheeks.

Like Eve, Pandora encapsulated male ambivalence about women's thirst for knowledge, and so was depicted frequently. Waterhouse followed the convention of showing the world's evils escaping from a chest, on which is chased a sun rising over water, symbol of the Hermetic Order of the Golden Dawn. Founded in 1888, this rosicrucian society sought to connect its adherents with supernatural forces through practices including alchemy, magic circles, invocations of Pan and the tree of life –

all relevant to Waterhouse's art. He decorated his best friend's grave-marker with a similar sun driving off the night stars, a clue that both men may have participated in the Order's rituals.[7]

Logically, Pandora would stand to open this large casket, yet her kneeling pose heightens the suspense and generates a sculptural effect emphasising her breast and figure. A sculptor himself, Waterhouse knew many of the so-called New Sculptors, whose idealised images of women in contemplation often bore Symbolist under-currents. Pandora and later Waterhouse pictures of heroines alone (see cat. 92) point towards the Art-Worker Harry Bates ARA (1850–1899) and his renowned marble Pandora (1891; Tate Britain). In 1900 the Waterhouses took 10 Hall Road, a large studio house in St John's Wood that had been expanded by Bates.

Another misogynistic myth is that of the Danaïdes, the 50 daughters of King Danaus married off to the sons of his rival. All but one followed their father's order to murder their husbands, and so were condemned in Hades to fill a leaking jar with water. Andrew Lloyd Webber's 1904 version (cat. 96) is the earlier of Waterhouse's two treatments, and both offer a disconcerting mix of melancholy and sensuality: one sister's breast, thrust forward by the weight of her vessel, is potentially arousing, even as the pale tone of her nipples evokes the modesty of a neoclassical marble. Waterhouse's masterly drawing of these figures can be appreciated fully in his sensitive preparatory study (cat. 91).

Waterhouse's only studio companions were models, mostly women, whose names he recorded in sketchbooks. Perpetuating an academic tradition, he transcended their particularities to create his own idealised, instantly recognisable type of female beauty, varied primarily by hair colour. Scholars' attention has focused on the woman who appears in more than 60 paintings from 1889 to the artist's death in 1917. The search for her name has pivoted on a drawing for the 1905 Lamia (Yale Center for British Art, New Haven) inscribed 'Miss Muriel Foster/Buxton Rd/Chingford', but this annotation is problematic and the search remains open.[8] Given their three-decade relationship, this 'Waterhouse girl' surely functioned as the artist's muse.

Perhaps she possessed the integrity of the noble 'Lady Clare' (1900; cat. 99), a poem that appears in

Cat. 91
John William Waterhouse RA
(1849–1917)
Study for 'The Danaïdes', c. 1904
Pencil heightened with blue and white
chalk on faded blue paper,
38.5 × 31 cm

Waterhouse's own decorated volume of Tennyson. Lord Ronald and Lady Clare are engaged, and he has brought her a 'lily-white doe' as a lover's token. Her nurse confesses to be Clare's mother, so the girl goes to return the doe and release her fiancé. But love prevails and Ronald marries his 'flower of the earth'. Particularly striking in Waterhouse's painting is Clare's direct gaze, an emblem of honesty. *The Lady Clare* is unusual in being one of 39 pictures painted for an exhibition at Agnew's by Academicians, including Alma-Tadema, Poynter and John Singer Sargent; Agnew's donated the admission fees to the Artists' General Benevolent Institution, which assisted indigent colleagues.

Although Waterhouse is best known for his Tennysonian scenes, he painted more episodes from Ovid's superbly pictorial *Metamorphoses*, including *The Awakening of Adonis* (1899; cat. 98). Like Ophelia and the Lady of Shalott, Ovid's characters act out the passionate awakenings, deaths and transfigurations that elevate their tales into myths conveying a hopeful message of regeneration. When Adonis' handsome looks sparked a quarrel between Venus and Persephone, queen of Hades,

it was decided that the youth should divide the year between them. After Adonis was gored to death by a boar, anemones sprouted where his blood spilled. Waterhouse presented the moment every spring when Venus rouses this human anemone from his wintry sleep. The critic F. G. Stephens correctly felt that Waterhouse saw the story 'with Venetian eyes that are inspired with neo-classic passion',[9] yet the artist's uncharacteristic use of golden-curled cherubs, rather than swarthy pans, sweetens the myth's profundity, while Adonis' effeminacy diminishes the erotic charge that makes *Hylas and the Nymphs* (1896; Manchester City Art Gallery) so memorable.

As taste turned against explicit narratives during the 1900s, Waterhouse painted more women seated by streams and picking flowers. Seemingly plotless, several canvases actually allude to the Ovidian abductions of Oreithyia and Persephone. Having enclosed his women in gardens and glades, Waterhouse now opened his pictures to expansive meadows drenched in silvery light. Around 1900 he painted at least four depictions of a girl leaning over a fence to pick flowers, of which Andrew Lloyd Webber has acquired the only watercolour (cat. 89). As there is no evidence that Waterhouse exhibited this beautiful series, he may have made them for his own enjoyment.

As early as 1886, critics praised Waterhouse's capacity to compose without exhaustive preparations. As cat. 91 suggests, he drew figures in the nude, and then he made lively oil sketches, three of which feature in Andrew Lloyd Webber's collection (cat. 92–4). Waterhouse purchased primed canvases and, in the French academic manner, stated the main lines of his composition with brushstrokes of dark, flowing paint mixed with an easy-to-handle medium containing a diluent such as spirit of turpentine. He then laid in the basic tonal relationships as blocks of thinned, translucent colour, such as pale green or fawn. Waterhouse painted his figures without fully articulating them, then added draperies. Cat. 93 shows how he mapped out the image with loose strokes and then concentrated on the face and hair. The sketch for *Nymphs Finding the Head of Orpheus* (cat. 94) reveals how he began to work out the foliage, especially the sinuous trees which so fascinated him.

Waterhouse worked intensively at the easel, applying as many as twelve layers of paint to achieve his desired effect. Microscopic sampling shows that he gathered up

Cat. 92
John William Waterhouse RA
(1849–1917)
The Necklace (Study for 'Lamia'),
c. 1909
Oil on canvas, 99 × 66 cm

Cat. 93
John William Waterhouse RA
(1849–1917)
Study of a Young Woman, c. 1909
Oil on canvas, 59.6 × 49.5 cm

to six different pigments in one brushload: the metalwork
he loved to depict (see cat. 96) appears brownish yellow
to the eye, but actually contains ultramarine, viridian,
yellow ochre, charcoal black, sienna and prismatic lead
white.[10] *St Cecilia* is one of at least four canvases containing
verdigris, and it also has an interleaving of ground gold
leaf. The presence of such expensive materials where
they cannot be seen confirms that Waterhouse compul-
sively added layers to refine his vision. In view of such
perfectionism, one understands why the collector James
Murray complained that 'W[aterhouse] & his wife have
no sense of time'.[11] Letters show that he rushed to
complete works for the Academy's 'sending-in day',
and his failure to let paint layers dry may account for
the distinctive crackling of many pictures' surfaces.

No longer considered progressive, Waterhouse's
recognisable style was still attracting patrons in the 1910s.
He was especially successful in cultivating the financier

Alexander Henderson, later 1st Baron Faringdon, whose
extended family owned more than 30 pictures by the
artist, including portraits. In 1912 Aberdeen Art Gallery
paid £1,400 for *Penelope and the Suitors,* and *St Cecilia* brought
a remarkable £2,415 at auction in 1913. *The Annunciation*
(1914; private collection), Waterhouse's only biblical scene,
marked a renewed emphasis on Pre-Raphaelite narratives
in historical settings. Several of these late works were
acquired by the soap magnate W. H. Lever: *The Enchanted*
Garden (Lady Lever Art Gallery, Port Sunlight) was on
the artist's easel when he died of liver cancer in 1917.

In its memorial tribute *The Studio* classed Waterhouse
'among the best of our romanticist painters' for 'the right
atmosphere of poetic suggestion',[12] yet *The Times* thought
eclecticism had limited his originality – a modernist
perspective anticipating the rapid decline in his reputation.[13] Attending Waterhouse's funeral were patrons such
as Murray and H. W. Henderson; the artists included

Cat. 94
John William Waterhouse RA
(1849–1917)
*Study for 'Nymphs Finding the Head
of Orpheus'*, c. 1900
Oil on canvas, 96.5 × 104.1 cm

Poynter, Herbert Draper and William Strang. He was interred at Kensal Green Cemetery, and instead of receiving his own memorial exhibition at Burlington House, as Alma-Tadema had, Waterhouse was represented in a 1922 show of recently deceased Academicians. Esther Waterhouse held a 100-lot sale in 1926, when the artist's work had become so unfashionable that the 1889 *Ophelia* sold for only £450. Since the 1960s more Waterhouse pictures have been reproduced commercially, and the 1888 version of *The Lady of Shalott* has become Tate's best-selling postcard. This revival of interest moved to a new level in 2000 when headlines worldwide announced that the Andrew Lloyd Webber Art Foundation had acquired *St Cecilia* for £6.6 million, still the highest price paid for a Victorian painting. Waterhouse would surely be delighted, if rather amazed, by the growing acclaim for his life's work.

1 *The World*, 8 May 1889; quoted in Stanley Weintraub, *Bernard Shaw on the London Art Scene, 1885–1950*, University Park, PA, 1989, p. 281.
2 *The Times*, 12 February 1917, p. 6.
3 Gleeson White, *The Master Painters of Britain*, London, 1898, vol. 4, p. 10.
4 *Academy* 1201, 11 May 1895, p. 407.
5 *Spectator*, 1 June 1895, p. 753, and 16 May 1891, p. 693.
6 *Academy* 1255, 23 May 1896, p. 432.
7 P. M. Feeney's grave-marker is at Thurne, Norfolk.
8 James K. Baker and Cathy L. Baker, 'Miss Muriel Foster: The John William Waterhouse Model', *The Journal of Pre-Raphaelite Studies* 8, autumn 1999, pp. 70–82.
9 *Athenaeum* 3784, 5 May 1900, p. 568.
10 Technical analysis was conducted for the author in 2000 by Libby Sheldon of University College, London.
11 Aberdeen Art Gallery Archive; annotation by Murray on a letter dated 25 December 1911 that he had received from Waterhouse.
12 A. L. Baldry, 'The Late J. W. Waterhouse, R.A.', *Studio*, June 1917, p. 10.
13 *The Times*, 12 February 1917, p. 6.

Cat. 95
John William Waterhouse RA
(1849–1917)
St Cecilia, first exhibited 1895
Oil on canvas, 123.2 × 200.7 cm
The Andrew Lloyd Webber Art
Foundation

 132

Cat. 96
John William Waterhouse RA
(1849–1917)
The Danaides, 1904
Oil on canvas, 152.4 × 111.9 cm

Cat. 97
John William Waterhouse RA
(1849–1917)
Pandora, 1896
Oil on canvas, 152.4 × 91.4 cm

Cat. 98
John William Waterhouse RA
(1849–1917)
The Awakening of Adonis, 1899
Oil on canvas, 95.9 × 188 cm

Cat. 99
John William Waterhouse RA
(1849–1917)
The Lady Clare, 1900
Oil on canvas, 76.2 × 61 cm

Cat. 100
John William Waterhouse RA
(1849–1917)
Ophelia, first exhibited 1910
Oil on canvas, 100.3 × 62.2 cm

'Tracing the finger of God': Landscape Painting in Victorian England

TIM BARRINGER

Vividly discernible in almost every landscape painting in the present exhibition is the influence of one man: the polymathic critic of art and society John Ruskin (1819–1900; fig. 1).[1] When Charlotte Brontë said of the first volume of Ruskin's *Modern Painters* (1843) 'this book seems to give me eyes' she spoke for an entire generation.[2] Ruskin's book was planned as a defence of J.M.W. Turner against his critics; yet its impassioned advocacy of intense naturalism was to inspire younger British painters to create works distant in style and subject from the grandiose academy canvases and ethereal studies of Turner. Ruskin's first volume concluded with an exhortation to young artists to be 'humble and earnest in following the steps of nature, and tracing the finger of God. . . . [They should] go to Nature in all singleness of heart, and walk with her laboriously and trustingly, having no other thoughts but how best to penetrate her meaning, and remember her instruction; rejecting nothing, selecting nothing and scorning nothing . . . and rejoicing always in the truth.'[3] Ruskin was as interested in the truths of science as he was in those of art and found in both the opportunity to praise God. The artist must be as attentive to natural forms as the botanist, the geologist or the climatologist; to fail to take reverent notice of every detail of creation would be an aesthetic form of blasphemy.

Ruskin's words were eagerly read by painters and public alike. Despite the Royal Academy's advocacy of history painting, landscape painting had long established itself, along with the portrait, as the quintessentially English art form. Largely as a result of *Modern Painters*, mid-Victorian Britain saw the creation of a radically new style of landscape painting, a new language of nature, whose focus and clarity can be identified as inherently modern.[4] Landscape is, paradoxically, a genre of art beloved of urbanised, industrialised cultures like Britain in the age of the Crystal Palace or the Dutch republic in the 17th century. Victorian landscape painters faced a dilemma: should they paint the urban landscape known to most

of their audience and evoked by contemporary novelists such as Charles Dickens, with its defiled, smoky atmosphere, which Ruskin presciently described as the 'storm-cloud of the nineteenth century';[5] or should they provide their viewers with a vision of pure nature, as Ruskin himself seemed to demand?

One imaginative solution was to explore mundane subject matter within reach of London, scenery which provided the backdrop for everyday life, as in Ford Madox Brown's extraordinary circular composition *Southend, Essex, Looking Towards Sheerness* (cat. 104). Born at Calais to British parents, Brown (1821–1893) enjoyed the benefits of a full academic training at the Antwerp Academy; his work, however, is strikingly unconventional. Although he noted that 'Southend is here represented as it was before the invasion of gas and railroad', the

Fig. 1 **Sir John Everett Millais Bt PRA**, *John Ruskin*, 1853–54. Oil on canvas, 78 × 68 cm. Private collection

quotidian scene of untidy buildings and shipping in the right distance bears the unmistakably imprint of modernity.[6] Modern, too, is Brown's vivid, almost hallucinatory, observation, which compresses a wealth of detail into a roundel less than 30 cm in diameter: it is a world seen through the wrong end of a telescope, in which commonplace events and objects take on a heightened intensity. Note the recalcitrant cow refusing to be led by a white-hatted boy as a bright red carriage passes; the scruffy pollarded trees silhouetted against hayfield, sea and sky; and the distant Nore lightship, visible in the Thames Estuary. Brown began the landscape in 1846 but extensively reworked it in 1858 and again in 1861. The brilliance of colour and precision of detail in *Southend* undoubtedly reflects the influence of a slightly younger group of painters, close friends of Brown, who in 1848 had founded the Pre-Raphaelite Brotherhood (PRB), notably William Holman Hunt (1827–1910; cat. 64, 67, 70, 103, 108, 109) and John Everett Millais (1829–1896; cat. 19–29), who became Ruskin's protégé in 1851. Millais's portrait of Ruskin (fig. 1) exemplifies the way in which the critic's aesthetic theory of landscape melded with the reformist energies of the young painters to create a wholly new approach to painting in which unflinching scrutiny of the natural world became the primary goal.

Hunt recalled in his autobiography trying, as a student in 1847, to paint a pool at Ewell, Surrey, at much the same time as he completed a workmanlike study of the local church (cat. 103). Struggling to capture the effect of light on water, Hunt noted 'the difference between the scene as it was presented to my untutored sight, and any single landscape by the great painters that I knew'.[7] A corrective to the errors of their contemporaries, so it was agreed by the founding members of the PRB in 1848, lay in the fresh and vivid work of the early masters of the quattrocento. But as Ruskin explained in a letter to *The Times* on 13 May 1851, while the PRB denounced the conventionalism of their teachers and peers, they had no intention of merely imitating early Italian works: 'They intend to return to early days in this one point only – that, as far as in them lies, they will draw either what they see, or what they suppose might have been the actual facts of the scene they desire to represent, irrespective of any conventional rules of picture-making'.[8]

Hunt's *Fairlight Downs (Sunlight on the Sea)* (1852–58; cat. 109) is a triumphant exercise in representing 'actual facts'. His visual analysis of bright sunlight and cloud shadows reflected on the sea is fearless in its attempt to match exactly the local colour of the viewed object with the hues applied to the canvas. The effect is richly chromatic, brazen in its disregard for those conventions of composition, tone and *chiaroscuro* which even such radical figures as Turner and Constable had generally respected. No detail is too trivial to be recorded with painstaking – even religious – fervour; Hunt expended vast labour on the ears of the sheep and on the dog chasing a stick in the foreground. The industrial world impinges on this blissful pastoral scene, however, in the form of a steam tug spilling out black smoke in the English Channel, then one of the busiest shipping lanes in the world.

Ruskin played an active role in advising, sometimes perhaps dominating, a group of younger artists inspired by the early achievements of the PRB. One such was John Brett (1831–1902), the son of an army officer, who entered the Royal Academy Schools in 1854. As early as 1853 he had written 'I am going on fast towards Preraphaelitism' and devoted himself to 'close childlike study of nature'.[9] But what to paint? Ruskin was troubled by the Pre-Raphaelites' fondness for the quotidian landscapes of London's hinterland, and suggested that young Brett, already his protégé in succession to Millais, should paint the Turnerian subject of the foothills on the Italian side of Mont Blanc. Here, the artist produced *The Val d'Aosta* (1858; cat. 107), one of the most single-minded and fastidious achievements of Victorian landscape painting.

From the lichen on the rocks in the foreground (reminiscent of Millais's *John Ruskin*) to the distant storm on Mont Blanc, *The Val d'Aosta* is even bolder than Hunt's view of Fairlight Downs in representing natural objects as they really appear in brilliant Alpine sunshine. All the Ruskinian hallmarks are here: concern for geology and botany; careful notation of clouds and their shadows; and avoidance of any hint of modern, industrial life. Above all the painting represented a *tour de force* of devoted, even devotional, artistic labour. On seeing the finished work, Ruskin exclaimed: 'Yes, here we have it at last – some close-coming to it at least – historical landscape, properly so called – landscape painting with a meaning and a use. We have had hitherto plenty of industry, precision quite

Cat. 101
Eugene von Guérard (1811–1901)
A View of Geelong, Victoria, Australia,
1856
Oil on canvas, 89 × 152.5 cm

unlimited – but all useless, or nearly so, being wasted in scenes of no majesty or enduring interest. Here is, at last, a scene worth painting'. He proceeded to give a long, detailed and admiring account of the painting's subject and its handling. Yet, alas for Brett, Ruskin did not stop there. For, as Turner's greatest advocate, he ultimately took issue with Brett's youthful masterpiece: 'A notable picture, truly. . . . Yet not . . . a noble picture. It has a strange fault, considering the school to which it belongs – it seems to me wholly emotionless. I cannot find from it that the painter loved, or feared, anything in all that wonderful piece of the world. . . . I never saw the mirror so held up to Nature – but it is Mirror's work, not Man's.'[10] Brett's effort to inscribe on canvas the precise appearance of nature was recognised by contemporaries as an attempt to emulate the new technology of the camera: Millais called it 'a wretched work like a photograph'.[11] Brett's anguish at Ruskin's remarks was, perhaps, assuaged by the

fact that the older man acquired the painting; indeed, it remained in his house at Herne Hill until his death in 1900.

Ruskin's influence spread swiftly throughout the Anglophone world. In the United States a generation of artists led by Frederic Edwin Church (1826–1900) turned in the 1850s to a meticulously detailed and scientifically rigorous landscape style, in works such as Church's *Twilight in the Wilderness* (1860; Cleveland Museum of Art), which often bore an implicit religious message. Ruskinian naturalism seemed especially appropriate to the representation of the unfamiliar landscape, flora and fauna of Britain's burgeoning imperial territories. Although the pioneering painter of Australian landscape, Eugene von Guérard (1811–1901), was trained in the famous Düsseldorf Academy, it is possible to discern the influence of Ruskin in his works of the 1850s. Von Guérard tried his hand at gold prospecting at Ballarat before settling in Melbourne in 1854.[12] One

Cat. 102
William Lionel Wyllie RA (1851–1931)
London from the Monument, 1870
Oil on canvas, 72.3 × 120.6 cm

of many possible conduits for Ruskin's ideas in Australia was Thomas Woolner (1825–1892), a founding member of the Pre-Raphaelite Brotherhood who had emigrated to Melbourne in 1852 (an event commemorated in Ford Madox Brown's great painting *The Last of England* of 1852–55; Birmingham Museum and Art Gallery). Von Guérard's panoramic view of Geelong (1856; cat. 101) combines the heritage of German Romantic landscape painting with a Ruskinian precision of finish and a particular interest in unique local botanical and geological forms. A landscape of settlement, the canvas documents the transformation of the fertile lands of Victoria under the hands of European cultivators. In other works, von Guérard, like the English expatriate John Glover, documented and lamented the fate of the dispossessed Aboriginal population.

An entire generation of landscape painters in Victorian England was influenced by Pre-Raphaelitism and by Ruskin's writing. Benjamin Williams Leader (1831–1923), for example – a prolific and skilled painter of verdant pastoral scenery – adopted something of the detailed finish of the Pre-Raphaelites in his fine, early work (cat. 112), but scrupulously avoided any hint of modern industrialism.[13] John Atkinson Grimshaw

(1836–1893), the son of a Leeds policeman, began his career as an amateur in the late 1850s, but by the next decade was producing fresh, spontaneous canvases of local subjects such as *Ghyll Beck, Barden, Yorkshire, Early Spring* (1867; cat. 111), replete with such favourite Ruskinian details as primroses, mossy tree trunks and foaming streams.[14] He also treated the grander scenery of the Lake District (cat. 110), where Ruskin lived, at Brantwood overlooking Coniston Water, for the last decades of his life. Grimshaw's lack of formal training freed him to adopt a range of unorthodox techniques, including the frequent use of photographs for his compositions. Unlike Ruskin, Grismshaw was also keenly aware of the mysterious beauty of Victorian industrial cities, as in *Lights on the Mersey* (1892; cat. 116). His elegiac studies of canals and docks, and of deserted suburban streets, often seen in the melancholy glow of gaslight, are among the most haunting images of the Victorian era.

Few British painters directly confronted the uncompromising modernity of the metropolitan scene. The panoramic *London from the Monument* (1870; cat. 102) by William Lionel Wyllie (1851–1931) is a rare exception, a hymn to the beauty of the industrial city and the heart of the Empire which makes no concession to acknowledged landmarks, reducing the Palace of Westminster to a spectral presence on the horizon while glorying in the dark silhouette of Canon Street Station and the smoke of a locomotive crossing the bridge towards it. In contrast to his vast output of pedestrian marine pieces, *London from the Monument* and his later masterpiece *Toil, Glitter, Grime and Wealth on a Flowing Tide* (Tate Britain, London), are inspired tributes to the energy and grandeur of the imperial capital. The painting marks an abandonment of Ruskinian principles; in addition to the urban subject, the brushwork is allusive rather than fiercely descriptive, the paint layer thicker and creamier than the enamel-like surfaces of Pre-Raphaelitism.

Ruskin's influence waned during the 1870s, dramatically so after the libel action in 1878 brought by James McNeill Whistler (1834–1903), of whom Ruskin had said: 'I never expected to hear a coxcomb ask two hundred guineas for flinging a pot of paint in the public's face'.[15] Ruskin was writing, in his 'letters to the workmen and labourers of Great Britain', *Fors Clavigera*, of Whistler's *Nocturne in Black and Gold: The Falling Rocket* (fig. 2), another Thames scene celebrating urban modernity. In Whistler's hands, smoke and cloud in the background, illuminated by flames, are evoked through swiftly scumbled black and blue paint, while the sparks and flashes of fireworks over Cremorne Gardens are captured in smudges and blobs of impasto. Ruskin profoundly objected not only to the urban subject, but to the absence of finish, of visible signs of labour in the painting, which flouted the notion of the artist as an honest, reverent workman who revealed the beauty of God's creation. Whistler's Aestheticism won the day at the trial, although the American was awarded only a farthing in damages and was bankrupted by his legal costs. Ambivalent though it was, the trial marked the end of a glorious quarter-century in which the Pre-Raphaelite generation, with Ruskin as their champion, had perfected a powerfully original landscape idiom.

Fig. 2 **James McNeill Whistler**, *Nocturne in Black and Gold: The Falling Rocket*, c. 1875. Oil on panel, 60.5 × 46.5 cm. Detroit Institute of Arts

1 For a more expansive version of some of the arguments offered here, see Tim Barringer, *Reading the Pre-Raphaelites*, New Haven and London, 1999.

2 *Macmillan's Magazine* 64, August 1891, p. 280; quoted in Tim Hilton, *John Ruskin: The Early Years*, New Haven and London, 1985, p.73.

3 John Ruskin, *Modern Painters*, vol. 1 (1843), in E. T. Cooke and A. Wedderburn (eds), *The Works of John Ruskin*, 39 vols, London, 1903–12, vol. 3, pp. 623, 624.

4 Jason Rosenfeld, 'New Languages of Nature in Victorian England: The Pre-Raphaelite Landscape, Natural History and Modern Architecture in the 1850s', Ph.D. diss., Institute of Fine Arts, New York University, 1999.

5 John Ruskin, *The Storm-cloud of the Nineteenth Century* (1884), in Cooke and Wedderburn (note 3), vol. 34, pp. 9–84.

6 Ford Madox Brown, *The Exhibition of WORK and other Paintings* (1865), repr. in K. Bendiner, *The Art of Ford Madox Brown*, University Park, PA, 1998, p. 139.

7 William Holman Hunt, *Pre-Raphaelitism and the Pre-Raphaelite Brotherhood*, vol. 1, London, 1905, pp. 71–2. See also Allen Staley, *The Pre-Raphaelite Landscape*, 2nd edn, New Haven and London, 2001, p. 73.

8 *The Times*, 13 May 1851, p. 8; repr. in Cooke and Wedderburn (note 3), vol. 12, p. 322.

9 John Brett, diary entry for 18 May 1853; quoted in Michael Hickox and Christiana Payne, 'Sermons in Stones: John Brett's *The Stonebreaker* Reconsidered', in Ellen Harding (ed.), *Re-Framing the Pre-Raphaelites: Historical and Theoretical Essays*, Aldershot, 1995, p. 101.

10 John Ruskin 'The Royal Academy 1858', in Cooke and Wedderburn (note 3), vol. 14, pp. 235–7.

11 Quoted in Cooke and Wedderburn (note 3), vol. 14, p. 22n.

12 *Eugen von Guérard*, Candice Bruce, exh. cat., Art Gallery of New South Wales, Sydney, 1980; Tim Bonyhady, *Images in Opposition: Australian Landscape Painting 1801–1890*, Melbourne, 1985, pp. 91–3.

13 For a fascinating exception, see Leader's *The Excavation of the Manchester Ship Canal: Eastham Cutting with Mount Mainsty in the Background* (National Trust, Tatton Park, Cheshire). *In Trust for the Nation: Paintings from National Trust Houses*, Alastair Laing, exh. cat., National Gallery, London, 1995, pp. 96–7.

14 Alexander Robertson, *Atkinson Grimshaw*, Oxford, 1988, pp. 25–8.

15 John Ruskin, *Fors Clavigera: Letters to the Workmen and Labourers of Great Britain*, vol. 7, letter 79 (July 1877), in Cooke and Wedderburn (note 3), vol. 29, p. 160. See also Linda Merrill, *A Pot of Paint: Aesthetics on Trial in Ruskin v Whistler*, Washington DC, 1992.

Cat. 103
William Holman Hunt OM
(1827–1910)
The Old Church at Ewell, 1847
Oil on canvas, 63.5 × 76.2 cm

Cat. 104
Ford Madox Brown (1821–1893)
*Southend, Essex, Looking Towards
Sheerness*, begun 1846, reworked
in 1858 and 1861
Oil on paper, diam. 29 cm

Cat. 105, 106
John Brett ARA (1831–1902)
Two Studies for 'The Val d'Aosta', 1858

105 Watercolour over pencil,
heightened with white and gum arabic,
on paper, 24.5 × 19.4 cm

106 Watercolour and gouache on
paper, 16.5 × 25.4 cm

FACING PAGE
Cat. 107
John Brett ARA (1831–1902)
The Val d'Aosta, 1858
Oil on canvas, 87.6 × 68 cm

Cat. 108
William Holman Hunt OM
(1827–1910)
Fairlight Downs (The Silver Lining), 1865
Pencil, watercolour and gouache
on paper, 12.7 × 17.5 cm

Cat. 109
William Holman Hunt OM
(1827–1910)
Fairlight Downs (Sunlight on the Sea),
1852–58
Oil on panel, 22.8 × 31.1 cm

OVERLEAF   Detail of cat. 109

Cat. 110
John Atkinson Grimshaw
(1836–1893)
A Shepherd with His Flock in
a Mountainous Landscape
(Lake Buttermere from Hassness), 1865
Oil on canvas, 44.5 × 59.7 cm

Cat. 111
John Atkinson Grimshaw
(1836–1893)
Ghyll Beck, Barden, Yorkshire,
Early Spring, 1867
Oil on canvas, 76.2 × 63.5 cm

Cat. 112
Benjamin Williams Leader RA
(1831–1923)
A River Landscape with a Fisherman
Making Eel Traps, 1864
Oil on canvas, 80 × 132 cm

Cat. 113
James Talmage White (1833–1907)
Ruins of the Temple of Hercules,
Capo di Sorrento, first exhibited 1867
Pencil, watercolour and gouache
on paper, 54.6 × 102.9 cm

Cat. 114
John Brett ARA (1831–1902)
Norbury on the Mole, 1862
Oil on canvas, 51 × 68.5 cm

Richard Dadd
Contradiction: Oberon and Titania

CHARLOTTE GERE

Richard Dadd (1817–1886) has been labelled a 'fairy painter' and a 'mad' artist, but his art eludes classification. He was born in Chatham and trained at the Royal Academy Schools. His promising artistic career was cut short after only six years, when he became deranged following a gruelling expedition to the Middle East with a wealthy traveller, Sir Thomas Phillips. Dadd murdered his father, under the illusion that he had been commanded to do so by the Egyptian god Osiris, and spent the rest of his life confined to asylums for the criminally insane.

Dadd's doctors encouraged his artistic activities and provided him with books and prints. His acknowledged masterpieces, the present painting and *The Fairy-Feller's Master-Stroke* (1855–64; Tate Britain, London), were both done in Bethlem Hospital (Bedlam). Strictly speaking, they are therefore 'mad' paintings (and were not seen in public until the 20th century), but they are also the work of a trained artist experienced in fairy subjects. *Contradiction: Oberon and Titania* was painted for Dr Charles Hood, Dadd's sympathetic physician. The subject, taken from Act II, scene 1 of *A Midsummer Night's Dream*, is the dispute between Oberon, the fairy king, and his consort, Titania, who refuses to give up her adopted Indian boy so that he may become Oberon's page. Dadd deploys a huge cast of characters, possibly influenced by Sir Joseph Noël Paton's *Reconciliation of Oberon and Titania* of 1847 and *Quarrel of Oberon and Titania* of 1849–50 (both National Gallery of Scotland, Edinburgh), which amazed contemporary audiences with their teeming crowds of fairy figures. The leaden airlessness and stark lighting of *Contradiction* recall the stage, and indeed fairy subjects were often theatrical in origin, many of them derived from Shakespeare's plays. Victorian fairy painting drew on a number of sources, however, including the grotesques of Hieronymus Bosch (*c.* 1450–1516), apparent here in the green, egg-shaped object at the upper right. Tradition identified fairyland with the Orient, and this, coupled with memories of his travels, explains the Orientalism of Dadd's characters and costume. The host of figures and the minutely depicted natural surroundings are a remarkable achievement for an artist who worked without models or access to flora and fauna. Dadd's reputation has been rescued from the 'insane genius' stereotype, but to execute a painting in such laborious detail over many years would scarcely have been possible for artists living under normal circumstances who relied on their profession for a livelihood. Dadd's asylum paintings resulted from a situation that promoted his special gifts.

Cat. 115
Richard Dadd (1817–1886)
Contradiction: Oberon and Titania, 1854/58
Oil on canvas, oval, 61 × 75.5 cm

John Atkinson Grimshaw

ALEXANDER ROBERTSON

The art of John Atkinson Grimshaw (1836–1893), who is best known as a painter of moonlight, was based on a close observation of nature and in many ways can be seen as a reaction to the materialism of Victorian life. On the occasion of a memorial exhibition held in 1897, one critic noted: 'His best work is characterised by a tender, poetic feeling; many of his canvases might well be described as "poems in paint". At the beginning of his career the Pre-Raphaelite brotherhood was exercising a decided influence upon the art of the day. Young Grimshaw fell a victim to it, and continued his allegiance to the end. In many of his pictures the detail is marvellous. . . . Moonlight effects next took his fancy, and so popular was his work in this line that the demand exceeded the supply. . . . Atkinson Grimshaw was a Bohemian, and, like many of the brotherhood, endowed with great natural ability.'[1]

Born in Leeds in 1836, Grimshaw grew up in a town that rapid industrialisation was turning into one of the leading manufacturing centres of England. His family moved briefly to Norwich, but had returned to Leeds by 1852, when Grimshaw became a clerk for the Great Northern Railway. As an artist, he seems to have been entirely self-taught, learning from works exhibited in local galleries and art shops. Of particular importance here were the paintings of the Pre-Raphaelite Brother-hood, which were collected avidly by a Leeds stockbroker, Thomas Plint.[2] Equally valuable to Grimshaw were the occasional exhibitions of work by his fellow Leeds artist John William Inchbold (1830–1888),[3] himself a member of the Brotherhood circle and a friend of the leading art critic of the day, John Ruskin (1819–1900).

Grimshaw married Theodosia Hubbarde, cousin of the animal painter Thomas Sidney Cooper (cat. 173), in 1858 and three years later gave up his job in order to paint full time. His early work consisted of careful studies from nature and still-lifes. By 1864 he had adopted a Pre-Raphaelite manner, using precise handling to depict minute detail in a palette of vibrant colours that were often applied to a white ground. Like many young artists at mid-century, he was attracted to Ruskin's notion of 'truth to nature'.[4] With its icy coolness and brilliant, crisp detail, *Ghyll Beck, Barden, Yorkshire, Early Spring* (1867; cat. 111) represents a high point of Grimshaw's early period, but this kind of imagery soon gave way to paintings with a more poetic atmosphere and an interest in moonlight.

In 1870 the Grimshaw family took up residence in Knostrop Old Hall, a Jacobean manor house on the outskirts of Leeds, surroundings which encouraged the artist to indulge his love of legend and poetry. The move heralded Grimshaw's most successful years as an artist, during which he developed his style and technique in subjects which became his trademark: suburban lanes, dock scenes in London and Liverpool, images derived from poetry, and compositions set in ancient Greece and Rome in the style of Lawrence Alma-Tadema (cat. 143–5). Over a ten-year period he also produced several interiors in the manner of the French artist James Tissot (cat. 128–35) which showed the modern woman 'at home'.

The 1870s and '80s saw Grimshaw taken up by the art dealers Agnew and Tooth in their London and regional galleries. In addition, work by him was accepted for exhibition at the Royal Academy from 1874 to 1886, while in 1885 he was invited to show a painting at the prestigious Grosvenor Gallery, which numbered the leading members of the Aesthetic Movement among its contributors. In the late 1870s Grimshaw rented a second house, in Scarborough, which he named Castle-by-the-Sea after Longfellow's poem, and early in the following decade took a studio in Manresa Road, Chelsea, London, both of which brought new subjects to his attention. He greatly increased his output in the 1880s, possibly to pay off the debts of a friend. The artist's last years saw him embracing new subject matter and a lighter palette in some delightful beach, estuary and, during the final winter of his life, snow scenes.

Images of suburban lanes formed a staple of the artist's repertoire for over twenty years, produced in endless variations that drew on the skills acquired from his close observation of nature during the first decade of his career. Detail is more generalised than in his early work, but remains essential to an understanding of the paintings. In *The Lovers* (1874; cat. 122), for example, the couple become a pivotal point of interest set against a curtain of branches amid the all-enveloping twilight. Moving out of the suburbs into the country provided Grimshaw with further subjects of this type. He returned to Stapleton Park, near Pontefract, West Yorkshire, on several occasions. In the painting shown here (1879; cat. 120) the zigzag of the road allowed a dramatic contrast of light and shade, a contrast echoed in the juxtaposition of autumnal greens and browns. Still more striking are the trees silhouetted against the golden light, a kind of inner glow that appears to emanate from the canvas. The degree of meticulously executed detail, and its sheer exuberance, make *Sixty Years Ago* (1879; cat. 121) one of Grimshaw's most impressive lane pictures. Golden light floods the whole scene, pouring through the screen of tree branches onto the stone walls and puddles. Holding together the composition of this *tour de force* of natural

observation is the figure of an elegantly dressed young lady, complete with lace gloves, daintily stepping across the lane. In combination with the image, Grimshaw's title suggests a more leisurely past, far removed from the cares of modern life.

Much of Grimshaw's work was produced for private patrons, but his figure paintings of the 1870s and '80s were painted for the art market in order to cater for the Victorian love for romantic and contemporary subjects. Alfred Tennyson's poem 'The Lady of Shalott' inspired several paintings by the artist. That included here (1878; cat. 125) shows the lady after the curse has befallen her. Cast off from her island, she drifts to Camelot in a boat and dies on the way. Grimshaw's treatment of light, sky and water provides a ghostly foil for the central group. In *Il Penseroso* (1875; cat. 118) he took the title of Milton's poem of 1632 as a starting point for the depiction of a contemporary woman seated among the exotic plants in the conservatory at Knostrop Old Hall. The central figure and the various props make it clear that this was an attempt to rival Tissot.

Grimshaw regarded *Dulce Domum* (1885; cat. 117) as one of his most important paintings and appended the following inscription to the reverse: 'Mostly painted

Cat. 116
John Atkinson Grimshaw
(1836–1893)
Lights on the Mersey, 1892
Oil on board, 25.4 × 50.8 cm

under great difficulties, but by God's grace finished 1885. LABOR OMNIA VINCIT'. T. W. H. Crosland wrote a poem based on the picture which includes the lines:

> This house is full of strange memories,
> Wondrously strange, God-wot-
> Dim wraithes of woe and ghosts of tragedies,
> But they disturb her not. . .[5]

Only a year before starting the painting three of the Grimshaws' children had died; two more followed in 1882. The 'sweet home' of the title is replete with artistic props. The *Times* critic singled out the painting of the woman's dress as evidence of the artist's technical skill,[6] but Grimshaw's gift for observation is to be seen everywhere in *Dulce Domum*.

When the artist took a studio in London in the early 1880s (and reputedly made the acquaintance of James McNeill Whistler) he became attracted not only to the city and the Thames as subjects, but also to the suburbs. A south London suburb provided the subject of *Wimbledon Park, Autumn After Glow* (1886; cat. 119). This is one of Grimshaw's most detailed paintings, notable for a mosaic-like pattern spreading across road and walls and for an intense feeling of autumn chill and damp soggy leaves, with the man raking up leaves forming an essential element of the composition. Another painting of a London suburb, this time to the north of the city (1881; cat. 126), reveals all the salient characteristics of the artist's mature style and technique. As so often in Grimshaw's work, the moon plays a dominant role in *On Hampstead Hill*, controlling the atmosphere of the painting. As the writer of one obituary of the artist noted: 'it was the mystery of the murky air, the tender hues of the dawn, or the mellow light of the moon thrown on all beneath it, a silvery radiance, that appealed to him most deeply'.[7]

Throughout the 1880s Grimshaw produced a series of commanding views of London. *Cornhill* (1885; cat. 127) evinces not just an interest in the light of the moon (in this case, a hidden light source), but also in the effects of artificial light from street lamps and shop windows as reflected in wet surfaces. In this he echoed Mrs Gaskell, who in *Mary Barton* (1848) had written: 'it is a pretty sight to walk through a street with lighted shops; the gas is so brilliant, the display of goods so much more vividly shown than by day'.[8]

Grimshaw's views of the ports of Glasgow, Hull, Liverpool, London and Whitby were perhaps his most popular paintings. *Liverpool* (1882; cat. 124) is notable for its sparse placing of figures and for the 'sketched in' nature of the buildings and the ships' masts and rigging. As in all his finest dock pictures, Grimshaw covers the grubby reality with a poetic sheen. Another example is *Home Again* (cat. 123), painted in the late 1870s, which depicts an embracing couple picked out by moonlight against a view of Whitby old town with St Hilda's Abbey. Whitby had been the setting for the artist's earliest moonlit images and remained a favourite venue. The dramatic effect of the sky and of the light seen through the fence and between the masts makes this one of Grimshaw's most evocative and poetic compositions, and it also includes a show of human emotion extremely rare in his work.

During the last years of his life Grimshaw's output declined sharply. One of the few dated paintings he produced at this time was *Lights on the Mersey* (1892; cat. 116). Carried out in two tones of blue with the merest hint of a shoreline, this picture reveals the greatest subtlety in using extreme simplicity of means to achieve the maximum effect. If this was a new direction Grimshaw was taking, his death aged only 57 is all the more regrettable.

1 *Leeds Mercury*, 12 November 1897, p. 7, reviewing *Loan Exhibition of Works by the Recently Deceased Local Artists Robert Atkinson, Atkinson Grimshaw, Edward March and Thomas Sutcliffe* at Leeds City Art Gallery.

2 Brian Lewis, 'Thomas Edward Plint: A Patron of Pre-Raphaelite Painters', *Leeds Museums and Galleries Review* 4, 2001–02, pp. 30–5.

3 *John William Inchbold*, Christopher Newall, exh. cat., Leeds City Art Gallery, 1993.

4 Expounded in *Modern Painters*, 3rd edn, 3 vols, London, 1846–60.

5 Typescript, supplied to the author by Grimshaw's grandson, Guy Phillips, in 1979. 'Dulce Domum' apparently appeared in a privately published four-page pamphlet. W. Sorley Brown, *The Life and Genius of T. W. H. Crosland*, London, 1928, p. 42.

6 *The Times*, 25 May 1885, p. 4.

7 *Leeds Mercury*, 1 November 1893, p. 5.

8 Elizabeth Gaskell, *Mary Barton*, Harmondsworth, 1986, p. 101.

Cat. 117
John Atkinson Grimshaw
(1836–1893)
Dulce Domum, 1885
Oil on canvas, 83.1 × 122.5 cm

Cat. 118
John Atkinson Grimshaw
(1836–1893)
Il Penseroso, 1875
Oil on board, 59.7 × 49.5 cm

Cat. 119
John Atkinson Grimshaw
(1836–1893)
Wimbledon Park, Autumn After Glow,
1886
Oil on canvas, 60.4 × 90.2 cm

Cat. 120
John Atkinson Grimshaw
(1836–1893)
Stapleton Park, 1879
Oil on canvas, 75 × 125.8 cm

Cat. 121

John Atkinson Grimshaw
(1836–1893)
Sixty Years Ago, 1879
Oil on canvas, 83 × 122 cm

Cat. 122
John Atkinson Grimshaw
(1836–1893)
The Lovers, 1874
Oil on panel, 46.5 × 56.7 cm

Cat. 123
John Atkinson Grimshaw
(1836–1893)
Home Again, late 1870s (?)
Oil on board, 42.5 × 63.8 cm

Cat. 124
John Atkinson Grimshaw
(1836–1893)
Liverpool, 1882
Oil on board, 30 × 49 cm

Cat. 125
John Atkinson Grimshaw
(1836–1893)
The Lady of Shalott, 1878
Oil on canvas, 82.5 × 122 cm

Cat. 126
John Atkinson Grimshaw
(1836–1893)
On Hampstead Hill, 1881
Oil on panel, 30.5 × 40.5 cm

Cat. 127
John Atkinson Grimshaw
(1836–1893)
Cornhill, 1885
Oil on canvas, 76.2 × 63.5 cm

James Joseph Tissot

NANCY ROSE MARSHALL

Born Jacques-Joseph Tissot in 1836, Tissot moved from his native Nantes to study art in Paris in 1856 or 1857.[1] Although he gained admission to the conservative Ecole des Beaux-Arts, Tissot cultivated a circle of avant-garde artists in Paris, including Edgar Degas, Edouard Manet and James McNeill Whistler. Around this time he anglicised his first name to James, perhaps as a token of his admiration for Whistler. Despite these friendships Tissot never joined the Impressionists, but instead sought success in the most prestigious art institution of the day, the Paris Salon. From 1859 his work appeared regularly at the Salon, and by 1866 Tissot was earning 70,000 francs a year and had built a house in a fashionable quarter of the city. During his Parisian career, he experimented with a range of subject matter, including *japoniste* genre scenes, popular society portraits, images of contemporary life and scenes set in the French Directoire period of the late 18th century.

In 1871, following the Franco-Prussian war, Tissot abruptly moved to London. The reasons for his relocation probably relate to his suspected involvement in the Commune, the temporary radical government set up in Paris that had been violently suppressed by the French authorities. In London from 1871 to 1882, Tissot quickly built a thriving career to rival the one he had left behind, exhibiting at the Royal Academy and the Grosvenor Gallery. Although at first he achieved success with 18th-century costume pictures, around 1873 Tissot began to work almost exclusively in subjects of modern English life. His artistic circle in London included George du Maurier, John Everett Millais (cat. 19–29) and Lawrence Alma-Tadema (cat. 143–5), whom he entertained in his villa in St John's Wood.[2]

In 1876 the Irish divorcée Kathleen Irene Kelly Newton moved into Tissot's house and became both his mistress and the model for many of his subsequent paintings, including several in the Andrew Lloyd Webber Collection. In 1882 Newton died of tuberculosis, and a grief-stricken Tissot returned almost immediately to Paris. Long interested in spiritualism, Tissot now began to consult mediums and even believed he had achieved contact with Newton's spirit during a seance in London in 1885. He died in 1902.

The paintings by Tissot in Lord Lloyd-Webber's collection all date from the artist's London period and represent themes of modern life that recur throughout his oeuvre. These include ships and harbours, boating on the Thames, mourning, children and gardens.

The Return from the Boating Trip (1873; cat. 133) depicts a man and a woman disembarking from a pleasure craft on the Thames at Maidenhead Bridge, a common picturesque destination for river tourists. The woman gazes out of the picture with an ambiguous pout; the man, rather than helping her up the steps, lags behind and turns away from her, suggesting tension or discord in their relationship. Images of couples rowing together were common in art and literature of the period, most often symbolising an actual or potential romantic union. Any difficulty with navigation was therefore a portent of future unhappiness, as for example in George du Maurier's amusing cartoon of 1875 'Now or Never! An Allegorical Sketch at Maidenhead' (fig. 1). Du Maurier's drawing resembles *The Return from the Boating Trip* in its theme, location and male attire, and may have been a direct reference to his friend's painting; even if not, the cartoon points to the fact that, for Victorian audiences, images of a man and a women with a boat awakened notions of courtship.[3]

The Captain and the Mate (1873; cat. 128) is one of a group of Tissot's works set on ships at harbour. On the left, the Captain, dressed in the uniform of a commercial shipping company, sits with a young woman who sports the same dress, hat and shawl as her counterpart in *The Return from the Boating Trip*. In the centre of the composition the Mate perches on the ship's gunwale, nervously twisting the hem of his coat in a gesture that underscores

"NOW, OR NEVER!"
(*An Allegorical Sketch of Maidenhead.*)

EMILY DISTINCTLY REFUSES TO TRUST HERSELF IN THE SAME BOAT WITH FRANK, UNLESS HE CONSENTS TO ROW BOW TO HER STROKE. WHAT IS TO BE DONE! TO YIELD, MIGHT BE A FATAL PRECEDENT FOR THE FUTURE; TO REFUSE, MIGHT BE TO JEOPARDISE THAT FUTURE ALTOGETHER!

the seriousness of the conversation he is having with the young lady.[4] He has apparently just asked a question, and as she ponders her answer she holds him – and the viewer – in suspense. By refusing to create a clear narrative – we know neither the question nor the response to it – Tissot was participating in the avant-garde experiments of his friends Degas and Whistler. The composition is also unconventional, as the people become subordinate to the objects in the foreground; on the right is the brass and wood ship's binnacle, which housed the steering compass.[5] To the left is a tray of refreshments, including soda water in its distinctive bottles. The accuracy of detail with which Tissot rendered such objects of shipboard life, as well as the extraordinary tangle of masts and rigging in the background, is typical of his polished style of this period, as is the unusual black and white tonality.

'Goodbye' – *On the Mersey* of c. 1881 (cat. 132) is another picture set in a harbour, this time the port of Liverpool. In the foreground several figures wave hats and handkerchiefs at an enormous Cunard steamer, presumably setting sail for New York. As viewers, we are positioned on the small local ferry with those remaining behind, so we identify with the sense of urgency with which the farewells are performed. Parting, loss and departure are recurrent themes in Tissot's work, and the sombre palette intensifies the melancholy mood of this picture.

The Widower (c. 1877; cat. 131) and *L'Orpheline* (first exhibited 1879; cat. 135) more explicitly explore the themes of loss and death, as both depict figures in mourning. The widower hoists his little girl up to admire a fruiting tree while he gazes sombrely at the flowering rhubarb and irises in the overgrown garden. Contemporary reviewers accurately perceived the luxuriant vitality of the man's surroundings as a stark contrast with his mood: as one commented, 'the rich summer vegetation is rife with thoughts of the summers that once brought blossoms of life and joy to him'.[6]

L'Orpheline, although somewhat similar in composition, puzzled its viewers, who were confused by its subject. The woman and girl, dressed in black, stand against a glowing curtain of yellow horse chestnut leaves in a thicket of reeds and cattails, leading one reviewer to complain that the 'place . . . suggests nothing short of suicide and by one of the muddiest of deaths. It would be hard to discover any meaning in this kind of picture beyond "an arrangement in black and green"'.[7] The use of the word 'arrangement' (or, in another case, 'harmony'[8]) suggests that reviewers were picking up on Tissot's similarities to Whistler, who included such words in the titles of his works in order to draw comparisons between art and music. Like Whistler, Tissot was exploring Aestheticism, a form of art that stressed beauty and colour harmony over narrative subject matter.

The models for *L'Orpheline* were Tissot's mistress, Kathleen Newton, and her niece Lilian Hervey, who also appear in *Uncle Fred* (c. 1879; cat. 129), *Quiet* (c. 1878/79; cat. 130), and *Le Banc de jardin* (1882; cat. 134). These three works are part of a large group of images, painted between 1877 and 1882, which were set in the garden of Tissot's St John's Wood villa. Collectively, the pictures convey the impression of family snapshots – seemingly unposed moments of playful leisure in peaceful, sunlit landscapes.

Uncle Fred depicts Hervey with Newton's brother Frederick Kelly. Wearing the same pink ribbons, Hervey peers over the fur-draped bench in *Quiet* as Newton reads to her. The seat appears in the large exhibition picture *Le Banc de jardin*, which portrays Newton, her daughter Violet, her niece Belle (behind the bench) and her son Cecil George. In this vivid work similarly rendered spots of rich colour pick out both dress patterns and lush flower beds, representing an unusual foray for Tissot

Fig. 2 **James Joseph Tissot**, *His First Breeches*, 1880. Etching and drypoint on laid paper, 17.9 × 7.5 cm (impression). Art Gallery of Ontario, Toronto (Gift of Allan and Sondra Gotlieb, 1994)

Cat. 128
James (Jacques) Joseph Tissot
(1836–1902)
The Captain and the Mate, 1873
Oil on panel, 53.6 × 76.2 cm

OVERLEAF Detail of cat. 128

into a range of different types of mark-making. Newton gazes fondly at Cecil, who boldly sits astride the back of the bench; her maternal watchfulness is suggested by the way she holds his hand and protectively touches his foot in order to balance him. Cecil and the girls all turn to look at the viewer, who in this case seems nearly identified with Tissot himself.

This picture was in Tissot's possession at his death, suggesting its importance to him, which may have included private aspects. Not only was it one of the last compositions for which Kathleen Newton modelled, but Cecil Newton may also have been Tissot's son.[9] Cecil is the focus of several works from this period, including the etching *His First Breeches* (1880; fig. 2), in which he wears the same outfit as in *Le Banc de jardin*. Tissot clearly seems to have been interested in the boy's progress to maturity and may have been subtly claiming paternity through his depictions of him.

1 The most complete accounts of Tissot's life are by Willard Misfeldt, 'James Jacques Joseph Tissot: A Biocritical Study', Ph.D. diss., Washington University, 1971, and Michael Wentworth, *James Tissot*, Oxford, 1984. The following information is distilled from their research.

2 Jane Abdy, 'Tissot: His London Friends and Visitors', *James Tissot*, Krystyna Matyjaszkiewicz (ed.), exh. cat., Barbican Art Gallery, London, 1984, pp. 40–52.

3 Du Maurier's couple have been quarrelling over which of them is to row 'Bow to the other's Stroke', and the man worries that giving way to the woman at this point would 'set a precedent'. *Punch*, 10 July 1875, p. 6.

4 Unusually for him, Tissot chose authentic models for his shipboard works: Captain John Freebody, his wife Margaret Kennedy Freebody and her brother, Mate Lumley Kennedy, sat for this picture. *James Tissot* (note 2), p. 110.

5 I am indebted to Teddy Archibald for the information about the company uniforms and to Drs Hugh Richmond and David Cordingly for identifying the binnacle. The pointed chimneys on this instrument are ventilators for the heat and smoke of the lamps that illuminated it at night.

6 *The Times*, 1 May 1877, p. 10.

7 *The Times*, 2 May 1879, p. 3. The picture was first exhibited at the Grosvenor Gallery, under the title *Orphans*.

8 The reviewer describes the work as 'a pleasant "harmony"' in gold, green and black'. *Kensington*, June 1879, p. 385.

9 The contents of Tissot's studio at his death are listed in *J.J. Tissot: Prints from the Gotlieb Collection*, Willard Misfeldt, exh. cat., Dixon Gallery and Gardens, Memphis, TE, 1991, p. 164.

Cat. 129
James (Jacques) Joseph Tissot
(1836–1902)
Uncle Fred, c. 1879
Oil on panel, 19.4 × 30.5 cm

Cat. 130
James (Jacques) Joseph Tissot
(1836–1902)
Quiet, c. 1878/79
Oil on panel, 31.7 × 21.6 cm

Cat. 131
James (Jacques) Joseph Tissot
(1836–1902)
The Widower, c. 1877
Oil on panel, 35.5 × 23.5 cm

Cat. 132
James (Jacques) Joseph Tissot
(1836–1902)
'Goodbye' – On the Mersey, c. 1881
Oil on panel, 34.2 × 22.8 cm

Cat. 133
James (Jacques) Joseph Tissot
(1836–1902)
The Return from the Boating Trip, 1873
Oil on panel, 61 × 43.1 cm

Cat. 134
James (Jacques) Joseph Tissot
(1836–1902)
Le Banc de jardin, 1882
Oil on canvas, 99.1 × 142.2 cm

Cat. 135
James (Jacques) Joseph Tissot
(1836–1902)
L'Orpheline (*Orphans*),
first exhibited 1879
Oil on canvas, 216 × 109.2 cm

Giovanni Boldini
The Marchesa Luisa Casati

ANN DUMAS

Giovanni Boldini (1842–1931) displayed a precocious talent and at the age of eighteen was already established as a portrait painter in his native Ferrara. Later, in Florence, he mixed with the progressive Macchiaoli group of artists before moving in 1871 to Paris, where he was to spend the rest of his life. At first, Boldini specialised in the popular genre of minutely executed 18th-century costume pieces, but soon turned to portraiture. By the end of the century he had attained a stellar reputation as a portraitist of high society, together with John Singer Sargent and James McNeill Whistler. Boldini was a virtuoso draughtsman and an accomplished exponent of etching and pastel, in which he learned from the example of his friend Edgar Degas.

The Marchesa Luisa Casati is a splendid example of Boldini's images of glamorous society women, a genre which he made particularly his own. Typically, he is less interested in capturing nuances of character than in a dazzling distillation of style. The Marchesa's face with her wide-eyed gaze and rouged lips is the only clearly defined element of the composition, in which pyrotechnic swirling lines suggest the plumed hat, fur boa and the rustle of fine stuffs. Boldini's painterly virtuosity reveals his debt to the great portraitists of the past, especially the 17th-century painters Velázquez, Hals and Van Dyck.

The Marchesa Luisa Casati, who was born into a wealthy family of Lombard textile manufacturers, was renowned for her extravagance. The poet Gabriele d'Annunzio once claimed that she was the only woman capable of surprising him. Boldini is supposed to have first met her in Venice, when he helped her retrieve pearls from a seven-metre-long necklace that had broken. Stylish beasts, like the greyhound in this portrait that complements the Marchesa's elegant allure, seem to have been among her regular accoutrements. She would parade through Venice dressed as a gondolier and accompanied by a cheetah on a leash.

Cat. 136
Giovanni Boldini (1842–1931)
The Marchesa Luisa Casati, 1908
Oil on canvas, 253.4 × 140.4 cm

Antonio Frilli

Nude Reclining in a Hammock

MARYANNE STEVENS

Little is known about Antonio Frilli. Neither the dates nor the locations of his birth and death are recorded. He was apparently active in Florence, where he ran a workshop producing, in marble, bronze and alabaster, busts, decorative items and free-standing pieces such as *Nude Reclining in a Hammock*. His work was first recorded at the 1883 Esposizione Nazionale in Rome, yet he seems to have had an international exhibiting career, showing at the Glasgow International Exhibition of 1888, the Exposition Universelle in Paris the following year, and the St Louis International Exhibition of 1904, at which the present sculpture was apparently purchased by William Goldman, a major theatrical entrepreneur.

Although Frilli's work is described in the *Dizionario degli Scultori dell'ottocento e primo novecento* (second edition) as being in the 'Stile Liberty', the Italian variant of Art Nouveau, there is little in *Nude Reclining in a Hammock* to suggest this. Rather, the virtuoso carving of the figure, whose weight is borne by a hammock somewhat precariously slung between two relatively slim uprights of classical design, places the piece more firmly within the neo-Baroque tradition of Italian sculpture represented by such contemporaries as Ercole Rosa (1846–1893) and Giulio Monteverde (1837–1917). Unlike the preceding generation of Italian sculptors, whose work had been dominated by the calm poise and austere monumentality of the neoclassical style practised by Antonio Canova (1757–1822), these younger artists turned to 17th-century exemplars, creating pieces in which the materiality of marble is challenged through mannered poses and richly worked and articulated surfaces.

Goldman placed *Nude Reclining in a Hammock* in his garden before transferring it in December 1932 to the Jules Mastbaum Theatre, Philadelphia (subsequently demolished). Here it joined an extensive art collection that formed part of the interior decoration of this movie palace, built in a 'wedding cake' style by Jules Mastbaum and opened to the public in 1929.

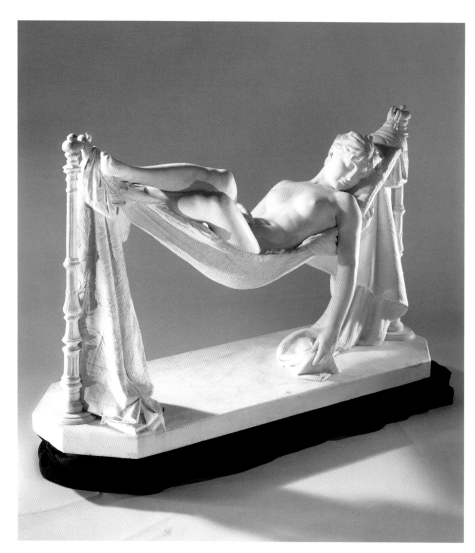

Cat. 137
Antonio Frilli (late 19th – early 20th century)
Nude Reclining in a Hammock,
c. 1883/1904
White marble, 109.9 × 188 cm

Academics and Classicists: Leighton, Alma-Tadema, Poynter, Moore and Others

ROBYN ASLESON

The Pre-Raphaelites had no sooner brought realism to the fore of Victorian art than the pendulum swung to the opposite pole and the next generation of daring young men ushered in an era of idealism. While remaining reasonably faithful to nature, this new group of revolutionaries drew their principal inspiration from art – specifically, the sculptures of classical antiquity and the paintings of Renaissance Italy. Aspiring to create works of equivalent grandeur of form and nobility of purpose, they raised contemporary British painting to an entirely new level of sophistication.

The rise of classical tendencies in late Victorian art owed much to the influence of Frederic Leighton (1830–1896), the charismatic President of the Royal Academy from 1878 to 1896. Having spent his cosmopolitan youth among the art museums and ateliers of continental Europe, Leighton was steeped in the academic tradition. His extreme competence as a figure painter distinguished him from the majority of British artists at mid-century, as did his dedication to working with the nude model. In addition to making exhaustive preparatory drawings from the nude, Leighton painted a succession of independent nudes. These ranged from large-scale pictures intended for exhibition, to the more intimate, impromptu study in the Andrew Lloyd Webber Collection (cat. 141). In the latter work Leighton's model adopts the pose of a *diadumenos*, or fillet binder, a subject frequently found in antique sculpture. The association with classical culture was meant to dignify the picture, but the sheer beauty of the woman's unclothed body is clearly Leighton's real subject, and he has painted it with singular sensitivity and evident pleasure.

By the turn of the century British artists were treating the nude with a sensuousness and eroticism that Leighton would never have attempted. Edward Poynter (1836–1919), a close colleague of Leighton and his successor as Royal Academy President, produced one of the most voluptuous treatments of the classical nude:

The Cave of the Storm Nymphs (cat. 142). An expanded version of a picture shown at the Royal Academy in 1902 (unlocated), the painting revisits the perennially popular theme of the amoral *femme fatale*: in this case, three siren-like nymphs whose beautiful music-making has lured a treasure-laden ship onto the rocks. A superb draughtsman, Poynter perfected the complex, sinuous poses through a series of meticulous chalk drawings from the live model. The slender, pubescent body type deviates from the classical ideal and reflects contemporary fetishisation of the child-woman. Although, like Leighton, Poynter tended to over-refine his flesh painting to a cold, unnatural polish, here the dramatic use of highlight and shadow makes the skin appear to pulsate with life.

At the time Leighton and Poynter were beginning their careers, the path to professional distinction lay not with the nude but with elaborately costumed history paintings. With such a picture Leighton, at the age of 34, secured his election as an Associate of the Royal Academy: *Dante in Exile* (cat. 138), a monumental canvas exhibited in 1864, depicts the fate of the Florentine poet in Verona, forced to endure the obtrusive attentions of a crowd of vapid merrymakers gathering for a festa. Though the subject suggests a lively and colourful scene, Leighton approached it with classical restraint, using the architectural elements of the staircase and framing walls to organise the figures into orderly, symmetrical groupings. His palette is equally restrained, limited to subdued blacks, browns, greens and whites, with a few eye-catching splashes of scarlet and gold striking notes of luxury and drama. The folds of green velvet cascading from the shoulders of the red-haired woman on the left demonstrate the artist's sensitivity to the classical language of drapery, while the well-defined legs and buttocks of her male companion, shifting into a contrapposto stance, attest to scrupulous study of classical sculpture and the nude model.

Leighton's association with the prestige of classicism and the lofty ideals of the academic tradition accelerated his professional ascent and won the admiration of younger British artists. Frank Dicksee (1853–1928) fell under Leighton's spell while studying at the Royal Academy Schools. In 1924 he followed in Leighton's and Poynter's footsteps as President of the Academy, but he began his professional career in the 1870s as an illustrator of books and periodical journals. His twelve illustrations to *Romeo and Juliet* (cat. 151), published in 1884 as part of Cassell's *Royal Shakspeare*, clearly reveal Leighton's influence. 'The Ball Scene' (cat. 151c), for example, rivals *Dante in Exile* in its use of architecture to impose order on a crowd of revellers. The torchbearer in the right middle distance (reminiscent of the young dandy seen from the rear in *Dante*) attests to Dicksee's close study of the nude model, as do the actively posed youths in 'Rival Factions', 'The Invitation' and 'The Death of Tybalt' (cat. 151a, b, f). Lessons learned from the skilfully arranged drapery of classical sculpture emerge in other scenes – most notably, 'Friar Laurence', 'Juliet's Chamber' and 'The Tomb' (cat. 151d–e, i, k). Even in episodes of violent action, Dicksee's illustrations are characterised by the same air of dignified restraint that Leighton cultivated in his work.

Although scenes from history and literature gained respect, it was through depictions of beautiful women that many late Victorian painters earned their bread. Serving no other purpose than to please the eye, such pictures gave artists free rein to indulge their personal ideas of beauty. Leighton, for instance, was prone to a rather confectionary treatment of lovely women and children in exotic settings. *Gulnihal* (cat. 150) is a particularly delightful example, exquisite in handling and charming in character. Despite the Oriental costume (brought back from the artist's travels in the Levant) and the Arabic title (which translates as 'beautiful rose'), the picture is not meant to represent a Middle Eastern subject (as the girl's northern European features make clear). It is, rather, an arrangement of beautiful things, beautifully painted.

The same might be said of Dicksee's fantasy of classical feminine beauty, *The Mirror* (cat. 149). An archaeologist would quibble with the ornate, mother-of-pearl throne, the peacock feather wall hanging and the richly patterned draperies, but they are bound together by the logic of beauty, rather than that of archaeology, and this is singularly appropriate in a painting whose subject is visual pleasure.

The Victorian preoccupation with ideal feminine beauty fuelled the popularity of a series of pictures commissioned by *The Graphic* magazine, in which artists were asked to depict classic types of womanhood. One set of paintings, 'The Graphic Gallery of Shakespeare's Heroines', yielded a particularly lovely work by Edmund Blair Leighton (1853–1922) (cat. 139). Though unrelated by birth to Frederic Leighton, Blair Leighton shared the classical sensibilities of the Royal Academy President. His *Olivia* (inspired by the heroine of Shakespeare's *Twelfth Night*) recreates authentic details of Renaissance dress, jewellery and décor, yet the woman's low brow and symmetrical features clearly derive from classical sculpture. Like many British artists of his generation, Blair Leighton had begun his art education with close study of the Elgin Marbles, and their ideal forms left a permanent imprint on his imagination.

The vogue for classicism in Victorian art coincided with a trend towards Aestheticism – the belief that beauty pursued for its own sake is the only appropriate aim of art and that all other concerns, whether historical, ethical or narrative, are irrelevant distractions. Classicism and Aestheticism coalesced in the work of Albert Moore (1841–1893), a highly idiosyncratic artist who conceived of his paintings as beautiful arrangements of beautiful things, without meaning or moral. The blend of ancient and modern elements in *Companions* (cat. 146) typifies Moore's provocative disregard for chronological consistency in assembling the elements of his paintings. He refined his compositions by means of elaborate under-drawings of diagonal, vertical and horizontal lines, traces of which are discernible in the background of *Companions*. Moore based these geometric diagrams on formal principles he believed responsible for beauty in art and nature.

On many occasions Moore deflected attempts to find narrative significance in his paintings by giving them deliberately non-allusive titles. *Red Berries* (cat. 147), for example, directs the viewer's attention to a seemingly meaningless inanimate object. The human figure is treated as just one element in a remarkably complex design, all but lost in the psychedelic intensity of the all-over surface patterning.

Towards the end of his career, Moore expanded his focus beyond the purely formal qualities of his canvases.

Cat. 138
Frederic, Lord Leighton PRA
(1830–1896)
Dante in Exile, first exhibited 1864
Oil on canvas, 152.5 × 254 cm

In late works such as *Lightning and Light* (cat. 148) he established human interest through the suggestion of incident and emotion, and substituted freely painted landscapes for the patently artificial, hermetic settings of previous pictures. Nevertheless, infinitesimal calculations and recalculations continued to determine the placement of each line and colour, all refined through exhaustive preparatory drawings and oil sketches. Even the decorative metal railing and inlaid bench frame were designed specifically for this painting.

Equally fastidious in execution, the classical paintings of Lawrence Alma-Tadema (1836–1912) embraced the narrative and archaeological elements that Moore eschewed. Extensive research at excavation sites and an immense collection of photographs and measured drawings contributed to the factual accuracy of paintings such as *Goldfish* (cat. 145), in which Alma-Tadema reconstructed the appearance of an ancient Roman atrium. Originally painted in 1872 (a year before the Dutch-born artist became a British citizen), *Goldfish* was extensively repainted in a more polished style at the request of the dealer who acquired the picture in 1899. Working with a miniaturist's touch, Alma-Tadema convincingly replicated the luminosity of marble, the sheen of silver, the delicate bloom of flowers and the dazzle of sunlight. The subject, a lovely young woman reclining in luxurious ease, recurs not only in his work, but also in much late Victorian painting – an embodiment of the values of beauty and repose that were then considered essential to art.

Cat. 139
Edmund Blair Leighton (1853–1922)
Olivia, 1887
Oil on canvas, 48.2 × 61 cm

Alma-Tadema's tremendous success encouraged other painters to work in a similar vein. Among the most prolific of his imitators was John William Godward (1861–1922), who gained a popular following (if not official honours) with his technically accomplished depictions of classically draped women surrounded by marble, water and sky. His *Dolce far niente* (cat. 140) revisits the theme of a languid woman reclining in pleasant repose. Like Alma-Tadema, Godward included recognisable sculptures and mosaics in his paintings to lend them an air of archaeological authenticity, and he lavished particular care on the luminous appearance of sunlit marble and water. Clinging drapery and sumptuous textures (such as the fur and feathers in *Dolce far niente*) add to the sensuous appeal of his pictures.

Few, if any, of Alma-Tadema's imitators could compete with the most celebrated aspect of his art: his monumental scenes of festivals and other public occasions, enriched with meticulously researched archaeological details and peopled with multitudes of figures. *The Coliseum* (cat. 144) is one of his most astonishing conceptions, demonstrating the artist's love of theatrical presentation and breathtaking shifts in scale and perspective. The painting also reveals Alma-Tadema's knack for capturing not only the grandeur that was Rome, but also a vivid sense of the human beings who lived there. The trio of figures in the foreground adds psychological and narrative interest to what might otherwise appear a dry assemblage of museum relics. Gazing at the procession gathering far below their perch on a balcony of the Baths of Titus, they draw us into the

Cat. 140
John William Godward (1861–1922)
Dolce far niente (A Pompeian Fishpond),
1904
Oil on canvas, 50.8 × 76.2 cm

picture and express the mingled emotions of curiosity and awe that we ourselves feel.

A similar grouping of foreground figures ushers us into the painting that Alma-Tadema himself considered his greatest achievement: *The Baths of Caracalla* (cat. 143). It took the artist two years to research and execute this extraordinarily detailed depiction of Romans enjoying the city's most opulent bathing establishment. Ever the perfectionist, Alma-Tadema continued to work on the canvas following its return from the Royal Academy

exhibition of 1899. The end result is a *tour de force* of illusionistic painting, as well as a learned disquisition on the building practices and social customs of ancient Rome.

When, in the early 20th century, the pendulum of artistic opinion inevitably swung against late Victorian classical and academic painting, it swung very firmly indeed. It is only in recent decades that newly appreciative audiences have rediscovered the technical mastery and thematic ambition of this important phase of British art.

Cat. 141
Frederic, Lord Leighton PRA
(1830–1896)
Standing Female Nude, date unknown
Oil on canvas, 54.6 × 25.4 cm

Cat. 142
Sir Edward John Poynter Bt PRA
(1836–1919)
The Cave of the Storm Nymphs, 1903
Oil on canvas, 148 × 112 cm

Cat. 143
Sir Lawrence Alma-Tadema OM RA
(1836–1912)
*Thermae Antoninianae (The Baths of
Caracalla)*, 1899
Oil on canvas, 152.5 × 95 cm

Cat. 144
Sir Lawrence Alma-Tadema OM RA
(1836–1912)
The Coliseum (A Roman Holiday), 1896
Oil on panel, 112 × 73.6 cm

Cat. 145
Sir Lawrence Alma-Tadema OM RA
(1836–1912)
Goldfish, 1900
Oil on panel, 18.7 × 40.6 cm

Cat. 146
Albert Joseph Moore (1841–1893)
Companions, first exhibited 1883
Oil on canvas, 43 × 23.4 cm

Cat. 147
Albert Joseph Moore (1841–1893)
Red Berries, first exhibited 1884
Oil on canvas, 49.5 × 116.2 cm

Cat. 148
Albert Joseph Moore (1841–1893)
Lightning and Light, first exhibited 1892
Oil on canvas, 87.6 × 145.6 cm

Cat. 149
Sir Frank Dicksee PRA (1853–1928)
The Mirror, 1896
Oil on canvas, 95.3 × 118.1 cm

Cat. 150
Frederic, Lord Leighton PRA
(1830–1896)
Gulnihal, first exhibited 1886
Oil on canvas, 55.2 × 40 cm

Cat. 151a–k
Sir Frank Dicksee PRA (1853–1928)
Eleven Scenes from 'Romeo and Juliet', c. 1881–82
Gouache *en grisaille* on paper
(four with arched tops); smallest: 17.2 × 11.1 cm;
largest: 31.1 × 43.9 cm

a 'Rival Factions'

b 'The Invitation'

c 'The Ball Scene'

d 'Friar Laurence'

e 'Friar Laurence'

f 'The Death of Tybalt'

g 'Friar Laurence's Cell'

h 'Juliet and Nurse'

i 'Juliet's Chamber'

j 'The Visit to the Apothecary'

k 'The Tomb'

Painted Fictions: Commemorating the Everyday in Victorian Art

SUSAN P. CASTERAS

Genre pictures, which explore the everyday aspects of life, were a well-established tradition by the time Victorian artists adapted them to their purposes. These paintings naturally transmitted cultural values and imperatives about a broad spectrum of topics — gender, morality, politics, class dynamics, country vs. city and so forth — and in the process reshaped public perceptions of contemporary life and issues as much as reflecting them.

Many narrative and genre paintings are more complex and paradoxical than they appear at first glance, while others are modest and simple. Inaccessible to personal memory, the Victorian era for 21st-century viewers is merely a visual legacy profoundly influenced by the art (and literature) of the period. The power of Victorian paintings derives primarily from the air of reality they project. Yet authenticity is not the same thing as realism; and in Victorian art it is the seemingly real appearance of people, situations and objects that amplifies their credibility and makes it seem that they mirror reality rather than offer visual testimony to their creators' skills of observation.

As often described by John Ruskin and other art critics, the goals of narrative art were to instruct and to uplift the spectator. Some paintings communicated a message or mood of reassurance, others anxiety or ambiguity; many offered upbeat glimpses of life that literally objectified Victorian existence. The change from an agrarian to an industrial economy shook the foundations of society, and many Victorian artists consciously offered a pleasant respite from the strains of such realities. Pictorial escapism, translating reality into palatable doses of nostalgia, proliferated, and a literal trope of the upheavals of contemporary life as well as the power of narrative art is encapsulated in W. A. Atkinson's *Upset Flower Cart* (early 1860s; cat. 160). Although little is known about this artist (fl. 1849–70), he produced one other image of metropolitan life, *The First Metropolitan Drinking Fountain* (Geffrye Museum, London), rendered

in a similarly minute, tight style and a brilliant palette that were undoubtedly indebted to Pre-Raphaelitism.

Atkinson's painting triggers the kind of close examination and story projections the Victorians relished. 'Clues' range from a signpost marked 'Caledonian Road' to the salient contrast — a common ploy — between wealthy and poor. The painting is replete with tacit class distinctions, ranging from attire to the disparity between the oval-faced, Madonna-like middle-class mother and her charitable daughter on the one hand to the irregular features, hair and expression of the vendor on the other.

The spectacle of viewing art was central to Victorian culture, whether on the walls of the Royal Academy or elsewhere, and genre pictures were ideal vehicles of this visuality as mini-theatres or stages on which character, incident, gesture and expression were played out. Although a modern preconception about the Victorian era fixes on its supposed generic emotional reserve, narrative art of the period suggests the opposite, since it required considerable emotional input and empathy to ponder actively, to judge and to provide 'scripts' for the visual dramas presented.

The power of Victorian public opinion was impressive, as myriad works attest, including *First Class — The Meeting* (1854; cat. 156) by Abraham Solomon (1824–1862) and *In Memoriam* by Noel Paton (1821–1901). Solomon's painting proved hugely successful, but only after he yielded to public censure of the original version. Initially, *First Class* (National Gallery of Canada, Ottawa) depicted an old man dozing while his young female charge covertly flirted with an admiring stranger. Spectators were outraged by the alleged improprieties of this encounter, so Solomon moved the elderly man to the middle and showed him conversing with the swain, who has become a respectable naval officer. The pendant, *Second Class — The Parting* (fig. 1), was deemed superior because of its explicit moral of filial/maternal love and its subliminal suggestion (when the works were engraved with reversed titles) that

Fig. 1 **Abraham Solomon**
Second Class – The Parting, 1854
Oil on canvas, 54.5 × 76.5 cm.
Southampton Art Gallery

hard work might yield social, economic and romantic rewards.[1]

In Memoriam (1858; cat. 157), by an artist singled out by his contemporaries for his superb fairy paintings, commemorates the Cawnpore Massacre of 1857, when scores of women and children in India were imprisoned and killed. Public memory of this was fresh when *In Memoriam* appeared, and in the first version Indian sepoys burst into the dungeon with their weapons (and an implied threat of death and sexual violation). In response to public indignation, Paton repainted the sepoys as Highlanders rescuing the Christian martyrs, personified by the central woman, who exudes fortitude, faith and courage.[2]

The meanings of narrative art were not always stable or resolvable and may be even less penetrable now. Submerged meanings were perhaps best unlocked by contemporary Victorians, who understood the preconceptions, signals and codes of their culture more fully than later audiences. Fortunately, however, genre pictures prove highly elastic, composed for a specific time, audience and culture yet still accessible to future beholders. Victorian love of detail and description abetted an intimate bonding between spectator and object by encouraging scrutiny and interpretation. Materiality and tangibly realised things in Victorian paintings exist on various levels, from the literal to the meaning-laden.

Paradoxically, the facts, although artificial, are convincing precisely because they *look* so real, and viewers willingly subscribed to this beguiling fiction.

Genre paintings, and the larger context of narrative art to which they belong, should not therefore be construed as visual reportage or representations of reality so much as approximations of them. In these carefully constructed worlds filled with visual evidence, canvases often highlight or blend several genres. One of the most significant in this category is animal painting, images that frequently had historical and documentary elements grafted onto them. John Frederick Herring (1795–1865), probably the era's best-known portraitist of racehorses, offers a classic adaptation of 18th-century profiled horses in the brightly hued *Start for the Derby (1834)* (1834; cat. 152). Despite the suspended animation of the central jockey atop the eventually victorious steed Plenipotentiary, the composition implies movement, with many runners identifiable. Slightly pre-Victorian in date, the painting is decidedly different from some Victorian interpretations of this topic; William Powell Frith (1819–1909) in *Derby Day* (1858; Tate Britain, London) and the Pre-Raphaelite John Everett Millais (1829–1896) in his 1853 drawing *At the Races* (Ashmolean Museum, Oxford), for example, focused not on the race or riders but on the sociological diversity and *mores* of the racegoers.

Cat. 152
John Frederick Herring Snr
(1795–1865)
The Start for the Derby (1834), 1834
Oil on canvas, 101.6 × 152.4 cm

The pre-eminent British animal painter of the 19th century was Edwin Landseer (1802–1873), who received many commissions from Queen Victoria to portray both her human and animal families. Landseer revitalised animal painting by letting his subjects, especially dogs, respond to certain situations in human emotional terms. *'Scarbro', An Old Cover Hack* (first exhibited 1848; cat. 172) includes genre elements in the array of carefully rendered still-life objects and in the peaceful 'clan' of animals, which suggests a state of natural harmony. Another of Landseer's pictorial paeans to the nobility and heroism of animals is *Refreshment* (first exhibited 1846; cat. 171), a straightforward genre picture in which a woman and a boy watch as their devoted helper satisfies his hunger while canine companions repose nearby.

Another prolific *animalier* was Thomas Sidney Cooper (1803–1902), whose *Near Herne Bay* (1884; cat. 173), shown at the 1885 Royal Academy exhibition, adds animals and people to a rocky coastal landscape on a sunny day. The inclusion of a genre element in the form of a working-class picnic is unusual: though a popular pictorial subject, picnics were more typically depicted in bucolic pastoral settings.

Recreational moments were favourite genre vignettes, but so was the bustle, if not pandemonium, of ordinary life. The perfect exponent was Frith, who gained widespread public acclaim in 1854 with the first of three commanding panoramas of modern life (and crowds), which proved show-stopping at the Royal Academy, where it required railings and police protection. One of the paintings was *The Railway Station* (Royal Holloway College, Egham), and the present reduced replica (apparently by Marcus Stone) features a Paddington platform teeming with a cross-section of people and mini-dramas (1862; cat. 155). Like the beach, the railway station was a place where classes mingled, and the painting chronicles a potpourri of social and national types. The original included a cast of eighty characters, a surging intersection of classes with distinctive phsyiognomies, apparel and circumstances, ranging from gentlemen and middle-class families to porters, recruits and even a criminal apprehended by detectives as a result of the first-ever official use of the telegraph.[3]

Images of rural and maritime life, often seen through rose-coloured spectacles, tended to rely on stock characters embodying humility, sincerity and incorruptibility. Class distinctions take countless guises. In *The Old Sailor's Yarn* (probably first exhibited 1859; cat. 158) by James Campbell (*c.* 1825/28–1893), one of numerous Liverpool artists directly influenced by Pre-Raphaelitism, the implied drama pits old age against youth, a weathered 'old salt' relating adventures to young, fashionable visitors. The relationship between the figures is unclear, but the interplay of gazes invites interpretation.

A similar doorway framing device occurs in *Christmas* (first exhibited 1858; cat. 159) by John Anster Fitzgerald (1823–1906), best known as a fairy painter. A boy hovers on the threshold of an affluent household, having literally and metaphorically come in from the cold. Bearing holly and oranges (an expensive holiday treat), and swathed in a vermilion scarf giving him an aspect both mysterious and amusing, he encounters the quasi-magical appearance of a disembodied hand offering drink and a plate of food.

The darker side of rustic existence manifested itself in Victorian art in such themes as emigration. This was a highly topical subject, since a huge exodus to Australia and North America took place at mid-century, often encouraged by government subsidies or schemes assisting 'deserving' working-class families. James Collinson (1825–1881), a founding member of the Pre-Raphaelite Brotherhood, treated this subject in *Answering the Emigrant's Letter* (fig. 2), an unofficial pendant to his *Emigration Scheme* (first exhibited 1852; cat. 162). Both present tense cottage interior scenes with some similar, meticulously rendered objects, but in *The Emigration Scheme* a family listens thoughtfully as a boy reads *The Australian News*.

One of the pictorial themes that flooded the Royal Academy and the art market throughout the Victorian period centred on femininity and domesticity. Sometimes the focus was girlhood, and numerous women artists contributed to this seminal iconology, including French-born Sophie Anderson (1823–1903). *The Lace Handkerchief* (1850s; cat. 153) was one of several canvases by her to feature a wide-eyed, rosebud-lipped, blonde little girl. A miniaturised adult in garb and demeanour, she balances idleness and industry with culturally endorsed feminine

Fig. 2 **James Collinson**, *Answering the Emigrant's Letter*, 1850. Oil on panel, 70 × 89 cm. Manchester City Art Gallery

Cat. 153
Sophie Anderson (1823–1903)
The Lace Handkerchief, 1850s
Oil on canvas, 30.5 × 41 cm

decorativeness. Ironically working on unravelling a handkerchief, she reposes amid the trappings of a well-to-do existence, to modern eyes perhaps a dreamy baby odalisque, a semi-invalid or passive, even bored, captive of exquisitely hermetic surroundings.

The four Hayllar sisters represent a notable exception to male dominance of the art world in the 19th century. They based many of their images on experiences, spaces and belongings at their family home of Castle Priory at Wallingford, south of Oxford. In *A Summer Shower* (1883; cat. 170) Edith Hayllar (1860–1948) uses handsome family objects, models and furnishings in an image of leisure revolving around mixed-doubles lawn tennis. Wearing fairly casual garb and shoes, a couple manages a tête-à-tête while others take refreshments and wait for intemperate skies to clear. The Hayllars all incorporated objects familiar to them in their pictures, as in *'A thing of beauty is a joy forever'* (1890; cat. 169), a dazzling watercolour by Kate Hayllar (fl. 1883–98) that takes its title from Keats's well-known line in *Endymion*. Before abandoning her career around 1900, she produced still-lifes, one of which had been purchased by Alexandra, Princess of Wales. A number of her paintings include copies of Old Masters, in the present case a print after Raphael's *Madonna della Sedia* in the Palazzo Pitti, Florence. Kate Hayllar here creates a mini-shrine to women's traditional

mission of motherhood, simultaneously alluding to more recent female roles as interior decorators, arbiters of taste and artists.

Scores of paintings situated women of all ages in attractive middle-class chambers. An example is *'Old Maid'* (1886; cat. 154) by Frederick Goodall (1822–1904), an artist better known for biblical and Egyptian subjects and for his studio-cum-palace designed by Norman Shaw. *'Old Maid'* combines genre elements with portraiture, depicting Goodall's daughter Maud and Alice Frederica Sambourne, offspring of the eminent *Punch* cartoonist, in an elegant room containing a table and a rug belonging to Linley Sambourne House.[4] The title refers both to the eponymous card game and, ironically, to the fact that the decorous protagonists are too youthful to be described as 'old maids' or 'losers' in the game of life.

In the 1870s narrative painting began to be infused with darker subject matter. Luke Fildes (1843–1927) was among the most important exponents of this, but after years of contributing sombre social realist illustrations to *The Graphic* and creating paintings that probed urban blight, destitution and crime, he turned to portraits, which were more lucrative, and away from scenes of social deprivation. His *Village Wedding* (1883; cat. 161), for example, is far lighter in palette and tone than the earlier *Doctor* (exhibited 1891; Tate Britain, London), invoking

Cat. 154
Frederick Goodall RA (1822–1904)
'Old Maid', 1886
Oil on canvas, 110.4 × 97.7 cm

a pre-industrial past with bright skies, rural pleasures and sentimentality. Fildes's parade of rural society streaming along a road of life, set in the 1830s, offers a counterpart to Frith's panoramas of urban society. Each character suggests a story, and all are cheerful, healthy and content, attesting to a stereotypical view of country life as paradisiacal and rural folk as straightforward, honest and innocent.

Fildes concurrently produced images of Venice inspired by his trips to that city and other places abroad. *Venetian Life* (1884; cat. 166) is one of several very well received, richly coloured canvases that perpetuated the happy mood of *The Village Wedding*. Here, too, the inhabitants are perceived not as downtrodden or morose, but as vivacious and charming. Evoking different stages of female existence, Fildes almost playfully

includes a river/canal of life where the Italian beauties gossip, toil and perform their toilette.

The starker direction of Victorian art that Fildes ultimately rejected was upheld by other artists. Some pursued the subject of religion; they included Charles Staniland (1838–1916), an illustrator for *The Graphic* whose work Vincent van Gogh admired. Religion remained a volatile concern throughout the period, the authority of the Church challenged from mid-century on by new scientific theories, the large-scale movement of the population to the cities and a general waning of belief. Staniland's *At the Back of the Church* (1876; cat. 164) belongs to a sub-genre of pew/sermon subjects, typically with the congregation comprising a mixture of classes and ages. Free seats for the poor were located at the back of churches, and the artist depicts an array of mostly psychologically isolated parishioners, from child to widow and old veteran. In the same vein, and perhaps influenced by Hubert von Herkomer's *The Last Muster* (1875; Lady Lever Art Gallery, Port Sunlight), is *The Sermon* (1888; cat. 163) by Walter Tyndale (1855–1943), who a few years later switched to watercolours and scenes of Egypt, Morocco and Japan. The painting offers a slice of life from the middle-class church of St Alphege's, Greenwich, where the pews were rented (and numbered). Sometimes a touch of humour or romance invaded pew scenes, but Tyndale's congregation seems unanimously earnest, if not lugubrious, as they listen to the unseen preacher.

A different kind of 'line-up' of humanity appears in two particularly arresting images of the stark type. In *Behind the Bar* (1883; cat. 168) John Henry Henshall (1856–1928), who exhibited widely, at the Royal Academy, the Salon and elsewhere, produced a candid *tour de force* that borrows openly from Edouard Manet's *Bar at the Folies-Bergères* (1881–82; Courtauld Institute Galleries, London). The patrons of Henshall's bar form a frieze-like conspectus of the oppressed. Besides the barmaid accepting a gift, a young man consoles an older one, a woman spoonfeeds a baby with liquor (perhaps as a sedative), a child grasps a bottle of alcohol and an injured man raises a tankard.[5] The subject reflects public concern with temperance issues, with intensive campaigns to reduce alcohol consumption among the poor undertaken from the 1850s on.

The French-born Adrien-Emmanuel Marie (1848–1891) was another notable contributor to the hard-hitting pages of *The Graphic* and he also exhibited at the Salon. *Feeding the Hungry after the Lord Mayor's Banquet* (1882; cat. 167), exactly contemporary with Henshall's composition, is similarly injected with a gritty realism that highlights a queue of weary figures. Here, too, there is a serving area barrier, in this instance long wooden tables of leftover food set aside for the needy. The Lord Mayor's Banquet has ended, and food distribution has transformed this part of the Great Hall in the medieval Guildhall into a kind of soup kitchen or casual ward. The view looks toward the west end, with of one of the city's effigies of the legendary giants Gog and Magog discernible at the rear, silhouetted against the window on the right. In the middle ground are monuments to William Pitt the Younger (twice Prime Minister) and William Beckford *père* (twice Lord Mayor of London).[6] According to an undated clipping on the canvas's reverse, remaining food was given to applicants with tickets. Selection was made by the members of the Lord Mayor's Committee and distribution undertaken by the Chairman. The mood is sombre, a subdued confrontation between haves and have-nots, with most recipients forlorn and downcast. As in other genre pictures, the range of humanity portrayed is diverse – from black-clad, elderly women to children, all pressing in at the doorway under the watchful gaze of a bobby maintaining order.

These last two paintings exude a spirit of acute social realism that shocked viewers even as they galvanised public consciousness of the misery and ills of Victorian society. While earlier art had generally attempted to convey didactic messages in controlled dosages that avoided offending viewers, artists such as Fildes and Henshall were more daring in some of their paintings.

Throughout Victoria's reign genre pictures retained their appeal and encompassed topics from the realms of class, gender, labour, leisure and ethnicity. Grounded in a meticulously detailed style, many glorified their subjects, but others were less positive in tone. In general, genre pictures perpetuated social myths while preserving a sense of time and place so strong that even today filmmakers turn to them as an index of period style and 'feel'. The accumulation of material particulars sustains an artifice which seems true but, paradoxically, is illusory. Some of the culture-inflected implications are lost to post-modern generations, yet genre pictures still embody a kind of visual nationalism and ideology that reveal a great deal about the ever-provocative Victorian era.

1 *Solomon: A Family of Painters*, Jeffrey Daniels et al., exh. cat., Geffrye Museum, London, 1985, pp. 52–3.

2 Joan M. Hichberger, *Images of the British Army: The Military in British Art 1815–1914*, New York, 1988, p. 174.

3 Mary Cowling, *Victorian Figurative Painting: Domestic Life and the Contemporary Social Scene*, London, 2000, pp. 114–24.

4 Confirmed by Reena Suleman of Linley Sambourne House.

5 *Hard Times: Social Realism in Victorian Art*, Julian Treuherz (ed.), exh. cat., Manchester City Art Gallery, 1987, p. 114.

6 I thank Naomi Allen of the Guildhall Art Gallery for these details.

Cat. 155
Marcus Stone RA (1840–1921) after
William Powell Frith RA (1819–1909)
The Railway Station, 1862
Oil on canvas, 71.7 × 153 cm

Cat. 156
Abraham Solomon (1824–1862)
First Class – The Meeting, 1854
Oil on canvas with arched top,
67.3 × 95.2 cm

Cat. 157
Sir Joseph Noel Paton (1821–1901)
In Memoriam, 1858
Oil on panel with arched top,
121.9 × 96.5 cm

Cat. 158
James Campbell (*c.* 1825/28–1893)
The Old Sailor's Yarn,
first exhibited 1859 (?)
Oil on canvas, 30.5 × 25.4 cm

Cat. 159
John Anster Fitzgerald (1823–1906)
Christmas, first exhibited 1858
Oil on canvas, 40 × 30.5 cm

Cat. 160
W. A. Atkinson
(exhibited London 1849–70)
The Upset Flower Cart, early 1860s
Oil on canvas, 92 × 71.8 cm

Cat. 161
Sir (Samuel) Luke Fildes RA
(1843–1927)
The Village Wedding, 1883
Oil on canvas,
151.8 × 255.3 cm

Cat. 162
James Collinson (1825–1881)
The Emigration Scheme,
first exhibited 1852
Oil on panel, 56.5 × 76.2 cm

Cat. 163
Walter Frederick Roofe Tyndale
(1855–1943)
The Sermon, 1888
Oil on canvas, 46 × 102.1 cm

Cat. 164
Charles Joseph Staniland
(1838–1916)
At the Back of the Church, 1876
Pencil and watercolour with touches of
white on paper, 51.1 × 91.4 cm

Cat. 165
Alessandro Battaglia (1870–1920)
The Schoolroom, 1897
Oil on canvas, 87.5 × 174.4 cm

Cat. 166
Sir (Samuel) Luke Fildes RA
(1843–1927)
Venetian Life, 1884
Oil on canvas, 214 × 158 cm

Cat. 167
Adrien-Emmanuel Marie
(1848–1891)
Feeding the Hungry after the Lord Mayor's
Banquet, Interior of Guildhall, 1882
Oil on canvas, 91.4 × 133.3 cm

Cat. 168
John Henry Henshall (1856–1928)
Behind the Bar, 1883
Oil on canvas, 62.2 × 111.1 cm

Cat. 169
Kate Hayllar (exhibited 1883–1898)
'A thing of beauty is a joy forever', 1890
Watercolour with pencil, pen and ink,
and touches of white and gum arabic
on paper, 34 × 24.8 cm

Cat. 170
Edith Hayllar (1860–1948)
A Summer Shower, 1883
Oil on panel, 53.4 × 44.2 cm

Cat. 171
Sir Edwin Henry Landseer RA
(1802–1873)
Refreshment, first exhibited 1846
Oil on panel, 99.1 × 127 cm

Cat. 172
Sir Edwin Henry Landseer RA
(1802–1873)
'Scarbro', An Old Cover Hack,
first exhibited 1848
Oil on canvas, 122.5 × 151.8 cm

Cat. 173
Thomas Sidney Cooper RA
(1803–1902)
Near Herne Bay (On the North-East
Coast of Kent), 1884
Oil on canvas, 121 × 182 cm

Decorative and Applied Arts

PETER CORMACK

In 1877 William Morris (1834–1896) gave his first public lecture. Originally entitled 'The Decorative Arts', it was later published as *The Lesser Arts*.[1] Morris's ironic purpose in renaming his lecture was to draw attention to the unhealthy polarisation between the Fine and Applied arts – and the consequent downgrading of the latter – that had taken place since the Middle Ages. Against the back-drop of ever-advancing industrialisation in 19th-century Britain, Morris, Augustus Welby Northmore Pugin (1812–1852), William De Morgan (1839–1917) and others re-awakened the applied arts to a creative engagement with fertile historical (and sometimes non-European) traditions of design and workmanship. The fruits of this process, culminating in the Arts and Crafts Movement, are richly represented in the Andrew Lloyd Webber Collection. Applied arts are, indeed, almost a necessary complement to the collection's paintings by the Pre-Raphaelites and their followers, for the era to which they looked back was one in which painters worked in many 'decorative' media. That a Victorian artist could, in spite of all the changed conditions, work with equal versatility was proved above all by Edward Burne-Jones in his 35 years of collaboration with Morris.

The Craven cabinet (cat. 180), made *c.* 1775 for the 6th Baron Craven, impressively demonstrates the technical virtuosity of Georgian furniture-makers. It also has just those qualities that inflamed the morally charged critique of 19th-century designers and critics. For men like Pugin and John Ruskin (1819–1900), such refined, classical formality proclaimed the 'Paganism' they associated with a degenerate social order. Yet in one significant respect, the Craven cabinet does have its place in the lineage of later developments in the decorative arts. Although flanked by depictions of Greek and Roman ruins, its central, inner marquetry decoration – views of medieval English and Welsh castles and abbeys based on engravings by Nathaniel and Samuel Buck – celebrates a characteristically British antiquarianism which, imaginatively stimulated by

Romanticism, was to give birth to the Gothic Revival. Here, it is still a matter of exquisite antiquarian 'taste'. Within a few decades, however, the genteel delight in picturesque ruins had evolved into a national cultural identification with the medieval past.

When Pugin, writing in the mid-1840s, claimed to 'have the whole weight of the [Gothic] revival on my shoulders',[2] he was scarcely exaggerating his pivotal role in promoting 'not a style, but a principle'.[3] Even today, through his prolific design work at the Palace of Westminster, Pugin continues to be a pervasive (if largely subconscious) presence in our public life. His character combined Byronic romanticism with a prodigiously Victorian energy for work, enabling him to complete a remarkable number of projects in both architecture and a diverse range of applied arts during his short career. The ultimate public recognition of his genius was the

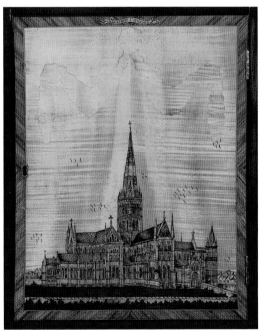

Detail of cat. 180

Mediaeval Court at the 1851 Great Exhibition. Enshrined somewhat incongruously in Paxton's Crystal Palace and surrounded by the 'Works of Industry of All Nations', Pugin's designs for metalwork, ceramics and furniture were acclaimed by the *Illustrated London News* as evidence of 'the applicability of Mediaeval Art . . . to the uses of the present day'.[4] The two inlaid octagonal tables (cat. 183, 184), made from Pugin's designs by J. G. Crace, closely resemble a prototype shown at the Medieval Court. Their overtly architectural and constructional form, which inspired the work of many subsequent designers, is convincingly Gothic, yet derived more from Pugin's study of medieval timber-framed buildings than from surviving ancient furniture.[5]

Despite Pugin's early death, the impetus he had given to the Gothic Revival ensured that it flourished among the succeeding generation of architect–designers. William Burges (1827–1881), who had close links with some of the Pre-Raphaelites, is credited with designing

some of the first fully painted furniture made since the Middle Ages, including the Sun Cabinet (1858–59; cat. 189) with its allegorical representations of metals painted by the young Edward Poynter (see cat. 142). Massive in its forms and free of complicated mouldings or carving, Burges's furniture is as 'architectural' as Pugin's but in a different way, its flat surfaces offering uninterrupted quasi-mural fields both for ornamental patterning, usually based on architectural motifs, and for figural decoration. The Philosophy Cabinet (1879; cat. 190), made for the designer himself and subsequently owned by John Betjeman and Evelyn Waugh, typifies Burges's bachelor wit with its paintings of 'the [domestic or conjugal] troubles of philosophers and literary men'.[6] Here, as in his lavish schemes of decoration at Cardiff Castle and Castell Coch, Burges relished the conceit of depicting classical and other non-Gothic subjects within the framework of his consistently medievalist idiom.

Philip Webb (1831–1915) was the principal furniture

Cat. 174
After **Sir Edward Coley Burne-Jones Bt ARA** (1833–1898)
Possibly painted by **Charles Fairfax Murray** (1849–1919)
Morris & Co., manufacturer
Cleopatra and *Lucretia* panels, c. 1875
Oil on varnished walnut,
each 54.5 × 37 cm

Cat. 175
William Morris (1834–1896), designer
Morris & Co., manufacturer
Small Hammersmith rug in blue, buff, red and green, 1879/81
Hand-knotted wool pile on worsted warp, 94 × 108 cm

designer among the partners of Morris, Marshall, Faulkner & Co., the firm founded by Morris and others in 1861. As the architect of Morris's Red House at Bexleyheath, Kent, Webb began his career as a 'Gothic man',[7] designing painted cabinets and settles in a manner similar to Burges's. For Webb and Morris, however, 'Gothic' became a broader and more inclusive term, embracing principles of design and craftsmanship discernible beyond the confines of Europe in the Middle Ages. Webb's circular table (cat. 187) and his adaptation of a traditional design for the Morris & Co. Sussex chairs (cat. 186) reveal his primary interest in simple, functional construction more than ornamentation, typifying a tendency away from full-blown, polychromatic medievalism after the mid-1860s. The *Cleopatra* and *Lucretia* panels (c. 1875; cat. 174), adapted from stained-glass designs by Burne-Jones, were made to be inset within the framework of a (now lost) Webb/Morris & Co. sideboard or cabinet.[8] Their rich but monochrome effect, of a type favoured by furniture-makers of the Aesthetic Movement, would have provided adornment without distracting from the furniture's overall structure.

Morris, wrote John D. Sedding, was Pugin's 'true lineal descendant'; he had 'not stopped at studio paper designs but . . . put an apron on, tucked up his sleeves, and set to work'.[9] No designer–craftsman has more self-evidently enjoyed his work, and perhaps this, above all, explains its enduring popularity. Throughout the 1870s, having set aside an early commitment to painting, Morris systematically experimented in, and then mastered, the various textile handicrafts. Although he claimed to find designing rugs and carpets 'mighty difficult', his output in this field, beginning with the relatively small Hammersmith rugs of c. 1880 (cat. 175), ranks among his most impressive work. Acutely conscious of the craft's historic Middle Eastern roots, Morris wrote of Persia as 'a holy land, for there in the process of time our art was perfected'.[10] His carpets consequently had to show 'enough of form and meaning . . . to justify our making [them] at all in these Western parts of the world . . . since as to the mere colour we are not likely to beat, and may well be pleased if we equal, an ordinary genuine Eastern specimen'.[11] That he succeeded is demonstrated by the saturated colour-mosaic of the Little Flower carpet (cat. 194): here is 'abstract' art of a high order. Morris's inventive powers were almost matched by his pupil John Henry Dearle (1860–1932), whose carpet designs (cat. 192, 193) confidently develop the 'Anglo-Persian' vocabulary of forms originated by his master.

The epic *Holy Grail* tapestries (cat. 191) were Morris's and Burne-Jones's supreme achievement in 'the noblest of the weaving arts'.[12] The original versions, designed by Burne-Jones in 1890–91, were woven for Stanmore Hall, Middlesex, the home of William Knox D'Arcy, an Australian mining millionaire. D'Arcy's business associate and fellow Australian George McCulloch commissioned the series included here,[13] woven in 1898–99 for his London house at 184 Queen's Gate, Kensington, where they were displayed along with fine Morris carpets (as they are in their present home) and stained glass. The tapestries convey the mystical intensity of the central legend of the Arthurian story perhaps more successfully than any contemporary works in other media. Their monumental scale, the dramatic stylisation of the figures and landscape, and the rich subtlety of colour and texture all amount to a triumphant vindication of the expressive potency of applied art. The McCulloch tapestries made

Cat. 176
After **Sir Edward Coley Burne-Jones
Bt ARA** (1833–1898)
Morris & Co., manufacturer (woven
by **John Martin** and **Walter Taylor**)
Love Leading the Pilgrim, 1910
High-warp tapestry: wool and silk weft
on cotton warp, 150 × 263.5 cm

a great impression when they were included in the British Pavilion at the 1900 Paris Exposition Universelle, and again at the British Empire Exhibition at Wembley in 1924–25.

Translating Burne-Jones's designs into tapestry, a process closely supervised by Morris, involved a number of intermediate stages and other hands. First, the artist's small-scale monochrome drawings of each subject were enlarged photographically to make full-size cartoons.[14] Burne-Jones then worked over these, refining and adding details, especially to the figures; meanwhile, Dearle produced drawings to show the colours throughout the series, as well as designing elements such as the flowers and the patterns on drapery. A final composite cartoon was then created for each tapestry, from which the weavers could work at the loom. As with Morris's carpets, the wools and silks used were coloured with vegetable

and other organic dyes, producing a remarkably vibrant and durable range of hues. Tapestry-weaving continued at Morris & Co.'s Merton Abbey workshops after the deaths of Morris and Burne-Jones, generally upholding their tradition of superlative craftsmanship. *Love Leading the Pilgrim* (cat. 176), woven in 1910, is one of several later tapestries closely based either on Burne-Jones's paintings (in this case an oil of 1896–97 now in Tate Britain, itself derived from an 1870s design for embroidered hangings) or on his stained-glass designs.

The Stanmore Hall piano (cat. 188) is – appropriately for a musician-collector – the single most spectacular applied art object in the Andrew Lloyd Webber Collection. The piano's angular shape, reminiscent of early keyboard instruments rather than the swollen curves and bulbous legs of the modern 'grand', was suggested to the manufacturer John Broadwood & Sons by Burne-Jones in the 1870s. Several versions were subsequently decorated for Morris & Co. in gilded and silvered gesso (low-relief plaster) by Kate Faulkner (1841–1898), sister of Charles Faulkner, one of the original partners in the Morris firm.[15] Of these variants, the Stanmore Hall piano, commissioned by William Knox D'Arcy, is by far the most elaborate. It epitomises the collaborative spirit that was so much part of the Arts and Crafts ethos, for Kate Faulkner designed and executed the decoration with help from Morris, who contributed the poetic inscription around the piano's sides,[16] and from Philip Webb, who drew the bird on the outer lid and assisted with parts of the ornamental design. The piano was Kate Faulkner's last major project, and embodies her own poignant story. The delicate but messy processes of modelling and carving the gesso-work began in October 1891 at her London family home, 35 Queen Square, Bloomsbury, but were soon interrupted by the death of her brother Charles, whom she had nursed for years after he had been paralysed by a stroke. Moving to nearby Caroline (now Mecklenburgh) Place, she resumed work and the piano was eventually completed in early 1894. In their correspondence Morris and Webb comment sympathetically on the slow progress of the commission as Kate's own health deteriorated. Despite 'all the hard disabilities of her state',[17] she nevertheless produced one of the Arts and Crafts Movement's most glorious artefacts, described

by W. R. Lethaby as 'simply the most beautiful piece of modern ornamental work known to me'.[18] The piano's disciplined profusion of flowers and plants — vines and poppies on the lid, cow parsley on the front and an encircling briar — calls to mind May Morris's childhood memories of the Faulkners' Queen Square home: 'a delicious country atmosphere of freshness and roses . . . all as if there were no soot in the gardens out there'.[19]

A typical 'William Morris' interior would, for many, be incomplete without the ceramics of Morris's friend William De Morgan, the Royal Academy-trained painter who became the leading Arts and Crafts ceramicist but ended his career as a successful novelist. Andrew Lloyd Webber's collection includes outstanding examples of all periods of De Morgan's pottery, particularly the metallic-sheened lustreware. Equipped with boyish enthusiasm, an intense interest in chemistry and much-needed perseverance (he was undeterred by such interruptions as 'setting the house on fire and burning the roof off'[20]), De Morgan experimented with glazes and firing methods to achieve results that truly rival the work of his predecessors in the Hispano-Moresque, the Middle Eastern Iznik and the Italian Renaissance traditions. As in Morris's case, his empirical experience of handicraft processes engendered a creative identification with historical tradition, not simply imitation. Inventively blending motifs from various sources, De Morgan's pots and tiles present, with an

Detail of cat. 188

Cat. 177
William Morris (1834–1896), designer
William De Morgan & Co., manufacturer
66-tile panel with foliage and floral design, 1876
Hand-painted underglaze colours on earthenware blanks made by
the Architectural Pottery, Poole, 164 × 91 cm (including frame)

appealing dimension of humour (see the Eagle's Supper charger, cat. 254), a whole decorative cosmology made up of beasts and birds, heraldically ferocious or quizzical, rhythmically dwelling amid exotic blooms and foliage or stylised seascapes.

Morris and De Morgan occasionally worked on joint commissions, their largest collaboration being a set of tile panels designed for Membland House, Devon (cat. 177), in which the glazed colours of the Morris pattern skilfully evoke the dyes used in his fabrics. As both colourist and

technician, De Morgan's crowning achievement is the triple-lustred Sunset and Moonlight Suite (see cat. 255–8). Made in the 1890s, these dishes combine silver, copper and gold decoration on grounds of iridescent pearl-grey or dark blue – 'darker than the Egyptian night sky' wrote May Morris, 'but full of that luminosity'.[21]

Morris believed that, after a well designed and furnished house, the next most important and desirable work of art was 'A beautiful Book'. For medieval scribes, printers and readers, he thought, books were like fine buildings, 'a comely body fit for the habitation of the dead man who was speaking to them'; 19th-century books by contrast were 'makeshifts . . . revoltingly ugly and vulgar' in their appearance.[22] Throughout his career, Morris characteristically pursued all available means of achieving well-crafted books: he worked with commercial printers, designed bindings, learned wood-engraving and calligraphy and, by the mid-1870s, had produced arguably the most beautiful illuminated manuscripts since the 16th century.

While Burne-Jones was working with Morris on the manuscript of Virgil's *Aeneid* (begun 1874–75; cat. 259), he quipped that 'it would put an end to printing',[23] so ambitious was the combination of script, ornament and illustrations. Inspired throughout by 15th-century Italian art, which for both men was still essentially part of the medieval rather than the Renaissance canon, the *Aeneid* is one of numerous undertakings which sustained and deepened their friendship and common interests. After a year or so of intensive work, however, the book was left unfinished, attaining its present splendid form 'post-humously', as an act of piety on the part of its subsequent owner, Charles Fairfax Murray (1849–1919), who in the 1900s worked with the scribe Graily Hewitt (1864–1953) and the illuminator Louise Powell (1882–1956) to bring the manuscript substantially nearer to completion. Although the *Aeneid* marked the end of his career in calligraphy, the design skills Morris had taught himself, creating legible and beautiful letter forms and con-structing pages of richly decorated (or sometimes quite plain) text, were at the heart of his final five-year 'adventure'[24] in the handicrafts.

In 1891 Morris founded the Kelmscott Press to print small editions, on vellum or handmade paper, of his own poetry and prose and of literary works by his favourite authors. Manually operated presses were used, not much

Cat. 178
William De Morgan (1839–1917),
designer and manufacturer
Tile panel composed of two tiles
painted with an exotic bird,
Chelsea period (1872–81)
Hand-painted underglaze colours on
earthenware tiles, 40.5 cm × 19.5 cm

Cat. 179
William De Morgan (1839–1917),
designer and manufacturer
Seven-tile frieze of an eagle in flight,
late Merton Abbey/early Fulham period
(*c.* 1885–92)
Hand-painted underglaze colours on
earthenware blanks, 15.5 × 110 cm

different from those employed by William Caxton in the 15th century, and Morris's collection of 15th-century books – 'always beautiful by force of the mere typography, even without the added ornament' – provided models for his general approach.[25] Many pages, especially in the Press's most famous book, *The Works of Geoffrey Chaucer* (cat. 267), are bordered by densely interwoven and scrolling foliage, the distilled perfection of a lifetime's mastery of organic pattern-design. Yet there are just as many page openings – and sometimes whole books, such as the little *Gothic Architecture* volume (cat. 260) – where Morris's art lies simply in the forthright clarity of the typeface and its judicious placing within generous margins.

Lethaby predicted that no one of Morris's stature would ever again work 'in the minor arts'.[26] In fact, the Arts and Crafts Movement proved to be not the hoped-for rebirth, but a final blossoming, of the handicraft tradition. This gives the objects created by those 19th- and early 20th-century idealists all the greater poignancy, for, unlike the products of 'functionalism' and of the vapid novelty-seeking spawned by our own design culture, they still resonate with profoundly human values. The writer Percy Lubbock once tried to capture in words how his experience was enhanced by 'the magic' of Morris's genius: 'It brings . . . strangeness and rarity into your own life, the life that *you* lead', he wrote, 'it allows you to work, and live as usual, as before, but with romance: the breathable air'.[27]

1 It appeared in 1882 with four other lectures in the volume *Hopes & Fears for Art*.
2 Letter to the Rev. J. R. Bloxam, *c.* 1845; quoted in Roderick O'Donnell, 'Pugin as a Church Architect', in Paul Atterbury and Clive Wainwright (eds), *Pugin: A Gothic Passion*, New Haven and London, 1994, p. 65.
3 *An Apology for the Revival of Christian Architecture in England* (1843); quoted in Atterbury and Wainwright (note 2), p. 15.
4 Quoted in Alexandra Wedgwood, 'The Mediaeval Court', in Atterbury and Wainwright (note 2), p. 244.
5 Both tables are discussed in Megan Aldrich, 'Marquetry in the Medieval Court: The Octagonal Tables of Pugin and Crace', *The Decorative Arts Society Journal* 25, 2001, pp. 55–7.
6 J. Mordaunt Crook, *William Burges and the High Victorian Dream*, London, 1981, p. 323.
7 W. R. Lethaby, *Philip Webb and His Work*, Oxford, 1935, p. 38.
8 A letter of 11 March 1875 from William Morris to Charles Fairfax

Murray (Norman Kelvin [ed.], *The Collected Letters of William Morris*, 4 vols, Princeton, 1984–96, vol. 1, pp. 245–7) might possibly refer to these panels. If so, they were painted by Murray for a sideboard subsequently owned, according to Morris's biographer J. W. Mackail (Mackail Notebooks, William Morris Gallery, London, vol. 1, p. 79), by George Campfield, Morris & Co.'s foreman glass-painter.
9 John D. Sedding, 'Things Amiss with our Arts and Industries', in *Transactions of the National Association for the Advancement of Art and Its Application to Industry, Liverpool Meeting, 1888*, London, 1888, p. 355.
10 'The History of Pattern Designing', in May Morris (ed.), *The Collected Works of William Morris*, 24 vols, London, 1910–15, vol. 22, p. 216.
11 'Some Hints on Pattern-Designing', ibid., pp. 194–5.
12 William Morris, 'Textiles', in *The Arts & Crafts Exhibition Society: Catalogue of the First Exhibition*, London, 1888, p. 17.

13 This lacks *The Summons*, the first tapestry from the sequence of five, which was sold separately and purchased by Birmingham City Museum and Art Gallery in 1980. Helen Proctor, *The Holy Grail Tapestries*, Birmingham, 1997, pp. 10–11.
14 The surviving photo-cartoons, in fragmentary condition, are in the collection of the William Morris Gallery, London.
15 The best known of Kate Faulkner's decorated pianos is that commissioned in the mid-1880s by Alexander Ionides and now in the Victoria and Albert Museum, London. It is illustrated in Linda Parry (ed.), *William Morris*, London, 1996, p. 179.
16 The text is from Morris's romance *The Roots of the Mountains*, London, 1890, p. 413.
17 Kelvin (note 8), vol. 3, pp. 433–4.
18 Lethaby (note 7), p. 189.
19 Morris (note 10), vol. 3, p. xxv.
20 William De Morgan, 'Lustre Ware', *Journal of the Society of Arts* 40, 24 June 1892, p. 759.

21 May Morris, in the *Burlington Magazine*, 1917; quoted in Mark Hamilton, *Rare Spirit: A Life of William De Morgan 1839–1917*, London, 1997, p. 43.
22 'Some Thoughts on the Ornamented Manuscripts of the Middle Ages' (1892); quoted in Christine Poulson (ed.), *William Morris on Art & Design*, Sheffield, 1996, pp. 142–3.
23 G[eorgiana] B[urne]-J[ones], *Memorials of Edward Burne-Jones*, 2 vols, London, 1904, vol. 2, p. 56.
24 S. C. Cockerell (ed.), *A Note by William Morris on His Aims in Founding the Kelmscott Press*, London, 1898, p. 1.
25 Ibid.
26 Lethaby (note 7), p. 62.
27 Quoted in May Morris (ed.), *The Art of William Morris: Artist, Writer, Socialist*, vol. 1, Oxford, 1936, p. 38.

Cat. 180
Attributed to **Ince & Mayhew**,
cabinetmakers of Golden Square, Soho
(fl. 1760–1800)
Cabinet and stand, c. 1775
Satinwood with marquetry in engraved,
stained and shaded woods, the drawer
fronts crossbanded with tulipwood and
ebony mouldings, 103 × 51 × 213 cm

Cat. 181
After (?) **Augustus Welby Northmore Pugin**
(1812–1852), designer
Attributed to Messrs Crace, under the direction of
John Gregory Crace (1809–1889), manufacturer
Writing table, c. 1850
Carved oak with footrest/stretcher upholstered in
woollen needlework, 80 × 147 × 84 cm

Cat. 183
After **Augustus Welby Northmore Pugin**
(1812–1852), designer
Messrs Crace, under the direction of **John Gregory
Crace** (1809–1889), manufacturer
Octagonal table, c. 1855
Burr-walnut, inlaid with sycamore, holly and boxwood,
73 × 148 × 148 cm

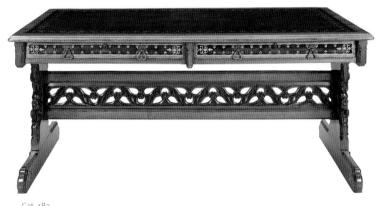

Cat. 182
Augustus Welby Northmore Pugin (1812–1852), designer
Messrs Crace, under the direction of **John Gregory Crace**
(1809–1889), manufacturer
Inlaid writing table, c. 1850
Walnut inlaid with sycamore, holly and boxwood, with leather
top and brass fittings, 76 × 168 × 82 cm

Cat. 184
After **Augustus Welby Northmore Pugin** (1812–1852), designer
Messrs Crace, under the direction of **John Gregory Crace**
(1809–1889), manufacturer
Octagonal table, c. 1853
Burr-walnut inlaid with sycamore, holly and boxwood,
73 × 148 × 148 cm
Stamped *CRACE* on the underside

Cat. 185
Attributed to **Dante Gabriel Rossetti** (1828–1882),
designer (copying/adapting a traditional model)
Morris, Marshall, Faulkner & Co., manufacturer
Rossetti armchair, in production from c. 1863
Ebonised wood (beech?), rush-seated, 89 × 50 × 47 cm

Cat. 186
Philip (Philippe) Speakman Webb (1831–1915),
designer (adapting a traditional model)
Morris, Marshall, Faulkner & Co., manufacturer
Sussex armchair, in production from the early 1860s
Ebonised wood (beech?), rush-seated, 86 × 53 × 43 cm

Cat. 188 (FACING PAGE)
Catherine (Kate) Faulkner (1841–1898), designer
and gesso-worker, assisted by **Philip Webb** (1831–1915)
John Broadwood & Sons, manufacturer of case
(with mechanism by **Julius Blüthner**, Leipzig,
installed in 1912)
The Stanmore Hall piano, 1891–94
Wooden case and trestle base decorated with
painted and gilded gesso-work, 94 × 140 × 260 cm

Cat. 187
Philip (Philippe) Speakman Webb (1831–1915), designer
Morris, Marshall, Faulkner & Co., manufacturer
Circular table, c. 1865
Walnut, 74 × 122 cm

Cat. 189
William Burges (1827–1881), designer
Painting of the figures attributed to
Sir Edward John Poynter Bt PRA
(1836–1919)
Possibly made by **Harland & Fisher**
The Sun Cabinet, 1858–59
Softwood (pine?) painted in oil colours,
with marble top, 105.5 × 94 × 56.5 cm

Cat. 190
William Burges (1827–1881), designer
Possibly painted by **Fred Weekes** (1833–1893)
Campbell & Smith, manufacturer
The Philosophy Cabinet, 1879
Softwood (pine?) painted in oil colours and gilded, with brass fittings, 240 × 130 × 50 cm

a

b

c

d

Cat. 191a–d
Sir Edward Coley Burne-Jones Bt ARA (1833–1898),
William Morris (1834–1896) and **John Henry Dearle**
(1860–1932), designers
Morris & Co., manufacturer (woven by **Robert Ellis**,
John Keich, **John Martin** and **George Merritt**)
Designed 1890–93, woven 1898–99
High-warp tapestry: wool and silk weft on cotton warp

Four *Holy Grail* tapestries
a *The Arming and Departure of the Knights*, 242 × 430 cm
b *The Failure of Sir Gawaine*, 238 × 189 cm
c *The Failure of Sir Lancelot to Enter the Chapel*, 239 × 180 cm
d *The Attainment: The Vision of the Holy Grail to Sir Galahad,*
   Sir Bors and Sir Perceval, 242 × 714 cm

OVERLEAF Details from cat. 191b and 191d

Cat. 192
John Henry Dearle (1860–1932), designer
Morris & Co., manufacturer
Square carpet with floral pattern
in pink, blue and green, 1890s
Hand-knotted wool on cotton warp,
212 × 214 cm

Cat. 193
John Henry Dearle (1860–1932), designer
Morris & Co., manufacturer
Carpet with repeating pattern of flowering
plants in blue, green, red and buff, 1890s
Hand-knotted wool on cotton warp,
345 × 520 cm

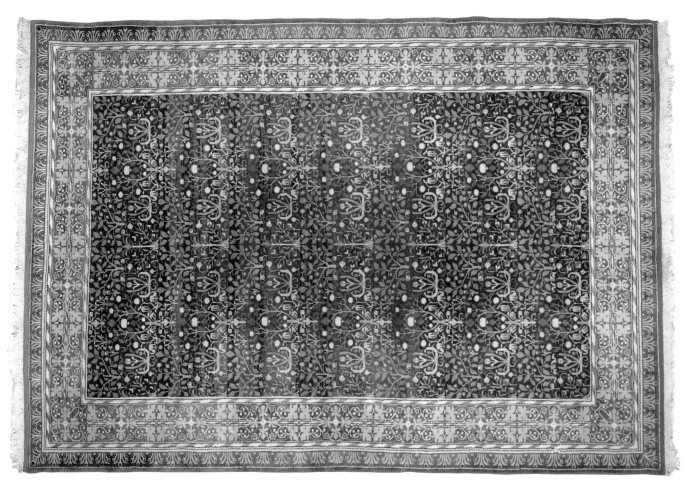

Cat. 194
William Morris (1834–1896), designer
Morris & Co., manufacturer
Little Flower carpet in russet-red
and green, 1890s
Hand-knotted wool on cotton warp,
198 × 478 cm

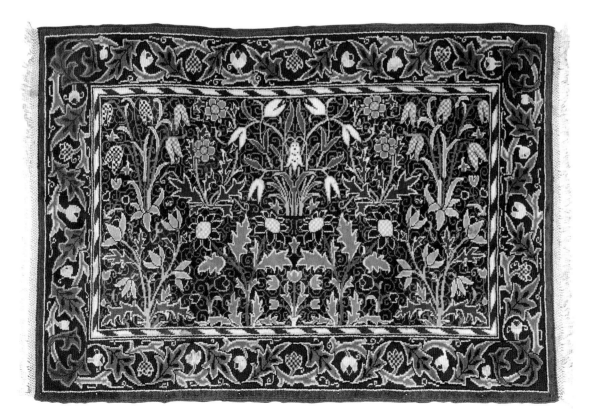

Cat. 195
John Henry Dearle (1860–1932), designer
Morris & Co., manufacturer
Rug with floral pattern in blue-violet,
red and pale buff, 1890s
Hand-knotted wool on cotton warp,
160 × 246 cm

OVERLEAF Detail of cat. 206

Cat. 196
William De Morgan (1839–1917), designer and manufacturer
Painted by **Charles Passenger**
Charger painted with a fabulous winged beast, Fulham period (1888–98)
Hand-painted underglaze colours on earthenware, diam. 53 cm

Cat. 197
William De Morgan (1839–1917), designer and manufacturer
Painted by **Charles Passenger**
Iznik charger painted with central hare and mythical bear and a scrolling
floral border, Fulham period (1888–98)
Hand-painted underglaze colours on earthenware, diam. 49.5 cm

Cat. 198
William De Morgan (1839–1917), designer and manufacturer
Painted by **Charles Passenger**
Plate painted with Renaissance designs,
Fulham period (1888–98)
Hand-painted underglaze colours on earthenware, diam. 20 cm

Cat. 199
William De Morgan (1839–1917), designer and manufacturer
Painted by **Charles Passenger**
Iznik rice dish, early Fulham period (1888–98)
Hand-painted underglaze colours on earthenware,
diam. 39 cm

Cat. 200
William De Morgan (1839–1917), designer and manufacturer
Painted by **Charles Passenger**
Iznik dish painted with an undulating river and swimming fish,
with a boat in the centre, Fulham period (1888–98)
Hand-painted underglaze colours on earthenware,
diam. 41.5 cm

Cat. 201
William De Morgan (1839–1917), designer and manufacturer
Painted by **Charles Passenger**
Iznik rice dish painted with winged mythical beasts in
stylised foliage, the central dome with mythical beasts,
Fulham period (1888–98)
Hand-painted underglaze colours on earthenware, diam. 41 cm

Cat. 202
William De Morgan (1839–1917), designer and manufacturer
Footed punch bowl in Iznik colours with an outer pattern based
on the BBB tile pattern, Fulham period (1888–98)
Hand-painted underglaze colours on earthenware,
h. 28 cm, diam. 41 cm

Cat. 203
William De Morgan (1839–1917), designer and
manufacturer
Iznik dish painted with a sailing ship within a border
of snakes, Merton Abbey period (1881–88)
diam. 21 cm

Cat. 204
William De Morgan (1839–1917), designer and
manufacturer
Iznik rice dish painted with bands of fish and with a raised
Tudor rose boss, Chelsea/Merton Abbey period (1872–88)
Hand-painted underglaze colours on earthenware,
diam. 23 cm

Cat. 205
William De Morgan (1839–1917), designer and
manufacturer
Iznik dish painted with a sailing ship and border
of fishes, Merton Abbey period (1881–88)
Hand-painted underglaze colours on earthenware,
diam. 20 cm

Cat. 206
William De Morgan (1839–1917), designer and
manufacturer
Painted and fired at the Cantagalli factory, Florence
The Apollo Charger, c. 1901
Hand-painted underglaze colours on earthenware,
diam. 50 cm

Cat. 207
William De Morgan (1839–1917), designer
and manufacturer
Maiolica vase, painted with grotesques and
winged *amorini* surrounded by foliage
reserved on a *berettino* banded ground
alternating with Latin inscriptions,
Fulham period (1888–98)
Hand-painted underglaze colours on
earthenware, h. 59 cm

Cat. 208
William De Morgan (1839–1917), designer and
manufacturer
Painted by **A. Farini**
Rice plate painted in bronze and yellow-green lustres,
Fulham period (1888–98)
Hand-painted underglaze colours on earthenware,
diam. 29 cm

Cat. 209
William De Morgan (1839–1917), designer and
manufacturer
Decorated by **A. Farini**
Lustre charger with relief decoration of petals and leaves
on a deep blue ground, Fulham period, c. 1891
Hand-painted underglaze colours on earthenware,
diam. 29.5 cm

Cat. 210
William De Morgan (1839–1917), designer and manufacturer
Painted by **Fred Passenger**
Gold-ground lustre vase painted with fish, Fulham period (1888–98)
Hand-painted underglaze colours on earthenware, h. 26 cm

Cat. 211
William De Morgan (1839–1917), designer and manufacturer
Painted by **Fred Passenger**
Gold-ground lustre vase and cover painted with birds, trees and flowers, Fulham period (1888–98)
Hand-painted underglaze colours on earthenware, h. 26 cm

Cat. 212
William De Morgan (1839–1917), designer and
manufacturer
Ruby lustre charger decorated with a galleon and swans,
Chelsea/Merton Abbey period (1872–88)
Hand-painted underglaze colours on earthenware,
diam. 35.5 cm

Cat. 213
William De Morgan (1839–1917), designer and
manufacturer
Lustre dish painted with a galleon in full sail, late
Chelsea/early Merton Abbey period (1878–85)
Hand-painted underglaze colours on earthenware,
diam. 36 cm

Cat. 214
William De Morgan (1839–1917), designer and
manufacturer
Lustre dish painted with a galleon with single main-sail,
late Chelsea/early Merton Abbey period (1878–85)
Hand-painted underglaze colours on earthenware,
diam. 36 cm

Cat. 215
William De Morgan (1839–1917), designer
and manufacturer
Painted by **John Hersey**
Lustre vase painted with birds among foliage,
Fulham period (1888–98)
Hand-painted underglaze colours on
earthenware, h. 16.5 cm

Cat. 216
William De Morgan (1839–1917), designer and
manufacturer
Lustre dish painted with fish on a scrolling ground,
late Chelsea/early Merton Abbey period (1878–85)
Hand-painted underglaze colours on earthenware,
diam. 35.5 cm

Cat. 217
William De Morgan (1839–1917), designer and
manufacturer
Ruby lustre dish with winged beasts, late Merton
Abbey/early Fulham period (c. 1885–92)
Hand-painted underglaze colours on earthenware,
diam. 36 cm

Cat. 218
William De Morgan (1839–1917), designer and
manufacturer
Ruby and gold lustre dish painted with an eagle grasping
a snake, Fulham period (1888–98)
Hand-painted underglaze colours on earthenware,
diam. 36 cm

Cat. 219
William De Morgan (1839–1917), designer and
manufacturer
Gold-ground red lustre dish painted with a naked maiden
riding a fabulous animal, the verso with trailing foliage,
late Chelsea/early Merton Abbey period (1878–85)
Hand-painted underglaze colours on earthenware,
diam. 35.5 cm

Cat. 220
William De Morgan (1839–1917), designer and
manufacturer
Red lustre charger painted with a doe suckling her fawn,
within a border of fishes, late Chelsea/early Merton Abbey
period (1878–85)
Hand-painted underglaze colours on earthenware,
diam. 42 cm

Cat. 221
William De Morgan (1839–1917), designer and
manufacturer
Painted by **Charles Passenger**
Charger painted with an angry stag, Merton Abbey period
(1881–88)
Hand-painted underglaze colours on earthenware,
diam. 37.5 cm

Cat. 222
William De Morgan (1839–1917), designer and manufacturer
Painted by **Charles Passenger**
Ruby and pink lustre dish painted with peacock, Fulham period
(1888–98)
Hand-painted underglaze colours on earthenware, diam. 21 cm

Cat. 223
William De Morgan (1839–1917), designer and manufacturer
Painted by **Charles Passenger**
Lustre charger painted with grotesque beasts and winged serpents,
Merton Abbey period (1881–88)
Hand-painted underglaze colours on earthenware, diam. 36.5 cm

Cat. 224
William De Morgan (1839–1917), designer and manufacturer
Dish inspired by a Persian original, the centre with a peacock above
the inscription *Omnia Vanitas* within a daisy and bird border, the
reverse with scrolling foliage, Chelsea period (1872–81)
Hand-painted underglaze colours on earthenware, diam. 34 cm

Cat. 225
William De Morgan (1839–1917), designer and manufacturer
Red and yellow lustre dish painted with stylised dolphin,
Fulham period (1888–98)
Hand-painted underglaze colours on earthenware, diam. 36 cm

Cat. 226
William De Morgan (1839–1917),
designer and manufacturer
Lustre vase painted with a band of figures
around the Wheel of Fortune, the reverse
with a winged cherub escaping from chains,
Chelsea period (1872–81)
Hand-painted underglaze colour on
moulded earthenware body, 46 × 27 cm

Cat. 227
William De Morgan (1839–1917), designer and manufacturer
Painted by **Charles Passenger**
Ruby lustre bowl painted with stylised cornflowers on the interior
and fish on the exterior, Fulham period (1888–98)

Cat. 228
William De Morgan (1839–1917),
designer and manufacturer
Lustre vase and cover painted with
stylised birds, Merton Abbey period
(1881–1888)
Hand-painted underglaze colours
on earthenware, h. 19 cm

Cat. 229
Halsey Ricardo (1854–1928), designer
William De Morgan & Co., manufacturer
Lustre vase moulded in relief with a frieze of storks against a red
lustre ground of fruiting trees and fish swimming among waves,
Fulham period (1888–98)
Hand-painted underglaze colours on earthenware, h. 26 cm

Cat. 230
William De Morgan (1839–1917), designer and manufacturer
Ruby lustre dish painted with winged symmetrical mythical beasts
and foliage, late Merton Abbey/early Fulham period (1885–92)
Hand-painted underglaze colours on earthenware, diam. 36 cm

Cat. 231
William De Morgan (1839–1917), designer and manufacturer
Ruby lustre dish painted with two panthers, late Chelsea/early
Merton Abbey period (1878–85)
Hand-painted underglaze colours on earthenware, diam. 21.5 cm

Cat. 232
William De Morgan (1839–1917), designer and manufacturer
Red lustre dish painted with a pair of running antelopes, late
Chelsea/early Merton Abbey period (1878–85)
Hand-painted underglaze colours on earthenware, diam. 36 cm

Cat. 233
William De Morgan (1839–1917), designer
Ruby lustre dish painted with a peacock in full display,
late Merton Abbey/early Fulham period (c. 1885–92)
Hand-painted underglaze colour on earthenware, diam. 36.5 cm

Cat. 234
William De Morgan (1839–1917), designer and manufacturer
Painted by **John Hersey**
Ruby lustre vase painted with eagles riding the back
of a fabulous creature, Fulham period (1888–98)
Hand-painted underglaze colours on earthenware,
h. 20 cm

Cat. 235
William De Morgan (1839–1917),
designer and manufacturer
Painted by **Joe Juster**
Red lustre vase painted with birds,
Fulham period (1888–98)
Hand-painted underglaze colours on
earthenware, h. 21 cm

Cat. 236
William De Morgan (1839–1917), designer and manufacturer
Painted by **Fred Passenger**
Iznik vase painted with alternating eagles and serpents,
late Merton Abbey/early Fulham period (c. 1885–92)
Hand-painted underglaze colours on earthenware, h. 58 cm

Cat. 237
William De Morgan (1839–1917), designer and manufacturer
Painted by **Fred Passenger**
Iznik vase painted with peacocks, Merton Abbey period (1881–88)
Hand-painted underglaze colours on earthenware, h. 59 cm

Cat. 238
William De Morgan (1839–1917), designer and manufacturer
Iznik vase moulded in relief and painted with winged beasts, applied
serpent handles, late Merton Abbey/early Fulham period
(c. 1885–92)
Hand-painted underglaze colours on earthenware, h. 38 cm

Cat. 239
William De Morgan (1839–1917), designer and manufacturer
Painted by **John Hersey**
Iznik vase painted with a Damascus leaf design bordered by
lizards and winged creatures, Merton Abbey period (1881–88)
Hand-painted underglaze colours on earthenware, h. 36 cm

Cat. 240
William De Morgan (1839–1917), designer and manufacturer
Iznik vase painted with a winged serpent among fruiting trees,
Chelsea period (1872–81)
Hand-painted underglaze colours on earthenware, h. 34 cm

Cat. 241
William De Morgan (1839–1917), designer
and manufacturer
Painted by **Fred Passenger**
Iznik vase and cover painted with a Damascus abstract
design of birds and carnations, Fulham period (1888–98)
Hand-painted underglaze colours on earthenware, h. 31 cm

Cat. 242
William De Morgan
(1839–1917), designer
and manufacturer
Painted by **Joe Juster**
Iznik vase painted with
a continuous scrolling
flowering branch, Fulham
period (1888–98)
Hand-painted underglaze
colours on earthenware,
h. 29.5 cm

Cat. 243
William De Morgan (1839–1917), designer and manufacturer
Iznik ewer and cover decorated with fish, Fulham period (1888–98)
Hand-painted underglaze colours on earthenware, h. 23 cm

Cat. 244
William De Morgan
(1839–1917), designer
and manufacturer
Painted by **Joe Juster**
Iznik' vase painted with herons,
Fulham period (1888–98)
Hand-painted underglaze colours
on earthenware, h. 29 cm

Cat. 245
William De Morgan
(1839–1917), designer
and manufacturer
Painted by **Halsey Ricardo**
Persian vase painted with
fish swimming among waves,
Fulham period (1888–98)
Hand-painted underglaze
colours on earthenware,
h. 32.5 cm

Cat. 246
William De Morgan
(1839–1917), designer
and manufacturer
Painted by **John Hersey**
Iznik vase and cover
decorated with peacocks,
Fulham period (1888–98)
Hand-painted underglaze
colours on earthenware,
h. 37 cm

Cat. 247
William De Morgan (1839–1917), designer and manufacturer
Painted by **Joe Juster**
Vase and cover painted with red fishes on a wavy blue background, Fulham period (1888–98)
Hand-painted underglaze colours on earthenware, diam. 21 cm

Cat. 248
William De Morgan (1839–1917), designer and manufacturer
Iznik jardinière painted with sparrows in a fruiting tree, Fulham period (1888–98)
Hand-painted underglaze colours on earthenware, h. 18 cm

Cat. 249
William De Morgan (1839–1917), designer and manufacturer
Painted by **Joe Juster**
Iznik vase painted with birds, Fulham period (1888–98)
Hand-painted underglaze colours on earthenware, h. 13 cm

Cat. 250
William De Morgan (1839–1917), designer and manufacturer
Iznik vase (inspired by Damascus wares) painted with tulips, Fulham period (1888–98)
Hand-painted underglaze colours on earthenware, h. 19 cm

Cat. 251
William De Morgan
(1839–1917), designer
and manufacturer
Painted by **Charles Passenger**
Pair of Iznik dishes painted with
Damascus decoration of cornflowers,
Fulham period (1888–98)
Hand-painted underglaze colours on
earthenware, each diam. 19.5 cm

Cat. 252
William De Morgan
(1839–1917), designer and manufacturer
Iznik bowl painted with stylised cornflowers
and tulips, Fulham period (1888–98)
Hand-painted underglaze colours
on earthenware, diam. 18 cm

Cat. 254
William De Morgan (1839–1917),
designer and manufacturer
Painted by **Charles Passenger**
Eagle's Supper charger, Fulham period (1888–98)
Hand-painted underglaze colours on
earthenware, diam. 53.5 cm

Cat. 253
William De Morgan
(1839–1917), designer
and manufacturer
Painted by **Charles Passenger**
Tazza painted with a winged lion,
late Chelsea/early Merton Abbey period
(1878–85)
Hand-painted underglaze colours on
earthenware, h. 21 cm, diam. 25 cm

Cat. 255
William De Morgan (1839–1917), designer and manufacturer
Painted by **Charles Passenger**
Sunset and Moonlight Suite saucer dish painted with a swan with three cygnets, late Fulham period (after 1892)
Hand-painted underglaze colours on earthenware, diam. 23.5 cm

Cat. 256
William De Morgan (1839–1917), designer and manufacturer
Painted by **Charles Passenger**
Sunset and Moonlight Suite saucer dish painted with an eagle feeding two eaglets in a nest, late Fulham period (after 1892)
Hand-painted underglaze colours on earthenware, diam. 23.5 cm

Cat. 257
William De Morgan (1839–1917), designer and manufacturer
Painted by **Charles Passenger**
Sunset and Moonlight Suite saucer dish painted with an eagle and serpent set against starry sky, late Fulham period (after 1892)
Hand-painted underglaze colours on earthenware, diam. 28 cm

Cat. 258
William De Morgan (1839–1917), designer and manufacturer
Painted by **Charles Passenger**
Sunset and Moonlight Suite saucer dish painted with a galleon, late Fulham period (after 1892)
Hand-painted underglaze colours on earthenware, diam. 30 cm

Cat. 259 (ABOVE AND FACING PAGE)
William Morris (1834–1896) with **Sir Edward Coley
Burne-Jones Bt ARA** (1833–1898) and **Charles Fairfax
Murray** (1849–1919); later work by **Graily Hewitt**
(1864–1953) and **Louise Powell** (1882–1956)
The Aeneid of Virgil, 1874–75 and 1904 – c. 1910
Binding by **J. & J. Leighton** of London, 34.9 × 26 cm

P. VIRGILII MARONIS

a [ ] clo soliti; tum facta silentia tectis
[ ] hospitibus nam te dare jura loquuntur
hunc lætum Tyriisque diem rojaque profectis
esse velis nostroque hujus meminisse minores
adsit lætitiae Bacchus dator et bona juno
et vos o coetum Tyrii celebrate faventes
ixit, et in mensam laticum libavit honorem
primaque libato summo tenus attigit ore
tum Bitiae dedit increpitans; ille impiger hausit
spumantem pateram et pleno se proluit auro
post alii proceres: cithara crinitus Iopas
personat aurata docuit quem maximus Atlas
hic canit errantem lunam solisque labores
unde hominum genus et pecudes unde imber et ignes
Arcturum pluviasque Hyades geminosque Triones
quid tantum oceano properent se tingere soles
hiberni vel quae tardis mora noctibus obstet
ingeminant plausu Tyrii Troesque sequuntur
et non et vario noctem sermone trahebat
infelix Dido longumque bibebat amorem
multa super Priamo rogitans super Hectore multa
nunc quibus Aurorae venisset filius armis
nunc quales Diomedis equi nunc quantus Achille
MMO age et a prima dic hospes origine nobis
insidias, inquit, Danaum casusque tuorum
erroresque tuos; nam te jam septima portat
omnibus errantem terris et fluctibus aestas

28

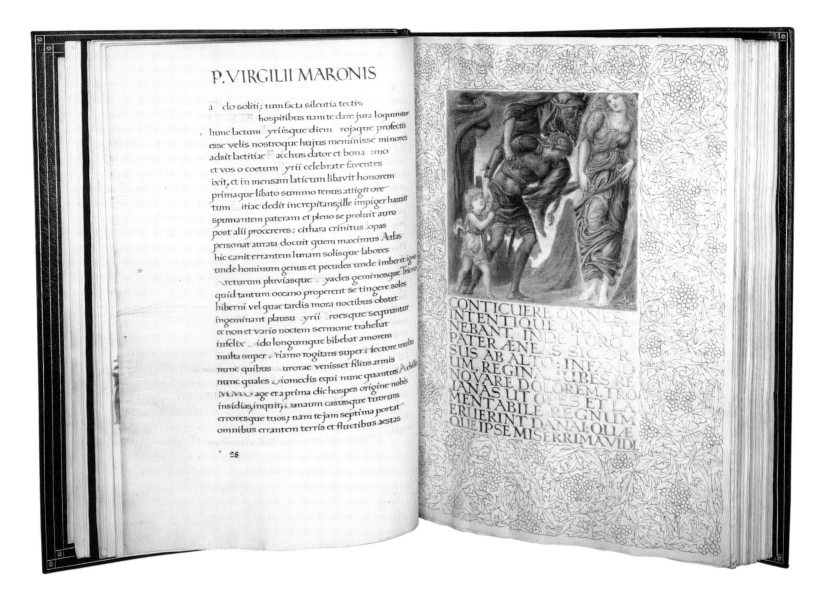

CONTICUERE OMNES,
INTENTIQUE ORA TE
NEBANT. INDE TORO
PATER ÆNEAS SIC OR
SUS AB ALTO: INFAND
UM, REGINA, IUBES RE
NOVARE DOLOREM, TRO
IANAS UT OPES ET LA
MENTABILE REGNUM
ERUERINT DANAI, QUÆ
QUE IPSE MISERRIMA VIDI.

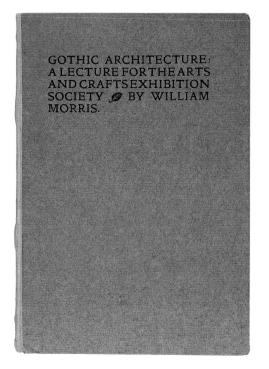

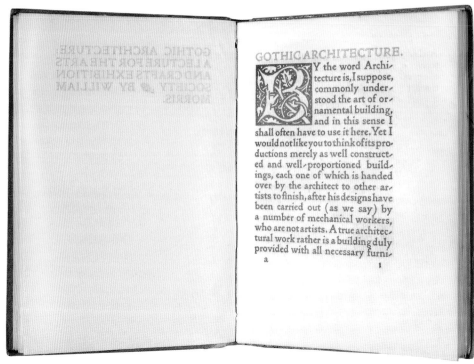

Cat. 260
William Morris, *Gothic Architecture: A Lecture for the Arts and Crafts Exhibition Society*
Published and printed by **William Morris** (1834–1896) at the Kelmscott Press, Hammersmith, 1893
Page size 14.3 × 10.4 cm

Cat. 261
John Ruskin, *The Nature of Gothic: A Chapter of the Stones of Venice*, with a Preface by William Morris
Published by **George Allen** and printed by **William Morris** (1834–1896) at the Kelmscott Press, Hammersmith, 1892
Page size 20 × 14.1 cm

Cat. 262
William Morris, *News from Nowhere: Or, an Epoch of Rest,*
being Some Chapters from a Utopian Romance
Published by **Reeves & Turner** and printed by **William Morris**
(1834–1896) at the Kelmscott Press, Hammersmith, 1893
Frontispiece illustration of Kelmscott Manor by **Charles**
March Gere (1869–1957) within a full woodcut border
designed by Morris
Page size 20.5 × 14 cm

Cat. 263
The Tale of King Florus and the Fair Jehane,
translated by William Morris
Published and printed by **William Morris** (1834–1896)
at the Kelmscott Press, Hammersmith, 1893
Page size 14.6 × 10.4 cm
The copy contains an inscription by Jenny Morris

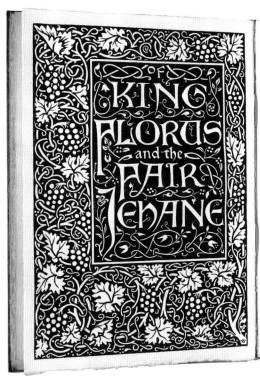
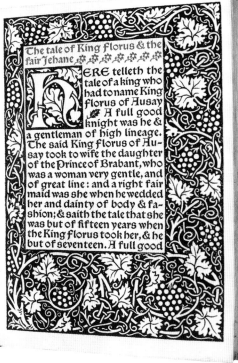
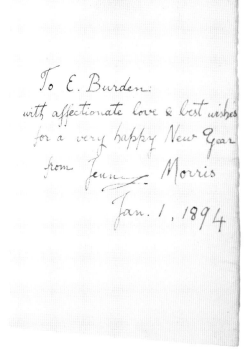

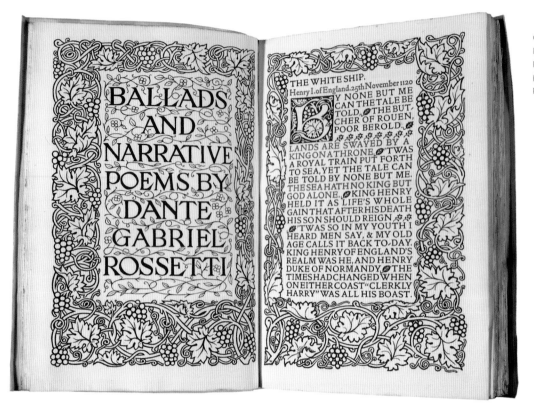

Cat. 264
Dante Gabriel Rossetti, *Ballads and Narrative Poems*
Published by **Ellis & Elvey** and printed by **William Morris**
(1834–1896) at the Kelmscott Press, Hammersmith, 1893
Page size 20.5 × 14 cm

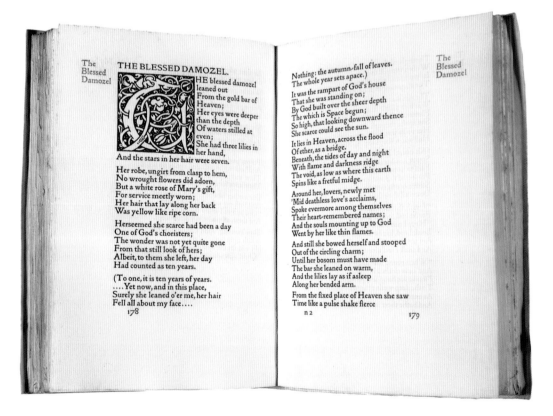

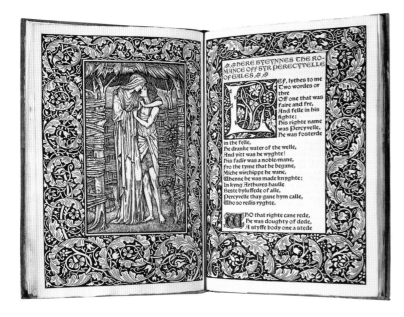

Cat. 265
Sir Perecyvelle of Gales, edited by F. S. Ellis
Published and printed by **William Morris** (1834–1896)
at the Kelmscott Press, Hammersmith, 1895
Page size 14.6 × 10.4 cm

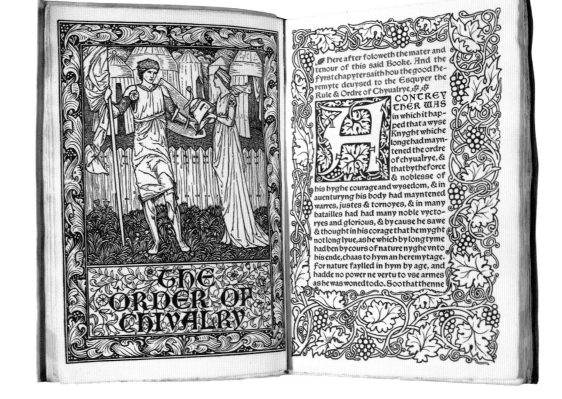

Cat. 266
The Order of Chivalry, translated from the French by
William Caxton and reprinted from his edition of 1484;
edited by F. S. Ellis; with *L'Ordene de Chevalerie* in a
verse translation from the French by William Morris
Published by **Reeves & Turner** and printed by
William Morris (1834–1896) at the Kelmscott Press,
Hammersmith, 1893
Frontispiece illustration by **Sir Edward Coley Burne-Jones
Bt ARA** (1833–1898) within a full woodcut border,
and with several partial page borders and initial capitals,
all designed by Morris
Page size 20 × 13.8 cm

Cat. 267
The Works of Geoffrey Chaucer, edited by F. S. Ellis
Published and printed by **William Morris** (1834–1896)
at the Kelmscott Press, Hammersmith, 1896
87 woodcut illustrations after designs by
Sir Edward Coley Burne-Jones Bt ARA (1833–1898)
Binding probably by the **W. H. Smith Bindery** under
the direction of Douglas Cockerell
Page size 42.5 × 29.2 cm

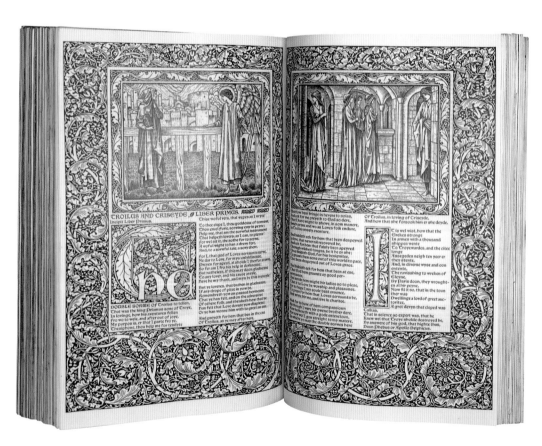

Cat. 268
Sir Edward Coley Burne-Jones Bt ARA, *The Flower Book:*
Reproductions of Thirty-Eight Watercolour Designs
Printed by **Henri Piazza & Co.** and published by
the Fine Art Society Ltd., London, 1905
Binding by the **W. H. Smith Bindery**
under the direction of Douglas Cockerell
Page size 33 × 26.5 cm

The Early 20th Century:
Munnings, Lowry and Spencer

JUDITH COLLINS

Munnings, Lowry and Spencer were great individualists and independents who painted the places and people that they loved with evident affection and authenticity. The localities where they lived and worked, Munnings in rural East Anglia, Lowry in the suburbs of Manchester and Spencer at Cookham village in Berkshire, have come to be identified with them, and all have permanent galleries devoted to their accomplishments. Their careers span the first half of the 20th century, Lowry's even longer, since he lived until 1976. Their work in this exhibition covers a 50-year period, from a 1902 canvas by Munnings painted during the Edwardian era to a transfigured crowd scene by Spencer painted in the mid-1950s, when a young Elizabeth II sat on the throne. British art changed greatly during this half-century, but the more avant-garde aesthetic innovations and developments of that period are not obviously found in these artists' canvases. All were content and confident in the strength of their own particular expression and vision, and saw no need to experiment with or alter trusted ways of working. In some respects they looked backwards in art history for inspiration, Munnings to Constable, Stubbs and the Impressionists, Lowry to the Impressionists and the Pre-Raphaelites, Spencer to Giotto and the Italian Renaissance via the Pre-Raphaelites. All seem to have avoided including anything notably modern in their paintings, so that their work celebrates a sense of unchanging time, even as the decades pass.

Munnings was probably the most adventurous of the trio, studying not only in his native East Anglia, but also at the Académie Julian in Paris and the Newlyn Art School in Cornwall. Lowry and Spencer felt no need to travel far in order to study. Lowry was taught by a French artist, Adolphe Valette (1876–1942), at Manchester School of Art and learned from him a low-keyed Impressionism, which he soon rejected. Spencer attended the Slade School of Art in London, where the emphasis was on draughtsmanship and imaginative composition.

Both Spencer and Lowry made synthetic paintings – that is, their works are constructed from detailed local observation but are imbued with emotion and imagination. Munnings's canvases appear to have less interior content and fewer layers of symbolism. All three artists, in their own way, still adhered to the 'truth to nature' outlook of the Pre-Raphaelite painters and the Impressionists. Munnings, Lowry and Spencer were ambitious for their work, and exhibited it regularly, especially at the Royal Academy, where all were elected Academicians, Munnings in 1926, Lowry in 1962, Spencer in 1932 (and again in 1950, following his resignation fifteen years previously). Both Lowry and Spencer were signed up with top London dealers – the Lefevre Gallery and Tooths respectively – who showed and sold their work, while Munnings relied more on commissions, particularly of the equestrian kind. Art is always autobiographical in some way, and the groups of people each man painted can be read as symbols of themselves. Munnings's people enjoy themselves in rural secular pastimes where the refreshment tent is always near; Lowry's people are absorbed in their private urban isolations where hardship plays its part, while Spencer's appear as the rapt chorus to a Passion play, which is both spiritual and erotic.

Alfred Munnings (1878–1959) was born in Mendham, near Harleston, Norfolk, the son of a miller and the grandson of a farmer. He admired the landscape art of earlier East Anglian painters such as Constable, Crome and Cotman, and the animal paintings of Stubbs and Ben Marshall. In 1899, aged 21, Munnings launched himself as a painter of landscapes and horses, emulating those artists whom he admired, and he began well, showing two works in the Royal Academy's Summer Exhibition that year. For the next 60 years he painted the same subjects with broad, juicy brushstrokes and a great sense of movement. He painted quickly, often as many as three or four canvases a day, and liked to work with a model in front of him. In 1944 he was elected President of the Royal Academy, a post he held for five years, during which he gained a reputation as an outspoken opponent of the avant-garde. *A Country Horse Fair* (1902; cat. 275) was one of the first of a series of paintings of East Anglian horse fairs and Saturday farm markets. Munnings loved the equestrian characters, plying their business among the striped tents and painted caravans. In his autobiography, published in 1950, he describes with enthusiasm the horse dealers, gypsies, jockeys and animals that he painted. *Shrimp and the White Pony* (1909; cat. 272) portrays Shrimp, a small gypsy boy called Fountain Page, driving Munnings's beloved white pony Augereau. Shrimp became one of Munnings's favourite models, once sitting for three paintings in a single day. He learned to clean the artist's brushes, and Munnings rewarded him with a caravan and a pony of his own. *The Ford* (c. 1912; cat. 273) also depicts Shrimp and Augereau, but this time with a large supporting cast of other riders, horses and a caravan. Having grown up beside a river, Munnings loved to paint water and here he catches the ripples in the stream as deftly as Monet. *Country Races – The Start* (c. 1915; cat. 274) depicts Munnings's favourite subject, the country racecourse scene, full of action, colour and noise.

L. S. Lowry (1887–1976) was born in Rusholme, a suburb of Manchester, the son of a rent collector. In 1909 the family moved to Pendlebury in Salford, and Lowry became obsessed with its topography and people, painting nothing else for 30 years. He had a full-time job, working as a rent collector and clerk for the Pall Mall Property Company, Manchester, and as a result painted in his spare

time, usually at night by electric light, and at weekends. He developed a remarkable sense of tone, working in oils in harmonies of black, grey and white. He is close to Whistler in the way his paintings suggest states of mind through their subtle or dramatic tonalities and their restrained compositional devices. On his death it was revealed that he owned 23 Pre-Raphaelite paintings and drawings, including fifteen by D. G. Rossetti and one by Ford Madox Brown. *St Augustine's Church, Pendlebury* (1920; cat. 270) is one of the earliest of Lowry's depictions of churches, and probably the most dramatic. The church is a Grade-I listed building, designed by George Frederick Bodley and built from 1871 to 1874. It was largely financed by a local banker, Edward Heywood, who built it for the benefit of the coal mining industry which surrounded it. Lowry exaggerates its scale and paints it towering above the land and the diminutive people in the churchyard, making it seem like a stern vision of heaven. In the churchyard is a memorial to the 178 men and boys who died in the explosion of a nearby colliery on 18 June 1885, 64 of whom are buried there, and this mining tragedy will have added an emotional layer to Lowry's response to his subject.

Stanley Spencer (1891–1959) was born in Cookham, Berkshire, the son of a piano teacher and church organist. He recognised early in his career that he painted two kinds of picture – landscapes and portraits rendered in a detailed and realistic manner, and imaginative paintings, in which the content often dictated the form. We know his feelings about his work from his unfinished autobiography, over

Cat. 269
Sir Alfred James Munnings PRA
(1878–1959)
Three Gypsy Scenes, dates unknown

a *The Grey Horse*
Oil on canvas, 63.5 × 76.8 cm

b *Gypsy Caravan*
Oil on canvas, 50.8 × 61.5 cm

c *The Caravan*
Oil on canvas, 63.8 × 76.2 cm

Cat. 270
Laurence Stephen Lowry RA
(1887–1976)
St Augustine's Church, Pendlebury, 1920
Oil on panel, 39.3 × 55.8 cm

three million poetic and muddled words held in the Tate Archive, which are a testament to his inner vision. His fertile imagination fused the Bible stories he knew well with the topography of his village to produce a series of paintings that portrayed Cookham and its inhabitants as a sacred paradise, a heaven on earth. In the 1930s he began to make paintings for his 'Church-House of me', which occupied him for the rest of his life. This was an ambitious scheme whereby his paintings would be housed in the equivalent of a large parish church and surrounding houses, and arranged by themes, bringing together his religious and his erotic pictures. There were to be chapels devoted to all the women he loved, his two wives, Hilda and Patricia, and his mistresses. At the end of his life he began an ambitious series of paintings depicting Christ preaching in Cookham, also for the Church-House project. Spencer held unorthodox spiritual and social views, particularly about marriage, and he was attracted by oriental religions such as Hinduism, which believes that human sexual intercourse is a symbolic act echoing the divine intercourse between

worshipper and God. Munnings, by then ex-President of the Royal Academy, was so incensed by the frankness and nudity of some of Spencer's drawings of his women that in 1950 he tried to have Spencer (recently re-elected an Academician) prosecuted for obscenity.

The Garage (1929; cat. 279) was painted as the result of a commission to make poster designs for the Empire Marketing Board, the body responsible for colonial trade, on the theme of Industry and Peace. *Burghclere* (c. 1932; cat. 276) is a distant view of the village Spencer stayed in while painting the walls of the Sandham Memorial Chapel nearby, a decorative commission that fulfilled his desire to paint chapels like his hero Giotto. *Cottage Garden, Leonard Stanley* (1939; cat. 277) was painted while Spencer was displaced from his Cookham home by his second wife, Patricia Preece. He lodged at the White Hart Inn in the village of Leonard Stanley, Gloucestershire, at the invitation of two artist friends, George and Daphne Charlton. *On the Tiger Rug* (cat. 281) dates from the beginning of 1940 and was set in Spencer's rented room at the inn. Daphne Charlton and Spencer became lovers at this time, while George Charlton was away teaching at the Slade School, which moved to Oxford during the Second World War. Spencer wanted this painting to convey 'the rapt staring of two people awakened in paradise. How near is the meaning of resurrection and sexual union'.

The subject of the Resurrection of the Dead was dear to Spencer's heart and he painted many interpretations of it, among them *The Resurrection: Waking Up (Triptych)* (1945; cat. 271). His was not the version found in the New Testament, where Christ judges those who have died, and sends the sinners to Hell and the faithful to Heaven. Spencer offers Heaven and a new life of bliss to all resurrected souls, irrespective of the lives they have led, and in doing so invests his paintings with a redemptive power.

Spencer painted a number of self-portraits at intervals throughout his career, all of which are revealingly direct and honest. The first was in 1914; others followed in 1936, 1939, 1949, 1951 (two, including cat. 278) and the last in 1959, only months before his death.

From Up the Rise (1937/56; cat. 280) is part of the projected Marriage at Cana theme in Spencer's Church-House project. Villagers from Cookham Rise have stopped on the edge of Cookham Moor before going on as guests to the wedding feast at Cana, which is why they are wearing their Sunday best clothes. They gaze out of the picture in the direction of their travel and share an intensity of purpose and focus. They are about to witness the first miracle of Christ enacted in their beloved village.

Cat. 271
Sir Stanley Spencer RA (1891–1959)
The Resurrection: Waking Up (Triptych),
1945
Oil on three canvases,
76.2 × 50.8 cm (central panel),
50.8 × 76.2 cm (side panels)

Cat. 272
Sir Alfred James Munnings PRA
(1878–1959)
Shrimp and the White Pony, 1909
Oil on canvas, 63.5 × 77 cm

Cat. 273
Sir Alfred James Munnings PRA
(1878–1959)
The Ford, c. 1912
Oil on canvas, 76.2 × 101.6 cm

Cat. 274
Sir Alfred James Munnings PRA
(1878–1959)
Country Races – The Start, c. 1915
Oil on canvas, 50.8 × 61 cm

Cat. 275
Sir Alfred James Munnings PRA
(1878–1959)
A Country Horse Fair, 1902
Oil on canvas, 34.9 × 52 cm

Cat. 276
Sir Stanley Spencer RA (1891–1959)
Burghclere, c. 1932
Oil on canvas, 50.8 × 71.1 cm

Cat. 277
Sir Stanley Spencer RA (1891–1959)
Cottage Garden, Leonard Stanley, 1939
Oil on canvas, 50.8 × 76.2 cm

Cat. 278
Sir Stanley Spencer RA (1891–1959)
Self-portrait, 1951
Oil on canvas, 55.8 × 45 cm

Cat. 279
Sir Stanley Spencer RA
(1891–1959)
The Garage, 1929
Oil on canvas,
101.6 × 152.4 cm
The Andrew Lloyd Webber
Art Foundation

Cat. 280
Sir Stanley Spencer RA (1891–1959)
From Up the Rise, 1937/56
Oil on canvas, 80 × 106.6 cm

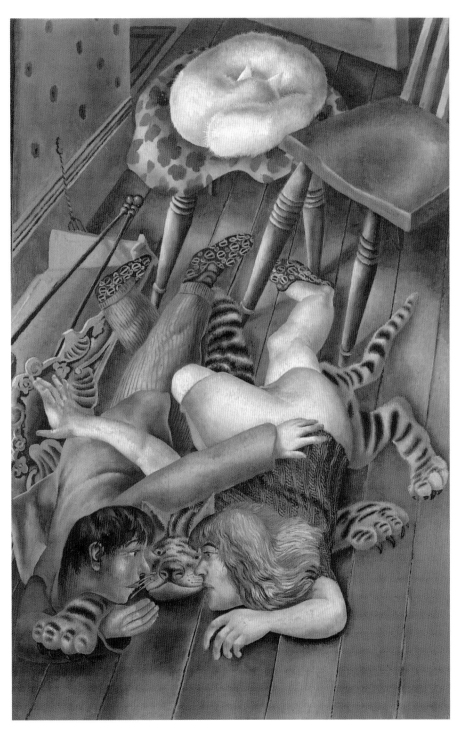

Cat. 281
Sir Stanley Spencer RA (1891–1959)
On the Tiger Rug, 1940
Oil on canvas, 91.5 × 61 cm

Pablo Picasso
Angel Fernández de Soto

ROBERT S. LUBAR

In February 1900 the nineteen-year-old Pablo Ruíz Picasso had his first one-man exhibition in Barcelona, at the Quatre Gats café, where he showed portraits of his intimate circle of friends. Among the little-known figures in this 'gallery of bohemians'[1] whom he immortalised in charcoal and ink was his friend Angel Fernández de Soto.

Angel de Soto entered Picasso's circle sometime in 1899, when the two met at the Edèn Concert, a cabaret in Barcelona's gothic quarter. The son of a father from a small town near Madrid and a mother from Barcelona, Angel was a self-styled bohemian and one-time artist who earned a meagre living working for Mir i Estrada, a firm in the Carrer Princessa that imported spices and other colonial products. Despite his modest circumstances, Angel, who died in 1938 during the Spanish Civil War, fashioned himself as a dandy and man-about-town who occasionally worked as an extra in the theatre to supplement his income.[2] Described by Josep Palau i Fabre as 'slender and elegant . . . and almost always surrounded by women',[3] this latter-day Don Juan was Picasso's ideal companion. In 1902 the two friends briefly shared a studio next to the Edèn Concert, but Angel's appetite for women and his penchant for entertaining during the evening hours prevented Picasso from working.[4]

Angel de Soto appears in a number of images by Picasso, culminating in the magnificent oil portrait of 1903 in the Andrew Lloyd Webber Collection. This is one of the most accomplished and moving paintings from Picasso's Blue Period, which lasted from autumn 1902 to spring 1904 and was characterised by images redolent of isolation and social alienation that are among the most deeply felt of the artist's career. Picasso approaches his sitter with the eye of a caricaturist, emphasising his lithe physique and somewhat effete countenance, and exaggerating his prominent chin, elegant hands and crooked nose. The portrait is a *tour de force* of thick, loose brushwork that recalls the work of Vincent van Gogh. De Soto's ghostlike face, with its heavily incised features, emerges from a deep, Prussian blue background. The elegantly dressed sitter appears to scrutinise the viewer with an intense, melancholic, yet curiously suspicious gaze, his inner agitation suggested by the forceful brushstrokes and the cloud of smoke hovering above him at the upper right. This is a striking study in psychological introspection, the mood of which is established by abstract harmonies of colour.

1 John Richardson, *A Life of Picasso*, vol. 1: *1881–1906*, New York, 1991, p. 145.
2 Ibid., pp. 115–16.
3 Josep Palau i Fabre, *Picasso y els seus amics catalans*, Barcelona, 1971, p. 56.
4 Richardson (note 1), p. 233.

Cat. 282
Pablo Picasso (1881–1973)
Angel Fernández de Soto, 1903
Oil on canvas, 69.5 × 55.2 cm
The Andrew Lloyd Webber Art Foundation

Canaletto
London: The Old Horse Guards from St James's Park

ELIZABETH EINBERG

Canaletto, arguably the greatest view painter of the
18th century, spent most of his working life in his native
Venice. The son of a distinguished designer and painter of
stage scenery, Canaletto began his career in that profession,
but soon abandoned it for painting views after nature.
To this he brought an unprecedented ability to master
illusionistic aerial perspective and to bathe his views in
brilliant Italian sunlight. From the 1720s his works were
avidly collected by the rich, mostly British, visitors who
flocked to Venice on their Grand Tour. Yet as the War of
the Austrian Succession began to spread across Europe
after 1741, the number of visitors to Venice declined.
Canaletto's sound business sense is thought to have
prompted his decision to move to London, not only to
find new clients, but also to invest his money in what was
rapidly becoming the largest and most vibrant commercial
centre in Europe. Canaletto arrived in London in May
1746 and, with the exception of two visits to Venice in
1750–51 and 1753–54, remained here until 1755.

Among the two dozen or so views of London that
Canaletto produced during this period, this is one of the
largest and most spectacular.[1] It commemorates the last
remnant of Stuart Whitehall before its demolition in
1750, to be replaced by the present New Horse Guards
(which Canaletto also painted). The decayed brick
buildings are flanked by the proud new structures of the
Georgian age: the Admiralty on the left, with the spire of
St Martin's behind, and, on the right, a glimpse of the York
Buildings water tower and William Kent's Treasury, with
the grand residences of Downing Street in the foreground.
Peopled with innumerable precisely characterised figures,
both rich and poor, with the Guards drilling on the
parade ground, servants going about their business,
men relieving themselves against any available wall and
children playing by the Canal, St James's Park presents a
delightfully well-observed slice of daily life in London.

1 For a more extensive discussion of
the painting, see the present author's

*Canaletto: 'The Old Horse Guards
from St James's Park'*, London, 1992.

Cat. 283
**Giovanni Antonio Canal, called
Canaletto** (1697–1768)
*The Old Horse Guards, London,
from St James's Park*, c. 1749
Oil on canvas, 117 × 236 cm
The Andrew Lloyd Webber
Art Foundation

Sir Joshua Reynolds

The Prince of Wales, later George IV

MARTIN POSTLE

Sir Joshua Reynolds (1723–1792) was born in Plympton, Devon, the son of a cleric and schoolmaster. Following a brief apprenticeship to the portrait painter Thomas Hudson, Reynolds set up independently as a portraitist in London. In 1749 he visited Italy. The three years he spent there formed the bedrock of his subsequent painting style, as he strove to endow his portraits with a classical grandeur drawn from the Old Masters. In 1768 Reynolds was elected first President of the Royal Academy and was knighted, despite the enmity of George III, who disliked his art and his politics. Increasingly, during the 1770s, Reynolds became identified with the Whig party and with the acolytes of the young Prince of Wales, who stood in opposition to the Court party. Reynolds continued to work assiduously until 1789, when ill health and failing sight forced him to stop painting. He died in February 1792, and was buried in St Paul's Cathedral.

George, eldest son of George III and Queen Charlotte, probably posed for the present portrait in 1783. It was exhibited by Reynolds at the Royal Academy in 1784. The Prince, who was not otherwise renowned for settling his debts, paid Reynolds 300 guineas for the painting and immediately presented it to the notoriously dissolute Peniston Lamb, 1st Lord Melbourne, with whose wife he was then conducting an affair. (George Lamb, born in July 1784, was rumoured to have been the offspring of Lady Melbourne and the Prince.)

The extravagant Baroque composition recalls the great equestrian portraits of Reynolds's 17th-century predecessors Rubens and Van Dyck. At the same time the dramatic pose of the Prince, silhouetted against a stormy sky, anticipates the sense of drama found in such works as *Portrait of an Officer of the Chasseurs* by the French Romantic painter Théodore Géricault (1812; Louvre, Paris). Prince George, sword drawn as if prepared for battle, sports the uniform of a British army officer, adorned with the order of the Star of the Garter, the blue Garter ribbon visible beneath. The Prince's proud martial bearing was a reflection of his personal vanity and his passion for dressing up, since in reality the King forbade him to participate in any sort of military service. This did not prevent the Prince from claiming in later life that he had helped to win the battle of Waterloo.

Cat. 284
Sir Joshua Reynolds PRA (1723–1792)
George, Prince of Wales,
first exhibited 1784
Oil on canvas, 238.7 × 266.7 cm

Catalogue

NOTE

The only professional membership noted after an artist's name at the head of each entry is of the Royal Academy of Arts, London (RA): ARA = Associate; RA = Member; PRA = President.

A distinction is made between dates separated by a dash and those separated by an oblique stroke. Hence '1861–65' signifies a work begun in the former year and completed in the latter, while '1861/65' signifies one created either in both the given years and/or in any in between.

Only known owners and sales are listed under 'Provenance'; gaps in knowledge are not noted. All auctions and dealers are in London unless otherwise stated.

Only the opening year and venue of an exhibition are given under 'Exhibitions'.

The 'Selected references' include neither publications associated with sales nor catalogues of the exhibitions listed in the entry. It may be assumed, however, that many exhibition catalogues since the 1970s contain new research. Items listed in abbreviated form here and in the notes at the end of an entry are given in full either within the text of the entry or in the Selected Bibliography (p. 315).

Remarks at the end of an entry generally contain only information of immediate relevance to the work concerned, referring for example only to other items closely related to it. Relatively unimportant drawings and studies, and copies by other artists, are not usually listed.

Paintings, Drawings, Sculpture

NICHOLAS TROMANS

Sir Lawrence Alma-Tadema OM RA (1836–1912)

144
The Coliseum (A Roman Holiday), 1896
Oil on panel, 112 × 73.6 cm
Inscribed lower left centre, on cushion: *L Alma Tadema op CCCXXXVI*; on frame: *And here the buzz of eager nations ran, / In murmur'd pity, or loud-roar'd applause* (Byron, 'Childe Harold's Pilgrimage' IV, 139)

PROVENANCE
Commissioned by Tooth & Sons, 1896; sold 1897, bought Knoedler & Sons, New York; sold 1897, bought J. D. Archbold, New York; by descent; Sotheby's Parke-Burnet, New York, 3 October 1975, lot 230, bought in by executors, by whom given to a monastical school, 1976; sold William Doyle Galleries, New York, 17 May 1984, lot 26; private collection, USA; acquired 1993

EXHIBITIONS
RA, 1896, no. 291; International Exhibition, St Louis, 1904, no. 291; *British and American Paintings*, Auburn University, AL, 1976, no. 2

SELECTED REFERENCES
Academy, 23 May 1896, p. 432; *Art Journal*, 1896, pp. 168–70; *Athenaeum*, 2 May 1896, pp. 587–8; *Magazine of Art*, 1896, p. 298; *Royal Academy Illustrated*, London, 1896, p. 291 ill.; Henry Blackburn (ed.), *Academy Notes*, London, 1896, pp. 12, 65 ill.; *Munsey's Magazine*, December 1896, p. 325 ill.; Frederick Dolman, 'Illustrated Interviews', *Strand Magazine*, December 1899, p. 613; Helen Zimmern, *Sir Lawrence Alma-Tadema*,

London, 1902, pp. 62–6, 72 ill.; Percy Cross Standing, *Sir Lawrence Alma-Tadema*, London, 1905, pp. 100–1; Vern G. Swanson, *Sir Lawrence Alma-Tadema: The Painter of the Victorian Vision of the Ancient World*, London, 1977, pl. 19; Swanson, 1990, no. 374; Barrow, 2001, pp. 147 (confused with *Caracalla and Geta*), 155 and pl. 154

143
Thermae Antoninianae (The Baths of Caracalla), 1899
Oil on canvas, 152.5 × 95 cm
Inscribed lower left, on bench leg: *L Alma Tadema op CCCLVI*

PROVENANCE
Commissioned by Arthur Tooth & Sons, 1899; sold 1903, bought Knoedler & Sons, New York; sold January 1904, bought Judge S. L. Bronson, New Haven, CT; sold American Art Association, New York, 15 March 1907, lot 73, bought Scott & Fowles; Leon Mandel; his sale, American Art Association, New York, 17 January 1917, lot 171, bought Henry Reinhardt & Sons; Cleve Bonner, Beverley Hills, CA; Allen Funt, New York; his sale, Sotheby's, 6 November 1973, lot 28, bought Messrs Charles Jerdein; sold to Lord Londonderry, 1974; sold to Fine Art Society, 1981; Owen Edgar Gallery, 1984; private collection, USA; acquired 1993

EXHIBITIONS
RA, 1899, no. 238; *Victorians in Togas: Paintings by Sir Lawrence Alma-Tadema from the Collection of Allen Funt*, Metropolitan Museum of Art, New York, 1973, no. 28; *Great Victorian Pictures*, Leeds City Art Gallery (Arts Council of Great Britain), 1978, no. 2

SELECTED REFERENCES
Athenaeum, 28 January 1899, p. 119; 1 April 1899, p. 408; and 29 April 1899, p. 536; *The Times*, 29 April 1899, p. 14; *Art Journal*, 1899, pp. 162–3; *Magazine of Art*, 1899, p. 388; Henry Blackburn (ed.), *Academy Notes*, London, 1899, p. 81; Frederick Dolman, 'Illustrated Interviews', *Strand Magazine*, December 1899, p. 613; idem, 'Pictures Preferred by their Painters', *Strand Magazine*, July 1901, p. 1; *New York Times*, 24 March 1907; Rudolf Dircks, 'The Later Work of Sir Lawrence Alma-Tadema', *Art Annual*, 1910, p. 32; Vern G. Swanson, *Sir Lawrence Alma-Tadema: The Painter of the Victorian Vision of the Ancient World*, London, 1977, pp. 38, 44, 141 and pl. 24; Christopher Wood, *Olympian Dreamers*, London, 1983, p. 124 and fig. 18; Swanson, 1990, no. 392; *Sir Lawrence Alma-Tadema*, exh. cat., Van Gogh Museum, Amsterdam, 1996, pp. 34, 42 ill., 262; *Imagining Rome: British Artists and Rome in the Nineteenth Century*, Michael Liversidge and Catherine Edwards (eds), exh. cat., Bristol City Museum and Art Gallery, 1996, p. 168 and fig. 34; Barrow, 2001, pp. 177, 185 and pl. 175; Elizabeth Prettejohn, 'Lawrence Alma-Tadema and the Modern City of Ancient Rome', *Art Bulletin*, March 2002, pp. 122–3, 125, 126, 127

145
Goldfish, 1900
Oil on panel, 18.7 × 40.6 cm
Inscribed upper left: *L. Alma-Tadema op. CCCLIX*

PROVENANCE
Mrs Dunkels, London, by 1913; James Coats Gallery, New York, by 1964; James Graham & Sons, New York, 1965; Lillian Bostwick Phipps; acquired 1993

EXHIBITIONS
RA, 1900, no. 226; RA, Winter 1913, no. 153; Lady Lever Art Gallery, Port Sunlight (date unknown); Memorial Art Gallery, Rochester, NY (date unknown); *Artists of Victoria's England*, Cummer Art Gallery, Jacksonville, FL, 1965, no. 2

SELECTED REFERENCES
Malcolm Bell, *Academy Review*, London, 1900, p. 14 ill.; *Royal Academy Illustrated*, London, 1900, p. 226 ill.; Henry Blackburn (ed.), *Academy Notes*, London, 1900, pp. 16 ill., 71; Swanson, 1990, no. 396; Barrow, 2001, pp. 91

Painted over an earlier version of the same subject (*Opus CVII*, 1872), created for Frederick Goodall and acquired by Tooth & Sons from Christie's, 24 June 1899, lot 111. Cat. 145 was commissioned by Tooth in 1900.

Sophie Anderson (1823–1903)

153
The Lace Handkerchief, 1850s
Oil on canvas, 30.5 × 41 cm
Signed lower right edge

PROVENANCE
Acquired 1994

EXHIBITION
Perhaps Society of British Artists, 1857, no. 445 (as *'I am helping Mamma'*)

W. A. Atkinson (exhibited London 1849–1870)

160
The Upset Flower Cart, early 1860s
Oil on canvas, 92 × 71.8 cm
Signed lower left

PROVENANCE
Evelyn Waugh; his trustees' sale, Sotheby's, 19 October 1971, lot 58; acquired 1992

EXHIBITION
Loan Exhibition of Victorian Paintings, Agnew's, London, 1961, no. 95

SELECTED REFERENCES
Graham Reynolds, *Painters of the Victorian Scene*, London, 1953, pp. 26, 85 and pl. 65; William Gaunt, *The Restless Century*, London, 1972, pl. 105; Christopher Wood, 'Evelyn Waugh: A Pioneer Collector', *Connoisseur*, September 1981, fig. 2, 3; Cowling, 2000, pp. 8 ill., 22–3

A version in oil, 49.5 × 39.3 cm, was sold at Christie's, 16 March 1973, lot 189.

Alessandro Battaglia (1870–1940)

165
The Schoolroom, 1897
Oil on canvas, 87.5 × 174.4 cm
Signed, dated and inscribed *ROMA* lower right

PROVENANCE
Acquired 1987

Giovanni Boldini (1842–1931)

136
The Marchesa Luisa Casati, 1908
Oil on canvas, 253.4 × 140.4 cm
Signed and dated lower left

PROVENANCE
Sold by the artist to Baron Maurice de Rothschild; acquired 1995

EXHIBITIONS
Salon, Paris, 1909, no. 119; *Esposizione d'Arte della Secessione*, Rome, 1914, no. 11

SELECTED REFERENCE
Tiziano Panconi, *Giovanni Boldini: L'Opera completa*, Florence, 2002, p. 496 (with further bibliography)

John Brett ARA (1831–1902)

107
The Val d'Aosta, 1858
Oil on canvas, 87.6 × 68 cm
Signed and dated

PROVENANCE
Bought by John James Ruskin (died 1864) at the instigation of his son, John Ruskin, for £200, November 1859 (J.J. Ruskin added a further £50 the following year); put up for sale by John Ruskin at Christie's, 15 April 1869, lot 47, but bought in at 245 guineas and remained with him; given by him to Arthur Severn, by 1880; acquired by (Sir) Richard Powell Cooper soon after Ruskin's death in 1900; by descent; acquired 1989

EXHIBITIONS
RA, 1859, no. 908; Liverpool Academy, 1859, no. 33; International Exhibition, London, 1862, no. 481; First Loan Exhibition, Douglas, Isle of Man, 1880, no. 10 (lent by Severn, but with catalogue entry by Ruskin); International Exhibition, Glasgow, 1901; Art and Industrial Exhibition, Wolverhampton, 1902, Fine Art section, no. 98; Franco-British Exhibition, White City, London, 1908, Oil Paintings by Deceased British Masters, no. 104; International Fine Arts Exhibition, Rome, 1911, Oil Paintings by Deceased British Masters, no. 3; Birmingham City Museum and Art Gallery, *The Pre-Raphaelite Brotherhood*, 1947, no. 2; *First Hundred Years, 1769–1868*, RA, Winter 1951, no. 283; Loan Exhibition of Victorian Paintings, Agnew's, London, 1961, no. 18; Bicentenary Exhibition, RA, Winter 1968, no. 76; *Zwei Jahrhundert englische [sic] Malerei: Britisch Kunst und Europa 1680 bis 1880*, Haus der Kunst, Munich, 1979, no. 233; *The Pre-Raphaelites*, Tate Gallery, London, 1984, no. 99; *Ruskin, Turner and the Pre-Raphaelites*, Tate Britain, London, 2000, no. 207

SELECTED REFERENCES
Critic, 1859, p. 544; *Fraser's Magazine*, June 1859, p. 666; Millais, 1899, vol. 1, p. 342; Percy Bate, *Art at the Glasgow International Exhibition 1901*, London, 1901, p. 44; Ruskin, 1903–12, vol. 7, p. 360; vol. 13, p. 572; vol. 14, frontispiece ill., pp. xxiii, xxvii–xxviii, 22 n.2, 172, 234–8 (*Academy Notes*, 1859), 293; Robin Ironside and John Gere, *Pre-Raphaelite Painters*, London, 1948, pp. 45–6 and pl. 79; Graham Reynolds, *Victorian Painting*, London, 1966, pp. 154–5; Timothy Hilton, *The Pre-Raphaelites*, London, 1970, pp. 120–2 and fig. 84; Robert Rosenblum and H. W. Janson, *Art of the Nineteenth Century*, London, 1984, pp. 297–8 and fig. 237; Bennett, 1988, pp. 17–18; Simon Taylor, 'Ruskin, John Brett and the Val d'Aosta', *Ruskin Gazette* 1, 3, 1989, pp. 34–8; Simon Taylor, 'John Brett's *Val d'Aosta*', *Antique Collector*, June 1989, pp. 114–15; Michael Hickox, 'The Unpublished Correspondence of Ruskin and Brett', *Ruskin Gazette* 1, 8, 1995, pp. 1–25; Michael Hickox, 'John Brett and Ruskin', *Burlington Magazine*, August 1996, pp. 521–5; Staley, 2001, pp. 174–9 and pl. 140; Christopher Newall, 'John Brett: The Pre-Raphaelite Years', in Ann Sumner (ed.), *John Brett: A Pre-Raphaelite on the Shores of Wales*, exh. cat., National Museum of Wales, Cardiff, 2001, pp. 19–20 and fig. 4

Two related studies are included here (cat. 105, 106); others are in the National Maritime Museum, London, Brett sketchbooks, nos 2, 3, 4, 5.

105, 106
Two Studies for 'The Val d'Aosta', 1858

105
Watercolour over pencil, heightened with white and gum arabic, on paper, 24.5 × 19.4 cm

PROVENANCE
Given by the artist's widow to their son Jasper;
Susan Oliver; acquired 1991

106
Watercolour and gouache on paper, 16.5 × 25.4 cm
PROVENANCE
Maas Gallery; acquired 1989

114
Norbury on the Mole, 1862
Oil on canvas, 51 × 68.5 cm
Signed and dated lower right
PROVENANCE
G. R. Burnett; Christie's, 4 March 1864, lot 73, bought
P. M. Martineau; acquired 2001
EXHIBITIONS
[Rejected RA, 1863]; Artist's studio, Pump Court,
Temple, London, 1863
SELECTED REFERENCES
The Times, 7 May 1863, p. 7; *Athenaeum*, 9 May 1863,
pp. 619–20; *Saturday Review*, 9 May 1863, pp. 592–3;
Michael Hickox, 'The Royal Academy's Rejection of
Brett's Florence', *Review of the Pre-Raphaelite Society*
3, 1, Spring 1995, pp. 10–16; Philip McEvansoneya,
'The Cosmopolitan Club Exhibition of 1863: The British
Salon des refusés', in Ellen Harding (ed.), *Re-Framing
the Pre-Raphaelites*, Aldershot, 1996, p. 29 (as *Scene
at Dorking*); Christopher Newall, 'John Brett: The
Pre-Raphaelite Years', in Ann Sumner (ed.), *John Brett:
A Pre-Raphaelite on the Shores of Wales*, exh. cat.,
National Museum of Wales, Cardiff, 2001, pp. 21, 26
n. 50

Related drawings are at the National Maritime
Museum, London, Brett sketchbooks, nos. 10, 11

Ford Madox Brown (1821–1893)

104
Southend, Essex, Looking Towards Sheerness, begun
1846, reworked in 1858 and 1861
Oil on paper, diam. 29 cm
Signed and inscribed lower left: *SOUTHEND*; label on
backboard inscribed *1858*
PROVENANCE
Purchased from the artist after 1861 by Thomas
Hedley (d. 1890); probably passed to Hedley's
daughter Margaret, Lady Wilson; acquired 1986
EXHIBITIONS
Hogarth Club, London, January 1859; *Winter Exhibition
of Sketches*, Gambart, London, November 1859; Royal
Scottish Academy, Edinburgh, 1860, no. 663; Liverpool
Academy, 1860, no. 687; Society for the
Encouragement of the Fine Arts, Mansion House,
London, May 1861; Brown's one-man exhibition,
191 Piccadilly, 1865, no. 23 (with brief description by
the artist; repr. in Bendiner, 1998, p. 139)
SELECTED REFERENCES
The Times, 24 November 1859; Ford M. Hueffer, *Ford
Madox Brown: A Record of His Life and Work*, London,
1896, pp. 156, 159, 434; Mary Bennett, 'Ford Madox
Brown at Southend in 1846: Some Lost Paintings',
Burlington Magazine, February 1973, pp. 74–8; Lynn
Roberts, 'Nineteenth-century English Picture Frames,
I: The Pre-Raphaelites', *The International Journal of
Museum Management and Curatorship* 4, 2, June 1985,
p. 159 and fig. 8; Teresa Newman and Ray Watkinson,
Ford Madox Brown, London, 1991, pp. 28, 51, 68, 116
and fig. 107; Kenneth Bendiner, *The Art of Ford Madox
Brown*, University Park, PA, 1998, pp. 17, 118, 139 and
fig. 19; Staley, 2001, pp. 35–6 and pl. 17

Sir Edward Coley Burne-Jones Bt ARA
(1833–1898)

30a–g
Seven Illustrations for 'The Fairy Family', 1854/56
Pen and ink on paper: two rectangular (14.5 × 9.8 cm),
one oval (7.4 × 5.8 cm), four circular (diam. 6.1 cm,
7.2 cm, 6.1 cm, 5.9 cm),
One inscribed: *The Sun. . .*
PROVENANCE
Mrs Eccles-Williams; acquired 1972
SELECTED REFERENCES
Burne-Jones, 1904, vol. 1, pp. 100, 120, 135–6; John
Christian, 'Burne-Jones's Drawings for "The Fairy
Family"', *Burlington Magazine*, February 1973,
pp. 93–100; Harrison and Waters, 1989, pp. 13, 16–19

Commissioned by Archibald Maclaren in 1853 as
illustrations to his volume of fairy stories. Burne-Jones
worked on dozens of drawings from 1854 to 1856,
but the book appeared in 1857 with only three
(unattributed) illustrations (London, 1975, no. 8).
The present group has become separated from
an album of some 41 further drawings, which also
survives (Pierpont Morgan Library, New York).

36
*Triptych: The Adoration of the Kings and the
Annunciation*, 1860–61
Oil on three canvases: 108 × 156.5 cm (central panel),
108 × 77.3 cm (side panels)
Frame, probably by Morris, Marshall, Faulkner & Co.,
inscribed: IN THE SIXTH MONTH THE ANGEL GABRIEL
WAS SENT / FROM GOD UNTO A CITY OF GALILEE NAMED
NAZARETH. (left panel); TO A VIRGIN ESPOUSED TO
A MAN WHOSE NAME WAS JOSEPH / OF THE HOUSE OF
DAVID AND THE VIRGIN'S NAME WAS MARY. (right panel);
NOW WHEN JESUS WAS BORN IN BETHLEHEM IN THE DAYS
OF HEROD THE KING BEHOLD THERE CAME WISE MEN
FROM THE EAST / SAYING WHERE IS HE THAT IS BORN KING
OF THE JEWS FOR WE HAVE SEEN HIS STAR IN THE EAST
AND ARE COME TO WORSHIP HIM. (central panel)
PROVENANCE
St Paul's Church, Brighton; acquired 1993
EXHIBITIONS
*Burne-Jones: The Paintings, Graphic and Decorative
Work of Sir Edward Burne-Jones 1833–98*, Hayward
Gallery, London, 1975, no. 67; on loan to Brighton
Museum and Art Gallery, 1976–93
SELECTED REFERENCES
Burne-Jones, 1904, vol. 1, pp. 223–4; Ronald Parkinson,
'Two Early Altar-pieces by Burne-Jones', *Apollo*,
November 1975, pp. 320–3

Painted for St Paul's Church, Brighton, at the instigation of the architect G. F. Bodley. A first version (oil on
canvas, 109 × 302 cm, 1860, Tate) was felt by the artist
to be too highly finished for viewing at a distance.

39
The Annunciation (The Flower of God), 1863
Watercolour and gouache on paper, 61 × 53.3 cm
Signed on label on reverse of frame
PROVENANCE
Edward Dalziel's sale, Christie's, 19 June 1886, lot 5,
bought William Coltart; A. M. Coltart; Maas Gallery,
1967; Lady Gibson; acquired 1992
EXHIBITIONS
Society of Painters in Water-Colours, London, 1864,
no. 200; Royal Jubilee Exhibition, Manchester, 1887,
no. 1300; Burne-Jones exhibition, New Gallery, London,
1892, no. 5; Burne-Jones exhibition, New Gallery,
London, 1898, no. 59; International Exhibition,
Glasgow, 1901, no. 1026; *Works by Pre-Raphaelite
Painters from Collections in Lancashire*, Tate Gallery,
London, 1913, no. 55; *Victorian Paintings*, Mappin
Gallery, Sheffield, 1968, no. 49; *The Pre-Raphaelites as*

Painters and Draughtsmen, Fermoy Art Gallery, King's
Lynn, 1971, no. 5; *Burne-Jones: The Paintings, Graphic
and Decorative Work of Sir Edward Burne-Jones
1833–98*, Hayward Gallery, London, 1975, no. 43;
Edward Burne-Jones: Victorian Artist–Dreamer,
Metropolitan Museum of Art, New York, 1998, no. 27
SELECTED REFERENCES
Athenaeum, 30 April 1864, p. 618; *Art Journal*, 1864,
p. 170; [Edward Clifford], *Broadlands as it Was*, London,
1890, p. 56; Bell, 1901, pp. 32–3, 129; George and
Edward Dalziel, *The Brothers Dalziel: A Record of Fifty
Years' Work*, London, 1901, pp. 164, 166, 254; de Lisle,
1904, pp. 63–4, 121, 180; Burne-Jones, 1904, vol. 1,
p. 261; Harrison and Waters, 1989, pp. 145, 180 and
col. pl. 10

Painted for the wood-engravers George and Edward
Dalziel as a 'private commission', i.e. not as a model
for a print. A smaller version, also painted in watercolour, for Burne-Jones' physician, Dr Radcliffe, was
with Agnew's in 1968.

37
Zephyrus and Psyche, 1865
Watercolour and gouache with gum arabic,
37 × 25.5 cm
Signed and dated on reverse
PROVENANCE
William Graham; his sale, Christie's, 3 April 1886,
lot 141; Gertrude, Countess of Pembroke, 1899;
Countess Brownlow; Christie's, 15 June 1971, lot 138;
Leger Galleries; Robert Walker, Paris; acquired 1993
EXHIBITIONS
Society of Painters in Water-Colours, London, 1866,
no. 304; Burne-Jones exhibition, New Gallery, London,
1898, no. 60; *Victorian Painting*, Fine Art Society,
London, 1977, no. 3
SELECTED REFERENCES
Art Journal, 1866, p. 174; *The Times*, 9 May 1866, p. 6;
Athenaeum, 5 May 1866, p. 604; de Lisle, 1904, pp. 85,
181; Bell, 1901, p. 35; Harrison and Waters, 1989, p. 84
and fig. 108

Based on a design for an unrealised illustration to
William Morris's poem 'Cupid and Pysche' (pen
and ink over pencil on paper, 10.8 × 8.6 cm, 1864,
Ashmolean Museum, Oxford; ill. Harrison and Waters,
1989, fig. 100).

38
The Princess Sabra Led to the Dragon, 1865–66,
reworked 1895
Oil on canvas, 108 × 96.6 cm
Initialled and dated 1866 lower left
PROVENANCE
Myles Birket Foster sale, Christie's, 28 April 1894,
lot 48/4, bought Agnew's; Major C. S. Goldman,
by 1898; Agnew's, 1901; Charles T. Yerkes, New York,
1910; Capt. J. R. De Lamar sale, American Art
Association, New York, 29 January 1920, lot 74;
Leander McCormick; Christie's, New York,
27 October 1982, lot 288; private collection, USA;
acquired 1991
EXHIBITIONS (shown with rest of St George series)
Thomas McLean Gallery, London, 1895, no. 4;
Gooden's Gallery, London, 1896; VII. Internationale
Kunstausstellung, Munich, 1897 (Gold Medal winner);
Burne-Jones exhibition, New Gallery, London, 1898,
no. 100
SELECTED REFERENCES
Bell, 1901, pp. 35–7; Burne-Jones, 1904, vol. 1,
pp. 295–6, 304; New York, 1998, p. 103 ill.

The fourth of seven paintings illustrating the legend
of St George and the Dragon, commissioned in 1865
by the artist Myles Birket Foster (see New York, 1998,
nos 31–6).

43
The Lament, after 1866
Oil on canvas, 27.9 × 38.7 cm
PROVENANCE
O. V. Watney; Mrs Blanche Watney; Christie's, 4 July 1967,
lot 57; acquired 1988

A later version of a work dated 1866 (watercolour
and gouache on paper, 47.5 × 79.5 cm) in the William
Morris Gallery, London (exhibited New York, 1998, no. 44).

47
Caritas, 1867/71, 1885
Watercolour and gouache, heightened with gold paint,
on paper, 152 × 68.5 cm
Inscribed lower left: *EB-J / LONDON MDCCCLXVII*
PROVENANCE
Purchased from the artist c. 1871/72 by F. S. Ellis; his
sale, Christie's, 16 May 1885, lot 92, bought Lord
Wantage, and still in his collection in 1902; Christie's,
15 June 1973, lot 69; Michael Hasenclever, Munich;
acquired 1993
EXHIBITIONS
Burne-Jones exhibition, New Gallery, London, 1892,
no. 35; *Fair Children*, Grafton Galleries, London, 1895,
no. 192; Burne-Jones exhibition, New Gallery, London,
1898, no. 105; *Burne-Jones: The Paintings, Graphic and
Decorative Work of Sir Edward Burne-Jones 1833–98*,
Hayward Gallery, London, 1975, no. 113; *Burne-Jones
and His Followers*, Isetan Museum of Art, Tokyo, 1987,
no. 16
SELECTED REFERENCES
Bell, 1901, pp. 41–2 and ill. facing p. 40; *Catalogue of
the . . . Collection of Lord and Lady Wantage*, London,
1902, no. 32; de Lisle, 1904, p. 104; George Charles
Williamson, *Murray Marks and his Friends*, London,
1919, pp. 100–2; Sewter, 1974–75, vol. 2, p. 86

Apparently a reworking of the cartoon for a stained-
glass window for the Old West Kirk at Greenock,
Renfrewshire. A small study for the composition
(watercolour on paper) was sold at Christie's, 23 July
1974, lot 65.

48
The Mirror of Venus, 1867–77
Oil on canvas, 79 × 122 cm
PROVENANCE
Purchased from the artist by William Graham; his sale,
Christie's, 3 April 1886, lot 159, bought Charles Butler
for £819; by descent; acquired 1983
EXHIBITION
Mirror Image: Jonathan Miller on Reflection, National
Gallery, London, 1998
SELECTED REFERENCES
Bell, 1901, pp. 39, 57, 130; de Lisle, 1904, pp. 101, 181;
Jonathan Miller, *On Reflection*, London, 1998, p. 59;
Kate Flint, 'Edward Burne-Jones's *The Mirror of Venus*:
Surface and Subjectivity in the Art Criticism of the
1870s', in Elizabeth Prettejohn (ed.), *After the Pre-
Raphaelites: Art and Aestheticism in Victorian England*,
Manchester, 1999, pp. 152–64 (on the reception of
the larger version at the Grosvenor Gallery in 1877)

Other versions: oil on canvas, 122 × 199.5 cm,
1873–77, Gulbenkian Foundation, Lisbon (exhibited
Grosvenor Gallery, London, 1877); oil on canvas,
76.2 × 121.9 cm, c. 1868 (virtually monochrome nude
study), Forbes Collection sale, Christie's, 19 February
2003, lot 24

49a–d
Pygmalion and the Image, 1868/70
a: 'The heart desires'
b: 'The hand refrains'
c: 'The godhead fires'
d: 'The soul attains'

Oil on four canvases, each 66 × 51 cm
All initialled, 49a dated 1868, 49c and 49d dated 1870
All possibly retouched in 1883

PROVENANCE
Commissioned by Euphrosyne Cassavetti, 1868;
by descent; Sotheby's, 11 October 1967, lots 12, 13;
Joseph Setton; Julian Hartnoll Ltd; acquired 1993

EXHIBITION
Viktorianische Malerei von Turner bis Whistler, Neue
Pinakothek, Munich, 1993, no. 71

SELECTED REFERENCES
Harrison and Waters, 1989, p. 84 and col. pl. 20–3;
Stephen Wildman, in New York, 1998, p. 221 n. 2 (on
1883 possible retouching)

A repetition of the series, all 99 × 76.3 cm, 1875–78,
in the Birmingham City Museum and Art Gallery
(exhibited New York, 1998, no. 87).

40
Night, 1870
Watercolour and gouache on paper, 79 × 56 cm
Signed and dated lower right

PROVENANCE
Frederick Craven; his sale, Christie's, 18 May 1895,
lot 53; H. W. Henderson; Agnew's, 1967; E. M. W.
Griffith; acquired 1998

EXHIBITIONS
Society of Painters in Water-Colours, London, 1870,
no. 136; *Burne-Jones: The Paintings, Graphic and
Decorative Work of Sir Edward Burne-Jones 1833–98*,
Hayward Gallery, London, 1975, no. 103; *Burne-Jones
and his Followers*, Isetan Museum, Tokyo, 1987, no. 11;
*The Age of Rossetti, Burne-Jones and Watts: Symbolism
in Britain, 1860–1910*, Tate Gallery, London, 1997, no. 27

41
Vesper (The Evening Star), 1872–73
Watercolour, gouache and gold paint on paper,
79 × 56 cm
Initialled lower left

PROVENANCE
Frederick Craven; his sale, Christie's, 18 May 1895,
lot 52; H. W. Henderson; Agnew's, 1967; E. M. W.
Griffith; acquired 1998

EXHIBITIONS
Burne-Jones exhibition, New Gallery, London, 1898,
no. 80; *Burne-Jones: The Paintings, Graphic and
Decorative Work of Sir Edward Burne-Jones 1833–98*,
Hayward Gallery, London, 1975, no. 102; *The Pre-
Raphaelites*, Tate Gallery, London, 1984, no. 247;
Burne-Jones and His Followers, Isetan Museum, Tokyo,
1987, no. 12; *The Age of Rossetti, Burne-Jones and
Watts: Symbolism in Britain, 1860–1910*, Tate Gallery,
London, 1997, no. 26

SELECTED REFERENCES
Bell, 1901, p. 50; Burne-Jones, 1904, vol. 2, p. 29

Another version, *Evening* (same media and dimensions,
dated 1870), has the figure dressed in white, head
turned away; ex-collection Earl of Carlisle; exhibited
Society of Painters in Water-Colours, London, 1870,
no. 45; ill. in Harrison and Waters, 1989, col. pl. 28.

34
The Judgement of Paris, early 1870s
Oil on canvas, 107.2 × 69.2 cm

PROVENANCE
The artist's second studio sale, Christie's, 5 June 1919,
lot 186, bought Gooden & Fox; acquired 1978

SELECTED REFERENCES
Bell, 1901, p. 25; Harrison and Waters, 1989, p. 108

Probably developed from the abandoned *Troy Triptych*,
designed in 1870, which was to have had this subject
as its central panel, although the *modello* for the

whole work shows a different composition (this
was largely the work of T. M. Rooke: oil on canvas,
275 × 298 cm, Birmingham City Museum and Art
Gallery; ill. Harrison and Waters, 1989, fig. 144, and
New York, 1998, no. 50). A drawing of a similar
composition to cat. 34 (pencil on paper, 16 × 9 cm)
was sold at Sotheby's, 20 March 1979, lot 9 (as
A Study for 'The Judgement of Paris').

31
Love and Beauty, 1874
Chalks on paper, 89 × 118 cm
Initialled and dated lower right; inscribed:
THE GARDEN OF / IDLENESSE (upper right),
LOVE (centre), *BEAUTE* (upper left)

PROVENANCE
Acquired 1994

SELECTED REFERENCES
Harrison and Waters, 1989, p. 117; New York, 1998,
pp. 180–7, ill. p. 181

Relates to the tapestry 'The Pilgrim in the Garden of
Idlenesse' from the series *The Romaunt of the Rose*,
William Morris Gallery, London (exhibited New York,
1998, no. 72).

42
Music, 1876
Oil on canvas, 68.9 × 45.1 cm
Initialled and dated lower left

PROVENANCE
Sold by the artist to a Mr Benjamin, 1876; Mrs R. H.
Benson, by 1898; Christie's, 21 June 1929, lot 94,
bought David Croal Thomson for 105 guineas;
Mortimer Brandt Gallery, New York, by 1950, when
purchased by Mrs Amalie Nelson; her daughter
Mrs Molly Williams of Morrilton, AR; acquired 1997

EXHIBITIONS
Burne-Jones exhibition, New Gallery, London, 1898,
no. 75; on loan to Arkansas Art Center, 1994, 1996

SELECTED REFERENCES
The Work of Edward Burne-Jones: 91 Photogravures,
London, 1901, no. 3; Bell, 1901, p. 130; de Lisle, 1904,
p. 184 (as a watercolour)

A version in oil, painted in 1877 for William Graham,
was sold at Christie's, 13 April 1934, lot 33.

61a, b
a: *The Vision of St Catherine*, c. 1878
b: *The Entombment of St Catherine*, c. 1878
Grey and brown wash with gouache on buff paper,
90 × 61.7 cm (a) and 89.7 × 61.3 cm (b)

PROVENANCE
Mrs Aglaia Coronio, by 1898; acquired 1980

EXHIBITION
Burne-Jones exhibition, New Gallery, London, 1898,
nos 185, 186

SELECTED REFERENCE
Sewter, 1974–75, vol. 1, fig. 530, 532; vol. 2, p. 146

Cartoon for a window in Christ Church Cathedral,
Oxford.

52
Philip Comyns Carr, 1882
Oil on canvas, 71 × 48.5 cm
Monogrammed and dated; inscribed on cartouche:
Philip Comyns Carr / London / to CAJ

PROVENANCE
J. Comyns Carr, 1898; Major C. S. Goldman; by descent;
acquired 1989

EXHIBITIONS
Grosvenor Gallery, London, 1883, no. 83; Burne-Jones
exhibition, New Gallery, London, 1892, no. 25; Burne-
Jones exhibition, New Gallery, London, 1898, no. 67

SELECTED REFERENCES
Art Journal, 1883, p. 203; Cosmo Monkhouse, in *The
Academy*, 5 May 1883, p. 316; Eve Adam (ed.), *Mrs. J.
Comyns Carr's Reminiscences*, London, 1925, pp. 60–2,
ill.; Bell, 1901, p. 62; Burne-Jones, 1904, vol. 1, p. 128

35
King Cophetua and the Beggar Maid, 1883
Gouache and gum arabic on paper, 72.3 × 37 cm
Initialled and dated lower left corner (faded or
erased); initialled and dated above earlier inscription

PROVENANCE
The artist's daughter Margaret; by descent; acquired
1990

EXHIBITION
Burne-Jones exhibition, New Gallery, London, 1898,
no. 139

SELECTED REFERENCES
W. S. Taylor, 'King Cophetua and the Beggar Maid',
Apollo, February 1973, pp. 148–55; Harrison and
Waters, 1989, fig. 200; New York, 1998, p. 253 ill.

Other versions: oil on canvas, 293.4 × 135.9 cm, dated
1884, Tate (exhibited Grosvenor Gallery, London,
1884); oil on panel, 154 × 71 cm, Sotheby's, New York,
23–24 May 1996, lot 160; gouache, chalks and gold
paint on paper, 290 × 132 cm, Birmingham City
Museum and Art Gallery; mixed media on paper,
75 × 31 cm, private collection (exhibited *Burne-Jones,
dal Preraffaellismo al simbolismo*, Galleria Nazionale
d'Arte Moderna, Rome, 1986, no. 58).

58
Christ Enthroned, 1883/84
Pastel, gouache and gold paint on paper,
68.6 × 42.5 cm

PROVENANCE
The artist's daughter Margaret; by descent; Christie's,
17 November 1970, lot 175, bought Piccadilly Gallery;
Michael Hasenclever, Munich; acquired 1979

EXHIBITIONS
On loan to Leighton House, London, 1927–70; *Burne-
Jones*, Mappin Art Gallery, Sheffield, 1971, no. 164

SELECTED REFERENCES
Bell, 1901, pp. 85–6; de Lisle, 1904, pp. 145–6; Richard
Dorment, 'Burne-Jones's Roman Mosaics', *Burlington
Magazine*, February 1978, pp. 73–82; Maria Teresa
Benedetti, 'Il mosaico della chiesa di S. Paolo entro
le Mura', in *Burne-Jones, dal Preraffaellismo al
simbolismo*, exh. cat., Galleria Nazionale d'Arte
Moderna, Rome, 1986, pp. 185–91, ill. p. 188

A design for the mosaic decoration installed in 1885
in the apse of the American Episcopal Church of
St Paul's Within-the-Walls, Rome (see also cat. 59, 62).

59
The Archangel Zophiel, 1883/84
Gouache on board, 51.5 × 26.5 cm
Inscribed lower right: *ZOPHIEL*

PROVENANCE
The artist's daughter Margaret; by descent; Christie's,
17 November 1970, lot 176, bought Agnew's; Dr and
Mrs Robert Mandelbaum, New York; acquired 1980

EXHIBITION
On loan to Leighton House, London, 1927–70

SELECTED REFERENCES
See cat. 58

A design for the mosaic decoration installed in 1885
in the apse of the American Episcopal Church of
St Paul's Within-the-Walls, Rome (see also cat. 58, 62).

44
Flamma Vestalis, 1886
Oil on canvas, 107.9 × 37.4 cm
Initialled and dated lower right

PROVENANCE
Sir Horace Davey, by 1892; Sir Henry Tate; by descent
to Mrs Robert Grosvenor; Sotheby's, 19 November 1969,
lot 160; private collection, Switzerland; acquired 1996

EXHIBITIONS
Grosvenor Gallery, London, 1886, no. 1; St Jude's,
Whitechapel, London, 1889, no. 40; Burne-Jones
exhibition, New Gallery, London, 1892, no. 22;
Burne-Jones exhibition, New Gallery, London, 1898,
no. 129; *Burne-Jones: The Paintings, Graphic and
Decorative Work of Sir Edward Burne-Jones 1833–98*,
Hayward Gallery, London, 1975, no. 154

SELECTED REFERENCES
Theodore Child, 'Pictures in London and Paris',
Fortnightly Review, June 1886, pp. 789–90; *Magazine
of Art*, 1886, pp. 347–8; *Illustrated London News*,
8 May 1886, p. 498; Cartwright, 1894, pp. 23–5; Bell,
1901, p. 63; Burne-Jones, 1904, vol. 2, p. 165

A version in oil on canvas, 65 × 43 cm, dated 1896,
with a half-length figure (exhibited New Gallery,
London, 1898, no. 64) was sold at Sotheby's, 20 June
1989, lot 72.

46
The Sleeping Princess, 1886/88
Gouache with gold paint on paper, 96.5 × 147.5 cm
Inscribed lower left: *EB-J to MJM 1886–1888*

PROVENANCE
Given by the artist to his daughter Margaret (the
model for the princess), apparently on her marriage
to J. W. Mackail, 1888; by descent; Sotheby's, 23 March
1981, lot 23; acquired 1988

EXHIBITIONS
Burne-Jones exhibition, New Gallery, London, 1892,
no. 120; Burne-Jones exhibition, New Gallery, London,
1898, no. 62; Burne-Jones centenary exhibition, Tate
Gallery, London, 1933, no. 28; *Burne-Jones: The
Paintings, Graphic and Decorative Work of Sir Edward
Burne-Jones 1833–98*, Hayward Gallery, London, 1975,
no. 181; on loan to Mappin Art Gallery, Sheffield, 1980

SELECTED REFERENCE
Harrison and Waters, 1989, fig. 208

A simplified version of the 'Rose Bower' composition
from the *Briar Rose* series. Other versions: from the
small *Briar Rose* series for William Graham, oil on
canvas, 60 × 115 cm, dated 1871, Museo de Arte de
Ponce, Puerto Rico (exhibited New York, 1998, no. 58);
watercolour and gold paint on vellum, 27 × 37.6 cm,
dated 1871, Manchester City Art Gallery (ill. Harrison
and Waters, 1989, fig. 128); oil on canvas, 125 × 231
cm, 1886–90, Faringdon Collection, Buscot Park
(National Trust); oil on canvas, 126 × 237 cm, 1894,
Hugh Lane Gallery, Dublin

55
Study for 'Katie Lewis', c. 1886
Black chalk on buff paper, 52 × 120.5 cm

PROVENANCE
Sir George Lewis, the sitter's father; by descent;
acquired 1995

Study for the portrait of Katie Lewis reading, 1886,
oil on canvas, 61 × 127 cm (same provenance to 1995),
Christie's, 14 June 2000, lot 20 (exhibited New York,
1998, no. 118).

57
The Adoration of the Magi (The Star of Bethlehem),
1887/88
Watercolour, gouache and gold paint on paper,
64.5 × 98.5 cm

PROVENANCE
The artist's daughter Margaret, and by descent;
Christie's, 7 March 1972, lot 147; bought Leger;
Sotheby's, 1 October 1979, lot 14; acquired 1993

EXHIBITIONS
Burne-Jones Drawings and Studies, Burlington Fine Arts Club, London, 1899, no. 83; *English Watercolours*, Leger Galleries, London, 1972, no. 64; *Morris and Company*, Fine Art Society, London, 1979, no. 184

SELECTED REFERENCES
Strand Magazine, 1895, p. 25; Stephen Wildman, in New York, 1998, p. 293 and under nos 141, 142

A study for the Morris & Co. tapestry made for Exeter College, Oxford (exhibited London, 1975, no. 226), using a full-scale cartoon photographically enlarged from this study (Victoria and Albert Museum, London). Another version was commissioned by Birmingham Corporation in 1887 (fig. 3, p. 70)

56a–f
Six Studies for 'The Adoration of the Magi (The Star of Bethlehem)', 1887
a: *The Virgin*, 30.8 × 18.7 cm
b: *Melchior*, 33.7 × 16.5 cm
c: *Gaspar*, 32.3 × 23.2 cm
d: *Joseph*, 33.7 × 16.5 cm
e: *Gaspar*, 33.7 × 16.5 cm
f: *Balthazar*, 33.7 × 16.5 cm
Chalks with gold paint on buff paper
Each initialled and dated

PROVENANCE
Sir J. Stirling-Maxwell; Agnew's; Sotheby's, acquired 1993

EXHIBITIONS
Burne-Jones exhibition, New Gallery, London, 1898, nos 165, 166, 170 (three only); *Burne-Jones Drawings and Studies*, Burlington Fine Arts Club, London, 1899

SELECTED REFERENCE
Stephen Wildman, in New York, 1998, pp. 294, 296 n. 12

From a group of seven studies of individual figures for the *Adoration of the Magi* tapestries and the Birmingham watercolour (see fig. 3, p. 70); the seventh, *Balthazar*, is in Birmingham City Museum and Art Gallery.

51
Dorothy Mattersdorf, 1893
Oil on canvas, 64 × 42.5 cm
Initialled and dated lower left

PROVENANCE
Acquired 1992

SELECTED REFERENCE
Burne-Jones, 1904, vol. 2, p. 235 ('The work-list for 1893 includes mention of four portraits in hand – an unusual thing')

50
Amy Gaskell, 1893
Oil on canvas, 96.5 × 52 cm
Initialled and dated lower left; inscribed on reverse: AMY GASKELL, 1893 / painted by EDWARD BURNE-JONES / and given to her Mother

PROVENANCE
Helen Mary Gaskell, mother of the sitter; by descent; Sotheby's, 23 March 1981, lot 27; acquired 1993

EXHIBITIONS
New Gallery, London, 1894, no. 155; Burne-Jones exhibition, New Gallery, London, 1898, no. 85; Burne-Jones centenary exhibition, Tate Gallery, London, 1933, no. 16; *Burne-Jones: The Paintings, Graphic and Decorative Work of Sir Edward Burne-Jones 1833–98*, Hayward Gallery, London, 1975, no. 245

SELECTED REFERENCES
Art Journal, 1894, p. 191; Cartwright, 1894, pp. 26–7; Robert de La Sizeranne, *La Peinture anglaise contemporaine*, Paris, 1895, p. 194; Bell, 1901, p. 68; de Lisle, 1904, p. 155; *The Age of Rossetti, Burne-Jones and Watts: Symbolism in Britain, 1860–1910*, exh. cat., Tate Gallery, London, 1997, p. 32 ill.

62
The Fall of Lucifer, 1894
Gouache and gold paint on paper laid down on canvas and stretched over board, 245 × 118 cm
Initialled and dated lower right; frame inscribed with Vulgate text of *Revelation XII*, 7–12

PROVENANCE
Artist's first studio sale, Christie's, 16 July 1898, lot 90, bought Agnew's, but apparently also in second studio sale, Christie's, 5 June 1919, lot 143; David Grieg, by 1933; Sotheby's, 14 April 1965, lot 48; Robert Walker, by 1973; acquired 1981

EXHIBITIONS
New Gallery, London, 1895, no. 106; Burne-Jones exhibition, New Gallery, London, 1898, no. 119; Japan–British Exhibition, White City, London, 1910 (see *Official Report*, 1911, p. 330, for photograph of installation); Burne-Jones centenary exhibition, Tate Gallery, London, 1933, no. 2; *Burne-Jones: The Paintings, Graphic and Decorative Work of Sir Edward Burne-Jones 1833–98*, Hayward Gallery, London, 1975, no. 190

SELECTED REFERENCES
Cartwright, 1894, p. 32; *Magazine of Art*, 1895, pp. 285–6; Bell, 1901, p. 69; de Lisle, 1904, p. 186; Burne-Jones, 1904, vol. 2, pp. 257–8; Harrison and Waters, 1989, p. 134 and col. pl. 33

A rejected design for the mosaic decoration of St Paul's-Within-the-Walls, Rome (see cat. 58, 59).

54
Study for 'The Sleeping Princess', 1894
Red chalk heightened with white on pink paper, 26 × 31.7 cm
Initialled and dated lower left

PROVENANCE
Acquired 1997

Apparently relates to the attendant seated lower right in the 'Rose Bower' from the *Briar Rose* series, the last version of which has been dated to 1894 (see cat. 46).

32
The Challenge in the Wilderness, c. 1894/98
Oil on canvas, 129.5 × 96.5 cm

PROVENANCE
Artist's studio sale, Christie's, 16 July 1898, lot 80, bought Agnew's; Sir John T. Middlemore; sold by the Middlemore Trustees, 1973; Hartnoll & Eyre; Christie's, 19 May 1978, lot 243; acquired 1993

EXHIBITIONS
On loan to Birmingham City Museum and Art Gallery prior to sale in 1973; *Burne-Jones: The Paintings, Graphic and Decorative Work of Sir Edward Burne-Jones 1833–98*, Hayward Gallery, London, 1975, no. 191; *Burne-Jones and His Followers*, Isetan Museum of Art, Tokyo, 1987, no. 30; *Edward Burne-Jones: Victorian Artist–Dreamer*, Metropolitan Museum of Art, New York, 1998, no. 42

SELECTED REFERENCES
Cartwright, 1894, p. 31; Harrison and Waters, 1989, col. pl. 39

Begun by 1894, the painting remained unfinished. It is derived from one of a series of pictures painted for George Howard, Earl of Carlisle, and now in Birmingham City Museum and Art Gallery (exhibited New York, 1998, no. 40b). A drawing of the composition of cat. 32 (black chalk on paper, 28 × 20.6 cm) was sold at Christie's, 15 May 1984, lot 177.

53
Cicely Horner (later Mrs George Lambton), 1895
Oil on canvas, 73.3 × 45.2 cm

PROVENANCE
Commissioned by the sitter's father, (Sir) John Horner, as a present for his wife; by descent until sold at Sotheby's, 1 July 1975, lot 37; acquired 1995

SELECTED REFERENCES
Harrison and Waters, 1989, col. pl. 46; Penelope Fitzgerald, *Burne-Jones: A Biography*, London, 1975, p. 261

The sitter (1883–1972) was a granddaughter of Burne-Jones's patron William Graham.

60
St Luke, 1890s (?)
Gouache and charcoal on canvas, 141 × 68.6 cm

PROVENANCE
Artist's second studio sale, Christie's, 5 June 1919, lot 163/2 (as *St John*); Christie's, 19 November 1965, lot 42 (as *St John*); Maas Gallery; Sally Oliver; acquired 2001

EXHIBITIONS
Morris & Company in Cambridge, Fitzwilliam Museum, Cambridge, 1980, no. 55; *Burne-Jones, Dal preraffaelismo al simbolismo*, Galleria Nazionale d'Arte Moderna, Rome, 1986, no. 96; *Edward Burne-Jones: Victorian Artist–Dreamer*, Metropolitan Museum of Art, New York, 1998, no. 68

SELECTED REFERENCE
Sewter, 1974–75, vol. 1, pl. 424; vol. 2, p. 43

Reprise of a motif used in 1872 in a cartoon for a stained-glass window at Jesus College, Cambridge (pencil, pastel and gouache on paper, 122.4 × 51.6 cm, Tate).

45a, b
Two Studies of a Woman's Head, date unknown
Pencil on paper, each 22.5 × 16.5 cm

PROVENANCE
D. H. Idwal Jones; acquired 1972

James Campbell (c. 1825/1828–1893)

158
The Old Sailor's Yarn, first exhibited 1859 (?)
Oil on canvas, 30.5 × 25.4 cm

PROVENANCE
Christopher Wood Gallery; acquired 1995

EXHIBITIONS
Probably Liverpool Academy, 1859, no. 292 (as *A Visit to the Old Sailor*).

Giovanni Antonio Canal, called Canaletto (1697–1768)

283
The Old Horse Guards, London, from St James's Park, c. 1749
Oil on canvas, 117 × 236 cm
The Andrew Lloyd Webber Art Foundation

PROVENANCE
John Roberts, 4th Earl of Radnor, Cross Deep, Twickenham, Middlesex, by 1756; bequeathed by him to James Harris MP, 1757; by descent to the Earls of Malmesbury; acquired for the Andrew Lloyd Webber Art Foundation, 1992

EXHIBITIONS
Canaletto's lodgings, Silver St (now Beak St), London, 1749; Burlington Fine Arts Club, London, 1926, no. 36; *Pictures from Hampshire House*, Winchester, 1938, no. 33; *Coronation Exhibition of 35 Masterpieces of Venetian Painting*, Agnew's, London, 1953, no. 8; *European Masters of the Eighteenth Century*, RA, London, 1954, no. 7; *Canaletto*, Art Gallery of Ontario, Toronto, 1964, no. 104; *I vedutisti veneziani del settecento*, Palazzo Ducale, Venice, 1967, no. 75; on loan to the Tate Gallery, London, after 1992 sale; *Canaletto and England*, Birmingham City Museum and Art Gallery, 1993, no. 19

SELECTED REFERENCES
Daily Advertiser, 25 July 1749; George Vertue, *Notebooks*, vol. 3 (Walpole Society, 1933–34), p. 151; William T. Whitley, *Artists and their Friends in England, 1700–1799*, London, 1928, vol. 1, pp. 115–6; J. G. Links, *Canaletto: The Complete Paintings*, London, 1981, no. 219; W. G. Constable, rev. J. G. Links, *Canaletto*, Oxford, 1989, vol. 2, no. 415; Elizabeth Einberg, *Canaletto: The Old Horse Guards from St. James's Park*, London, 1992; J. G. Links, *Canaletto*, London, 1994, pp. 172–3 and pl. 152

A related drawing is in the British Museum, London (pen and ink on paper, 34.6 × 68.8 cm; Constable, 1989, no. 734). A different view (oil on canvas, 47.3 × 76.8 cm) was sold at Christie's, 17 November 1989, lot 4.

James Collinson (1825–1881)

162
The Emigration Scheme, first exhibited 1852
Oil on panel, 56.5 × 76.2 cm

PROVENANCE
Bought from the Liverpool Academy exhibition by William King; by descent; Sotheby's, 15 March 1967, lot 92; acquired 1994

EXHIBITIONS
National Institution (Portland Gallery), London, 1852, no. 286; Liverpool Academy, 1852, no. 238; *Narrative Pictures*, Leger Galleries, London, 1937, no. 51; *Victorian Life*, Leicester Galleries, London, 1937, no. 107; Burlington Fine Arts Club, London, 1938, no. 120; *The Pre-Raphaelites*, Birmingham City Museum and Art Gallery, 1947, no. 18; *British Life*, New Burlington Galleries, London (Arts Council of Great Britain), 1953, no. 90; *Victorian Paintings*, Festival Club, Aldeburgh (Arts Council of Great Britain), 1962, no. 10; *Victorian Painting*, Agnew's, London, 1961, no. 131

SELECTED REFERENCES
William Michael Rossetti, in *Spectator*, 1 May 1852, p. 422; *Art Journal*, 1852, p. 140; Thomas Bodkin, 'James Collinson', *Apollo*, May 1940, p. 132, fig. v; Graham Reynolds, *Painters of the Victorian Scene*, London, 1953, p. 73 and pl. 44; Alastair Grieve, *The Art of Dante Gabriel Rossetti, 1: 'Found'; 2: The Pre-Raphaelite Modern-Life Subject*, Norwich, 1976, pp. 21–2 and fig. 2; Wood, 1976, pp. 221–2 and pl. 233; Ronald Parkinson, 'James Collinson', in London, 1984, pp. 70, 241 n. 25; R.W. Peattie, 'W. M. Rossetti's Reviews of James Collinson', *The Journal of Pre-Raphaelite Studies* 5, 2, May 1985, pp. 101–2, 104

Thomas Sidney Cooper RA (1803–1902)

173
Near Herne Bay (On the North-East Coast of Kent), 1884
Oil on canvas, 121 × 182 cm
Signed and dated

PROVENANCE
J. D. Allcroft of Stokesay Court, Shropshire; acquired 1994

EXHIBITION
RA, 1885, no. 84

SELECTED REFERENCES
Kentish Gazette, 31 March 1885; Thomas Sidney Cooper, *My Life*, 2nd edn, London 1891, p. 400 (listed)

Richard Dadd (1817–1886)

115
Contradiction: Oberon and Titania, 1854/58
Oil on canvas, oval, 61 × 75.5 cm
Signed and dated lower left; inscribed on reverse: *Contradiction / Oberon & Titania / Midsummer Night's*

Dream Act. 2. Scene. 2 [sic] / Painted for W. C. Hood. Esqre. MD. &c. / by Rd. Dadd. / A.D. 1854–58

PROVENANCE

Dr William Charles Hood; his sale, Christie's, 28 March 1870, lot 332A, bought Holl for 136 guineas; Arthur Crossland; Thomas Laughton; Sotheby's, 18 March 1964, lot 42; R. F. Needler, Hull; Sotheby's, 15 March 1983, lot 25; Regis Collection, Minneapolis; Myron Kunin, Chicago; acquired 1992

EXHIBITIONS

Jubilee Exhibition, Art Gallery, Bradford, 1930, no. 468; *Victorian Paintings*, Mappin Art Gallery, Sheffield, 1968, no. 58; *Collectors' Choice*, Ferens Art Gallery, Hull, 1970, no. 49; *The Late Richard Dadd*, Tate Gallery, London, 1974, no. 172; *Zwei Jahrhunderte englische [sic] Malerei: Britisch Kunst und Europa 1680 bis 1880*, Haus der Kunst, Munich, 1979, no. 325; on loan to the Minneapolis Institute of Arts, from 1983; *Objects of Adornment*, Minneapolis Institute of Arts, 1986; on loan to the Art Institute of Chicago, 1991–92; *Victorian Fairy Painting*, RA, 1997, no. 26

SELECTED REFERENCES

Laurence Binyon, 'A Note on Richard Dadd', *Magazine of Art*, 2 February 1937, p. 125; Sacheverell Sitwell, *Narrative Pictures*, London, 1937, p. 72; Jeremy Maas, *Victorian Painters*, London, 1969, pp. 151–2; David Greysmith, *Richard Dadd: The Rock and Castle of Seclusion*, London, 1973, pp. 66, 76, 81, 82, 121, 124, 179 and pl. 89; Patricia Allderidge, *Richard Dadd*, London, 1974, pp. 29–31, 97–8 and col. pl. VII; Patricia Allderidge, in *The Late Richard Dadd*, exh. cat., Tate Gallery, London, 1974, frontispiece (photograph of Dadd working on the picture), pp. 30, 35, 42–3, 114–17, 120; Peter Fuller, 'Richard Dadd', *Arts Review*, 28 June 1974, p. 395; Robert Hughes, 'From the dark garden of the mind', *Time Magazine*, 8 July 1974, pp. 64–5; Peter Fuller, 'Richard Dadd: A Psychological Interpretation', *Connoisseur*, July 1974, pp. 172, 176–7; Keith Roberts, in the *Burlington Magazine*, August 1974, pp. 488–9; Allen Staley, 'Richard Dadd of Bedlam', *Art in America*, November–December 1974, pp. 80, 82; John M. MacGregor, *The Discovery of the Art of the Insane*, Princeton, NJ, 1989, pp. 126, 127 and pl. 9

Painted for Dr William Charles Hood, physician superintendent of the Bethlem Hospital, London, where the artist was an inmate.

Evelyn De Morgan (1855–1919)

87

The World's Wealth (The Crown of Glory), 1896
Oil on canvas, 104.7 × 53.7 cm
Initialled and dated lower right

PROVENANCE

Bought from the artist by William Imrie; his sale, Christie's, 28 June 1907, lot 127, bought Boswell; Vaughan-Lee family; Christie's, 29 November 1985, lot 96; Sotheby's, 21 November 1989, lot 59; acquired 1991

EXHIBITIONS

Evelyn De Morgan, Wolverhampton Art Gallery, 1907, no. 27; *Evelyn De Morgan*, Russell-Cotes Art Gallery, Bournemouth, 1996, no. 46

SELECTED REFERENCE

Anna M. W. Stirling, *William De Morgan and his Wife*, London, 1922, p. 192

Sir Frank Dicksee PRA (1853–1928)

151a–k

Eleven Scenes from 'Romeo and Juliet', c. 1881–82
a: 'Rival Factions'
b: 'The Invitation'
c: 'The Ball Scene'
d: 'Friar Laurence'
e: 'Friar Laurence'

f: 'The Death of Tybalt'
g: 'Friar Laurence's Cell'
h: 'Juliet and Nurse'
i: 'Juliet's Chamber'
j: 'The Visit to the Apothecary'
k: 'The Tomb'

Gouache *en grisaille* on paper (four with arched tops); smallest: 17.2 × 11.1 cm; largest: 31.1 × 43.9 cm
All initialled, three dated 1882

PROVENANCE

Volkins & Co.; acquired 1989

EXHIBITION

Dudley Gallery, London, 1881, nos 236, 238

SELECTED REFERENCE

E. Rimbault Dibdin, 'Frank Dicksee, RA: His Life and Work', *The Art Annual*, 1905, p. 8

Commissioned by the publisher Cassell to be reproduced in photogravure for their 1884 edition of Shakespeare's play.

149

The Mirror, 1896
Oil on canvas, 95.3 × 118.1 cm
Signed and dated lower right

PROVENANCE

Sir Edward Waterlow; Philip H. Waterlow, by 1905; Frost & Reed; Castano Galleries, Boston; Priscilla Juvelis, Boston; acquired 1993

EXHIBITION

RA, 1896, no. 202

SELECTED REFERENCES

Art Journal, 1896, p. 172; Henry Blackburn (ed.), *Academy Notes*, London, 1896, p. 10; *The Studio*, 1896, p. 110; E. Rimbault Dibdin, 'Frank Dicksee, RA: His Life and Work', *The Art Annual*, 1905, pp. 13, 15–16

Sir (Samuel) Luke Fildes RA (1843–1927)

161

The Village Wedding, 1883
Oil on canvas, 151.8 × 255.3 cm
Signed and dated lower left

PROVENANCE

Bought from the artist by Agnew's for 2,500 guineas; Edward K. Harrison, Shortlands; Christie's, 8 May 1886, lot 131, bought Thomas McLean Gallery for 1,050 guineas; Edward Brooke, 1887; by descent to Mrs S. A. Birkbeck; her sale, Christie's, 26 November 1982, lot 340; Christopher Wood Gallery; Richard Manney, New York; acquired 1992

EXHIBITIONS

RA, 1883, no. 515; Royal Jubilee Exhibition, Manchester, 1887, Fine Arts section, no. 222; Centenary Exhibition, Southport, 1892; International Exhibition, Glasgow, 1901; loan exhibition, Municipal Art Gallery, Hull, 1904, no. 83; *Historical Exhibition of Liverpool Art*, Walker Art Gallery, Liverpool, 1908, no. 77

SELECTED REFERENCES

Manuscript correspondence between Fildes and his brother-in-law Henry Woods RA, 1881–82, National Art Library, London, 86.PP.3; *Athenaeum*, 5 May 1883, p. 576; *Illustrated London News*, 12 May 1883, pp. 470–1; Henry Blackburn (ed.), *Academy Notes*, London, 1883, p. 50; *Manchester Royal Jubilee Exhibition: Critical Notices of the Exhibition*, London, 1887, pp. 23–4; Sir Walter Armstrong, *Celebrated Pictures at the Manchester Exhibition*, London, 1888, p. 31; 'Illustrated Interviews, XXV: Mr. Luke Fildes, RA', *Strand Magazine*, 1893, pp. 115–16; David Croal Thomson, 'Luke Fildes RA: His Life and Work', *Art Annual*, 1895, pp. 9–11, 32; L. V. Fildes, *Luke Fildes, R.A.: A Victorian Painter*, London, 1968, pp. 71–5, 77, 79, 82–3, 85–6, 92, 99, 109 and ill. facing p. 82; Wood, 1976, fig. 77A; Christopher Wood, *Paradise Lost*, London, 1988, pp. 16, 206.

166

Venetian Life, 1884
Oil on canvas, 214 × 158 cm
Signed and dated lower right

PROVENANCE

John Aird; acquired 1989

EXHIBITIONS

RA, 1884, no. 390; RA, Winter 1928; on loan to Keele University to 1988

SELECTED REFERENCES

Magazine of Art, 1884, p. 351; *The Times*, 3 May 1884, p. 7, and 12 May 1884, p. 4; *Art Journal*, 1884, p. 24; L. V. Fildes, *Luke Fildes, R.A.: A Victorian Painter*, London, 1968, pp. 92, 96, 99

John Anster Fitzgerald (1823–1906)

159

Christmas, first exhibited 1858
Oil on canvas, 40 × 30.5 cm
Signed

PROVENANCE

Acquired 1990

EXHIBITION

RA, 1858, no. 900

Edward Reginald Frampton (1872–1923)

84

The Passage of the Holy Grail to Sarras, 1907
Oil on canvas, 122 × 152.5 cm
Signed and dated lower right

PROVENANCE

Acquired 1988

EXHIBITIONS

New Gallery, London, 1907, no. 58; Autumn Exhibition, Liverpool, 1907; Salon, Paris, 1911, no. 756

SELECTED REFERENCES

Pictures of 1907 (*Pall Mall Magazine Extra*), p. 111; Rudolf Dircks, in *Art Journal*, 1907, pp. 291, 296

Part of the inscription on the plaque on the frame reads 'Exhibited at Birmingham, Bristol, New and Latin Galleries', but the exhibitions have not been identified.

Antonio Frilli (late 19th – early 20th century)

137

Nude Reclining in a Hammock, c. 1883/1904
White marble, 109.9 × 188 cm
Inscribed on top of base: *A. Frilli / Firenze*

PROVENANCE

William Goldman, Philadelphia (who installed it in the Jules Mastbaum theatre, Philadelphia, 1932); by descent; acquired 1994

EXHIBITION

International Exhibition, St Louis, 1904

SELECTED REFERENCES

Frank Brookhouser, in *Sunday Bulletin* (Philadelphia), 5 March 1967; M. H. Orodenker, in *Box Office*, 12 March 1979

Another version (white marble, 121.9 × 201.9 cm) was sold at Sotheby's, New York, 3 November 1999, lot 62.

William Gale (1823–1909)

73

The Wounded Knight, 1853
Oil on panel, 50.2 × 67.2 cm
Signed and dated lower right

Frame inscribed with lines from Spenser's *Faerie Queene* VI, ii, 41: *And there beside him sate upon the ground / His wofull Ladie, piteously complayning / With loud laments that most unluckie stound, / And her sad*

selfe with carefull hand constrayning / To wype his wounds, and ease their bitter payning.

PROVENANCE

Christie's, 13 March 1949, lot 120; Cooling Castle, Rochester, Kent; acquired 1995

EXHIBITION

RA, 1854, no. 55

John William Godward (1861–1922)

140

Dolce far niente (A Pompeian Fishpond), 1904
Oil on canvas, 50.8 × 76.2 cm
Signed and dated upper right

PROVENANCE

Thomas McLean Gallery; Major N. S. Horne; Sotheby's, 20 June 1972, lot 110, bought Mrs Blond; Sotheby's, 8 March 1977, lot 59, bought Roy Miles Ltd; acquired 1995

EXHIBITIONS

Thomas McLean Gallery, London, 1904, 1905; Roy Miles Gallery, London, 1977

SELECTED REFERENCE

Vern G. Swanson, *John William Godward: The Eclipse of Classicism*, Woodbridge, 1997, p. 211, no. 1904.4

Godward produced at least seven pictures with this title.

Frederick Goodall RA (1822–1904)

154

'Old Maid', 1886
Oil on canvas, 110.4 × 97.7 cm
Monogrammed and dated

PROVENANCE

Private collection, New York; acquired 1990

EXHIBITION

RA, 1886, no. 266

SELECTED REFERENCES

Art Journal, 1886, p. 222; Henry Blackburn (ed.), *Academy Notes*, London, 1886, p. 8; *The Reminiscences of Frederick Goodall*, London, 1902, p. 387 (identifies the girls as the daughters of Goodall and Edward Linley Sambourne).

John Atkinson Grimshaw (1836–1893)

110

A Shepherd with His Flock in a Mountainous Landscape (Lake Buttermere from Hassness), 1865
Oil on canvas, 44.5 × 59.7 cm
Signed and dated lower left

PROVENANCE

Bonhams, 10 April 1980, lot 260; Sotheby's, 20 June 1989, lot 39; acquired 1991

111

Ghyll Beck, Barden, Yorkshire, Early Spring, 1867
Oil on canvas, 76.2 × 63.5 cm
Signed and dated lower left

PROVENANCE

Edward Simpson; Sotheby's, 23 June 1981, lot 24; acquired 1994

EXHIBITION

Works of Recently Deceased Local Artists, Leeds City Art Gallery, 1897, no. 200

SELECTED REFERENCE

Robertson, 1988, pp. 25–6 and pl. 17

Other pictures of this motif are dated 1878 and 1885.

122

The Lovers, 1874
Oil on panel, 46.5 × 56.7 cm
Signed and dated lower left; inscribed on reverse: *Sculby Lane End / Near Scarborough*

PROVENANCE
Jane, Lady Abdy; Eric Jourdan, Paris, by 1970; acquired 2001

118
Il Penseroso, 1875
Oil on board, 59.7 × 49.5 cm
Signed and dated lower left

PROVENANCE
Acquired 1975

EXHIBITIONS
Atkinson Grimshaw, Alexander Gallery, London, 1976, no. 11; *Atkinson Grimshaw*, Leeds City Art Gallery, 1979, no. 25

SELECTED REFERENCE
Robertson, 1988, p. 39 and pl. 46

123
Home Again, late 1870s (?)
Oil on board, 42.5 × 63.8 cm
Signed and inscribed HKM lower left

PROVENANCE
W. A. H. Harding; Jane, Lady Abdy; Bury Street Gallery, 1988; acquired 1993

EXHIBITIONS
Works of Recently Deceased Local Artists, Leeds City Art Gallery, 1897, no. 173; *Atkinson Grimshaw*, Ferrers Gallery, London, 1970, pp. 28–9; *Atkinson Grimshaw*, Alexander Gallery, London, 1976, no. 14; *Atkinson Grimshaw*, Leeds City Art Gallery, 1979, no. 44; Maritime England exhibition, Crescent Art Gallery, Scarborough, 1982, no. 4; *Atkinson Grimshaw*, Crescent Art Gallery, Scarborough, 1993 (ex cat.)

SELECTED REFERENCE
Robertson, 1988, p. 70 and ill. title page

125
The Lady of Shalott, 1878
Oil on canvas, 82.5 × 122 cm
Signed and dated lower left; inscribed on reverse: *painted by Atkinson Grimshaw / at 'The Castle by the Sea' / Scarborough* followed by lines from Tennyson's 'The Lady of Shalott'

PROVENANCE
The Pre-Raphaelite Trust; acquired 1991

EXHIBITION
The Pre-Raphaelites and Their Times, Isetan Museum, Tokyo, 1985, no. 24

SELECTED REFERENCE
Robertson, 1988, p. 59

A similar composition (oil on canvas, 61 × 91.4 cm) is in a private collection (exhibited *Atkinson Grimshaw*, Ferrers Gallery, London, 1970, pp. 26–7).

121
Sixty Years Ago, 1879
Oil on canvas, 83 × 122 cm
Signed and dated lower right

PROVENANCE
Acquired 1999

SELECTED REFERENCE
Robertson, 1988, p. 94 and pl. 85

120
Stapleton Park, 1879
Oil on canvas, 75 × 125.8 cm
Signed and dated lower right

PROVENANCE
Acquired 1972

Numerous versions of this composition are known, with various dimensions and dated between 1877 and 1883.

126
On Hampstead Hill, 1881
Oil on panel, 30.5 × 40.5 cm
Signed and dated lower right

PROVENANCE
W. P. Bowman; acquired 1972

Other versions include: oil on board, 30.5 × 51 cm, dated 1881, Christie's, 25 July 1986, lot 218; oil on board, 34 × 44 cm, dated 1881, Sotheby's, New York, 5 May 1999, lot 133; oil on board, 36.8 × 53.7 cm, dated 1882, Tate; oil on board, 50.8 × 76.2 cm, dated 1883, photograph in Witt Library, Courtauld Institute of Art, London.

124
Liverpool, 1882
Oil on board, 30 × 49 cm
Signed and dated lower left

PROVENANCE
Acquired 1994

127
Cornhill, 1885
Oil on canvas, 76.2 × 63.5 cm
Signed and dated lower right

PROVENANCE
Acquired 1998

117
Dulce Domum, 1885
Oil on canvas, 83.1 × 122.5 cm
Signed and dated lower left; inscribed on reverse: *'Dulce Domum', 'Harmony'. Painted by Atkinson Grimshaw at / his home Knostrop Hall, nr. Leeds. Yorks. Commenced and named / 1876. Finished January 1885. Painted as a sequel to a picture called 'A Question of Colour' by the same painter & Mostly / painted under great difficulties, but by God's grace finished / 1885. LABOR OMNIA VINCIT.*

PROVENANCE
Bought from the 1885 Manchester exhibition by Walter Battle, Leeds; Auktionsverk, Gothenburg, 6 November 1980, lot 660; Sotheby's, New York, 27 May 1982, lot 68; acquired 1992

EXHIBITIONS
RA, 1885, no. 947; Autumn Exhibition, Manchester City Art Gallery, 1885, no. 143; inaugural exhibition, Leeds City Art Gallery, 1888, no. 21; *Works of Recently Deceased Local Artists*, Leeds City Art Gallery, 1897, no. 141; *Japan and Britain: An Aesthetic Dialogue 1850–1930*, Barbican Art Gallery, London, 1991, no. 91

SELECTED REFERENCES
The Times, 25 May 1885, p. 4; *Athenaeum*, 13 June 1885, p. 766; *Art Journal*, 1885, p. 257; Peter Thornton, *Authentic Decor: The Domestic Interior 1620–1920*, London, 1983, pl. 465; Robertson, 1988, pp. 39, 46, 50 and pl. 34, 40, 110

119
Wimbledon Park, Autumn After Glow, 1886
Oil on canvas, 60.4 × 90.2 cm
Signed and dated lower left

PROVENANCE
Acquired 1972

116
Lights on the Mersey, 1892
Oil on board, 25.4 × 50.8 cm
Signed, dated and inscribed T23 lower right

PROVENANCE
Sotheby's, 19 October 1971, lot 23; Christie's, 16 March 1973, lot 19; Christopher Wood Gallery; Christie's, 11 November 1999, lot 25

EXHIBITION
Atkinson Grimshaw, Richard Green Gallery, London, 1990, no. 34

Eugene von Guérard (1811–1901)

101
A View of Geelong, Victoria, Australia, 1856
Oil on canvas, 89 × 152.5 cm
Signed and inscribed *Melbourne 1856* lower right

PROVENANCE
Bought by Frederick Gonnerman Dalgety, Melbourne, 1856; taken by him to Lockerley Hall, Hampshire; by descent; acquired 1996

EXHIBITIONS
Maclachlan's, Melbourne, 1856; International Exhibition, London, 1862; *Eugen von Guérard*, Art Gallery of New South Wales, Sydney, 1980, p. 103

SELECTED REFERENCES
Argus (Melbourne), 9 April 1856, p. 5; *Age* (Melbourne), 5 May 1856, p. 3, and 3 June 1856, p. 3; *Australian News*, 27 July 1867, p. 8; Candice Bruce et al., *Eugene von Guérard 1811–1901: A German Romantic in the Antipodes*, Martinborough, New Zealand, 1982, pl. 7

Michael Frederick Halliday (1822–1869)

79
The Measure for the Wedding Ring, 1855
Oil on canvas, 90.1 × 67.3 cm
Signed and dated lower left

PROVENANCE
Evelyn Waugh; acquired 1971

EXHIBITION
RA, 1856, no. 568

SELECTED REFERENCE
Christopher Wood, 'Evelyn Waugh: A Pioneer Collector', *Connoisseur*, September 1981, fig. 11

The background of the picture was painted by John Everett Millais (cat. 19–29).

78
The Blind Basket-maker with His First Child, 1856
Oil on canvas, 94 × 56 cm
Signed and dated lower right

PROVENANCE
Acquired 1994

EXHIBITION
RA, 1858, no. 459

SELECTED REFERENCES
Art Journal, 1858, p. 169; *Art Journal*, 1869, p. 272

Another version (oil on panel, 25.4 × 14.9 cm, dated 1858) was sold at the Forbes Collection sale, Christie's, 20 February 2003, lot 115.

Edith Hayllar (1860–1948)

170
A Summer Shower, 1883
Oil on panel, 53.4 × 44.2 cm
Signed and dated lower left

PROVENANCE
Christie's, 10 July 1970, lot 60; acquired 2003

EXHIBITIONS
RA, 1883, no. 420; *The Art and Mind of Victorian England*, University of Minnesota Gallery, Minneapolis, 1974, no. 17; *The Royal Academy Revisited*, Metropolitan Museum of Art, New York, 1975, no. 22; *Women Artists 1550–1950*, Los Angeles County Museum of Art, 1977, no. 103; *The Substance or the Shadow: Images of Victorian Womanhood*, Yale Center for British Art, New Haven, CT, 1982, no. 38; *The Pre-Raphaelites and Their Times*, Isetan Museum, Tokyo, 1985, no. 71; *The Painter was a Lady*, Forbes Magazine Galleries, New York, 1986, no. 13a; *Love All: The Romance of Tennis*, Wimbledon Lawn Tennis Museum, London, 1989; *Viktorianische Malerei von Turner bis Whistler*, Neue Pinakothek, Munich, 1993, no. 105;

A Struggle for Fame: Victorian Women Artists and Authors, Yale Center for British Art, New Haven, CT, 1994, p. 60; *The Pursuit of Leisure*, Djanolgly Art Gallery, Nottingham University, 1997, no. 46; *The Defining Moment: Narrative Paintings from the FORBES Magazine Collection*, Mint Museum, Charlotte, NC, 2000, no. 16

SELECTED REFERENCES
Christopher Wood, 'The Artistic Family Hayllar', *Connoisseur*, April 1974, p. 4, and May 1974, pp. 6–7; Wood, 1976, p. 186 and pl. 197; Susan P. Casteras, *Images of Victorian Womanhood in English Art*, Rutherford, NJ, 1987, p. 157 and pl. 130; Christopher Wood, *Paradise Lost*, London, 1988, pp. 192, 194 and pl. 171; Julian Treuherz, *Victorian Painting*, London, 1993, p. 178 and fig. 144; Lionel Lambourne, *Victorian Painting*, London, 1999, p. 228 and pl. 279; Mary Cowling, *Victorian Figurative Painting*, London, 2000, p. 82 and pl. 57

Kate Hayllar (exhibited 1883–1898)

169
'A thing of beauty is a joy forever', 1890
Watercolour with pencil, pen and ink, and touches of white and gum arabic on paper, 34 × 24.8 cm
Signed and dated lower right

PROVENANCE
Christie's, 22 July 1927, lot 12; Phillips, Ipswich, 5 April 1990, lot 53; acquired 2003

EXHIBITIONS
RA, 1890, no. 1190; *A Struggle for Fame: Victorian Women Artists and Authors*, Yale Center for British Art, New Haven, CT, 1994, p. 61; *The Defining Moment: Narrative Paintings from the FORBES Magazine Collection*, Mint Museum, Charlotte, NC, 2000, no. 19

John Henry Henshall (1856–1928)

168
Behind the Bar, 1883
Oil on canvas, 62.2 × 111.1 cm
Signed lower right

PROVENANCE
Newman Gallery, London; Anthony Body, London; acquired 1992

EXHIBITIONS
First exhibition of the Institute of Painters in Oil Colours, London, 1883, no. 231; *Hard Times: Social Realism in Victorian Art*, Manchester City Art Gallery, 1987, no. 95

SELECTED REFERENCES
Art Journal, 1883, p. 166; Wood, 1976, fig. 6

A version in watercolour on paper, 40.2 × 72 cm, is in the Museum of London (Water Colour Exhibition, Dudley Gallery, London, 1883, no. 112).

John Frederick Herring Snr (1795–1865)

152
The Start for the Derby (1834), 1834
Oil on canvas, 101.6 × 152.4 cm
Signed and dated

PROVENANCE
Commissioned from the artist by David Robertson; Scott & Fowles, Inc., New York; Raymond R. Guest, Powhatan Plantation, VA; acquired 1997

SELECTED REFERENCE
Memoir of John Frederick Herring, Sheffield, 1848, p. 9

Arthur Hughes (1832–1915)

71
Ophelia, 1852/57
Oil on lunette-shaped panel, 50.8 × 91.4 cm

Signed lower right; frame, inscribed with lines from *Hamlet* IV, vii

PROVENANCE

Sir Walter James, by 1862; by descent; acquired 1994

EXHIBITIONS

Russell Place, Fitzroy Square, London, 1857, no. 34; *British Art*, National Academy of Design, New York, 1857, no. 85; French Gallery, London, 1858, no. 68; International Exhibition, London, 1862, Fine Art section, no. 38A / 466; on loan to two Girls' Clubs, Dover, 1940s–60s; *The Pre-Raphaelite Brotherhood*, Birmingham City Museum and Art Gallery, 1947, no. 25; *The Pre-Raphaelites*, Whitechapel Art Gallery, London, 1948, no. 27

SELECTED REFERENCES

Critic, 15 June 1857, p. 280; *Crayon* (New York), November 1857, p. 343; *New York Monthly Magazine*, January 1858, p. 54; *Spectator*, 6 November 1858, p. 1171; *Art Journal*, 1858, pp. 354–5; Susan P. Casteras, 'The 1857–8 Exhibition of English Art in America', in *The New Path: Ruskin and the American Pre-Raphaelites*, exh. cat., Brooklyn Museum, New York, 1985, p. 122; Leonard Roberts and M. V. Evans, '"Sweets to the Sweet": Arthur Hughes's Versions of *Ophelia*', *Journal of Pre-Raphaelite and Aesthetic Studies* 1, 2, 1988; Susan P. Casteras, *English Pre-Raphaelitism and its Reception in America in the Nineteenth Century*, Rutherford, NJ, 1990, p. 58; Roberts, 1997, no. 10.3

The frame was designed by the artist. Another version of the painting is in Manchester City Art Gallery: oil on canvas, 68.5 × 124 cm (exhibted RA, 1852).

72
April Love, c. 1855/56
Oil on panel, 45.5 × 26 cm
Signed lower right

PROVENANCE

Arthur James Lewis, by c. 1864; his sale, Christie's, 1 April 1871, lot 285; A. Campbell Blair, by 1911; J. R. Cookson; acquired John Gere, 1948; acquired 1995

EXHIBITIONS

Russell Place, Fitzroy Square, London, 1857, no. 37; *British Art*, National Academy of Design, New York, 1857, no. 87; *Ford Madox Brown and the Pre-Raphaelites*, Manchester City Art Gallery, 1911, no. 253; *Works by Pre-Raphaelite Painters from Collections in Lancashire*, Tate Gallery, London, 1913, no. 25; *The Pre-Raphaelites*, Whitechapel Art Gallery, London, 1948, no. 28; *Victorian Paintings*, Festival Club, Aldeburgh (Arts Council of Great Britain), 1962, no. 29; *Victorian Painting*, Agnew's, London, 1961, no. 60

SELECTED REFERENCES

Crayon (New York), November 1857, p. 343; *Athenaeum*, 8 April 1871, p. 440; William Michael Rossetti (ed.), *Ruskin: Rossetti: Preraphaelitism; Papers 1854–62*, London, 1899, pp. 182, 188; Robin Ironside and John Gere, *Pre-Raphaelite Painters*, London, 1948, p. 43; Virginia Surtees (ed.), *Sublime and Instructive: Letters from John Ruskin*, London, 1972, p. 166; Susan P. Casteras, *English Pre-Raphaelitism and Its Reception in America in the Nineteenth Century*, Rutherford, NJ, 1990, p. 58; Roberts, 1997, no. 29.5

Another version is owned by the Tate: oil on canvas, 88.9 × 49.5 cm, exhibited RA, 1856, no. 578 (accompanied by lines from Tennyson's 'Miller's Daughter').

69
The King's Orchard, 1858
Oil on canvas, 66 × 50.8 cm
Signed lower right

PROVENANCE

Bought from the artist by Thomas Plint; his sale, Christie's, 8 March 1862, lot 233, bought Agnew's; Cunliffe Brooks; John Brearley sale, Christie's,

17 December 1928, lot 79; Waugh (not Evelyn); Mrs O. Devitt; by descent; acquired 1988

EXHIBITIONS

[Rejected RA, 1858]; RA, 1859, no. 609 (with lines from Browning's 'Pippa Passes' [1841])

SELECTED REFERENCES

John Ruskin, *Academy Notes*, London, 1858, pp. 22–3 (Ruskin, 1903–12, vol. 14, p. 163); *Athenaeum*, 7 May 1859, p. 617; *The Times*, 18 May 1859, p. 12; *Critic*, 21 May 1859, p. 497, and 28 May 1859, p. 520; John Ruskin, *Academy Notes*, London, 1859, p. 31 (Ruskin, 1903–12, vol. 14, p. 232); *Athenaeum*, 15 March 1862, pp. 367–8; *Art Journal*, 1862, p. 105; William Michael Rossetti, 'English Painters of the Present Day', *Portfolio*, August 1870, p. 115; Helen Allingham and E. Baumer Williams (eds), *Letters to William Allingham*, London, 1911, p. 66; Robin Gibson, 'Arthur Hughes: Arthurian and Related Subjects of the Early 1860s', *Burlington Magazine*, July 1970, p. 452; John Christian, '"A Serious Talk": Ruskin's Place in Burne-Jones's Artistic Development', in London, 1984, p. 193 (not named); James Taylor and John Dabney, 'Arthur Hughes' "King's Orchard"', *Antique Collector*, November 1988, pp. 113–16; Kate Flint, 'Arthur Hughes as Illustrator for Children', in Gillian Avery and Julia Briggs (eds), *Children and their Books*, Oxford, 1989, p. 202; Roberts, 1997, no. 35

Other versions: oil on paper, 28.5 × 29.2 cm, Fitzwilliam Museum, Cambridge (Roberts, 1997, no. 35.2); watercolour, unlocated (exhibited French Gallery, London, 1862; Roberts, 1997, no. 35.3).

74
The Knight of the Sun, c. 1859/60
Oil on canvas, 101.6 × 132 cm
Signed lower right; inscribed on frame: *Better a death when work is done / Than earth's most favoured birth* (from George MacDonald's poem 'Better Things', 1857)

PROVENANCE

Purchased from the artist by Thomas Plint; his sale, Christie's, 8 March 1862, lot 220, bought Agnew's; Jacob Burnett sale, Christie's, 25 March 1876, lot 97; William Graham; Mrs Quintin Hogg, by 1903; by descent; Sotheby's, 4 November 1953, lot 37, but remained in Hogg family until acquired in 1984

EXHIBITIONS

British Association for the Advancement of Science, Newcastle-upon-Tyne, 1863; Fine Art loan exhibition, Institute of Fine Arts, Glasgow, 1878, no. 145; loan exhibition, Nottingham Art Gallery, 1900; Winter Exhibition, Whitechapel Art Gallery, London, 1903, no. 279; *British Art Fifty Years Ago*, Whitechapel Art Gallery, London, 1905, no. 442; *Ford Madox Brown and the Pre-Raphaelites*, Manchester City Art Gallery, 1911, no. 251; *Arthur Hughes*, National Museum of Wales, Cardiff, 1971, no. 9; *The Pre-Raphaelites*, Tate Gallery, London, 1984, no. 110

SELECTED REFERENCES

Athenaeum, 31 March 1860, p. 448 (noting intention to send picture to RA, 1860); *Critic*, 9 June 1860, p. 723; *Athenaeum*, 15 March 1862, p. 367; *Art Journal*, 1862, p. 105; George MacDonald, *The Seaboard Parish*, London, 1868, vol. 3, pp. 252–4; William Michael Rossetti, 'English Painters of the Present Day', *Portfolio*, August 1870, p. 115; *Athenaeum*, 20 September 1873, p. 374; *Athenaeum*, 1 April 1876, p. 471; *Art Journal*, 1876, p. 334; William E. Fredeman (ed.), *A Pre-Raphaelite Gazette: The Penkill Letters of Arthur Hughes to William Bell Scott and Alice Boyd, 1886–97*, London, 1967, pp. 50, 54–5; Robin Gibson, 'Arthur Hughes: Arthurian and Related Subjects of the Early 1860s', *Burlington Magazine*, July 1970, pp. 451–6; R. Cooper, 'Arthur Hughes's "La Belle Dame Sans Merci" and the Femme Fatale', *Art Bulletin of Victoria*, 1986, pp. 14, 17, 25; Roberts, 1997, no. 43; Staley, 2001, pp. 113–14 and pl. 84

Other versions (see Roberts, 1997, nos 43.2–8) include: oil on board, 28 × 39.5 cm, Sotheby's, 18 April 1978, lot 60 (exhibited *McCormick Collection*, Yale Center for British Art, New Haven, CT, 1984, no. 17; Roberts, 1997, no. 43.6); watercolour on paper, 22.5 × 32 cm, Ashmolean Museum, Oxford (Roberts, 1997, no. 43.8).

68
Bed-Time, c. 1861
Oil on canvas laid down on panel, 71.1 × 58 cm
Signed lower right

PROVENANCE

Lawrence W. Hodson; his sale, Christie's, 25 June 1906, lot 150, bought Colnaghi for George Howard, 9th Earl of Carlisle; by descent to his grandson Wilfred Roberts, by 1968; acquired 1988

EXHIBITIONS

George Howard and His Circle, Carlisle Art Gallery, 1968, no. 173; *Pre-Raphaelites: Painters and Patrons in the North-East*, Laing Art Gallery, Newcastle-upon-Tyne, 1989, no. 53

SELECTED REFERENCE

Roberts, 1997, no. 57.2

Another version is in the Harris Art Gallery, Preston: oil on paper laid down on canvas, 103 × 132 cm, exhibited RA, 1862, no. 598.

77
Silver and Gold, 1863
Oil on canvas, 99 × 67.3 cm
Signed lower right

PROVENANCE

Bought from the artist by John Hamilton Trist, 1863; his sale, Christie's, 9 April 1892, lot 74; remained in the Trist family until offered at Christie's, 23 April 1937, lot 79, when it passed to another family member; Christie's, 15 December 1972, lot 133, bought Hartnoll & Eyre; The Pre-Raphaelite Trust; acquired 1991

EXHIBITIONS

RA, 1864, no. 486; loan exhibition, Guildhall Art Gallery, London, 1900, no. 82; *British Art Fifty Years Ago*, Whitechapel Art Gallery, London, 1905, no. 392; *Arthur Hughes*, National Museum of Wales, Cardiff, 1971, no. 16; *Arthur Hughes: The Lady with the Lilacs*, Art Gallery of Ontario, Toronto, 1988

SELECTED REFERENCES

The Times, 30 April 1864, p. 14; *Athenaeum*, 7 May 1864, p. 651; *Art Journal*, 1864, p. 161; *Fraser's Magazine*, July 1864, p. 70; Francis Turner Palgrave, *Essays on Art*, London, 1866, p. 63; Cosmo Monkhouse, in *Magazine of Art*, 1883, pp. 69–70; Percy H. Bate, *The English Pre-Raphaelite Painters*, London, 1899, pp. 71–2; Robin Gibson, review of Cardiff, 1971, exhibition, *Burlington Magazine*, December 1971, p. 761; Karen Finlay, in Toronto, 1988, exh. cat., *passim*, esp. pp. 3–10; Roberts, 1997, no. 59

The frame was designed by the artist. The following works relate to the painting: *The Lady with the Lilacs* (study for the girl), oil on panel, 44.5 × 22.5 cm, Art Gallery of Ontario, Toronto (Roberts, 1997, no. 59.3); sketch of the composition, oil on paper, 34 × 23.5 cm, ex-collection Vita Sackville-West (Roberts, 1997, no. 59.5); two unlocated sketches (Roberts, 1997, nos 59.2,4).

Edward Robert Hughes (1851–1914)

76
Bertuccio's Bride, 1895
Pencil and watercolour on paper, 100.3 × 76.1 cm
Signed and dated lower left; inscribed on label on backboard with lines from W. G. Waters's translation of the *Nights of Straparola*

PROVENANCE

Mrs Weir; Christie's, 23 June 1944, lot 40; Peter Nahum Gallery, 1989; acquired 1991

EXHIBITIONS

Royal Society of Painters in Water-Colours, London, 1895, no. 59; *Burne-Jones, the Pre-Raphaelites and their Century*, Peter Nahum Gallery, London, 1989, no. 155

Based on one of a series of designs commissioned to illustrate Waters's 1894 translation of the 16th-century collection of novellas *Nights of Straparola*.

William Holman Hunt OM (1827–1910)

103
The Old Church at Ewell, 1847
Oil on canvas, 63.5 × 76.2 cm
Inscribed lower left centre, on tombstone: EWELL / OLD CHURCH / Painted in June / 1847 / FOR THE REV^D / SIR G. L GLYN BAR^T / LAY RECTOR AND / VICAR / BY W H HUNT

PROVENANCE

Sir George L. Glyn, 1847; by descent until at least 1942; Mrs Kathleen Constance Warner, 1972; acquired 1994

EXHIBITION

The Pre-Raphaelites, Tate Gallery, London, 1984, no. 4

SELECTED REFERENCES

Hunt, 1905, vol. 1, p. 72; J. P., letter to *The Times*, 12 September 1910, p. 11

109
Fairlight Downs (Sunlight on the Sea), 1852–58
Oil on panel, 22.8 × 31.1 cm
Monogrammed and inscribed lower left FAIRLIGHT and, on the reverse, *Sunlight on the Sea / Fairlight Downs*

PROVENANCE

Bought from the artist for £120, 1858, probably by A. H. Novelli, who had the picture by 1886; Christie's, 19 June 1897, lot 69, bought by Colnaghi for Sir Max Waechter; given by him to his wife, Armatrude, on her birthday, 20 May 1915; Peter Nahum Ltd, 1985; acquired 1995

EXHIBITIONS

Winter Exhibition, French Gallery, London, 1858, no. 71; *The Pictures of Mr. Holman Hunt*, Fine Art Society, London, 1886, no. 23; *The Pre-Raphaelites*, Tate Gallery, London, 1984, no. 52; Peter Nahum Gallery, London, 1985; *Viktorianische Malerei von Turner bis Whistler*, Neue Pinakothek, Munich, 1993, no. 51

SELECTED REFERENCES

Athenaeum, 30 October 1858, p. 558; *Critic*, 30 October 1858, p. 736; *Illustrated London News*, 27 November 1858, p. 508; *Art Journal*, 1 December 1858, p. 355; [William Michael Rossetti], *Spectator*, 6 November 1858, p. 1171, repr. in his *Fine Art, Chiefly Contemporary*, London, 1867, p. 244; [Frederic George Stephens], *William Holman Hunt and His Works*, London, 1860, pp. 53–5; Philip Gilbert Hamerton, *A Painter's Camp in the Highlands, and Thoughts about Art*, London, 1862, vol. 2, pp. 209–11; William Holman Hunt, 'The Pre-Raphaelite Brotherhood: A Fight for Art', *Contemporary Review*, June 1886, p. 822; Hunt, 1905, vol. 1, p. 336; Janet Camp Troxell (ed.), *Three Rossettis: Unpublished Letters to and from Dante Gabriel, Christina, William*, Cambridge, MA, 1937, p. 36; Judith Bronkhurst, in *A Celebration of British and European Painting of the 19th and 20th Centuries*, exh. cat., Peter Nahum, London, [1985], pp. 12–17; Staley, 2001, pp. 79, 82, 91, 122, 154 and pl. 54

108
Fairlight Downs (The Silver Lining), 1865
Pencil, watercolour and gouache on paper, 12.7 × 17.5 cm
Monogrammed and dated lower right; inscribed on a label on the reverse: *Fairlight Down*

PROVENANCE
Still with the artist, 1884; Henry Haslam, by 1894; by descent; acquired 2002

EXHIBITIONS
Modern Pictures, Walker Art Gallery, Liverpool, 1884, no. 456; Fine Art loan exhibition, St Jude's, Whitechapel, London, 1894, no. 189; *Collective Exhibition of the Art of William Holman Hunt*, Free Public Library, Museum, and Walker Art Gallery, Liverpool, 1907, no. 53 (as *The Silver Lining*)

67
Morning Prayer, 1866
Oil on panel, 25.5 × 18.5 cm
Monogrammed and dated lower left

PROVENANCE
Joseph Morby (a London dealer); Agnew's, 1866; John Fowler, 1867; his sale, Christie's, 6 May 1899, lot 57; Alfred Yarrow, by 1905; by descent until 1945; acquired 1995

EXHIBITIONS
International Exhibition, London, 1871, no. 443; Franco-British Exhibition, White City, London, 1908, no. 376; International Fine Arts Exhibition, Rome, 1911, no. 37

SELECTED REFERENCES
Athenaeum, 9 December 1865, p. 811; Hunt, 1905, vol. 1, ill. facing p. 60; Otto von Schleinitz, *William Holman Hunt*, Leipzig, 1907, pp. 58, 60 and pl. 57; Diana Holman-Hunt, *My Grandmothers and I*, London, 1960, p. 94; Diana Holman-Hunt, *My Grandfather, His Wives and Loves*, London, 1969, p. 205 (figure identified, apparently mistakenly, as Annie Miller); Mary Bennett, 'Footnotes to the Holman Hunt Exhibition', *Liverpool Bulletin*, 1970, p. 35

Begun in 1865 as a design for an illustration to Isaac Watts's poem 'A Morning Star', to be included in a new edition of the poet's *Divine and Moral Songs for Children*.

64
The Shadow of Death, 1873
Oil on panel, 104.5 × 82 cm
Monogrammed and inscribed *1870.3* and, lower right: *JERUSALEM copy made by whh 1873*

PROVENANCE
John Heugh; Christie's, 17 March 1877, lot 56, bought Agnew's; John T. Middlemore, Birmingham, 1896; Agnew's, 1973; acquired 1994

EXHIBITIONS
Centennial International Exhibition, Melbourne, 1888, no. 51; on loan to Birmingham City Museum and Art Gallery, 1935–73; *William Holman Hunt*, Walker Art Gallery, Liverpool, 1969, no. 46; *Painting in England 1630–1870*, Agnew's, London, 1973, no. 63; *Präraffaeliten*, Staatliche Kunsthalle, Baden-Baden, 1973, no. 48

SELECTED REFERENCES
Argus (Melbourne), 9 August 1888, p. 11, and 19 November 1888, p. 8; Hunt, 1905, vol. 2, pp. 310, 382; Michael Davie (ed.), *The Diaries of Evelyn Waugh*, London, 1976, p. 738 (notes seeing the picture at Birmingham, 1955); Evelyn Waugh, in *Spectator*, 14 October 1960, p. 567; James H. Coombs et al. (eds), *A Pre-Raphaelite Friendship: The Correspondence of William Holman Hunt and John Lucas Tupper*, Ann Arbor, MI, 1986, pp. 182, 183, 185, 186, 190, 191, 222, 236, 237, 239, 244

Frame designed by the artist. This is the third version of the composition, commissioned by Agnew's in 1873 as a model for Frederick Stacpoole's engraving (published 1877), completed the following year and painted in London despite the inscription. Other versions are: oil on canvas, 92.7 × 73 cm, begun in Palestine in 1869, Leeds City Art Gallery; oil on canvas, 214.2 × 168.2 cm, begun in Jerusalem in 1870,

Manchester City Art Gallery (the model for cat. 64); sketch for landscape background, oil on canvas, 31.8 × 72.3 cm, private collection (exhibited Liverpool, 1969, no. 48).

70
Master Hilary – The Tracer, 1886
Oil on canvas, 122.2 × 66 cm
Monogrammed and dated lower left centre; inscribed on backboard: *For Hilary on his 21st Birthday / W.H.H. / Given May 6th 1900 / W.H.H.*

PROVENANCE
Given to the sitter, the artist's son, on his 21st birthday, 1900; by descent; acquired 1994

EXHIBITIONS
Grosvenor Gallery, London, 1887, no. 208 (with motto '"Be sure before painting to make a correct outline" – Old-fashioned Manual of Art'); Autumn Exhibition, Royal Birmingham Society of Artists, Birmingham, 1887, no. 219; Fine Art loan exhibition, St Jude's, Whitechapel, London, 1888, no. 51*; *Collective Exhibition of the Art of William Holman Hunt*, Free Public Library, Museum, and Walker Art Gallery, Liverpool, 1907, no. 8; Autumn Exhibition, Walker Art Gallery, Liverpool, 1923, no. 824; Hunt exhibition, Walker Art Gallery, Liverpool, 1969, no. 57

SELECTED REFERENCES
Daily Telegraph, 2 May 1887, p. 3; *Pall Mall Gazette*, 2 May 1887, p. 5; *Athenaeum*, 7 May 1887, p. 613; *Spectator*, 7 May 1887, p. 621; *Illustrated London News*, 14 May 1887, p. 552; *The Times*, 27 May 1887, p. 8; *Birmingham Daily Post*, 14 September 1887, p. 4; Hunt, 1905, vol. 2, p. 335 and ill. facing p. 418 (showing the picture before changes made by E. R. Hughes); Otto von Schleinitz, *William Holman Hunt*, Leipzig, 1907, p. 117 and pl. 116; Diana Holman-Hunt, *My Grandmothers and I*, London, 1960, p. 100

Changes were made to the costume after 1905 by Hunt's studio assistant, E. R. Hughes.

Sir Edwin Henry Landseer RA (1802–1873)

171
Refreshment, first exhibited 1846
Oil on panel, 99.1 × 127 cm

PROVENANCE
C. J. Nieuwenhuys; F. Barchard, by 1874; Tooth & Sons, by 1961; Sotheby's, New York, 4 June 1993, lot 78, bought Coyne; acquired 2001

EXHIBITIONS
RA, 1846, no. 291; Landseer memorial exhibition, RA, Winter 1874, no. 215; loan exhibition, Royal Pavilion, Brighton, 1884

SELECTED REFERENCES
Art Journal, 1846, p. 178; Frederic George Stephens, *The Early Works of Sir Edwin Landseer*, London, 1869, p. 155; Algernon Graves, *Catalogue of the Works of the Late Sir Edwin Landseer, R.A.*, London, [1874], pp. 28, 46 and no. 349; Campbell Lennie, *Landseer: The Victorian Paragon*, London, 1976, p. 111

172
'Scarbro', An Old Cover Hack, first exhibited 1848
Oil on canvas, 122.5 × 151.8 cm

PROVENANCE
Painted for Richard Heathcote, the owner of the horse; by descent until sold at Christie's, 6 November 1959, lot 97, bought Rivett for 1,200 guineas; Sotheby's, 19 April 1961, lot 143, bought Agnew's; acquired 1992

EXHIBITIONS
RA, 1848, no. 229; Landseer memorial exhibition, RA, Winter 1874, no. 233

SELECTED REFERENCES
Algernon Graves, *Catalogue of the Works of the Late Sir Edwin Landseer, R.A.*, London, [1874], p. 28, no. 358; John Ruskin, *Modern Painters*, vol. 2: *Addenda* (Ruskin, 1903–12, vol. 4, p. 335)

The picture has always been kept and sold together with a case containing Scarbro's tail.

Benjamin Williams Leader RA (1831–1923)

112
A River Landscape with a Fisherman Making Eel Traps, 1864
Oil on canvas, 80 × 132 cm
Signed and dated

PROVENANCE
Acquired 1984

Edmund Blair Leighton (1853–1922)

139
Olivia, 1887
Oil on canvas, 48.2 × 61 cm
Signed and dated lower left

PROVENANCE
The Graphic; Christie's, 9 March 1889, lot 299, bought Took; acquired 1990

Commissioned by *The Graphic* magazine to be reproduced in 'Goupilgravure' in *The Graphic Gallery of Shakespeare's Heroines* (1888).

Frederic, Lord Leighton PRA (1830–1896)

138
Dante in Exile, first exhibited 1864
Oil on canvas, 152.5 × 254 cm

PROVENANCE
Bought from the artist by Gambart for 1,000 guineas, 1864; F. W. Cosens sale, Christie's, 17–19 May 1890, lot 132, bought Tooth; Christie's, 27 May 1893, lot 102, bought Ward; Christie's, 10 February 1894, lot 84, bought Lister; Mrs Tania Gordon; British Rail Pension Fund; acquired 1990

EXHIBITIONS
RA, 1864, no. 194 (with verses from Cary's translation of the *Paradiso* xvii, 56–64: 'Thou shalt prove / How salt the savour is of others' bread . . .'); International Exhibition, Dublin, 1865, no. 143; on loan to Leighton House, London, 1981–89; *Frederic Leighton*, RA, 1996, no. 29

SELECTED REFERENCES
Art Journal, 1864, pp. 157–8; *Athenaeum*, 1864, p. 616; *The Times*, 30 April 1864, p. 14; *Examiner*, 30 April 1864, p. 280; *Spectator*, 30 April 1864, p. 506; 21 May 1864, p. 592; *Daily Telegraph*, 4 May 1864, p. 5; *Illustrated London News*, 7 May 1864, p. 455; *Saturday Review*, 14 May 1864, p. 593; *Fraser's Magazine*, July 1864, p. 71; *Art Student*, June 1864, p. 82; William Michael Rossetti, in *Fine Art Quarterly Review* 3, 1864–65, p. 29; Frederic George Stephens, introduction to Ernest Rhys, *Sir Frederic Leighton*, 1st edn, London, 1895, pp.12–13; Ernest Rhys, *Frederic Lord Leighton: An Illustrated Record*, 2nd edn, London, 1898, pp. 17–18, 73, 85; Alice Corkran, *Frederic Leighton*, London, 1904, pp. 56–57, 193; Mrs Russell (Emilia) Barrington, *The Life, Letters and Work of Frederic Leighton*, London, 1906, vol. 2, pp. 114, 123; Ormond, 1975, pp. 59–61, 155 and no. 100; Newall, 1990, p. 48 and pl. 27

Ormond, 1975, lists as no. 101 an unlocated oil sketch measuring 6 × 9 in. (15.2 × 22.9 cm) that relates to the painting.

150
Gulnihal, first exhibited 1886
Oil on canvas, 55.2 × 40 cm

PROVENANCE
Baron Rothschild; P. Polak; Christie's, 24 April 1936, lot 29 (as *Contemplation*); Frost & Reed; Sotheby's, 15 October 1969, lot 109 (as *Contemplation*); Stone Gallery, Newcastle-upon-Tyne; Sotheby's, 25 November 1987, lot 31; acquired 1992

EXHIBITIONS
RA, 1886, no. 354; *Frederic Leighton*, RA, 1996, no. 94

SELECTED REFERENCES
Henry Blackburn (ed.), *Academy Notes*, London, 1886, p. 10; *Athenaeum*, 1 May 1886, p. 590; *Art Journal*, 1886, p. 222; Ernest Rhys, *Frederic, Lord Leighton: An Illustrated Record*, 2nd edn, London, 1898, p. 35; Ormond, 1975, nos 328 (*Gulnihal*) and 406 (*Contemplation*) with the provenance given as above, the confusion arising from the retitling of the picture; Newall, 1990, p. 109 and pl. 76

141
Standing Female Nude, date unknown
Oil on canvas, 54.6 × 25.4 cm

PROVENANCE
John Postle Heseltine; his sale, Sotheby's, 27 May 1935, lot 80 (as by Poynter); W. P. Beck; Major the Hon. John Stourton; Christie's, 28 January 1977, lot 13; acquired 1988

EXHIBITION
Frederic Leighton, RA, 1996, no. 106

SELECTED REFERENCE
Newall, 1990, p. 101 and pl. 69

The painting was consistently misattributed to Poynter (cat. 142) until 1990.

Laurence Stephen Lowry RA (1887–1976)

270
St Augustine's Church, Pendlebury, 1920
Oil on panel, 39.3 × 55.8 cm
Signed and dated lower right

PROVENANCE
Bought from the artist by the Rev. Geoffrey Bennett, 1956; Christie's, 7 June 1985, lot 234; acquired 2001

EXHIBITION
Lowry, RA, 1976, no. 29

SELECTED REFERENCE
Judith Sandling and Mike Leber, *Lowry's City: A Painter and his Locale*, Salford, 2000, pp. 22–3

Adrien-Emmanuel Marie (1848–1891)

167
Feeding the Hungry after the Lord Mayor's Banquet, Interior of Guildhall, 1882
Oil on canvas, 91.4 × 133.3 cm
Signed and dated lower right

PROVENANCE
Sir John Holder, to 1927; Sotheby's, 19 March 1979, lot 40; acquired 1993

EXHIBITION
On loan to the Guildhall, London, 1981–93

SELECTED REFERENCE
Art Journal, 1883, p. 95

Sir John Everett Millais Bt PRA (1829–1896)

20
James Wyatt and His Granddaughter Mary Wyatt, 1849
Oil on panel, 35.5 × 45 cm
Monogrammed and dated lower right

PROVENANCE
Commissioned by James Wyatt, and given by him to Mary Wyatt (later Mrs Standen); by descent; acquired 1999

EXHIBITIONS
RA, 1850, no. 429; Millais exhibition, Grosvenor Gallery, London, 1886, no. 2; Millais exhibition, RA, 1898, no. 32; *The Pre-Raphaelite Brotherhood*, Birmingham City Museum and Art Gallery, 1947, no. 46; *The Pre-Raphaelites*, Whitechapel Art Gallery, London, 1948, no. 41; *British Portraits*, RA, 1956, no. 443; *Paintings and Drawings by Victorian Artists in England*, National Gallery of Canada, Ottawa, 1965, no. 89; Millais exhibition, RA, 1967, no. 20; *The Pre-Raphaelites*, Tate Gallery, London, 1984, no. 28; *Millais: Portraits*, National Portrait Gallery, London, 1999, no. 4

SELECTED REFERENCES
Art Journal, 1850, p. 173; Spielmann, 1898, pp. 87–8; Millais, 1899, vol. 1, pp. 41, 53, 88; vol. 2, p. 467; William Michael Rossetti (ed.), *Preraphaelite Diaries and Letters*, London, 1900, p. 225; Hunt, 1905, vol. 1, p. 194; Robin Ironside and John Gere, *Pre-Raphaelite Painters*, London, 1948, p. 39 and pl. 47; Fredeman, 1975, pp. 20, 39, 42, 50, 70

21
Four Children of the Wyatt Family, 1849
Oil on panel, 45.7 × 30.5 cm
Monogrammed and dated indistinctly lower right

PROVENANCE
Christie's, 30 November 1907, lot 118 (with incorrect identification of sitters); Christie's, 21 January 1921, lot 114, bought Sir Hugh Blaker; Christie's, 5 November 1948, lot 40, bought Abbot & Barnett, Hurstpierpoint, Sussex; acquired by Florence Maud Williams (née Standen), daughter of Mary Wyatt, 1950s; acquired 1994

EXHIBITION
Works from the Blaker Collection, Platt Hall, Manchester, 1929

SELECTED REFERENCE
Funnell and Warner, 1999, p. 50 ill.

25
A Huguenot, c. 1852/55
Oil on board with arched top, 24.7 × 17.7 cm
Monogrammed lower left
A note dated 4 July 1896, and signed by the artist, is pasted to the reverse: *I painted this small copy of the 'Huguenot' shortly after the original picture but I cannot give the exact date*

PROVENANCE
Thomas Plint; his sale, Christie's, 8 March 1862, lot 322, bought D. White; John Morley sale, Christie's, 16 May 1896, lot 44, bought Agnew's; J. Pierpont Morgan, 1896; Christie's, 31 March 1944, lot 80, bought W. J. Burningham, who still had it in 1967; Sotheby's, 19 March 1979, lot 24; acquired 1990

EXHIBITIONS
Millais exhibition, RA, 1898, no. 200; Millais exhibition, RA, 1967, no. 36

SELECTED REFERENCES
Spielmann, 1898, pp. 168, 183 and no. 30; Alfred Lys Baldry, *Sir John Everett Millais: His Art and Influence*, London, 1899, p. 113; Millais, 1899, vol. 2, p. 468; *Connoisseur*, 1906, p. 219

A smaller replica of the painting shown at the RA, 1852 (fig. 1, p. 46). The letter on the reverse is written in the hand of the artist's brother-in-law, Albert Gray, who had brought cat. 25 to show the dying artist from the London house of its new owner, J. Pierpont Morgan. Millais appended his own signature to the letter.

63
Sir John Everett Millais Bt PRA and Michael Frederick Halliday (1822–1869)
Scrapbook of Painting Tours, 1850–55
Sketches and inscriptions cut from notebooks and mounted in a scrapbook of 61 leaves, 44.9 × 32 cm, containing:
'An Artistic Stay at Winchilsea [*sic*] in 1854 by Millais'
'A Short Tour in the Highlands in 1853 [by Millais]'
'A Sporting Trip to the Ardennes in 1850 [by Halliday]'
'A Visit to the Crimea in 1855 by M. F. H.'

PROVENANCE
Acquired 1993

EXHIBITION
Millais exhibition, RA, 1898, nos 189, 197 (?)

SELECTED REFERENCES
Millais, 1899, vol. 1, p. 238 (on the Winchelsea trip), and with reproductions of similar drawings; vol. 2, p. 491; Mary Lutyens and Malcolm Warner (eds), *Rainy Days at Brig O'Turk: The Highland Sketchbooks of John Everett Millais 1853*, Westerham, 1983

24
The Proscribed Royalist, 1651, 1852–53
Oil on canvas framed with arched top, 102.8 × 73.6 cm
Signed and dated lower right

PROVENANCE
Commissioned by Lewis Pocock, May 1852; Foster's, 18 March 1857, lot 83; Gambart, 1858; Thomas Plint, by 1861; his sale, Christie's, 8 March 1862, lot 330, bought Agnew's; Sir John Pender; his sale, Christie's, 29 May 1897, lot 54; James Ogston; his niece Mrs Marjorie Mary Yates; acquired 1983

EXHIBITIONS
RA, 1853, no. 520; Millais exhibition, Grosvenor Gallery, London, 1886, no. 125; *Loan Collection of Modern Pictures*, Birmingham City Museum and Art Gallery, 1891, no. 193; loan exhibition, Guildhall Art Gallery, London, 1894, no. 106; Millais exhibition, RA, 1898, no. 45; *King or Parliament*, Wolverhampton Art Gallery, 1978, no. 8; on loan to the National Gallery of Scotland, Edinburgh, 1980–83; *The Pre-Raphaelites*, Tate Gallery, London, 1984, no. 46

SELECTED REFERENCES
Art Journal, 1853, p. 149; Spielmann, 1898, pp. 30, 93–4, 104, 160, 168, 181; Millais, 1899, vol. 1, pp. 56, 145, 148, 160, 164–6, 169–78, 190, 348, 365, and vol. 2, pp. 468, 487; Alfred Lys Baldry, *Sir John Everett Millais: His Art and Influence*, London, 1899, pp. 29, 40, 43, 44, 47, 69, 81, 111; Percy H. Bate, *The English Pre-Raphaelite Painters*, London, 1899, pp. 13, 35, 38, 81, 88; William J. Stillman, *The Autobiography of a Journalist*, New York, 1901, vol. 1, p. 177; Amy Woolner (ed.), *Thomas Woolner, R.A.: His Life in Letters*, London, 1917, pp. 53–4; Henry William Shrewsbury, *Brothers in Art: Studies in Holman Hunt and Millais*, London, 1920, pp. 39–40; Gerald Reitlinger, *The Economics of Taste*, London, 1961, vol. 1, pp. 389–90; Mary Lutyens, *Millais and the Ruskins*, London, 1967, pp. 38, 45; Fredeman, 1975, p. 98; Roy Strong, *And When Did You Last See Your Father? The Victorian Painter and British History*, London, 1978, pp. 144–5; Susan P. Casteras, *English Pre-Raphaelitism and Its Reception in America in the Nineteenth Century*, Rutherford, NJ, 1990, p. 23; Staley, 2001, p. 57

Another version (oil, 25 × 18 cm) was sold at Christie's, 28 January 1972, lot 155.

19
Design for a Gothic Window, 1853
Charcoal and gouache on grocery paper mounted on canvas with arched top, 213.4 × 276.8 cm

PROVENANCE
By descent from the artist to Sir Ralph Millais; Mrs J. G. Links, by 1967; Christie's, 14 July 1972, lot 108, bought Maas Gallery; acquired 1974

EXHIBITIONS
Millais exhibition, RA, 1898, no. 222; Millais exhibition, RA, 1967, no. 324; *Präraffaeliten*, Staatliche Kunsthalle, Baden-Baden, 1973, no. 69

SELECTED REFERENCES
Millais, 1899, vol. 1, pp. 204–6, and vol. 2, p. 491; Hunt, 1905, vol. 1, pp. 363–5; Ruskin, 1903–12, vol. 12, p. xxviii; Mary Lutyens, *Millais and the Ruskins*, London, 1967, pp. 81–2; Timothy Hilton, *The Pre-Raphaelites*, London, 1970, p. 74 and fig. 44

23
A Dream of the Past: Sir Isumbras at the Ford, c. 1857
Oil on panel, 27.3 × 36.5 cm

PROVENANCE
Perhaps the 'small sketch' taken by Millais to the dealer D. T. White, July 1859; sold from the John Knowles Collection, Manchester, 1877; John Morley; his sale, Christie's, 16 May 1896, lot 43 (as *The Good Knight*); Howard Morley, by whom bequeathed to Lord Lawrence of Kingsgate; Mrs R. Ades, 1967; acquired 1998

SELECTED REFERENCES
Spielmann, 1898, pp. 178, 183 (as *The Good Knight*); Millais, 1899, vol. 2, p. 486 (as the *The Good Knight*); Mary Bennett, in Millais exh. cat., RA, 1967, pp. 42–3 (as collection of Mrs R. Ades); Bennett, 1988, p. 137 n. 3

A sketch for the painting exhibited RA, 1857 (oil on canvas, 125.5 × 171.5 cm, Lady Lever Art Gallery, Port Sunlight), which has various subsequent additions not featured in the present version. Another version (watercolour on paper, 14 × 17.7 cm) is also in the Lady Lever Art Gallery.

22
Ophelia, 1865–66
Watercolour with gouache, 17.8 × 25.4 cm
Monogrammed lower left

PROVENANCE
Commissioned by Agnew's for £100; John Fleming sale, Christie's, 22 March 1879, lot 36, bought William Quilter; his sale, Christie's, 18 May 1889, lot 84, bought Agnew's; Edward Quilter; Major J. Inglis Jones, 1967; acquired 1987

EXHIBITION
Millais exhibition, Grosvenor Gallery, London, 1886, no. 155

SELECTED REFERENCE
Millais, 1899, vol. 2, p. 487

A replica of the picture exhibited RA, 1852 (oil on canvas, 76.2 × 111.8 cm, Tate).

28
Chill October, 1870
Oil on canvas, 141 × 186.7 cm
Monogrammed and dated lower left

PROVENANCE
Purchased by Agnew's, February 1871; sold by them to Samuel Mendel, May 1871; his sale, Christie's, 24 April 1875, lot 431, bought Agnew's for £3,255; William (Lord) Armstrong of Newcastle, by 1886; his sale, Christie's, 24 June 1910, no. 76, bought Agnew's for £5,040; acquired 1991

EXHIBITIONS
RA, 1871, no. 14; Royal Scottish Academy, Edinburgh, 1873, no. 431; Exposition Universelle, Paris, 1878, British section, no. 171; Millais exhibition, Fine Art Society, London, 1881, no. 13; Millais exhibition, Grosvenor Gallery, London, 1886, no. 21; Guildhall Art Gallery, London, 1890, no. 7; Guildhall Art Gallery, London, 1897, no. 18; Millais exhibition, RA, 1898, no. 108; International Exhibition, Glasgow, 1901, no. 194; International Exhibiton, St Louis, 1904, no. 88; Millais exhibition, RA, 1967, no. 76; *The Discovery of Scotland*, National Gallery of Scotland, Edinburgh, 1978, no. 12.2; *Landscape in Britain 1850–1950*, Hayward Gallery, London, 1983, no. 30; *The Pre-Raphaelites*, Tate Gallery, London, 1984, no. 140; *Pre-Raphaelites: Painters and Patrons in the North-East*, Laing Art Gallery, Newcastle-upon-Tyne, 1989, no. 72; *Van Gogh in England*, Barbican Art Gallery, London, 1992, no. 75; on loan to the Perth Art Gallery and Museum, until 1991

SELECTED REFERENCES
The Times, 29 April 1871; *Athenaeum*, 29 April 1871, p. 531; *Graphic*, 29April 1871, p. 387, and 6 May 1871, p. 414; *Illustrated London News*, 6 May 1871, p. 447; William Bell Scott, 'The Royal Academy Exhibition', *The Academy*, 15 May 1871, p. 261; *Spectator*, 27 May 1871, p. 638; *Illustrated London News*, 3 June 1871, p. 551; Lucy H. Hooper, 'The Pictures at the Paris Exhibition, 1: The English Section', *The Art Journal* (New York) 4, 1878, pp. 221–2; Spielmann, 1898, pp. 57, 118; Millais, 1899, vol. 2, pp. 26–7, 29–30 (prints a letter from the artist dated 18 May 1882, then on the reverse of the picture, describing its motif and execution), 474; Vincent van Gogh, *Complete Letters*, London, 1958, vol. 1, pp. 129, 417; vol. 2, p. 300; vol. 3, pp. 322, 366; Anne Helmreich, 'Poetry in Nature: Millais's Pure Landscape', in Debra N. Mancoff (ed.), *John Everett Millais: Beyond the Pre-Raphaelite Brotherhood*, London, 2001, pp. 150–7 and col. pl. IX; Staley, 2001, p. 71 and pl. 46

27
'Yes', 1877
Oil on canvas, 152.4 × 116.8 cm
Monogrammed and dated lower left

PROVENANCE
Purchased from the artist by Agnew's, 1877; James Hall Renton; his sale, Christie's, 30 April 1898, lot 91; Agnew's, 1898; Mrs A. Bannister; Christie's, 23 June 1944, lot 9; Parke-Burnet, New York, 25 September 1968, lot 25; Sotheby's, 19 November 1969, lot 157; Sir Billy Butlin; Christie's, 25 July 1975, lot 103; Douglas Wing; acquired 1989

EXHIBITIONS
RA, 1877, no. 409; Millais exhibition, RA, 1898, no. 116; on loan to Barreau Art Gallery St Helier, Jersey, 1973

SELECTED REFERENCES
Athenaeum, 5 May 1877, p. 581; Henry Blackburn (ed.), *Academy Notes*, London, 1877, p. 38; *Art Journal*, 1877, p. 186; *Gazette des Beaux-Arts*, September 1877, p. 291; François Guillaume Dumas, *Millais*, London, 1882, p. 40; Spielmann, 1898, pp. 121–2, 173, 181; Millais, 1899, vol. 2, pp. 88, 478; J. Eadie Reid, *Sir J. E. Millais*, London, 1909, pp. 80, 178; Henry James, *The Painter's Eye: Notes and Essays on the Pictorial Arts*, John L. Sweeney (ed.), London, 1956, p. 151; Debra N. Mancoff, 'Introduction', in idem (ed.), *John Everett Millais: Beyond the Pre-Raphaelite Brotherhood*, London, 2001, p. 8 and fig. 5.

26
Cinderella, 1881
Oil on canvas, 125.7 × 88.9 cm
Monogrammed and dated lower left

PROVENANCE
Charles J. Wertheimer; Sir J. B. Robinson; his daughter, the Princess Labia; Sotheby's, 20 June 1972, lot 138; acquired 1978

EXHIBITIONS
RA, 1881, no. 270; Exposition Internationale, Paris, 1889, British section, no. 105; *Fair Women*, Grafton Galleries, London, 1894, no. 153; Millais exhibition, RA, 1898, no. 182; *The Robinson Collection*, RA, 1958, no. 70

SELECTED REFERENCES
Athenaeum, 30 April 1881, p. 598; *Art Journal*, 1881, p. 186; *Graphic*, 7 May 1881; Henry Blackburn (ed.), *Academy Notes*, London, 1881, p. 34; Spielmann, 1898, p. 142; Millais, 1899, vol. 2, pp. 128, 131

A similar image of Cinderella, in which she appears older (oil on canvas, 100.5 × 73.5 cm) was sold at Sotheby's, 10 July 1973, lot 67.

29
The Old Garden, 1888
Oil on canvas, 114.5 × 174 cm
Monogrammed and dated lower right

PROVENANCE
Charles J. Wertheimer; Sir J. B. Robinson, by 1900;
by descent; acquired 1988

EXHIBITIONS
RA, 1889, no. 242; Millais exhibition, RA, 1898,
no. 181; Whitechapel Art Gallery, London, 1898,
no. 35; Exposition Internationale, Paris, 1900, no 179;
The Robinson Collection, RA, 1958, no. 77

SELECTED REFERENCES
Athenaeum, 4 May 1889, p. 573; Spielmann, 1898,
p. 142; Claude Phillips, in *Nineteenth Century*, March
1898; Millais, 1899, vol. 2, pp. 203–7, 401, 457; Alfred
Lys Baldry, *Sir John Everett Millais: His Art and Influence*,
London, 1899, pp. 59, 82; Anne Helmreich, 'Poetry in
Nature: Millais's Pure Landscape', in Debra N. Mancoff
(ed.), *John Everett Millais: Beyond the Pre-Raphaelite
Brotherhood*, London, 2001, pp. 170–2 and fig. 61

A smaller version (oil on canvas, 66 × 89 cm) was
painted in 1891 and sold at Sotheby's, 16 April 1986,
lot 230 (as *Winter Garden*).

Albert Joseph Moore (1841–1893)

146
Companions, first exhibited 1883
Oil on canvas, 43 × 23.4 cm
Inscribed lower left with anthemion

PROVENANCE
Christie's, 1887; Thomas L. Devvitt, by 1894; Leggatt
Bros; Christie's, 25 March 1955, lot 138, bought Dent
for 14 guineas; acquired 1995

EXHIBITIONS
Dowdeswell, Bond St, London, 1883; Moore memorial
exhibition, Grafton Galleries, London, 1894

SELECTED REFERENCES
Art Journal, 1894, p. 89; Baldry, 1894, pp. 54, 59, 82, 104

Other versions: *Topaz*, oil on canvas, 91.3 × 43.1 cm,
private collection (Asleson, 2000, pl. 147); *Companions*,
watercolour on paper, 43.4 × 22.3 cm, Fogg Art
Museum, Harvard University, Cambridge, MA (exhibited
Royal Institute of Painters in Water-Colours, London,
1885, no. 605).

147
Red Berries, first exhibited 1884
Oil on canvas, 49.5 × 116.2 cm
Inscribed lower left with anthemion

PROVENANCE
T. G. Arthur, Glasgow; Claude Joseph, 1894; Joseph
Chamberlain; John L. MacFarlane, 1901; The Pre-
Raphaelite Trust; acquired 1995

EXHIBITIONS
Grosvenor Gallery, London, 1884, no. 158; Institute of
Fine Arts, Glasgow, 1888, no. 24; Institute of Fine Arts,
Glasgow, 1901; Royal Glasgow Institute, 1911; *Victorian
High Renaissance*, Manchester City Art Gallery, 1978,
no. 81; *Viktorianische Malerei von Turner bis Whistler*,
Neue Pinakothek, Munich, 1993, no. 78

SELECTED REFERENCES
Baldry, 1894, pp. x, 57, 82, 105 and ill. facing p. 58; D. S.
MacColl, *Nineteenth Century Art*, Glasgow, 1902, p. 185
(as *The Reader*); Asleson, 2000, p. 168 and pl. 161

148
Lightning and Light, first exhibited 1892
Oil on canvas, 87.6 × 145.6 cm
Inscribed with anthemion pattern in railing

PROVENANCE
Mrs Linton Bogle Hammond Smith, by 1912; her sale,

American Art Association, New York, 24 January 1928,
lot 136; Sotheby's, New York, 31 October 1985, lot 59;
Fine Art Society; Forbes Collection; acquired 2003

EXHIBITIONS
RA, 1892, no. 672; Society of Artists, Birmingham,
Spring 1904, no. 196; *The Moore Family of York*, York,
1912, no. 204; *Victorian Dreamers*, Isetan Museum,
Tokyo, 1989, no. 54; 150th anniversary exhibition,
Heatherley School of Fine Art, London, 1996, no. 31;
The Victorian Imagination, Bunkamura Museum of Art,
Tokyo, 1998, no. 47

SELECTED REFERENCES
The Times, 21 May 1892, p. 6; *Athenaeum*, 21 May 1892,
p. 672; *Art Journal*, 1892, pp. 217–18; Baldry, 1894, pp. 21,
65, 80, 106; Asleson, 2000, pp. 189–91, 196 and pl. 181

A version in pastel on paper, 78 × 139 cm, was sold
in the Forbes Collection sale, Christie's, 20 February
2003, lot 136.

Sir Alfred James Munnings PRA (1878–1959)

274
Country Races – The Start, c. 1915
Oil on canvas, 50.8 × 61 cm
Signed lower left

PROVENANCE
Acquired 1995

EXHIBITION
Probably RA, 1915, no. 727

273
The Ford, c. 1912
Oil on canvas, 76.2 × 101.6 cm
Signed lower left

PROVENANCE
Bought from the artist by the Rev. Harvey W. G.
Thursby, 1912; by descent; bequeathed by J. H. Thursby
to the National Horseracing Museum, Newmarket,
1991; private collection, New York; acquired 2003

SELECTED REFERENCES
Alfred J. Munnings, *An Artist's Life*, London, 1950,
p. 239; Stanley Booth, *Sir Alfred Munnings 1878–1959*,
London, 1978, p. 88

Other versions: oil on canvas, 137.2 × 162.6 cm,
unlocated (exhibited RA, 1911); oil on canvas, same
dimensions, Wolverhampton Art Gallery; oil on canvas,
same dimensions, Munnings Museum, Dedham
(exhibited *Munnings: An English Idyll*, Sotheby's,
London, 2001, no. 22).

272
Shrimp and the White Pony, 1909
Oil on canvas, 63.5 × 77 cm
Signed and dated lower right

PROVENANCE
Stanley Howes; given by his widow to the Norwich
Arts Trust, 1970; acquired 1995

SELECTED REFERENCE
Jean Goodman, *What a Go! The Life of Alfred Munnings*,
London, 1988, pp. 84–8 (on Shrimp)

275
A Country Horse Fair, 1902
Oil on canvas, 34.9 × 52 cm
Signed and dated lower right

PROVENANCE
Richard Green Gallery, London, 1968; acquired 1999

269
Three Gypsy Scenes, dates unknown

a: *The Grey Horse*
Oil on canvas, 63.5 × 76.8 cm
Signed lower left

b: *Gypsy Caravan*
Oil on canvas, 50.8 × 61.5 cm
Signed lower left

c: *The Caravan*
Oil on canvas, 63.8 × 76.2 cm
Signed lower left

PROVENANCE
Rev. Harvey W. G. Thursby; acquired 1998

Charles Fairfax Murray (1849–1919)

65
The Concert, first exhibited 1890
Oil on canvas, 63.5 × 243.8 cm
Initialled upper left

PROVENANCE
Bought by the architect Thomas Collcutt for Richard
d'Oyly Carte, as decoration for the foyer of the
latter's new Palace Theatre, Cambridge Circus, London
(opened 1891); acquired 1983

EXHIBITION
New Gallery, London, 1890, no. 252 (as *The Music Party*)

SELECTED REFERENCE
David B. Elliott, *Charles Fairfax Murray: The Unknown
Pre-Raphaelite*, Lewes, 2000, p. 115

Other versions: same composition: oil on panel,
20.5 × 73.5 cm, Andrew Lloyd Webber Collection;
'shorter' version with eleven heads (exhibited *Burne-
Jones and His Followers*, Isetan Museum, Tokyo, 1987,
p. 107); same proportions as cat. 65, but with ten
figures seated outside: Finarte auctions, Milan,
13 October 1987, lot 197 (as *Concerto campestre*).

Sir Joseph Noel Paton (1821–1901)

157
In Memoriam, 1858
Oil on panel with arched top, 121.9 × 96.5 cm
Monogrammed and dated lower left

PROVENANCE
I. Alexander Hill, 1858–67; Alexander Whitelaw, 1911;
acquired 1989

EXHIBITIONS
RA, 1858, no. 471; Royal Scottish Academy, Edinburgh,
1859, no. 146 (as *In Memoriam – Henry Havelock*);
Exposition Universelle, Paris, 1867, British section 1,
no. 91 (as *In Memoriam – India 1858*); International
Exhibition, Glasgow, 1888, no. 313; Scottish National
Exhibition, Glasgow, 1911, no. 243; *The Raj: India and
the British 1600–1947*, National Portrait Gallery,
London, 1990, no. 325

SELECTED REFERENCES
Art Journal, 1858, p. 169; *Illustrated London News*,
15 May 1858, p. 498; John Ruskin, *Academy Notes*,
London, 1858, p. 15 (Ruskin, 1903–12, vol. 14, pp.
155–6); *Art Review*, 17 March 1858, p. 17, and 30 April
1858, p. 23; *Athenaeum*, 8 May 1858, p. 597; *Saturday
Review*, 15 May 1858, p. 502; *Spectator*, 8 May 1858,
pp. 503–4; *Art Journal*, 1859, p. 111; *Athenaeum*, 10
March 1860, p. 346; *Art Journal*, 1867, p. 245; Ernest
Chesneau, *La Peinture anglaise*, Paris, 1882, pp. 208–11
(trans. L. N. Etherington as *The English School of
Painting*, London, 1885, with same pagination); William
D. McKay, *The Scottish School of Painting*, London,
1906, p. 328; Susan P. Casteras, *Images of Victorian
Womanhood in English Art*, Rutherford, NJ, 1987, p. 65;
J. M. W. Hichberger, *Images of the Army: The Military in
British Art, 1815–1914*, Manchester, 1988, pp. 168–9,
174–5; M.H. Noel-Paton and Jean P. Campbell, *Noel
Paton 1821–1901*, Edinburgh, 1990, pp. 19–20; Alison
Blunt, 'Embodying War: British Women and Domestic
Defilement in the Indian "Mutiny" 1857–58', *Journal of
Historical Geography*, 2000, pp. 403–28; Mary Cowling,
Victorian Figurative Painting, London, 2000, pp. 61–3

After the painting's showing at the RA in 1858,
mutinous sepoys shown intent on murder in the upper
left corner were replaced by soldiers of a Highland
regiment coming to the rescue. The broader sense of
the image was thus altered, from a commemoration
of the murdered women and children of Cawnpore
to a memorial to General Sir Henry Havelock, hero
of the relief of Lucknow.

Pablo Picasso (1881–1973)

282
Angel Fernández de Soto, 1903
Oil on canvas, 69.5 × 55.2 cm
Signed and dated upper right
The Andrew Lloyd Webber Art Foundation

PROVENANCE
Paul von Mendelssohn-Bartholdy, Berlin; Justin K.
Thannhauser, Lucerne; Knoedler & Co., New York, 1936;
William H. Taylor, West Chester, PA; Donald and Jean
Stralem, 1946; acquired for the Andrew Lloyd Webber
Art Foundation, 1995

EXHIBITIONS
French Art, Philadelphia Museum of Art, 1937; on loan
from William H. Taylor to the Pennsylvania Museum
of Art, Fairmount, PA; *Picasso and Man*, Art Gallery of
Ontario, Toronto, 1964, no. 17; *Pablo Picasso*, Museum
of Fine Arts, Dallas, 1967; Summer loan exhibitions,
Metropolitan Museum of Art, New York, 1962, 1968;
on loan to the Metropolitan Museum of Art, New York,
1990–91; on loan to the National Gallery, London,
after 1995 sale

SELECTED REFERENCES
Pierre Daix and Georges Boudaille, *Pablo Picasso
1900–1906: Catalogue raisonné de l'œuvre peint*, Paris,
1966, no. IX.20; John Richardson, *A Life of Picasso*,
London, 1991, vol. 1, p. 285 ill.

Sir Edward John Poynter Bt PRA
(1836–1919)

142
The Cave of the Storm Nymphs, 1903
Oil on canvas, 148 × 112 cm
Monogrammed and dated right edge, on rock in centre

PROVENANCE
James Gresham, Woodheys Park; Vivien Bell; Maas
Gallery; Christie's, 21 March 1969, lot 61; Sotheby's,
21 March 1981, lot 74; Christie's, 25 November 1988,
lot 119; acquired 1994

EXHIBITIONS
RA, 1903, no. 160 (with eight lines of verse by an
unidentified poet: 'Careless of wreck or ruin, still they
sing / Their light songs to the listening ocean caves
. . .'); International Exhibition, St Louis, 1904, British
section, no. 38; Autumn Exhibition, Manchester, 1909;
International Fine Art Exhibition, Rome, 1911, British
section, no. 287; *Victorian Dreamers*, Isetan Museum
of Art, Tokyo, 1989, no. 41

SELECTED REFERENCES
Art Journal, 1903, p. 168; *Magazine of Art*, 1903, p. 386;
Studio, 1903, pp. 42, 44; Malcolm Bell, *The Drawings of
Sir E. J. Poynter, bart., P.R.A.*, London, 1905, pl. XXXI,
XLIII, XLIV; Christopher Wood, *Olympian Dreamers*,
London, 1983, pp. 150, 153 and fig. 15; Joseph A.
Kestner, *Mythology and Misogyny*, Madison, WI, 1989,
pp. 225–6; Richard Jenkyns, *Dignity and Decadence*,
London, 1991, p. 28

A smaller version in oil on canvas was exhibited at the
RA, 1902, no. 149 (see *Royal Academy Pictures*, London,
1902, vol. 1, p. 50).

Valentine Cameron Prinsep (1836–1904)

82
Il Barbagianni (The Owl), first exhibited 1863
Oil on canvas, 77.5 × 54 cm

PROVENANCE
Cochran family, Tacoma, WA; acquired 1989

EXHIBITION
RA, 1863, no. 391

SELECTED REFERENCES
Athenaeum, 16 May 1863, p. 565; William Michael Rossetti, in *Fraser's Magazine*, 1863, p. 790

Sir Joshua Reynolds PRA (1723–1792)

284
George, Prince of Wales, first exhibited 1784
Oil on canvas, 238.7 × 266.7 cm

PROVENANCE
Bought by the sitter for 300 guineas, and given by him to Lord Melbourne of Brocket Hall, where the picture remained until acquired in 1996

EXHIBITIONS
RA, 1784, no. 70; Reynolds exhibition, British Institution, London, 1813, no. 95; Summer loan exhibition, British Institution, London, 1823, no. 1; Bicentenary Exhibition, RA, 1968, no. 73

SELECTED REFERENCES
The Gazetteer and New Daily Advertiser, 27 April 1784, p. 2; *Morning Herald*, 27 April 1784, p. 2; *Morning Chronicle*, 8 May 1784, p. 3; *Morning Post*, 14 May 1784, p. 3, and 18 May 1784, p. 2 (on the sitter's forgetting to attend the RA dinner); Ellis Waterhouse, *Reynolds*, London, 1941, p. 74; Christopher Gilbert, *The Life and Work of Thomas Chippendale*, London, 1978, p. 262 and fig. 19; Renate Prochno, *Joshua Reynolds*, Weinheim, 1990, p. 73 and pl. 32; David Mannings, *Sir Joshua Reynolds: A Complete Catalogue of His Paintings*, London, 2000, no. 719; John Sunderland and David H. Solkin, 'Staging the Spectacle', in Solkin (ed.), *Art on the Line: The Royal Academy Exhibitions at Somerset House, 1780–1836*, London, 2001, p. 25 and fig. 17, 22

Dante Gabriel Rossetti (1828–1882)

1
Giotto Painting the Portrait of Dante, 1852
Watercolour over pencil, heightened with gum arabic, on paper, 36.8 × 47 cm
Initialled and inscribed *Sept 1852* lower left centre

PROVENANCE
Thomas Seddon; his brother John Pollard Seddon; Rossetti studio sale, Christie's, 12 May 1883, lot 95, bought Agnew's; Sir John Aird; by descent; acquired 1991

EXHIBITIONS
Winter Exhibition, Society of Painters in Water-Colours, London, 1852, no. 7; Rossetti exhibition, RA, 1883, no. 365

SELECTED REFERENCES
Art Journal, 1884, p. 151; William Michael Rossetti, *Dante Gabriel Rossetti as Designer and Writer*, London, 1889, pp. 16–17; Frederic George Stephens, *Dante Gabriel Rossetti*, London, 1894, p. 32; William Michael Rossetti (ed.), *Dante Gabriel Rossetti: His Family-Letters*, London, 1895, vol. 1, pp. 159, 163, 179; Marillier, 1899, pp. 39–40, 53 and no. 26; Helen M. Rossetti, *The Life and Work of Dante Gabriel Rossetti (The Easter Art Annual)*, London, 1902, pp. 12–13; Surtees, 1971, no. 54; Alastair Grieve, *The Art of Dante Gabriel Rossetti: The Watercolours and Drawings of 1850–1855*, Norwich, 1978, pp. 13–16; David G. Riede, *Dante Gabriel Rossetti and the Limits of Victorian Vision*, Ithaca, 1983, pp. 60–3; Maria Teresa Benedetti, *Dante Gabriel Rossetti*, Florence, 1984, p. 173; Flavia Dietrich, 'Art

History Painted: The Pre-Raphaelite View of Italian Art: Some works by Rossetti', *The British Art Journal* 2, 1, Autumn 2000, pp. 61–9; William E. Fredeman (ed.), *The Correspondence of Dante Gabriel Rossetti: The Formative Years (1835–1862)*, Cambridge, 2002, vol. 1, p. 224 (Rossetti to Thomas Woolner, 8 January 1853)

A vertical-format version with text (pen and ink on paper, 19 × 16.8 cm) is owned by the Tate (Surtees, 1971, no. 54A).

2
The Virgin Mary Being Comforted, 1852
Pencil on paper, 22.2 × 27.3 cm
Inscribed lower left: *E. L. Bateman from his friend D. G. Rossetti Highgate. May 1852*, and lower right: *William Leiper from his friend E. L. Bateman. The Hermitage, Bute, May 1891*

PROVENANCE
Given by Rossetti to the artist Edward Latrobe Bateman, 1852; given by Bateman to the architect William Leiper, 1891; Allan McLean; his niece Marguerite Key, 1928; Claudia Naudi, 1966; acquired 1987

SELECTED REFERENCES
Surtees, 1971, no. 51; Alastair Grieve, *The Art of Dante Gabriel Rossetti: The Watercolours and Drawings of 1850–1855*, Norwich, 1978, pp. 39–40

13
My Lady Greensleeves, c. 1860/63
Pencil on paper, 36.8 × 31.7 cm
Inscribed on paper attached to verso: *bought from the artist May '66*

PROVENANCE
Bought from the artist by George P. Boyce, 1866; probably his sale, Christie's, 1 July 1897, although not identified in the catalogue; Sotheby's, 24 October 1978, lot 2; acquired 1993

SELECTED REFERENCE
John Christian, catalogue entry in 'The Ford Collection', *Walpole Society* 60, 1998, p. 232 (RBF 339)

Not in Surtees, 1971, but related to nos 161 (oil on canvas, dated 1863, Fogg Art Museum, Harvard University, Cambridge MA) and 161A (pencil on paper, ex-collection the late Sir Brinsley Ford).

3
How They Met Themselves, 1864
Watercolour with gum arabic on paper, 27.9 × 24.1 cm
Monogrammed and dated lower right

PROVENANCE
William Graham; his sale, Christie's, 3 April 1886, lot 106; R. Benson; S. Pepys Cockerell; by descent; acquired 1996

EXHIBITIONS
Rossetti exhibition, RA, 1883, no. 350; Rossetti exhibition, New Gallery, London, 1897, no. 64; *The Pre-Raphaelite Brotherhood*, Birmingham City Museum and Art Gallery, 1947, no. 111

SELECTED REFERENCES
Marillier, 1899, no. 160; Surtees, 1971, no. 118/R.2

The second watercolour replica of a drawing made for George P. Boyce (pen and ink on paper, 26.7 × 21 cm, inscribed *1851/1860*, Fitzwilliam Museum, Cambridge; Surtees, 1971, no. 118). Like the drawing, the first replica is in the Fitzwilliam Museum (watercolour on paper, 34 × 27 cm; Surtees, 1971, no. 118/R.1).

12
Fanny Cornforth, c. 1865
Pencil on paper, 39.3 × 26.6 cm
Monogrammed lower right

PROVENANCE
Bought from the artist by George P. Boyce, 1865; his

sale, Christie's, 1 July 1897, lot 22, bought Fairfax Murray; J. Dyson Perrins; acquired 1979

EXHIBITION
Rossetti exhibition, Burlington Fine Arts Club, London, 1883, no. 130

SELECTED REFERENCES
Marillier, 1899, under no. 163; Surtees, 1971, no. 178C (as untraced, measuring 20 × 14 in. [50.8 × 35.6 cm])

A study for *The Blue Bower* (fig. 1, 29; Surtees, 1971, no. 178), very close to another study for that painting (dated 1865, Birmingham City Museum and Art Gallery, acc. no. 59'31), which Surtees (1971, no. 554) connects instead with *The Beloved* (Tate).

4
Christina Rossetti, 1866
Coloured chalks on pale blue paper, 79 × 63.5 cm
Monogrammed, inscribed with sitter's name and dated *SEPTEMBER 1866* upper right

PROVENANCE
The sitter; her brother, William Michael Rossetti; by descent; acquired 1994

EXHIBITIONS
Rossetti exhibition, Burlington Fine Arts Club, London, 1883, no. 75; Rossetti exhibition, New Gallery, London, 1897, no. 70; *Rossetti and Madox Brown: Family Portraits*, Manchester City Art Gallery, 1920, no. 20; *Dante Gabriel Rossetti: Painter and Poet*, RA, 1973, no. 247; *Christina Rossetti, 1830–1894*, National Portrait Gallery, London, 1994, no. 2

SELECTED REFERENCES
Marillier, 1899, no. 363; Surtees, 1971 no. 429

18
Penelope, 1869
Monogrammed, dated and inscribed *PENELOPE* upper left
Coloured chalks on paper, 89 × 67 cm

PROVENANCE
James Leathart; by descent to Mrs Rodolfo Mele; Julian Hartnoll Ltd; acquired 1990

EXHIBITIONS
Rossetti exhibition, Burlington Fine Arts Club, London, 1883, no. 89; *Leathart Collection*, Laing Art Gallery, Newcastle-upon-Tyne, 1968, no. 67

SELECTED REFERENCES
William Sharp, *Dante Gabriel Rossetti: A Record and a Study*, London, 1882, pp. 174–5; Marillier, 1899, no. 220; William Michael Rossetti (ed.), *Rossetti Papers, 1862 to 1870*, London, 1903, p. 403; Surtees, 1971, no. 210.

9
Jane Morris, c. 1869/70
Black crayon on paper, 33 × 25.4 cm
Old label on verso inscribed: *no. 251*

PROVENANCE
Mrs Janet Camp Troxell, 1971; Agnew's; acquired 1988

SELECTED REFERENCE
Surtees, 1971, no. 375

The sale or exhibition to which the label on the verso refers has not been identified.

15
Marie Stillman (née Spartali), 1869
Coloured chalks on two pieces of grey-green paper, 62.2 × 47 cm
Monogrammed and dated lower right

PROVENANCE
The sitter; by descent to R. M. Ritchie; acquired 1992

EXHIBITION
Dante Gabriel Rossetti: Painter and Poet, RA, 1973, no. 295

SELECTED REFERENCES
Marillier, 1899, no. 370; Surtees, 1971, no. 519; Andrea Rose, *Pre-Raphaelite Portraits*, London, 1981, p. 106

A painting by the sitter is included here (cat. 83).

14
Portrait of a Lady, 1870
Coloured chalks on paper, 48.9 × 39.4 cm
Monogrammed and dated lower right

PROVENANCE
J. Redfern sale, Christie's, 16 October 1981, lot 87; Whitford & Hughes, Ltd, 1982; acquired 1993

7
La Ghirlandata, 1873
Coloured chalks on paper, 90.1 × 76.2 cm
Monogrammed and dated lower left

PROVENANCE
Charles A. Howell; Agnew's; James Worral, 1894; by descent; bought from Agnew's by Stone Gallery, Newcastle-upon-Tyne, 1968; acquired 1993

EXHIBITIONS
On loan to Wye College, Kent; *Dante Gabriel Rossetti: Painter and Poet*, RA, 1973, no. 356

SELECTED REFERENCES
Art Journal, 1884, p. 206; Marillier, 1899, under no. 257; Gale Pedrick, *Life with Rossetti, or No Peacocks Allowed*, London, 1964, pp. 140, 166; Surtees, 1971, no. 232A; Rowland Elzea (ed.), 'The Correspondence between Samuel Bancroft, Jr. and Charles Fairfax Murray, 1892–1916', *Delaware Art Museum Occasional Paper 2*, 1980, p. 46 and n. 8

A study for the picture, also dated 1873, now in the Guildhall Art Gallery, London (Surtees, 1971, no. 232), worked up for sale.

11
Blanzifiore (Snowdrops), 1873
Oil on canvas, 41.5 × 34 cm
Monogrammed and dated upper right; inscribed on reverse: *Blanzifiore*

PROVENANCE
Charles A. Howell; Mrs Toynbee; Major C. S. Goldman; by descent; Sotheby's, 23 June 1981, lot 101, bought in; Sotheby's, 22 November 1983, lot 74; Whitford & Hughes, Ltd, 1984; acquired 2000

EXHIBITION
Rossetti exhibition, Burlington Fine Arts Club, London, 1883, no. 95

SELECTED REFERENCES
William Michael Rossetti, *Dante Gabriel Rossetti as Designer and Writer*, London, 1889, pp. 87–8; Marillier, 1899, no. 254; Helen Rossetti Angeli, *Pre-Raphaelite Twilight*, London, 1954, p. 101; Surtees, 1971, no. 227

Cut down from an unfinished version of *Proserpine* (Surtees, 1971, under no. 233).

8
Study for 'The Blessed Damozel', 1873
Coloured chalks on paper, 78.7 × 89 cm
Monogrammed and dated lower right; inscribed upper right: *THE BLESSED DAMOZEL*

PROVENANCE
F. R. Leyland; his sale, Christie's, 28 May 1892, lot 11, bought Thomas McLean Gallery; the Marchioness of Normanby; by descent to Lady Elizabeth Davis; acquired 1995

EXHIBITIONS
Rossetti exhibition, RA, 1883, no. 328; Rossetti exhibition, RA, 1973, no. 353

SELECTED REFERENCES
Marillier, 1899, no. 259; Surtees, 1971, no. 244A; Rossetti, 1965–67, vol. 3, p. 1174 (Rossetti to Ford Madox Brown, 28 May 1873)

A study for the picture now in the Fogg Art Museum, Harvard University, Cambridge, MA (Surtees, 1971, no. 244).

5

The Damsel of the Sanct Grael, 1874
Oil on canvas, 92 × 57.7 cm
Monogrammed and dated lower right

Plaque on frame inscribed with lines derived from Malory's *Morte d'Arthur* XI, ii: 'Anon there came a dove, and in her bill a little censer of gold . . .'

PROVENANCE
Bought from the artist by George Rae, Birkenhead; by descent; Sotheby's, 23 June 1981, lot 100; acquired 1996

EXHIBITIONS
Rossetti exhibition, RA, 1883, lot 311; loan exhibition, Guildhall Art Gallery, London, 1895, no. 41

SELECTED REFERENCES
Marillier, 1899, no. 262; Rossetti, 1965–67, vol. 3, p. 1324 (Rossetti to T. Gordon Hake, 20 December 1874); Surtees, 1971, no. 91/R.1

A variant of a watercolour of 1857 (on paper, 34.9 × 12.7 cm, Tate; Surtees, 1971, no. 91).

16

The Spirit of the Rainbow, 1876
Black chalk on paper, 105.4 × 72.4 cm
Monogrammed and dated lower right; inscribed lower left: *THE RAINBOW*

PROVENANCE
Given by the artist to Theodore Watts-Dunton in return for professional services in connection with the transformation of Morris, Marshall, Faulkner & Co. into Morris & Co.; his widow's sale, Sotheby's, 22 March 1939, lot 63, bought Douglas Langton; Evelyn Waugh; acquired 2000

SELECTED REFERENCES
Marillier, 1899, no. 279; Thomas Hake and Arthur Compton Ricketts (eds), *The Life and Letters of Theodore Watts-Dunton*, London, 1916, vol. 2, p. 194; Kerrison Preston (ed.), *Letters from Graham Robertson*, London, 1953, p. 416; Surtees, 1971, no. 245

The iconography of the drawing derives from Theodore Watts-Dunton's sonnet 'The Wood-Haunter's Dream'.

6

A Vision of Fiammetta, 1878
Oil on canvas, 146 × 88.9 cm
Signed and dated lower left; frame inscribed with a sonnet by Boccaccio, in Italian at the top and in English translation at the bottom, where it is accompanied by a sonnet by Rossetti

PROVENANCE
William A. Turner; his sale, Christie's, 28 April 1888, lot 117; Charles Butler; by descent to his grandson, Patrick Butler; Christie's, 2 April 1965, lot 49; David Rust, Washington; acquired 1993

EXHIBITIONS
Royal Institute, Manchester, 1882; Rossetti exhibition, RA, 1883, no. 304; Fine Art and Industrial Exhibition, Technical School, Huddersfield, 1883, Central Hall, no. 296; Royal Jubilee Exhibition, Manchester, 1887, Fine Arts section, no. 703; loan exhibition, Guildhall Art Gallery, London, 1897, no. 143; New Gallery, London, 1897, no. 67; RA, Winter 1901, no. 53

SELECTED REFERENCES
Athenaeum, 5 October 1878, pp. 439–40; William Sharp, *Dante Gabriel Rossetti: A Record and a Study*, London, 1882, p. 237; William Michael Rossetti, in *Art Journal*, 1884, p. 207; *The Century Guild Hobby Horse*, July 1889, pp. 95–6; William Michael Rossetti, *Dante Gabriel Rossetti as Designer and Writer*, London, 1889, pp. 101–3, 109; Marillier, 1899, no. 285; William Michael

Rossetti (ed.), *The Works of Dante Gabriel Rossetti*, London, 1911, pp. 229, 413 (for the sonnets); Evelyn Waugh, *Rossetti: His Life and Works*, London, 1928, pp. 203–4; Helen Rossetti Angeli, *Dante Gabriel Rossetti: His Friends and Enemies*, London, 1949, p. 61; Rossetti, 1965–67, vol. 4, pp. 1533, 1541, 1542, 1546, 1564, 1566, 1570, 1572, 1574; Surtees, 1971, no. 252; Rowland Elzea (ed.), 'The Correspondence between Samuel Bancroft, Jr. and Charles Fairfax Murray, 1892–1916', *Delaware Art Museum Occasional Paper 2*, 1980, p. 47

17

Desdemona, c. 1878/81
Black chalk on paper, 69.8 × 50.8 cm

PROVENANCE
J. W. Marsdon, 1911; acquired 1971

EXHIBITION
Autumn Exhibition, Manchester, 1911

A study for *Desdemona's Death-song* (c. 1878–81; Surtees, 1971, no. 254). Possibly identical with Surtees, 1971, no. 254E (untraced, ex-studio sale, Christie's, 12 May 1883, lot 34); very close to a larger sheet in Birmingham City Museum and Art Gallery (Surtees, 1971, no. 254D).

10

La Donna della Finestra (Jane Morris), 1880
Coloured chalks on two sheets of buff paper, 83.8 × 71.1 cm
Monogrammed and dated lower left

PROVENANCE
William Graham; Major C. S. Goldman; Miss Alice Goldman; her nephew John Monck; Christie's, 16 November 1965, lot 19; Sally Oliver; Peter Nahum Gallery; acquired 1989

EXHIBITIONS
Rossetti exhibition, RA, Winter 1883, no. 324; *Burne-Jones, the Pre-Raphaelites and Their Century*, Peter Nahum Gallery, London, 1989, no. 23

SELECTED REFERENCES
Marillier, 1899, no. 294; Surtees, 1971, no. 255E

After the picture dated 1879 in the Fogg Art Museum, Harvard University, Cambridge, MA (Surtees, 1971, no. 255).

Frederick Sandys (1829–1904)

81

Perdita, c. 1866
Oil on panel, 33 × 27.9 cm

PROVENANCE
Philip Henry Rathbone of Liverpool, by 1886; Christie's, 24 February 1906, lot 120, bought Paterson; William Connal of Glasgow; his sale, Christie's, 14 March 1908, lot 79, bought Dunthorne; Maas Gallery; Dr Reinhard Horstel, Bremen, 1974; acquired 1991

EXHIBITIONS
Grosvenor Gallery, London, 1879, no. 121; Grand Loan Exhibition, Walker Art Gallery, Liverpool, 1886, no. 1163; *Stunners*, Maas Gallery, London, 1974, no. 24; *John Ruskin and His Circle*, Maas Gallery, London, 1991, no. 103

SELECTED REFERENCE
Betty Elzea, *Frederick Sandys 1829–1904: A Catalogue Raisonné*, Woodbridge, 2001, pp. 186–7, no. 2.A.95

Abraham Solomon (1824–1862)

156

First Class – The Meeting, 1854
Oil on canvas with arched top, 67.3 × 95.2 cm
Signed and dated lower left

PROVENANCE
Mrs Lefroy; Christie's, 29 July 1977, lot 142; Roy Miles Gallery; acquired 1981

SELECTED REFERENCES
Punch, 1854, p. 247 (on the Ottawa version); Graham Reynolds, *Victorian Painting*, London, 1966, p. 113; I. Lowe, in *National Gallery of Canada Bulletin* 5, September–October 1967, pp. 41–6; Wood, 1976, pp. 214–5 and fig. 225 (Ottawa version), 226 (Southampton version); *Solomon: A Family of Painters*, exh. cat., Geffrye Museum, London, 1985, frontispiece

A revised version of a picture exhibited RA, 1854 (oil on canvas, 69.8 × 96.8 cm, National Gallery of Canada, Ottawa), that was found offensive because it depicted a young lady taking advantage of her father's dozing to flirt with a fellow passenger. A full-size replica of cat. 156 (oil on canvas, 68.5 × 96.5 cm, dated 1855) is in the National Railway Museum, York (exhibited London, 1985, no. 11), a smaller replica (oil on canvas, 54.6 × 76.5 cm) in Southampton City Art Gallery.

Simeon Solomon (1840–1905)

80

Beatrice, 1860
Watercolour heightened with white and gum arabic on paper, 40.6 × 29.2 cm
Monogrammed and dated lower right
Old label on verso inscribed: *no. 12*

PROVENANCE
Mrs Anstead Browne; Hartnoll & Eyre, 1971; acquired 1974

EXHIBITIONS
Baillie Gallery, London, 1905, lot 73; on loan to Lady Lever Art Gallery, Port Sunlight

SELECTED REFERENCE
Harrison and Waters, 1989, col. pl. 6

Sir Stanley Spencer RA (1891–1959)

279

The Garage, 1929
Oil on canvas, 101.6 × 152.4 cm
The Andrew Lloyd Webber Art Foundation

PROVENANCE
One of five pictures on the theme 'Industry and Peace' commissioned by the Empire Marketing Board, 1929; bought from them by Sir Edward Beddington-Behrens, 1932; Sotheby's, 6 April 1960, lot 98; The National Motor Museum Trust; acquired 1999

EXHIBITION
Stanley Spencer, Tate Britain, London, 2001, no. 41

SELECTED REFERENCE
Bell, 1992, no. 128E

276

Burghclere, c. 1932
Oil on canvas, 50.8 × 71.1 cm

PROVENANCE
Purchased by Edward James, 1935; James Kirkman; Bernard Jacobson Gallery, 1989; acquired 1998

EXHIBITIONS
Twee Eeuwen Engelsche Kunst, Stedelijk Museum, Amsterdam, 1936; *Stanley Spencer*, Worthing Museum and Art Gallery, 1961, no. 12; *Stanley Spencer*, Bernard Jacobson Gallery, London, 1992, no. 3

SELECTED REFERENCE
Bell, 1992, no. 157

280

From Up the Rise, 1937/56
Oil on canvas, 80 × 106.6 cm

PROVENANCE
Tooth & Sons; Harvey Beit, USA, by 1958; acquired 2001

EXHIBITIONS
RA, 1956, no. 91; *La Peinture contemporaine*, Galerie Greuze, Paris, 1957, no. 88; Stanley Spencer exhibition, Cookham Church, 1958, no. 9

SELECTED REFERENCE
Bell, 1992, no. 416

277

Cottage Garden, Leonard Stanley, 1939
Oil on canvas, 50.8 × 76.2 cm

PROVENANCE
Tooth & Sons, 1940; Capt. Sir R. A. Hornby, 1942; acquired 1995

EXHIBITIONS
Stanley Spencer, Leicester Galleries, London, 1942, no. 42; *Stanley Spencer RA*, RA, 1980, no. 206

SELECTED REFERENCE
Bell, 1992, no. 309

281

On the Tiger Rug, 1940
Oil on canvas, 91.5 × 61 cm

PROVENANCE
Tooth & Sons; bought from them by W. Rees Jeffreys, 1941; his sale, Christie's, 26 November 1954, lot 72, bought Cunningham; by descent; acquired 1998

EXHIBITION
Stanley Spencer, Tate Britain, London, 2001, no. 68

SELECTED REFERENCES
Maurice Collis, *Stanley Spencer: A Biography*, London, 1962, p. 162; Kenneth Pople, *Stanley Spencer: A Biography*, London, 1991, pp. 408–9, 412; Bell, 1992, no. 294; Fiona MacCarthy, *Stanley Spencer: An English Vision*, exh. cat., Hirshhorn Museum and Sculpture Garden, Smithsonian Institution, Washington, 1997, p. 55

271

The Resurrection: Waking Up (Triptych), 1945
Oil on three canvases, 76.2 × 50.8 cm (central panel), 50.8 × 76.2 cm (side panels)

PROVENANCE
Mrs M. Corble, 1950; Mrs Ann Neville; Christie's, 9 March 1990, lot 300; Bernard Jacobson Gallery; acquired 1998

EXHIBITIONS
RA, 1950, no. 566; *Ten Decades of British Taste*, Institute of Contemporary Arts, London, 1951, no. 250; *Stanley Spencer Retrospective*, Tate Gallery, London, 1955, no. 69; *Stanley Spencer: Religious Paintings*, National Museum of Wales, Cardiff, 1965, no. 22; *Stanley Spencer RA*, RA, 1980, no. 237; *Stanley Spencer: The Apotheosis of Love*, Barbican Art Gallery, London, 1991, no. 54; *Stanley Spencer*, Bernard Jacobson Gallery, London, 1992, no. 17

SELECTED REFERENCES
R. H. Wilenski, *Stanley Spencer: Resurrection Pictures*, London, 1951, pp. 16–17 and pl. 7; Kenneth Pople, *Stanley Spencer: A Biography*, London, 1991, pp. 445, 450, 467; Bell, 1992, no. 358c

From the *Port Glasgow Resurrection* series.

278

Self-portrait, 1951
Oil on canvas, 55.8 × 45 cm

PROVENANCE
Given by the artist to Mrs Anny Lewinter Frankl; Sotheby's, 4 December 1963, lot 90; acquired 1999

EXHIBITIONS
Pictures from Ulster Homes, Ulster Museum, Belfast, 1961, no. 220; Stanley Spencer Gallery, Cookham, 1963–64

SELECTED REFERENCE
Bell, 1992, no. 365

John Roddam Spencer Stanhope

(1829–1908)

86

Orpheus and Eurydice on the Banks of the Styx, first exhibited 1878
Oil on panel, 100 × 140 cm

PROVENANCE
Joseph Moseley; acquired 1987

EXHIBITIONS
Exposition Universelle, Paris, 1878, no. 241; Royal Jubilee Exhibition, Manchester, 1887, no. 209

SELECTED REFERENCE
Henry Blackburn, *British Fine Art Section of the Universal Exhibition*, London, 1878, p. 32

85

Charon and Psyche, first exhibited 1883
Oil on canvas, 95.2 × 138.4 cm

PROVENANCE
T. G. Arthur; Sotheby's, 27 June 1978, lot 36; Sotheby's, 10 November 1981, lot 47; Johnny Van Haeften, Ltd; acquired 1993

EXHIBITIONS
Grosvenor Gallery, London, 1883, no. 175; International Exhibition, Glasgow, 1888, no. 215

SELECTED REFERENCES
Art Journal, 1883, p. 175; *Athenaeum*, 1883, p. 609

Charles Joseph Staniland (1838–1916)

164

At the Back of the Church, 1876
Pencil and watercolour with touches of white on paper, 51.1 × 91.4 cm
Signed and dated lower right

PROVENANCE
Acquired 1993

EXHIBITION
Institute of Painters in Water-Colours, London, 1876, no. 102 (as *On hard and narrow free-seat, / Sit the humble village poor*)

Marie Stillman (née Spartali) (1844–1927)

83

The Lady Prays-desire, first exhibited 1867
Watercolour with gold paint on paper, 41.9 × 30.5 cm
Monogrammed lower left and inscribed on scroll upper left: Σοφία σπαρτίον υρατει [presumably for κρατει] ('skill/wisdom controls/holds the line/balance')

PROVENANCE
Sotheby's, 10 November 1981, lot 42

EXHIBITION
Dudley Gallery, London, 1867, no. 606 (with two lines, inaccurately quoted, from Spenser's *Faerie Queene* II, ix, 38: 'Pensive I own I am, and sad of mien; / Tho' great desire of glory and of fame'; the lines are correctly: 'Pensive I yeeld I am, and sad in mind, / Through great desire of glory and of fame')

SELECTED REFERENCES
John Christian, 'Marie Spartali, Pre-Raphaelite Beauty', *Antique Collector*, March 1984, pp. 42–7, fig. 2; Marsh and Nunn, 1989, pp. 99, 182 and col. pl. 6; Dennis Lanigan, 'The Dudley Gallery: Water Colour Drawings Exhibitions 1865–1882', *The Journal of Pre-Raphaelite Studies* 12, Spring 2003, p. 92

Marcus Stone RA (1840–1921)

after **William Powell Frith RA** (1819–1909)

155

The Railway Station, 1862
Oil on canvas, 71.7 × 153 cm
Signed by Frith and dated 1862 lower right

PROVENANCE
L. V. Flatow; Christie's, 4 May 1867, lot 109; F. W. Cosens sale, Chrsitie's, 17 May 1890, lot 130; Thomas Miles Restell sale, Christie's, 17 February 1900, lot 113, bought Vokins; Arthur Cunliffe sale, Christie's, 20 June 1924, lot 137, bought Sampson; Sotheby's, 13 November 1945, lot 225, bought Agnew's; Sotheby's, 9 April 1980, lot 25; Owen Edgar Gallery; acquired 1993

EXHIBITION
Victorian exhibition, Birmingham City Museum and Art Gallery, 1937, no. 84

SELECTED REFERENCES
Art Journal, 1872, p. 224; *The Journals of Walter White*, London, 1898, p. 180 (records visit to Stone while he was making the copy); Michael Davie (ed.), *The Diaries of Evelyn Waugh*, London, 1976, p. 640; Mark Amory (ed.), *The Letters of Evelyn Waugh*, London, 1980, p. 216; Jeremy Maas, *Gambart: Prince of the Victorian Art World*, London, 1975, p. 136; Jeannie Chapel, *Victorian Taste: The Complete Catalogue of Paintings at the Royal Holloway College*, London, 1982, pp. 88, 90, 141–2; Oliver Millar, *The Victorian Pictures in the Collection of HM the Queen*, London, 1992, text vol., p. 76

The original by Frith (oil on canvas, 115.5 × 244.6 cm, dated 1862) is at Royal Holloway College, Egham. Other versions are known.

George Adolphus Storey RA (1834–1919)

75

The Bride's Burial, 1859
Oil on canvas, 104.2 × 86.3 cm
Monogrammed and dated

Label on verso inscribed with eight lines from *Romeo and Juliet*

PROVENANCE
Sotheby's, New York, 30 October 1980, lot 34; acquired 1988

EXHIBITION
RA, 1859, no. 831 (with six lines from a translation of the first sonnet in chapter VIII of Dante's *Vita Nuova*: 'Mark now what honour she received from love: / I saw him leaning o'er her beauteous corpse, / Lamenting in sincerity of grief; / And oft he cast a wistful look to heaven, / Where now that gentle spirit finds its rest, / That lady was of countenance so gay.')

SELECTED REFERENCES
George Adolphus Storey, *Sketches from Memory*, London, 1899, pp. 106, 117; Percy H. Bate, *The English Pre-Raphaelite Painters*, London, 1899, p. 90 and ill. between pp. 12 and 13

The verses from *Romeo and Juliet* were presumably inscribed on the label on the verso in ignorance of the picture's iconographical connection with Dante's *Vita Nuova*.

John Melhuish Strudwick (1849–1937)

88

The Gentle Music of a Byegone Day, first exhibited 1890
Oil on canvas, 80.2 × 63.8 cm

PROVENANCE
Joseph Dixon; Sotheby's, 17 March 1971, lot 138; Hartnoll & Eyre; The Pre-Raphaelite Trust; acquired 1993

EXHIBITIONS
New Gallery, London, 1890, no. 11; loan exhibition, Guildhall Art Gallery, London, 1892, no. 144; British Empire Exhibition, Wembley, 1924; *Burne-Jones et l'influence des Préraphaélites*, Galerie du Luxembourg, Paris, 1972, no. 30

SELECTED REFERENCES
Athenaeum, 3 May 1890, p. 577; *The Times*, 23 May 1890, p. 13; *Magazine of Art*, 1890, p. 311; Percy H. Bate, *The English Pre-Raphaelite Painters*, London, 1899, ill. facing p. 114; Richard Muther, *The History Modern Painting*, London, 1896, vol. 3, p. 622; Harrison and Waters, 1989, col. pl. 50

James (Jacques) Joseph Tissot (1836–1902)

133

The Return from the Boating Trip, 1873
Oil on panel, 61 × 43.1 cm
Signed and dated lower left

PROVENANCE
Christie's, 26 November 1982, lot 306; Gerald Ratner; acquired 1995

EXHIBITION
James Tissot, Barbican Art Gallery, London, 1984, no. 60

SELECTED REFERENCE
Wood, 1986, p. 73 and pl. 70

128

The Captain and the Mate, 1873
Oil on panel, 53.6 × 76.2 cm
Signed and dated lower left

PROVENANCE
Acquired 1995

EXHIBITIONS
In the Seventies: An Exhibition of Paintings by James Tissot, Leicester Galleries, London, 1933, no. 22; *James Tissot*, Barbican Art Gallery, London, 1984, no. 61

SELECTED REFERENCES
James Laver, *Vulgar Society: The Romantic Career of James Tissot*, London, 1936, pl. VII; Wentworth, 1984, pp. 31, 105, 107 and col. pl. III; Wood, 1986, p. 89 and pl. 61

131

The Widower, c. 1877
Oil on panel, 35.5 × 23.5 cm
Signed lower left

PROVENANCE
Pealing Hall, 1910; Sotheby's, 1 October 1979, lot 41; British Rail Pension Fund; Sotheby's, 19 June 1990, lot 42; acquired 1994

EXHIBITION
On loan to the Museum of Fine Arts, Detroit, 1980s

SELECTED REFERENCES
Wentworth, 1984, p. 138 n. 36; Wood, 1986, pl. 97

A smaller version of a picture exhibited Grosvenor Gallery, 1877 (oil on canvas, 116 × 74.3 cm; Art Gallery of New South Wales, Sydney). An etching was made of the composition (Wentworth, 1978, no. 28).

130

Quiet, c. 1878/79
Oil on panel, 31.7 × 21.6 cm
Old label on reverse inscribed: *No. 3*

PROVENANCE
Richard Donkin MP; by descent; acquired 1993

SELECTED REFERENCE
Misfeldt, 1982, p. 59, no. III–17 (as *The Tale* [*Le Conte*])

The sale or exhibition to which the label on the reverse refers has not been identified. A different composition, also entitled *Quiet* but with the figures shown from the front of the bench (oil on canvas, 68.9 × 91.4 cm), was exhibited RA, 1881 (private collection; *James Tissot*, Barbican Art Gallery, London, 1984, no. 134). A horizontal version of cat. 130, entitled *Reading a Story* (oil on panel, 19 × 28 cm, c. 1878/79), is in a private collection (Wood, 1986, pl. 116).

135

L'Orpheline (*Orphans*), first exhibited 1879
Oil on canvas, 216 × 109.2 cm
Signed lower left

PROVENANCE
Christie's, 12 February 1955, lot 101; Agnew's, until 1984; acquired 1993

EXHIBITION
Grosvenor Gallery, London, 1879, no. 96 (as *Orphans*)

SELECTED REFERENCES
The Times, 2 May 1879, p. 3; *Athenaeum*, 10 May 1879, p. 607; Henry Blackburn, *Grosvenor Notes*, London, 1879, p. 31; Misfeldt, 1982, p. 53, no. III–3; Wentworth, 1984, pp. 66, 113, 138, 145–7, 203 and pl. 138; Wood, 1986, pp. 108, 111, 113 and pl. 111

Another painted version (oil on canvas, 117.2 × 54.6 cm; Christie's, 4 November 1994, lot 101) and an etching (Wentworth, 1978, no. 44) are known.

129

Uncle Fred, c. 1879
Oil on panel, 19.4 × 30.5 cm
Signed lower right and inscribed on reverse: *No.1 / £100*

PROVENANCE
The artist's niece Jeanne Tissot; Château de Buillon sale, November 1964; private collection, Besançon; acquired 1994

EXHIBITIONS
Institute of Fine Arts, Glasgow, 1880, no. 517; Autumn Exhibition, Liverpool, 1880, no. 159; Royal Institution, Manchester, 1881, no. 1190; *James Tissot*, Barbican Art Gallery, London, 1984, no. 133

SELECTED REFERENCE
Misfeldt, 1982, p. 60, no. III–18

132

'Goodbye' – On the Mersey, c. 1881
Oil on panel, 34.2 × 22.8 cm
Signed lower right

PROVENANCE
Mrs M. E. Blackler sale, Christie's, 1 November 1957, lot 143, bought Agnew's; acquired 1997

EXHIBITION
Loan Exhibition of Victorian Painting, Agnew's, London, 1961, no. 97

SELECTED REFERENCE
Misfeldt, 1982, p. 58, no. III–13 (probably the large version)

A smaller version of a painting exhibited RA, 1881 (oil on canvas, 84.2 × 53.6 cm; Forbes Collection sale, Christie's, 19 February 2003, lot 21). A version in watercolour on paper (42.5 × 30.5 cm, dated 1880) was sold at Sotheby's, New York, 13 October 1993, lot 116.

134

Le Banc de jardin, 1882
Oil on canvas, 99.1 × 142.2 cm
Signed and dated lower left

PROVENANCE
Probably taken by the artist from London to France, 1882, and completed there; his niece Jeanne Tissot; Château de Buillon sale, November 1964; Christie's, 24 June 1983, lot 103; acquired 1994

EXHIBITIONS
Palais de l'Industrie, Paris, 1883, no. 8; Galerie Sedelmeyer, Paris, 1885, no. 20; *Victorian Fanfare*, Christopher Wood Gallery, London, 1983, no. 29; *Tissot*, Barbican Art Gallery, London, 1984, no. 148

SELECTED REFERENCE
Wood, 1986, p. 123 and pl. 126

Other versions: an oil sketch on canvas, 25.1 × 47.8 cm (Christie's, New York, 1 November 1999, lot 105; *James Tissot*, Barbican Art Gallery, London, 1984, p. 132, fig. 67), and a monochrome oil sketch with the composition reversed (private collection), made as the model for a mezzotint (Wentworth, 1978, no. 75).

Phoebe Anna Traquair (1852–1936)

66
Love's Testament, 1898
Oil on canvas, 53.3 × 35.5 cm
Monogrammed and dated lower right

PROVENANCE
Acquired 1993

Walter Frederick Roofe Tyndale (1855–1943)

163
The Sermon, 1888
Oil on canvas, 46 × 102.1 cm
Signed and dated lower left

PROVENANCE
Timothy Daniell, 1976; acquired 1978

EXHIBITION
RA, 1889, no. 761

SELECTED REFERENCE
Wood, 1976, pl. 88

John William Waterhouse RA (1849–1917)

90
Ophelia, first exhibited 1889
Oil on canvas, 98 × 158 cm
Signed lower right

PROVENANCE
The artist's widow's sale, Christie's, 23 July 1926, lot 14, bought Gooden & Fox; Christie's, 2 August 1956, lot 292, bought Dent for 16 guineas; acquired 2001

EXHIBITIONS
RA, 1889, no. 222; on loan to RA in place of delayed diploma picture, 1895–1901; *Works by Recently Deceased Members of the Royal Academy*, RA, Winter 1922, no. 62

SELECTED REFERENCES
Art Journal, 1889, p. 188; *Magazine of Art*, 1889, pp. 271–2; *Academy*, 11 May 1889, p. 328; George Bernard Shaw, in *World*, 8 May 1889, quoted in Stanley Weintraub, *Bernard Shaw on the London Art Scene, 1885–1950*, University Park, PA, 1989, p. 281; Hobson, 1980, pp. 96, 91, pl. 74 and no. 78; Trippi, 2002, pp. 93–7, 142, 233 and pl. 66–7

Another *Ophelia* in landscape format (oil on canvas, 49.5 × 90 cm) was sold at Sotheby's, 17 February 1971, lot 43.

95
St Cecilia, first exhibited 1895
Oil on canvas, 123.2 × 200.7 cm
The Andrew Lloyd Webber Art Foundation

PROVENANCE
Bought from the artist by George McCulloch, 1895; Christie's, 23 May 1913, lot 91; Sir Brodie Henderson; Myriam di Stefano, Rome; Maas Gallery, 1968; Robert Walker; sold back privately through Sotheby's to Maas Gallery, 1982; acquired for the Andrew Lloyd Webber Art Foundation, 2000

EXHIBITIONS
RA, 1895, no. 97 (with partial quotation of three lines from Tennyson's 'The Palace of Art' [1832]: 'In a clear walled city on the sea, / Near gilded organ pipes . . ./ . . . slept St. Cecily.'); Autumn Exhibition, Liverpool, 1895, no. 1035; loan exhibition, Guildhall Art Gallery, London, 1897, no. 152; *McCulloch Collection*, RA, Winter 1909, no. 61; International Exhibition, Rome, 1911, no. 353; *Works by Recently Deceased Members of the RA*, RA, Winter 1922, no. 100

SELECTED REFERENCES
Art Journal, 1895, p. 176; *The Times*, 4 May 1895, p. 12; *Academy*, 25 May 1895, p. 449; *Spectator*, 1 June 1895,

p. 753; *Magazine of Art*, 1895, pp. 284, 324; *Illustrated London News*, 18 May 1895, p. 620; A. G. Temple, *The Art of Painting in the Queen's Reign*, London, 1897, p. 203; Sketchley, 1909, pp. 18, 32; Jeremy Maas, *Victorian Painters*, London, 1969, p. 20; Hobson, 1980, pp. 91, 94–5, pl. 63 and no. 112; James K. and Cathy L. Baker, 'Miss Muriel Foster: The John William Waterhouse Model', *Journal of Pre-Raphaelite Studies* 8, Autumn 1999, pp. 72; Trippi, 2002, pp. 138–42, 168, 169–70, 180, 205, 234 and pl. 110, 137

97
Pandora, 1896
Oil on canvas, 152.4 × 91.4 cm
Signed and dated lower right

PROVENANCE
Alfred A. de Pass; given by him to the Royal Institution of Cornwall, 1922; Christie's, 17 December 1965, lot 106, bought Lord Lambton; British Rail Pension Fund; acquired 1990

EXHIBITIONS
RA, 1896, no. 271; Autumn Exhibition, Liverpool, 1896, no. 878; *The Victorian Era*, Earls Court, London, 1897, no. 99; Burne-Jones, Mappin Art Gallery, Sheffield, 1971, no. 226; *Waterhouse*, Mappin Art Gallery, Sheffield, 1978, no. 11

SELECTED REFERENCES
Art Journal, 1896, p. 170; *Academy*, 23 May 1896, p. 432; *Magazine of Art*, 1896, p. 355; *The Studio*, 1896, p. 110; Sketchley, 1909, p. 23; Hobson, 1980, p. 97, pl. 85 and no. 114; Christopher Wood, *Olympian Dreamers*, London, 1983, pp. 232–3; Hobson, 1989, pp. 57, 81, 85; Trippi, 2002, pp. 149–51, 234 and pl. 119

98
The Awakening of Adonis, 1899
Oil on canvas, 95.9 × 188 cm
Signed and dated

PROVENANCE
James Ogston; by descent; Christie's, 10 February 1956, lot 14; Christie's, 24 November 1989, lot 78; acquired 1998

EXHIBITION
RA, 1900, no. 155

SELECTED REFERENCES
Studio, 1900, p. 35; *Athenaeum*, 5 May 1900, p. 568; *Spectator*, 26 May 1900, p. 742; *Fortnightly Review*, 1900, p. 1028; *Magazine of Art*, 1900, p. 386; Hobson, 1980, p. 105, pl. 91 and no. 126; Trippi, 2002, pp. 158–60 and pl. 129

A sketch of the composition exists (oil on canvas, 34 × 67 cm; Hobson, 1980, no. 127; Hobson, 1989, pl. 49).

99
The Lady Clare, 1900
Oil on canvas, 76.2 × 61 cm
Signed and dated lower right

PROVENANCE
Bought at Agnew's exhibition by Ernest R. Moon, 1900; by descent; Maas Gallery; acquired 1986

EXHIBITION
Artists' Benevolent Fund Exhibition, Agnew's, London, 1900, no. 33

SELECTED REFERENCES
Sketchley, 1909, p. 17; Hobson, 1980, p. 106, pl. 96 and no. 129; Trippi, 2002, p. 173 and pl. 140

An unfinished study for the painting (oil on canvas, 107 × 81 cm) was sold at Christie's, 25 November 1983, lot 88 (Hobson, 1980, no. 130).

94
Study for 'Nymphs Finding the Head of Orpheus', c. 1900
Oil on canvas, 96.5 × 104.1 cm

PROVENANCE
Henry William Henderson (younger brother of Alexander Henderson, 1st Lord Faringdon, who owned the finished picture); by descent; acquired 1980

EXHIBITION
Waterhouse, Mappin Art Gallery, Sheffield, 1978, no. 20

SELECTED REFERENCES
Hobson, 1980, no. 137; Hobson, 1989, pl. 60

The finished picture (149 × 99 cm, dated 1900, exhibited RA, 1901) is in a private collection (Sheffield, 1978, no. 19; Trippi, 2002, pl. 141). A complementary study for the lower part of the composition (oil on canvas, 49.5 × 90 cm), depicting the head of Orpheus in a pool of water and perhaps once part of the same canvas as cat. 94, was sold at Sotheby's, 15 June 1982, lot 114 (Trippi, 2002, pl. 143).

89
Spring (The Flower Picker), c. 1900
Watercolour heightened with white on paper, 46.3 × 29.2 cm
Initialled lower left

PROVENANCE
Mrs G. C. Stevens; by descent; Belgravia Fine Art, 1992; acquired 1993

SELECTED REFERENCE
Trippi, 2002, p. 243 n. 21

Other versions: *The Flower Picker*, oil on canvas, 29.2 × 20.3 cm (Christie's, New York, 28 May 1982, lot 175; Trippi, 2002, pl. 153); a very rough oil sketch on board, 40.5 × 30.2 cm (Bonhams, 13 June 1996, lot 57 [as *Study for the Flower Picker*]); a watercolour on paper, 20.3 × 15.2 cm, dated 1900 (Sotheby's, 9 March 1976, lot 31; Hobson, 1980, pl. 44 and no. 335 [as *The Flower Picker*]); and a watercolour on paper, 22.9 × 15.2 cm (Bonhams, 21 June 1989, lot 154 [as *Spring*]).

96
The Danaïdes, 1904
Oil on canvas, 152.4 × 111.9 cm
Signed and dated lower right

PROVENANCE
Acquired 1995

SELECTED REFERENCES
Hobson, 1989, p. 101 and pl. 1, 79; Trippi, 2002, p. 243 n. 31

A version in oil on canvas, 162.5 × 127.4 cm, was exhibited RA, 1906 (Aberdeen Art Gallery; Trippi, 2002, pl. 164).

91
Study for 'The Danaïdes', c. 1904
Pencil heightened with blue and white chalk on faded blue paper, 38.5 × 31 cm

PROVENANCE
The artist's widow's sale, Christie's, 23 July 1926, lot 8; acquired 2002

92
The Necklace (Study for 'Lamia'), c. 1909
Oil on canvas, 99 × 66 cm

PROVENANCE
Artist's widow's sale, Christie's, 23 July 1926, lot 33; acquired 1980

SELECTED REFERENCES
Hobson, 1980, pl. 125 and no. 283; Hobson, 1989, p. 89 and pl. 73

Apparently an early idea for *Lamia* (showing figure with arms raised to hair), exhibited RA, 1909 (oil on canvas, 91 × 57 cm, private collection; Hobson, 1980, pl. 80 and no. 173).

93
Study of a Young Woman, c. 1909
Oil on canvas, 59.6 × 49.5 cm

PROVENANCE
Acquired 1980

Cat. 93 is close to *Veronica*, oil on canvas, 55 × 45 cm, dated 1909 (Hobson, 1980, pl. 116 and no. 174).

100
Ophelia, first exhibited 1910
Oil on canvas, 100.3 × 62.2 cm
Signed lower right

PROVENANCE
Colonel Fairfax Rhodes sale, Sotheby's, 11 July 1934, lot 125; Newman; W. R. Fasey; Julian Hartnoll Ltd, by 1989; acquired 1994

EXHIBITIONS
RA, 1910, no. 114; *The Pre-Raphaelites and Their Times*, Isetan Museum, Tokyo, 1985, no. 47; *The Last Romantics: The Romantic Tradition in British Art*, Barbican Art Gallery, London, 1989, no. 113; *Shakespeare in Western Art*, Isetan Museum, Tokyo, 1992, no. 80

SELECTED REFERENCES
Hobson, 1980, pl. 79 and no. 176 (confused with the other vertical-format *Ophelia*, 1894; ibid., no. 109); Trippi, 2002, pp. 210–13 and pl. 190

James Talmage White (1833–1907)

113
Ruins of the Temple of Hercules, Capo di Sorrento, first exhibited 1867
Pencil, watercolour and gouache on paper, 54.6 × 102.9 cm
Monogrammed lower left

PROVENANCE
Christie's, 13 March 1973, lot 105; acquired 2000

EXHIBITION
RA, 1867, no. 716

William Lionel Wyllie RA (1851–1931)

102
London from the Monument, 1870
Oil on canvas, 72.3 × 120.6 cm
Signed and dated lower right

PROVENANCE
J. A. Goudge, Reigate, 1933; acquired 1982

EXHIBITIONS
RA, 1870, no. 14; *Works by Late Members*, RA, Winter 1933, no. 596

SELECTED REFERENCES
Athenaeum, 1870, p. 713; *Art Journal*, 1870, p. 162; Marian Amy Wyllie, *We Were One: A Life of W. L. Wyllie*, London, 1935, p. 45

Decorative Arts

PETER CORMACK

Furniture

189
William Burges (1827–1881), designer
Painting of the figures attributed to **Sir Edward John Poynter Bt PRA** (1836–1919; see cat. 142)
Possibly made by **Harland & Fisher**
The Sun Cabinet, 1858–59
Softwood (pine?) painted in oil colours, with marble top, 105.5 × 94 × 56.5 cm

PROVENANCE
Made for Herbert George Yatman (d. 1911) of Haslemere; Winscombe Hall, Somerset; acquired 1983

SELECTED REFERENCE
Crook, 1981, pp. 295–6

The cabinet's name comes from the sculptured figure of the Sun, now lost, which was originally mounted on a bracket over the top. The Ancients thought metals derived from the sun's rays – hence the allegorical depictions of lead, brass, gold, silver, copper and iron.

190
William Burges (1827–1881), designer
Possibly painted by **Fred Weekes** (1833–1893)
Campbell & Smith, manufacturer
The Philosophy Cabinet, 1879
Softwood (pine?) painted in oil colours and gilded, with brass fittings, 240 × 130 × 50 cm
Inscribed on lower drawer: *WILLIAM BURGES AD MDCCCLXXIX*

PROVENANCE
Made for the Golden Chamber of Burges's Tower House, Melbury Road, Kensington, London; R. P. Pullan (Burges's brother-in-law); Sir John Betjeman, by whom given to Evelyn Waugh; by descent to Auberon Waugh; acquired 1983

EXHIBITION
The Strange Genius of William Burges 1827–1881, National Museum of Wales, Cardiff, 1981, no. B.24

SELECTED REFERENCES
R. P. Pullan, *The House of William Burges*, London, 1885, pl. 37; Crook, 1981, p. 323

The troubled 'philosophers and literary men' depicted on the front are Socrates, Luther, Aristotle and Diogenes, with St Paul and Virgil on the sides; their various female adversaries look down from the battlements above. A procession of animals, representing the natural world, is painted around the base.

174
After **Sir Edward Coley Burne-Jones Bt ARA** (1833–1898)
Possibly painted by **Charles Fairfax Murray** (1849–1919)
Morris & Co., manufacturer
Cleopatra and *Lucretia* panels, c. 1875
Oil on varnished walnut, each 54.5 × 37 cm

PROVENANCE
E. M. C. Luard of Bournemouth; Morris & Co., George Street, Hanover Square, London, by 1929; Estelle, Countess Doheny; Estelle Doheny Collection, The Edward Laurence Doheny Memorial Library, St John's Seminary, Camarillo, CA; acquired 1989

SELECTED REFERENCE
A. C. Sewter, *The Stained Glass of William Morris and his Circle*, vol. 1, New Haven and London, 1974, fig. 199, 200 (original stained-glass versions of the series)

In 1864 Burne-Jones designed a series of stained-glass windows depicting characters from Chaucer's *Legend of Goode Wimmen*. The designs were subsequently adapted for painted tiles and, as here (the only known instance), for panels to be inset into an unidentified piece of Morris & Co. furniture.

188
Catherine (Kate) Faulkner (1841–1898), designer and gesso-worker, assisted by **Philip (Philippe) Speakman Webb** (1831–1915)
John Broadwood & Sons, manufacturer of case (with mechanism by **Julius Blüthner**, Leipzig, installed in 1912)
The Stanmore Hall piano, 1891–94
Wooden case and trestle base decorated with painted and gilded gesso-work, 94 × 140 × 260 cm

PROVENANCE
Commissioned from Morris & Co. by William Knox D'Arcy of Stanmore Hall, Middlesex; by descent (?); acquired 1991

SELECTED REFERENCES
Letter from Philip Webb to May Morris, 6 April 1892, in 'Morris Letters', vol. 5, British Library, London, Add. Ms. 45342; John Broadwood & Sons, *Album of Artistic Pianofortes*, London, 1895, p. 52; Lethaby, 1935, pp. 189–90; Kelvin, 1996, pp. 433–4

Comparison of the piano's gesso decoration with Kate Faulkner's designs for wallpapers, textiles and tiles suggests that she was largely responsible both for its design and its execution. Although Philip Webb is known to have drawn the bird (based on a specimen in the Natural History Museum, London) on the upper lid, his letters to William and May Morris consistently stress Kate's central role in the work.

180
Attributed to **Ince & Mayhew**, cabinetmakers of Golden Square, Soho (fl. 1760–1800)
Cabinet and stand, c. 1775
Satinwood with marquetry in engraved, stained and shaded woods, the drawer fronts crossbanded with tulipwood and ebony mouldings, 103 × 51 × 213 cm

PROVENANCE
Made for William, 6th Baron Craven (1738–1791), Combe Abbey, Warwickshire; by descent to the 7th Earl Craven; Christie's, 28 June 1979, lot 111; acquired 1984

SELECTED REFERENCES
Beard and Gilbert, 1986, p. 595; Thomas J. McCormick, *Charles-Louis Clérisseau and the Genius of Neo-Classicism*, Cambridge, MA, 1990, pp. 157–9

The four views of classical ruins on the inside of the doors are after Charles-Louis Clérisseau (1721–1820). Twelve of the thirteen buildings depicted on the drawer fronts, which include Salisbury Cathedral, Malmesbury Abbey and the castles at Beaumaris, Durham and Kenilworth, are taken from views engraved by Nathaniel and Samuel Buck for their series *Buck's Antiquities* (published in 1774). The one exception, a view of the Craven family seat, Combe Abbey, is based on a 17th-century print.

182
Augustus Welby Northmore Pugin (1812–1852), designer
Messrs Crace, under the direction of **John Gregory Crace** (1809–1889), manufacturer
Inlaid writing table, c. 1850
Walnut inlaid with sycamore, holly and boxwood, with leather top and brass fittings, 76 × 168 × 82 cm

PROVENANCE
Acquired 2002

The table closely resembles those designed by Pugin for the Gothic Saloon at Eastnor Castle, Herefordshire (1849–50), and shown in the Mediaeval Court at the 1851 Great Exhibition (Atterbury and Wainwright, 1994, p. 138 and pl. 253; Aldrich, 2001, p. 48 and fig. 2).

181
After (?) **Augustus Welby Northmore Pugin** (1812–1852), designer
Attributed to Messrs Crace, under the direction of **John Gregory Crace** (1809–1889), manufacturer
Writing table, c. 1850
Carved oak with footrest/stretcher upholstered in woollen needlework, 80 × 147 × 84 cm

PROVENANCE
Acquired 1998

184
After **Augustus Welby Northmore Pugin** (1812–1852), designer
Messrs Crace, under the direction of **John Gregory Crace** (1809–1889), manufacturer
Octagonal table, c. 1853
Burr-walnut inlaid with sycamore, holly and boxwood, 73 × 148 × 148 cm
Stamped *CRACE* on the underside

PROVENANCE
Made for John Naylor of Leighton Hall, Welshpool, Powys; sold with the contents of Leighton Hall, 1931; acquired 1998

SELECTED REFERENCES
New York, 1995, p. 351, fig. 109 (a design by Pugin [Victoria and Albert Museum, London, MNE 1614–1912] for a table of this type); Aldrich, 2001, pp. 55–7

A similar table, shown in the Medieval Court at the 1851 Great Exhibition, is now in the Library of Lincoln's Inn, London. Although the present table and cat. 183 were both made after Pugin's death, they closely follow his designs, both in their monumental construction and their inlaid decoration. J. G. Crace retained a large quantity of Pugin's drawings at his premises in Little Welbeck Street, London, continuing to use them, with modifications, for his firm's decorative commissions in the Gothic style.

183
After **Augustus Welby Northmore Pugin** (1812–1852), designer
Messrs Crace, under the direction of **John Gregory Crace** (1809–1889), manufacturer
Octagonal table, c. 1855
Burr-walnut, inlaid with sycamore, holly and boxwood, 73 × 148 × 148 cm

PROVENANCE
Commissioned by Thomas Tufton Knyfton as a wedding present to his second wife, Georgina Colston, and made for the Gothic Drawing Room at Uphill Manor, Weston-super-Mare, Somerset; Greenslade Hunt Fine Art, Taunton, Uphill Manor house sale, 10–11 December 1992, lot 758; Jonathan Harris, from whom purchased

SELECTED REFERENCE
Aldrich, 2001, pp. 55–6, 58

185
Attributed to **Dante Gabriel Rossetti** (1828–1882), designer (copying/adapting a traditional model)
Morris, Marshall, Faulkner & Co., manufacturer
Rossetti armchair, in production from c. 1863
Ebonised wood (beech?), rush-seated, 89 × 50 × 47 cm

SELECTED REFERENCE
Parry, 1996, p. 176

186
Philip (Philippe) Speakman Webb (1831–1915), designer (adapting a traditional model)
Morris, Marshall, Faulkner & Co., manufacturer
Sussex armchair, in production from the early 1860s
Ebonised wood (beech?), rush-seated, 86 × 53 × 43 cm

SELECTED REFERENCE
Parry, 1996, p. 176

187
Philip (Philippe) Speakman Webb (1831–1915), designer
Morris, Marshall, Faulkner & Co., manufacturer
Circular table, c. 1865
Walnut, 74 × 122 cm

PROVENANCE
Acquired 1996

SELECTED REFERENCE
Parry, 1996, p. 175

The table became a standard Morris & Co. model and was supplied to several houses furnished by the firm, including Standen in Sussex, designed by Webb. It was derived from a somewhat simpler prototype of c. 1862 (ill. *Furniture & Works of Art*, exh. cat., H. Blairman & Sons, London, June 2003, pp. 7–8), made for Sandroyd, the house at Fairmile, Surrey, that Webb designed for the painter J. Roddam Spencer Stanhope (1829–1908; see cat. 85, 86) immediately after Morris's Red House.

Textiles

191
Sir Edward Coley Burne-Jones Bt ARA (1833–1898), **William Morris** (1834–1896) and **John Henry Dearle** (1860–1932), designers
Morris & Co., manufacturer (woven by **Robert Ellis**, **John Keich**, **John Martin** and **George Merritt**)
Four *Holy Grail* tapestries, designed 1890–93, woven 1898–99
High-warp tapestry: wool and silk weft on cotton warp
a: *The Arming and Departure of the Knights*, 242 × 430 cm
b: *The Failure of Sir Gawaine*, 238 × 189 cm
c: *The Failure of Sir Lancelot to Enter the Chapel*, 239 × 180 cm
d: *The Attainment: The Vision of the Holy Grail to Sir Galahad, Sir Bors and Sir Perceval*, 242 × 714 cm

PROVENANCE
Commissioned by George McCulloch for his house at 184 Queen's Gate, Kensington, London; Mrs Coutts Mitchie, from whom purchased by Lord Lee of Fareham, May 1927; Christie's, 30 April 1953; private collection, Italy; acquired 1994

EXHIBITIONS
British Pavilion, Exposition Universelle, Paris, 1900; Morris Room, British Empire Exhibition, Wembley, 1925

SELECTED REFERENCES
Vallance, 1894, pp. 98–101; Marillier, 1927, pp. 19–34; Parry, 1983, pp. 114–17; Parry, 1996, pp. 294–5; Proctor, 1997, pp. 25–6, 33

Based on Book XIII of *Le Morte d'Arthur* by Sir Thomas Malory (c. 1408–1471), cat. 191a depicts Ladies arming the Knights of the Round Table as they set off on the quest for the Holy Grail. Guenevere is shown on the left, handing Sir Lancelot his shield. Burne-Jones designed the figures; Dearle drew the foreground flowers and the drapery patterns. Morris's contribution, in addition to supervising the weaving, was the heraldic devices on the shields.

Cat. 191b (from Book XIII, chap. 16, of the *Morte d'Arthur*) shows Sir Gawaine and Sir Uwaine – 'Knyghtes full of evyll faith and of poore beleve' – being turned away from the Quest by an Angel. The door of the deserted chapel glows with the light of the Holy Grail within.

Cat. 191c illustrates an episode from Book XIII of *Le Morte d'Arthur* in which an Angel tells Sir Lancelot in a dream that his love of Guenevere makes him unworthy of the Grail.

As described by Malory in Book XVII of the *Morte d'Arthur*, only three knights succeed in the Quest, and of these Sir Galahad alone is permitted to see the Grail itself (cat. 191d). Three Angels stand between his companions and the mystic culmination of the story as Galahad kneels before the open door of the Grail Chapel.

176
After **Sir Edward Coley Burne-Jones Bt ARA**
(1833–1898)
Morris & Co., manufacturer (woven by **John Martin**
and **Walter Taylor**)
Love Leading the Pilgrim, 1910
High-warp tapestry: wool and silk weft on cotton
warp, 150 × 263.5 cm
Woven signature (Merton Abbey monogram) and
date lower right

PROVENANCE
Commissioned by the Rt. Hon. Stanley Baldwin MP,
1910; acquired 1973

SELECTED REFERENCES
C. Holme (ed.), *The Studio Yearbook of Decorative Art
1910*, London, 1910, p. 130; Marillier, 1927, pp. 21, 35,
pl. 22(ii); Parry, 1983, pp. 117–18

In the 1890s Morris and Burne-Jones planned a series
of tapestries illustrating Chaucer's *Romaunt of the
Rose*, basing the designs on their 1870s embroidered
panels for Rounton Grange, Yorkshire (now at the
William Morris Gallery, London), and on Burne-Jones's
paintings derived from them. The tapestries were
eventually woven, under J. H. Dearle's supervision,
in the 1900s. Another version of the present subject,
woven in 1909, is at Birmingham City Art Gallery.

193
John Henry Dearle (1860–1932), designer
Morris & Co., manufacturer
Carpet with repeating pattern of flowering plants in
blue, green, red and buff, 1890s
Hand-knotted wool on cotton warp, 345 × 520 cm

PROVENANCE
Commissioned by Robert and Joanna Barr Smith and
used in the dining room of their house Torrens Park,
Adelaide, South Australia; by descent; acquired 1993

SELECTED REFERENCE
Adelaide, 2002, pp. 148, 162 (photograph showing
this carpet in the 1890s under the table in the dining
room at Torrens Park)

192
John Henry Dearle (1860–1932), designer
Morris & Co., manufacturer
Square carpet with floral pattern in pink, blue and
green, 1890s
Hand-knotted wool on cotton warp, 212 × 214 cm

PROVENANCE
Commissioned by Robert and Joanna Barr Smith and
used in the drawing room of their country house,
Auchendarroch, Mount Barker, South Australia;
acquired 1993

SELECTED REFERENCES
Adelaide, 1994, p. 47 and pl. 142 (photograph of Mr
and Mrs Barr Smith c. 1897 seated at the bay window
in the drawing room at Auchendarroch showing this
carpet); Adelaide, 2002, pp. 149, 164

195
John Henry Dearle (1860–1932), designer
Morris & Co., manufacturer
Rug with floral pattern in blue-violet, red and pale
buff, 1890s
Hand-knotted wool on cotton warp, 160 × 246 cm

PROVENANCE
Commissioned by Robert and Joanna Barr Smith and
used in the morning room of their country house,
Auchendarroch, Mount Barker, South Australia;
acquired 1993

SELECTED REFERENCES
Adelaide, 1994, pl. 144 (photograph of Mrs Barr Smith
c. 1897 seated in the morning room at Auchendarroch
showing this carpet); Adelaide, 2002, p. 165

175
William Morris (1834–1896), designer
Morris & Co., manufacturer
Small Hammersmith rug in blue, buff, red and green,
1879/81
Hand-knotted wool pile on worsted warp, 94 × 108 cm
Woven mark depicting a hammer and wavy line

PROVENANCE
Acquired 1993

SELECTED REFERENCE
Parry 1996, pp. 278–9 (ill. of almost identical rug)

The woven mark stands for Hammersmith, where
Morris's early rugs and carpets were made in the
coach house next to his Thames-side home, Kelmscott
Manor. For another version of this design, with the
border in buff, see Toronto, 1993, p. 169. Small rugs
such as this could also be used as wall-hangings.
Morris's first experiments with hand-knotted rugs
date from 1878. The following year he set up looms
at Hammersmith for making larger carpets; in autumn
1881 the looms were transferred to Morris & Co.'s
newly acquired workshops at Merton Abbey.

194
William Morris (1834–1896), designer
Morris & Co., manufacturer
Little Flower carpet in russet-red and green, 1890s
Hand-knotted wool on cotton warp, 198 × 478 cm

PROVENANCE
One of a pair commissioned by Robert and Joanna
Barr Smith and used in the drawing room of their
country house, Auchendarroch, Mount Barker, South
Australia; by descent; acquired 1993

SELECTED REFERENCES
Vallance, 1897, pl. XXXII; Parry, 1983, p. 94; Adelaide,
1994, p. 47 and pl. 143 (photograph of Mrs Barr Smith
c. 1897 seated in the drawing room at Auchendarroch
showing this carpet); Adelaide, 2002, pp. 149, 164

Ceramics

226
William De Morgan (1839–1917), designer and
manufacturer
Lustre vase painted with a band of figures around the
Wheel of Fortune, the reverse with a winged cherub
escaping from chains, Chelsea period (1872–81)
Hand-painted underglaze colour on moulded
earthenware body, 46 × 27 cm

PROVENANCE
William Wiltshire Collection; acquired 1991

SELECTED REFERENCE
Greenwood, 1989, p. 227, pl. 179

240
William De Morgan (1839–1917), designer and
manufacturer
Iznik vase painted with a winged serpent among
fruiting trees, Chelsea period (1872–81)
Hand-painted underglaze colours on earthenware,
h. 34 cm

PROVENANCE
William Wiltshire Collection; acquired 1991

SELECTED REFERENCE
Greenwood, 1989, pp. 156, 232, pl. 214

A related design (for a tile panel) is in the Prints and
Drawings Department at the Victoria and Albert
Museum, London, acc. no. E455-1917.

224
William De Morgan (1839–1917), designer and
manufacturer

Dish inspired by a Persian original, the centre with a
peacock above the inscription *Omnia Vanitas* within
a daisy and bird border, the reverse with scrolling
foliage, Chelsea period (1872–81)
Hand-painted underglaze colours on earthenware,
diam. 34 cm

PROVENANCE
William Wiltshire Collection; acquired 1991

178
William De Morgan (1839–1917), designer and
manufacturer
Tile panel composed of two tiles painted with an
exotic bird, Chelsea period (1872–81)
Hand-painted underglaze colours on earthenware
tiles, 40.5 cm × 19.5 cm
Marked: W. DE MORGAN (impressed)

PROVENANCE
William Wiltshire Collection; acquired 1991

212
William De Morgan (1839–1917), designer and
manufacturer
Ruby lustre charger decorated with a galleon and
swans, Chelsea/Merton Abbey period (1872–88)
Hand-painted underglaze colours on earthenware,
diam. 35.5 cm

PROVENANCE
William Wiltshire Collection; acquired 1991

204
William De Morgan (1839–1917), designer and
manufacturer
Iznik rice dish painted with bands of fish and with a
raised Tudor rose boss, Chelsea/Merton Abbey period
(1872–88)
Hand-painted underglaze colours on earthenware,
diam. 23 cm

PROVENANCE
William Wiltshire Collection; acquired 1991

SELECTED REFERENCE
Gaunt and Clayton-Stamm, 1971, p. 90, pl. 68

214
William De Morgan (1839–1917), designer and
manufacturer
Lustre dish painted with a galleon with single
main-sail, late Chelsea/early Merton Abbey period
(1878–85)
Hand-painted underglaze colours on earthenware,
diam. 36 cm

PROVENANCE
William Wiltshire Collection; acquired 1991

231
William De Morgan (1839–1917), designer and
manufacturer
Ruby lustre dish painted with two panthers, late
Chelsea/early Merton Abbey period (1878–85)
Hand-painted underglaze colours on earthenware,
diam. 21.5 cm
Marked: 8 (impressed)

PROVENANCE
William Wiltshire Collection; acquired 1991

SELECTED REFERENCES
Gaunt and Clayton-Stamm, 1971, p. 107, pl. 92;
Greenwood, 1989, pp. 32, 207, pl. 25

The original design, without the ground, is in the
Prints and Drawings Department at the Victoria
and Albert Museum, London, acc. no. E1221-1917.

232
William De Morgan (1839–1917), designer and
manufacturer

Red lustre dish painted with a pair of running
antelopes, late Chelsea/early Merton Abbey period
(1878–85)
Hand-painted underglaze colours on earthenware,
diam. 36 cm

PROVENANCE
Dr and Mrs Warren Baker Collection; Sotheby's,
New York, 28 January 1982, lot 235; William Wiltshire
Collection; acquired 1991

SELECTED REFERENCE
Greenwood 1989, pp. 51, 209, pl. 37

The original design is in the Prints and Drawings
Department at the Victoria and Albert Museum,
acc. no. E1218-1917.

324
William De Morgan (1839–1917), designer and
manufacturer
Gold-ground red lustre dish painted with a naked
maiden riding a fabulous animal, the verso with
trailing foliage, late Chelsea/early Merton Abbey
period (1878–85)
Hand-painted underglaze colours on earthenware,
diam. 35.5 cm

PROVENANCE
William Wiltshire Collection; acquired 1991

SELECTED REFERENCE
Greenwood, 1989, p. 205, pl. 6

213
William De Morgan (1839–1917), designer and
manufacturer
Lustre dish painted with a galleon in full sail, late
Chelsea/early Merton Abbey period (1878–85)
Hand-painted underglaze colours on earthenware,
diam. 36 cm

PROVENANCE
William Wiltshire Collection; acquired 1991

SELECTED REFERENCE
Greenwood, 1989, pp. 51, 219, pl. 124

The original design, a transverse image, is in the Prints
and Drawings Department at the Victoria and Albert
Museum, London, acc. no. E1185-1917.

216
William De Morgan (1839–1917), designer and
manufacturer
Lustre dish painted with fish on a scrolling ground,
late Chelsea/early Merton Abbey period (1878–85)
Hand-painted underglaze colours on earthenware,
diam. 35.5 cm

PROVENANCE
William Wiltshire Collection; acquired 1991

220
William De Morgan (1839–1917), designer and
manufacturer
Red lustre charger painted with a doe suckling her
fawn, within a border of fishes, late Chelsea/early
Merton Abbey period (1878–85)
Hand-painted underglaze colours on earthenware,
diam. 42 cm

PROVENANCE
William Wiltshire Collection; acquired 1991

253
William De Morgan (1839–1917), designer and
manufacturer
Painted by **Charles Passenger**
Tazza painted with a winged lion, late Chelsea/
early Merton Abbey period (1878–85)
Hand-painted underglaze colours on earthenware,
h. 21 cm, diam. 25 cm
Marked: tulip and 4 (impressed) and C. P. (painted)

Part of the original design is in the Prints and Drawings Department at the Victoria and Albert Museum, London, acc. no. E1448-1917.

228
William De Morgan (1839–1917), designer and manufacturer
Lustre vase and cover painted with stylised birds, Merton Abbey period (1881–1888)
Hand-painted underglaze colours on earthenware, h. 19 cm
Marked: *W. DE MORGAN MERTON ABBEY* (oval, impressed)

PROVENANCE
William Wiltshire Collection; acquired 1991

221
William De Morgan (1839–1917), designer and manufacturer
Painted by **Charles Passenger**
Charger painted with an angry stag, Merton Abbey period (1881–88)
Hand-painted underglaze colours on earthenware, diam. 37.5 cm
Marked: *C. P.* (painted)

PROVENANCE
Sotheby's, 15 February 1973, lot 17; William Wiltshire Collection; acquired 1991

SELECTED REFERENCE
Greenwood, 1989, p. 209, pl. 41

The original design is in the Prints and Drawings Department at the Victoria and Albert Museum, London, acc. no. E1211-1917.

223
William De Morgan (1839–1917), designer and manufacturer
Painted by **Charles Passenger**
Lustre charger painted with grotesque beasts and winged serpents, Merton Abbey period (1881–88)
Hand-painted underglaze colours on earthenware, diam. 36.5 cm
Marked: *20* (impressed) and *C. P.* (painted)

PROVENANCE
William Wiltshire Collection; acquired 1991

SELECTED REFERENCE
Greenwood, 1989, p. 207, pl. 21

The original design is in the Prints and Drawings Department at the Victoria and Albert Museum, London, acc. no. E1208-1917.

203
William De Morgan (1839–1917), designer and manufacturer
Iznik dish painted with a sailing ship within a border of snakes, Merton Abbey period (1881–88)
Hand-painted underglaze colours on earthenware, diam. 21 cm

PROVENANCE
William Wiltshire Collection; acquired 1991

SELECTED REFERENCE
Greenwood, 1989, p. 220, pl. 132

205
William De Morgan (1839–1917), designer and manufacturer
Iznik dish painted with a sailing ship and border of fishes, Merton Abbey period (1881–88)
Hand-painted underglaze colours on earthenware, diam. 20 cm

PROVENANCE
William Wiltshire Collection; acquired 1991

SELECTED REFERENCE
Greenwood, 1989, p. 220, pl. 130

239
William De Morgan (1839–1917), designer and manufacturer
Painted by **John Hersey**
Iznik vase painted with a Damascus leaf design bordered by lizards and winged creatures, Merton Abbey period (1881–88)
Hand-painted underglaze colours on earthenware, h. 36 cm
Marked: tulip (impressed) and *J. H.* (painted)

PROVENANCE
William Wiltshire Collection; acquired 1991

SELECTED REFERENCE
Greenwood, 1989, pp. 119, 238, pl. 249

The original design for part of the vase is in the Prints and Drawings Department at the Victoria and Albert Museum, London, acc. no. E1460-1917.

237
William De Morgan (1839–1917), designer and manufacturer
Painted by **Fred Passenger**
Iznik vase painted with peacocks, Merton Abbey period (1881–88)
Hand-painted underglaze colours on earthenware, h. 59 cm
Marked: *F. P.* (painted)

PROVENANCE
Acquired 1991

179
William De Morgan (1839–1917), designer and manufacturer
Seven-tile frieze of an eagle in flight, late Merton Abbey/early Fulham period (c. 1885–92)
Hand-painted underglaze colours on earthenware blanks, 15.5 × 110 cm

PROVENANCE
William Wiltshire Collection; acquired 1991

SELECTED REFERENCES
Gaunt and Clayton-Stamm, 1971, pl. 55 (a similar, five-tile panel, installed as an overmantel at Debenham House, Kensington, London); Greenwood, 1989, p. 178 (a related design).

230
William De Morgan (1839–1917), designer and manufacturer
Ruby lustre dish painted with winged symmetrical mythical beasts and foliage, late Merton Abbey/early Fulham period (1885–92)
Hand-painted underglaze colours on earthenware, diam. 36 cm
Marked: *20* (impressed)

PROVENANCE
William Wiltshire Collection; acquired 1991

217
William De Morgan (1839–1917), designer and manufacturer
Ruby lustre dish with winged beasts, late Merton Abbey/early Fulham period (c. 1885–92)
Hand-painted underglaze colours on earthenware, diam. 36 cm

PROVENANCE
William Wiltshire Collection; acquired 1991

SELECTED REFERENCE
Greenwood, 1989, p. 207, pl. 20

The original design is in the Prints and Drawings Department at the Victoria and Albert Museum, London, acc. no. E1146-1917.

233
William De Morgan (1839–1917), designer and manufacturer
Ruby lustre dish painted with a peacock in full display, late Merton Abbey/early Fulham period (c. 1885–92)
Hand-painted underglaze colour on earthenware, diam. 36.5 cm

PROVENANCE
William Wiltshire Collection; acquired 1991

SELECTED REFERENCE
Greenwood, 1989, pp. 77, 215, pl. 93

The original design is in the Prints and Drawings Department at the Victoria and Albert Museum, London, acc. no. E1328-1917.

238
William De Morgan (1839–1917), designer and manufacturer
Iznik vase moulded in relief and painted with winged beasts, applied serpent handles, late Merton Abbey/early Fulham period (c. 1885–92)
Hand-painted underglaze colours on earthenware, h. 38 cm

PROVENANCE
William Wiltshire Collection; acquired 1991

SELECTED REFERENCE
Greenwood, 1989, p. 232, pl. 215

236
William De Morgan (1839–1917), designer and manufacturer
Painted by **Fred Passenger**
Iznik vase painted with alternating eagles and serpents, late Merton Abbey/early Fulham period (c. 1885–92)
Hand-painted underglaze colours on earthenware, h. 58 cm
Marked: *W DE MORGAN MERTON ABBEY* (oval, impressed) and *F. P.* (painted)

PROVENANCE
William Wiltshire Collection; acquired 1991

SELECTED REFERENCE
Greenwood, 1989, pp. 157, 233, pl. 216–17

The original design is in the Prints and Drawings Department at the Victoria and Albert Museum, London, acc. no. E460-1917.

199
William De Morgan (1839–1917), designer and manufacturer
Painted by **Charles Passenger**
Iznik rice dish, early Fulham period (1888–98)
Hand-painted underglaze colours on earthenware, diam. 39 cm
Marked: *W. DE MORGAN & CO. FULHAM* and *C. P.* (painted)

PROVENANCE
Clayton-Stamm Collection; William Wiltshire Collection; acquired 1991

SELECTED REFERENCES
Gaunt and Clayton-Stamm, 1971, p. 100, pl. 82; Greenwood, 1989, pp. 91, 206, pl. 17

The original design is in the Prints and Drawings Department at the Victoria and Albert Museum, London, acc. no. E1393-1917.

201
William De Morgan (1839–1917), designer and manufacturer
Painted by **Charles Passenger**

Iznik rice dish painted with winged mythical beasts in stylised foliage, the central dome with mythical beasts, Fulham period (1888–98)
Hand-painted underglaze colours on earthenware, diam. 41 cm
Marked: *C. P.* (painted)

PROVENANCE
William Wiltshire Collection; acquired 1991

200
William De Morgan (1839–1917), designer and manufacturer
Painted by **Charles Passenger**
Iznik dish painted with an undulating river and swimming fish, with a boat in the centre, Fulham period (1888–98)
Hand-painted underglaze colours on earthenware, diam. 41.5 cm
Marked: *W. D. M. FULHAM*, *C.P.*, *4100* and *34* (all painted)

PROVENANCE
William Wiltshire Collection; acquired 1991

SELECTED REFERENCE
Greenwood, 1989, p. 218, pl. 123

The design of the central boat is closely related to a tile design in the Prints and Drawings Department at the Victoria and Albert Museum, acc. no. E818-1917 (ill. Greenwood, 1989, p. 120).

202
William De Morgan (1839–1917), designer and manufacturer
Footed punch bowl in Iznik colours with an outer pattern based on the BBB tile pattern, Fulham period (1888–98)
Hand-painted underglaze colours on earthenware, h. 28 cm, diam. 41 cm

PROVENANCE
William Wiltshire Collection; acquired 1991

222
William De Morgan (1839–1917), designer and manufacturer
Painted by **Charles Passenger**
Ruby and pink lustre dish painted with peacock, Fulham period (1888–98)
Hand-painted underglaze colours on earthenware, diam. 21 cm
Marked: *C. P.* (painted)

PROVENANCE
William Wiltshire Collection; acquired 1991

SELECTED REFERENCE
Gaunt and Clayton-Stamm, 1971, p. 119, pl. 110

215
William De Morgan (1839–1917), designer and manufacturer
Painted by **John Hersey**
Lustre vase painted with birds among foliage, Fulham period (1888–98)
Hand-painted underglaze colours on earthenware, h. 16.5 cm
Marked: *J. H.* (painted)

PROVENANCE
William Wiltshire Collection; acquired 1991

210
William De Morgan (1839–1917), designer and manufacturer
Painted by **Fred Passenger**
Gold-ground lustre vase painted with fish, Fulham period (1888–98)
Hand-painted underglaze colours on earthenware, h. 26 cm
Marked: *F. P.* (painted)

PROVENANCE
Sotheby's, 30 November 1983, lot 231; William
Wiltshire Collection; acquired 1991

SELECTED REFERENCE
Greenwood, 1989, p. 222, pl. 145

211
William De Morgan (1839–1917), designer and
manufacturer
Painted by **Fred Passenger**
Gold-ground lustre vase and cover painted with birds,
trees and flowers, Fulham period (1888–98)
Hand-painted underglaze colours on earthenware,
h. 26 cm
Marked: *W DE MORGAN SANDS END POTTERY*
(circular, impressed), *2273* and *F. P.* (painted)

PROVENANCE
William Wiltshire Collection; acquired 1991

SELECTED REFERENCE
Greenwood, 1989, p. 238, pl. 6

235
William De Morgan (1839–1917), designer and
manufacturer
Painted by **Joe Juster**
Red lustre vase painted with birds, Fulham period
(1888–98)
Hand-painted underglaze colours on earthenware,
h. 21 cm
Marked: *W DE MORGAN SANDS END POTTERY*
(circular, impressed), *2312* and *J. J.* (painted)

PROVENANCE
William Wiltshire Collection; acquired 1991

SELECTED REFERENCE
Greenwood, 1989, pp. 92,199, 229, pl. 200

The original design is in the Prints and Drawings
Department at the Victoria and Albert Museum,
London, acc. no. E1397-1917.

234
William De Morgan (1839–1917), designer and
manufacturer
Painted by **John Hersey**
Ruby lustre vase painted with eagles riding the back
of a fabulous creature, Fulham period (1888–98)
Hand-painted underglaze colours on earthenware,
h. 20 cm
Marked: *W. DE MORGAN & CO., FULHAM* and *J. H.*
(painted)

PROVENANCE
William Wiltshire Collection; acquired 1991

196
William De Morgan (1839–1917), designer and
manufacturer
Painted by **Charles Passenger**
Charger painted with a fabulous winged beast,
Fulham period (1888–98)
Hand-painted underglaze colours on earthenware,
diam. 53 cm
Marked: *W. DE MORGAN & CO. FULHAM* and *C. P.*
(painted)

PROVENANCE
Sold at Phillips, Glasgow, autumn 1980; William
Wiltshire Collection; acquired 1991

SELECTED REFERENCE
Greenwood, 1989, pp. 75, 213

The original watercolour design is in the Prints and
Drawings Department at the Victoria and Albert
Museum, London, acc. no. E1131-1917.

254
William De Morgan (1839–1917), designer and
manufacturer

Painted by **Charles Passenger**
Eagle's Supper charger, Fulham period (1888–98)
Hand-painted underglaze colours on earthenware,
diam. 53.5 cm
Marked: *W.D.M. FULHAM* and *C. P.* (painted)

PROVENANCE
William Wiltshire Collection; acquired 1991

SELECTED REFERENCE
Greenwood, 1989, p. 215, pl. 97 (a similar design,
in the Victoria and Albert Museum, London, acc. no.
E1174-1917)

227
William De Morgan (1839–1917), designer and
manufacturer
Painted by **Charles Passenger**
Ruby lustre bowl painted with stylised cornflowers,
Fulham period (1888–98)
Hand-painted underglaze colours on earthenware,
diam. 28 cm
Marked: *W. DE MORGAN & CO. FULHAM* and *C. P.*
(painted)

PROVENANCE
William Wiltshire Collection; acquired 1991

218
William De Morgan (1839–1917), designer and
manufacturer
Ruby and gold lustre dish painted with an eagle
grasping a snake, Fulham period (1888–98)
Hand-painted underglaze colours on earthenware,
diam. 36 cm

PROVENANCE
Acquired 1991

225
William De Morgan (1839–1917), designer and
manufacturer
Red and yellow lustre dish painted with stylised
dolphin, Fulham period (1888–98)
Hand-painted underglaze colours on earthenware,
diam. 36 cm

PROVENANCE
Acquired 1991

207
William De Morgan (1839–1917), designer and
manufacturer
Maiolica vase, painted with grotesques and winged
amorini surrounded by foliage reserved on a *berettino*
banded ground alternating with Latin inscriptions that
translate 'Be far from here wicked men and wicked
cares. Do not yield to misfortunes but go boldly
against them' (Virgil, *Aeneid*) and 'The well-prepared
heart hopes in adversity for a change of fate, fears it
in prosperity' (Horace, *Odes*), Fulham period
(1888–98)
Hand-painted underglaze colours on earthenware,
h. 59 cm
Marked: *W DE MORGAN & CO., SANDS END POTTERY*
(large, floral, impressed)

PROVENANCE
William Wiltshire Collection; acquired 1991

SELECTED REFERENCE
Greenwood, 1989, pp. 71, 213, 232

The original design is in the Prints and Drawings
Department at the Victoria and Albert Museum,
London, acc. no. E1354-1917.

198
William De Morgan (1839–1917), designer and
manufacturer
Painted by **Charles Passenger**
Plate painted with Renaissance designs, Fulham
period (1888–98)

Hand-painted underglaze colours on earthenware,
diam. 20 cm
Marked: *W DE MORGAN & CO, 1086* and *C. P.* (painted)

PROVENANCE
Clayton-Stamm Collection; William Wiltshire
Collection; acquired 1991

SELECTED REFERENCE
Gaunt and Clayton-Stamm, 1971, p. 96, pl. 77

242
William De Morgan (1839–1917), designer and
manufacturer
Painted by **Joe Juster**
Iznik vase painted with a continuous scrolling
flowering branch, Fulham period (1888–98)
Hand-painted underglaze colours on earthenware,
h. 29.5 cm
Marked: *W DE MORGAN SANDS END POTTERY* and *J. J.*

PROVENANCE
Collection of Dr and Mrs Warren Baker; their sale,
Sotheby's, New York, 28 January 1982, lot 216; William
Wiltshire Collection; acquired 1991

SELECTED REFERENCE
Greenwood, 1989, p. 151

A closely related design (but with the addition of
a serpent) is in the Prints and Drawings Department
at the Victoria and Albert Museum, London, acc. no.
E454-1917.

249
William De Morgan (1839–1917), designer and
manufacturer
Painted by **Joe Juster**
Iznik vase painted with birds, Fulham period (1888–98)
Hand-painted underglaze colours on earthenware,
h. 13 cm
Marked: tulip (impressed) and *J. J.* (painted)

PROVENANCE
William Wiltshire Collection; acquired 1991

SELECTED REFERENCE
Greenwood, 1989, pp. 92, 229, pl. 200, 201

The original design is in the Prints and Drawings
Department at the Victoria and Albert Museum,
London, acc. no. E1397-1917.

250
William De Morgan (1839–1917), designer and
manufacturer
Iznik vase (inspired by Damascus wares) painted with
tulips, Fulham period (1888–98)
Hand-painted underglaze colours on earthenware,
h. 19 cm

PROVENANCE
William Wiltshire Collection; acquired 1991

243
William De Morgan (1839–1917), designer and
manufacturer
Iznik ewer and cover decorated with fish, Fulham
period (1888–98)
Hand-painted underglaze colours on earthenware,
h. 23 cm
Marked: *W DE MORGAN SANDS END POTTERY*
(circular, impressed)

PROVENANCE
William Wiltshire Collection; acquired 1991

SELECTED REFERENCE
Greenwood, 1989, p. 222, pl. 150

248
William De Morgan (1839–1917), designer and
manufacturer
Iznik jardinière painted with sparrows in a fruiting
tree, Fulham period (1888–98)

Hand-painted underglaze colours on earthenware,
h. 18 cm
Marked: tulip (impressed)

PROVENANCE
William Wiltshire Collection; acquired 1991

247
William De Morgan (1839–1917), designer and
manufacturer
Painted by **Joe Juster**
Vase and cover painted with red fishes on a wavy
blue background, Fulham period (1888–98)
Hand-painted underglaze colours on earthenware,
diam. 21 cm
Marked: *W DE MORGAN SANDS END POTTERY*
(circular, impressed) and *J. J.* (painted)

PROVENANCE
William Wiltshire Collection; acquired 1991

SELECTED REFERENCE
Gaunt and Clayton-Stamm, 1971, p. 103, pl. 87.

252
William De Morgan (1839–1917), designer and
manufacturer
Iznik bowl painted with stylised cornflowers and
tulips, Fulham period (1888–98)
Hand-painted underglaze colours on earthenware,
diam. 18 cm
Marked: *W. DE MORGAN & CO.* (painted)

PROVENANCE
William Wiltshire Collection; acquired 1991

245
William De Morgan (1839–1917), designer and
manufacturer
Painted by **Halsey Ricardo**
Persian vase painted with fish swimming among
waves, Fulham period (1888–98)
Hand-painted underglaze colours on earthenware,
h. 32.5 cm
Marked: tulip (impressed) and *H. R.* (painted)

PROVENANCE
William Wiltshire Collection; acquired 1991

SELECTED REFERENCE
Greenwood, 1989, p. 222, pl. 146

246
William De Morgan (1839–1917), designer and
manufacturer
Painted by **John Hersey**
Iznik vase and cover decorated with peacocks,
Fulham period (1888–98)
Hand-painted underglaze colours on earthenware,
h. 37 cm
Marked: *W DE MORGAN & CO., SANDS END POTTERY*
(circular, impressed) and *J. H.* (painted)

PROVENANCE
William Wiltshire Collection; acquired 1991

SELECTED REFERENCE
Greenwood, 1989, p. 231, pl. 209

197
William De Morgan (1839–1917), designer and
manufacturer
Painted by **Charles Passenger**
Iznik charger painted with central hare and mythical
bear and a scrolling floral border, Fulham period
(1888–98)
Hand-painted underglaze colours on earthenware,
diam. 49.5 cm
Marked: *W. D. M. FULHAM* and *C. P.* (painted)

PROVENANCE
William Wiltshire Collection; acquired 1991

241
William De Morgan (1839–1917), designer and manufacturer
Painted by **Fred Passenger**
Iznik vase and cover painted with a Damascus abstract design of birds and carnations, Fulham period (1888–98)
Hand-painted underglaze colours on earthenware, h. 31 cm
Marked: tulip (impressed) and *F. P.* (painted)

PROVENANCE
William Wiltshire Collection; acquired 1991

SELECTED REFERENCE
Greenwood 1989, pp.108, 228, pl. 184, 187

The original design is in the Prints and Drawings Department at the Victoria and Albert Museum, London, acc. no. E1370-1917.

251
William De Morgan (1839–1917), designer and manufacturer
Painted by **Charles Passenger**
Pair of Iznik dishes painted with Damascus decoration of cornflowers, Fulham period (1888–98)
Hand-painted underglaze colours on earthenware, each diam. 19.5 cm
Marked: *w de morgan & co.* and *C. P.* (painted)

PROVENANCE
William Wiltshire Collection; acquired 1991

SELECTED REFERENCE
Greenwood, 1989, p. 220, pl. 134

244
William De Morgan (1839–1917), designer and manufacturer
Painted by **Joe Juster**
Iznik vase painted with herons, Fulham period (1888–98)
Hand-painted underglaze colours on earthenware, h. 29 cm
Marked: *J. J.* (painted)

PROVENANCE
Sotheby's, 3 May 1985, lot 392; William Wiltshire Collection; acquired 1991

SELECTED REFERENCE
Greenwood, 1989, p. 222, pl. 146

208
William De Morgan (1839–1917), designer and manufacturer
Painted by **A. Farini**
Rice plate painted in bronze and yellow-green lustres, Fulham period (1888–98)
Hand-painted underglaze colours on earthenware, diam. 29 cm
Inscribed on reverse: *LONDON 1891*

PROVENANCE
William Wiltshire Collection; acquired 1991

SELECTED REFERENCE
Gaunt and Clayton-Stamm, 1971, p. 125, pl. 119

209
William De Morgan (1839–1917), designer and manufacturer
Decorated by **A. Farini**
Lustre charger with relief decoration of petals and leaves on a deep blue ground, Fulham period (*c.* 1891)
Hand-painted underglaze colours on earthenware, diam. 29.5 cm
Marked on reverse: *IN FABBRICA DE MORGAN & CO LONDON* and *F* within triangle monogram (painted)

PROVENANCE
William Wiltshire Collection; acquired 1991

SELECTED REFERENCE
Gaunt and Clayton-Stamm, 1971, p. 127, pl. 122–3

257
William De Morgan (1839–1917), designer and manufacturer
Painted by **Charles Passenger**
Sunset and Moonlight Suite saucer dish painted with an eagle and serpent set against starry sky, late Fulham period (after 1892)
Hand-painted underglaze colours on earthenware, diam. 28 cm
Marked: *C. P.* (painted)

PROVENANCE
Clayton-Stamm Collection; William Wiltshire Collection; acquired 1991

SELECTED REFERENCES
Gaunt and Clayton-Stamm, 1971, p. 134, pl. 132; Greenwood, 1989, p. 211, pl. 66

The original sepia and pencil design is in the Prints and Drawings Department at the Victoria and Albert Museum, London, acc. no. E1421-1917.

258
William De Morgan (1839–1917), designer and manufacturer
Painted by **Charles Passenger**
Sunset and Moonlight Suite saucer dish painted with a galleon, late Fulham period (after 1892)
Hand-painted underglaze colours on earthenware, diam. 30 cm
Marked: *C. P.* (painted)

PROVENANCE
William Wiltshire Collection; acquired 1991

Closely related to a design in the Prints and Drawings Department at the Victoria and Albert Museum, London, acc. no. E1266-1917 (ill. Greenwood, 1989, p. 51).

256
William De Morgan (1839–1917), designer and manufacturer
Painted by **Charles Passenger**
Sunset and Moonlight Suite saucer dish painted with an eagle feeding two eaglets in a nest, late Fulham period (after 1892)
Hand-painted underglaze colours on earthenware, diam. 23.5 cm
Marked: *C. P.* (painted)

PROVENANCE
William Wiltshire Collection; acquired 1991

SELECTED REFERENCES
Gaunt and Clayton-Stamm, 1971, p. 135, pl. 133; Greenwood, 1989, p. 42

The original design is in the Prints and Drawings Department at the Victoria and Albert Museum, London, acc. no. E1247-1917.

255
William De Morgan (1839–1917), designer and manufacturer
Painted by **Charles Passenger**
Sunset and Moonlight Suite saucer dish painted with a swan with three cygnets, late Fulham period (after 1892)
Hand-painted underglaze colours on earthenware, diam. 23.5 cm
Marked: *C.P.* (painted)

PROVENANCE
William Wiltshire Collection; acquired 1991

SELECTED REFERENCES
Gaunt and Clayton-Stamm, 1971, p. 134, pl. 136; Greenwood, 1989, p. 45, 211, pl. 65

The original sepia and pencil design is in the Prints and Drawings Department at the Victoria and Albert Museum, London, acc. no. E1245-1917.

206
William De Morgan (1839–1917), designer and manufacturer
Painted and fired at the **Cantagalli** factory, Florence
The Apollo Charger, *c.* 1901
Hand-painted underglaze colours on earthenware, diam. 50 cm
Marked on reverse: Acrosticon (painted)

PROVENANCE
Cantagalli Family Collection; Sotheby's, 9 December 1968, lot 128; Clayton-Stamm Collection; William Wiltshire Collection; acquired 1991

SELECTED REFERENCES
Gaunt and Clayton-Stamm, 1971, p. 141, pl. 139; Greenwood, 1989, p. 204, pl. 17

The Acrosticon mark was devised by De Morgan for his collaborations with the Cantagalli factory.

177
William Morris (1834–1896), designer
William De Morgan & Co., manufacturer
66-tile panel with foliage and floral design, 1876
Hand-painted underglaze colours on earthenware blanks made by the Architectural Pottery, Poole, 164 × 91 cm (including frame)

PROVENANCE
Commissioned by Edward Baring for Membland Hall, Devon; estate sale, 1916 (?); acquired 1991

SELECTED REFERENCES
Jon Catleugh, *William De Morgan Tiles*, Shepton Beauchamp, 1991, p. 104; Parry, 1996, p. 193

This is one of six tile panels made for a bathroom at Membland Hall, home of the banker Edward Baring (later 1st Lord Revelstoke). Another panel and Morris's original design are in the William Morris Gallery, London; a third panel belongs to the Victoria and Albert Museum, London.

229
Halsey Ricardo (1854–1928), designer
William De Morgan & Co., manufacturer
Lustre vase moulded in relief with a frieze of storks against a red lustre ground of fruiting trees and fish swimming among waves, Fulham period (1888–98)
Hand-painted underglaze colours on earthenware, h. 26 cm
Marked: *w. de morgan & co.* and *H. R.* (painted)

PROVENANCE
Charles Moore Collection; William Wiltshire Collection; acquired 1991

SELECTED REFERENCE
Greenwood, 1989, p. 194

The original design is in the Prints and Drawings Department at the Victoria and Albert Museum, London, acc. no. E1671-1917. De Morgan and the architect Halsey Ricardo went into partnership in 1888, the year in which the pottery moved from Merton Abbey to Sands End, Fulham. Ricardo produced a number of vases (such as this) and tiles with decoration in relief, sometimes adapting De Morgan's designs.

Books

259
William Morris (1834–1896) with **Sir Edward Coley Burne-Jones Bt ARA** (1833–1898) and **Charles Fairfax Murray** (1849–1919); later work by **Graily Hewitt** (1864–1953) and **Louise Powell** (1882–1956)
The Aeneid of Virgil, 1874–75 and 1904 – *c.* 1910

Manuscript in black ink in roman minuscule on vellum, with some lettering and borders in burnished gold, others in bodycolour; vi + 185 (paginated 1–370)

+ vi vellum leaves, 33.5 × 24 cm; binding in panelled brown morocco by **J. & J. Leighton** of London with gilt edges and turn-ins, vellum pastedowns and matching morocco case with gilt-lettered spine, 34.9 × 26 cm

PROVENANCE
Sold by William Morris to Charles Fairfax Murray, *c.* 1890; by descent to Fairfax Murray's son Arthur; anonymous sale, Sotheby's, 18 July 1928, lot 2; Mrs George W. Millard, from whom purchased by Mrs Estelle Doheny, 24 June 1932; Estelle Doheny Collection, The Edward Laurence Doheny Memorial Library, St John's Seminary, Camarillo, CA; acquired 1989

EXHIBITIONS
William Morris and the Art of the Book, The Pierpont Morgan Library, New York, 1976, no. 63; *William Morris*, Victoria and Albert Museum, London, 1996, no. N. 14; *Edward Burne-Jones: Victorian Artist–Dreamer*, Metropolitan Museum of Art, New York, 1998, no. 66

SELECTED REFERENCES
Mackail, 1899, vol. 1, pp. 328–30; Burne-Jones, 1904, vol. 2, p. 56; Morris, 1910–15, vol. 11, pp. xxi–xxvii; Anna Cox Brinton, *A Pre-Raphaelite Aeneid of Virgil in the Collection of Mrs Edward Lawrence Doheny of Los Angeles*, Los Angeles, 1934; Kelvin, 1984, pp. 254–5, 274; Parry, 1996, pp. 299–300, 308; David Elliott, *Charles Fairfax Murray: The Unknown Pre-Raphaelite*, Lewes, 2000, p. 58

Morris wrote out 177 pages of the manuscript and began a number of the illuminated borders. The writing was later completed by Hewitt, who also executed the burnished gold initials, capital texts and one border. Fairfax Murray painted, but never completed, the miniatures after designs (now in the Fitzwilliam Museum, Cambridge) by Burne-Jones. Powell completed only four of the full-page foliate borders, leaving the others as outline drawings.

261
John Ruskin, *The Nature of Gothic: A Chapter of the Stones of Venice*, with a Preface by William Morris
Published by **George Allen** and printed by **William Morris** (1834–1896) at the Kelmscott Press, Hammersmith, 1892

One of 500 copies printed in Morris's Golden type on handmade paper, the first text page with a full woodcut border designed by Morris; bound in original stiff vellum with silk ties and gilt-lettered spine, page size 20 × 14.1 cm

PROVENANCE
Estelle Doheny Collection, The Edward Laurence Doheny Memorial Library, St John's Seminary, Camarillo, CA; acquired 1989

SELECTED REFERENCES
Cockerell, 1898, pp. 19, 23–4; Mackail, 1899, vol. 2, p. 289; Peterson, 1984, pp. 12–14

In his preface Morris writes that Ruskin's chapter, with its central assertion that 'art is the expression of man's pleasure in labour', was 'one of the very few necessary and inevitable utterances of the century'.

262
William Morris, *News from Nowhere: Or, an Epoch of Rest, being Some Chapters from a Utopian Romance*
Published by **Reeves & Turner** and printed by **William Morris** (1834–1896) at the Kelmscott Press, Hammersmith, 1893

One of 10 copies on vellum of a total edition of 310, printed in Morris's Golden type; the frontispiece illustration of Kelmscott Manor by **Charles March Gere** (1869–1957) within a full woodcut border designed by Morris; bound in original limp vellum with silk ties and gilt-lettered spine, page size 20.5 × 14 cm

PROVENANCE
Estelle Doheny Collection, The Edward Laurence Doheny Memorial Library, St John's Seminary, Camarillo, CA; acquired 1989

SELECTED REFERENCES
Cockerell; 1898, pp. 29–30; Peterson, 1984, pp. 33–6

Sydney Cockerell, Morris's secretary and later also secretary of the Kelmscott Press, suggested that a view of Kelmscott Manor, the setting for the novel's closing episode, should be used as an illustration. Printing of the text had already been completed when Gere visited the house to make drawings in January 1893, so publication was delayed for some months until the frontispiece – which has since become one of the best-known images associated with Morris – had been engraved.

266

The Order of Chivalry, translated from the French by William Caxton and reprinted from his edition of 1484; edited by F. S. Ellis; with *L'Ordene de Chevalerie* in a verse translation from the French by William Morris
Published by **Reeves & Turner** and printed by **William Morris** (1834–1896) at the Kelmscott Press, Hammersmith, 1893

One of 225 copies of an edition of 235, printed in Morris's Chaucer type in black and red on handmade paper; the frontispiece illustration by **Sir Edward Coley Burne-Jones Bt ARA** (1833–1898) within a full woodcut border, and with several partial page-borders and initial capitals, all designed by Morris; bound in original limp vellum with silk ties and gilt-lettered spine, page size 20 × 13.8 cm

PROVENANCE
Estelle Doheny Collection, The Edward Laurence Doheny Memorial Library, St John's Seminary, Camarillo, CA; acquired 1989

SELECTED REFERENCES
Cockerell, 1898, p. 30; Mackail, 1899, vol. 2, pp. 294–5; Peterson, 1984, pp. 36–9

This was one of several Kelmscott Press titles which were Morris's tribute to Caxton, the first English printer. The inclusion of the second text, a 13th-century French poem, was an afterthought. A prose translation was originally intended but, realising that the Kelmscott Press 'kept a poet of its own', Morris translated it into verse in a few weeks.

260

William Morris, *Gothic Architecture: A Lecture for the Arts and Crafts Exhibition Society*
Published and printed by **William Morris** (1834–1896) at the Kelmscott Press, Hammersmith, 1893

One of 45 copies on vellum of a total edition of 1545, printed in Morris's Golden type in black and red, with initial capitals designed by Morris; bound in original holland-backed blue paper boards, page size 14.3 × 10.4 cm

PROVENANCE
William Morris (this copy has his bookplate); sold to Henry Gamman, August 1897; Estelle Doheny Collection, The Edward Laurence Doheny Memorial Library, St John's Seminary, Camarillo, CA; acquired 1989

SELECTED REFERENCES
Cockerell, 1898, pp. 32–3; H. Halliday Sparling, *The Kelmscott Press and William Morris Master-Craftsman*, London, 1924, p. 87; Peterson, 1984, pp. 48–50

Gothic Architecture was the first book printed in the small 16mo format by the Kelmscott Press and is one of its most delightful productions. During October and November 1893, a press was moved to the Arts & Crafts Exhibition at the New Gallery in Regent Street, London, and copies 'were printed in public, under the eyes of an interested and constantly renewed crowd'.

264

Dante Gabriel Rossetti, *Ballads and Narrative Poems*
Published by **Ellis & Elvey** and printed by **William Morris** (1834–1896) at the Kelmscott Press, Hammersmith, 1893

One of 310 copies of a total edition of 316, printed in Morris's Golden type in black and red on handmade paper, with a woodcut title page and other ornaments designed by Morris; bound in original limp vellum with silk ties and gilt-lettered spine, page size 20.5 × 14 cm

PROVENANCE
Estelle Doheny Collection, The Edward Laurence Doheny Memorial Library, St John's Seminary, Camarillo, CA; acquired 1989

SELECTED REFERENCES
Cockerell, 1898, p. 33; Peterson 1984, pp. 53–5

William Michael Rossetti, the artist–poet's brother, read the proofs both for this volume and for a companion volume of D.G. Rossetti's *Sonnets and Lyrical Poems* issued by the Kelmscott Press in April 1894.

263

The Tale of King Florus and the Fair Jehane, translated by William Morris
Published and printed by **William Morris** (1834–1896) at the Kelmscott Press, Hammersmith, 1893

One of 350 copies of a total edition of 365, printed in Morris's Chaucer type in black and red on handmade paper, with a woodcut title page and other ornaments designed by Morris; bound in original holland-backed blue paper boards, page size 14.6 × 10.4 cm

PROVENANCE
Estelle Doheny Collection, The Edward Laurence Doheny Memorial Library, St John's Seminary, Camarillo, CA; acquired 1989

SELECTED REFERENCES
Cockerell, 1898, p. 34; Mackail, 1899, vol. 2, pp. 297–8; Peterson, 1984, pp. 56–8

Morris translated the text from an 1856 edition of 13th-century French romances which he regarded as 'among the most beautiful works of the Middle Ages'. This copy is inscribed 'To E. Burden with affectionate love & best wishes for a happy New Year from Jenny Morris Jan. 1, 1894'. Elizabeth Burden (Jane Morris's sister and Jenny's aunt) was an accomplished embroiderer who worked for Morris & Co. and taught at the Royal School of Needlework in London. She lived with the Morrises from 1860 until the mid-1870s.

265

Sir Perecyvelle of Gales, edited by F. S. Ellis
Published and printed by **William Morris** (1834–1896) at the Kelmscott Press, Hammersmith, 1895

One of 350 copies of a total edition of 358, printed in Morris's Chaucer type in black and red on handmade paper, with a woodcut frontispiece after a design by **Sir Edward Coley Burne-Jones Bt ARA** (1833–1898) and with borders and other ornaments designed by Morris; bound in original holland-backed blue paper boards, page size 14.6 × 10.4 cm

PROVENANCE
Estelle Doheny Collection, The Edward Laurence Doheny Memorial Library, St John's Seminary, Camarillo, CA; acquired 1989

SELECTED REFERENCES
Cockerell, 1898, p. 40; Peterson, 1984, pp. 86–7

On a miniature scale, Burne-Jones's frontispiece echoes the intense Arthurian atmosphere of the *Holy Grail* tapestries (cat. 191). *Sir Perecyvelle* was the first of three Kelmscott Press versions of medieval romances taken from a manuscript in the library of Lincoln Cathedral. All three had first been published

in 1844 and, according to S. C. Cockerell, were 'a favourite with Mr Morris from his Oxford days'.

267

The Works of Geoffrey Chaucer, edited by F.S. Ellis
Published and printed by **William Morris** (1834–1896) at the Kelmscott Press, Hammersmith, 1896

One of 13 copies on vellum of a total edition of 438, printed in Morris's Chaucer and Troy types in double columns in black and red, with 87 woodcut illustrations after designs by **Sir Edward Coley Burne-Jones Bt ARA** (1833–1898) and with borders and other ornaments designed by Morris; bound in quarter brown morocco over oak boards, blind-tooled with Celtic interlace and gilt-lettered on spine, probably by the **W. H. Smith Bindery** under the direction of Douglas Cockerell, page size 42.5 × 29.2 cm

PROVENANCE
Estelle Doheny Collection, The Edward Laurence Doheny Memorial Library, St John's Seminary, Camarillo, CA; acquired 1989

SELECTED REFERENCES
Cockerell, 1898, pp. 44–7; Mackail, 1899, vol. 2, pp. 321, 325, 330, 337–8, 341–2; Peterson, 1984, pp. 101–15; Parry, 1996, pp. 330–6; New York, 1998, pp. 308–11

The most ambitious of all the Kelmscott Press editions, the *Chaucer* was planned soon after the founding of the press in 1891 but was completed only four months before Morris's death. It was immediately acclaimed as his 'crowning achievement' as a printer and it remains a landmark in the history of modern book production. Burne-Jones famously likened it to 'a pocket cathedral', with Morris as master-mason and himself as 'carver of images'.

33

Sir Edward Coley Burne-Jones Bt ARA (1833–1898), *Manuscript volume of illustrated letters and humorous drawings sent to Helen Mary Gaskell*, 1897–98

104 pages including some blank; bound in white tooled and gilt-lettered vellum at the **Doves Bindery**, Hammersmith, by **Stella Cobden-Sanderson** and gilt-stamped with her initials, c. 1905, size of binding 18 × 12.5 × 2 cm

PROVENANCE
Mrs Helen Mary Gaskell; by whom given to Lord Balniel (Earl of Crawford and Balcarres), October 1938; acquired 2002

SELECTED REFERENCES
London, 1975, p. 79; New York, 1998, pp. 250

Burne-Jones first met Helen Mary Gaskell, wife of Captain Gaskell of the 9th Lancers, in 1892. She became one of several close female friends to whom the artist sent comic letters and drawings. Archaeology is the theme of these letters, with Burne-Jones inventing spurious German experts, including Professors Bung and Dustflopper and a Dr Paulus Schwumpff, and illustrating their fictional discussions with drawings of recent 'finds'. One drawing of an obviously late-medieval (and very Burne-Jonesian) helmet with an owl as its crest is supposed to be 'the handwork of Pheidias at the zenith of his power and represents the chryselephantine statue of Athena Promachos'.

268

Sir Edward Coley Burne-Jones Bt ARA, *The Flower Book: Reproductions of Thirty-Eight Watercolour Designs*
Printed by **Henri Piazza & Co.** and published by the **Fine Art Society Ltd**, London, 1905

Number 39 of an edition of 300, printed in full-colour facsimile from Burne-Jones's original watercolours, with an introductory text by Georgiana Burne-Jones and a 4-page facsimile of the artist's own list of

flower names at the end; bound in green morocco with gilt-lettered spine by the **W. H. Smith Bindery** under the direction of Douglas Cockerell, page size 33 × 26.5 cm

PROVENANCE
Miss Katie Lewis of Wychwood, Broadway, Worcestershire; the Hon. A. L. Baldwin, Twyning, Tewkesbury, Gloucestershire; acquired 1989

SELECTED REFERENCES
Burne-Jones, 1904, vol. 2, pp. 118–19; London, 1975, p. 89; New York, 1998, pp. 285–6

In 1882 Burne-Jones began a series of circular watercolour designs inspired by the traditional names of flowers, working on them at irregular intervals until his death in 1898. The flowers themselves are not shown; instead, each image is, in Lady Burne-Jones's words, 'a kind of magic mirror' capturing the symbolic and poetic associations of the names. The facsimile printing perfectly matches the qualities of the originals, which were given to the British Museum in 1909.

Selected Bibliography

Adelaide, 1994
Morris & Company: Pre-Raphaelites and the
Arts & Crafts Movement in South Australia,
Christopher Menz, exh. cat., Art Gallery of
South Australia, Adelaide, 1994

Adelaide, 2002
Morris & Co., Christopher Menz, exh. cat.,
Art Gallery of South Australia, Adelaide, 2002

Aldrich, 1994
Megan Aldrich, Gothic Revival, London, 1994

Aldrich, 2001
Megan Aldrich, 'Marquetry in the Medieval
Court: The Octagonal Tables of Pugin and
Crace', The Decorative Arts Society Journal 25,
2001, pp. 48–58

Asleson, 2000
Robyn Asleson, Albert Moore, London, 2000

Atterbury and Wainwright, 1994
Paul Atterbury and Clive Wainwright (eds),
Pugin, New Haven and London, 1994

Baldry, 1894
Alfred Lys Baldry, Albert Moore: His Life and
Works, London, 1894

Barrow, 2001
R.J. Barrow, Lawrence Alma-Tadema, London,
2001

Beard and Gilbert, 1986
Geoffrey Beard and Christopher Gilbert (eds),
Dictionary of English Furniture Makers
1660–1840, Leeds, 1986

Bell, 1901
Malcolm Bell, Sir Edward Burne-Jones: A Record
and Review, London, 1901

Bell, 1992
Keith Bell, Stanley Spencer: A Complete
Catalogue of the Paintings, London, 1992

Bennett, 1988
Mary Bennett, Artists of the Pre-Raphaelite
Circle: The First Generation – Catalogue of
Works in the Walker Art Gallery, Lady Lever Art
Gallery and Sudley Art Gallery, London, 1988

Brown, 1981
The Diary of Ford Madox Brown, Virginia Surtees
(ed.), New Haven and London, 1981

Burne-Jones, 1904
G[eorgiana] B[urne]-J[ones], Memorials of
Edward Burne-Jones, 2 vols, London, 1904

Cardiff, 1981
The Strange Genius of William Burges 'Art-
Architect', J. Mordaunt Crook (ed.), exh. cat.,
National Museum of Wales, Cardiff, 1981

Cartwright, 1894
Julia Cartwright, The Life and Work of Sir Edward
Burne-Jones, London, 1894.

Cockerell, 1898
S. C. Cockerell (ed.), A Note by William Morris
on His Aims in Founding the Kelmscott Press,
London, 1898

Cowling, 2000
Mary Cowling, Victorian Figurative Painting:
Domestic Life and the Contemporary Social
Scene, London, 2000

Crook, 1981
J. Mordaunt Crook, William Burges and the
High Victorian Dream, London, 1981

de Lisle, 1904
Fortunée de Lisle, Burne-Jones, London, 1904

Fredeman, 1975
William Fredeman (ed.), The PRB Journal:
William Michael Rossetti's Diary of the Pre-
Raphaelite Brotherhood, 1849–1953. . .,
Oxford, 1975

Funnell and Warner, 1999
Millais: Portraits, Peter Funnell and Malcolm
Warner (eds), exh. cat., National Portrait
Gallery, London, 1999

Gaunt and Clayton-Stamm, 1971
William Gaunt and M. D. E. Clayton-Stamm,
William De Morgan, London, 1971

Greenwood, 1989
Martin Greenwood, The Designs of William
De Morgan, Shepton Beauchamp, 1989

Harrison and Waters, 1989
Martin Harrison and Bill Waters, Burne-Jones,
2nd edn, London, 1989

Hilton, 2002
Timothy Hilton, John Ruskin, New Haven and
London, 2002

Hobson, 1980
Anthony Hobson, The Art and Life of J. W.
Waterhouse RA, 1849–1917, London, 1980

Hobson, 1989
Anthony Hobson, J. W. Waterhouse, Oxford,
1989

Hunt, 1905
William Holman Hunt, Pre-Raphaelitism and
the Pre-Raphaelite Brotherhood, 2 vols, London,
1905

Kelvin, 1984
Norman Kelvin (ed.), The Collected Letters
of William Morris, vol. 1, Princeton, 1984

Kelvin, 1996
Norman Kelvin (ed.), The Collected Letters
of William Morris, vol. 3, Princeton, 1996

Lethaby, 1935
W. R. Lethaby, Philip Webb and His Work,
Oxford, 1935

London, 1975
Burne-Jones: The Paintings, Graphic and
Decorative Work of Sir Edward Burne-Jones
1833–98, John Christian (ed.), exh. cat.,
Hayward Gallery, London, 1975

London, 1984
The Pre-Raphaelites, Leslie Parris (ed.), exh. cat.,
Tate Gallery, London, 1984

London, 1989
The Last Romantics: The Romantic Tradition in
British Art, Burne-Jones to Stanley Spencer,
John Christian (ed.), exh. cat., Barbican Art
Gallery, London, 1989

Mackail, 1899
J. W. Mackail, The Life of William Morris, 2 vols,
London, 1899

Marillier, 1899
H. C. Marillier, Dante Gabriel Rossetti, An
Illustrated Memorial of His Art and Life, London,
1899

Marillier, 1927
H. C. Marillier, History of the Merton Abbey
Tapestry Works, London, 1927

Marsh and Nunn, 1989
Jan Marsh and Pamela Gerrish Nunn, Women
Artists and the Pre-Raphaelite Movement,
London, 1989

Millais, 1899
John Guille Millais, The Life and Letters of
Sir John Everett Millais, 2 vols, London, 1899

Misfeldt, 1982
Willard E. Misfeldt, The Albums of James Tissot,
Bowling Green, OH, 1982

Morris, 1910–15
May Morris (ed.), The Collected Works of
William Morris, 24 vols, London, 1910–15

New York, 1995
A. W. N. Pugin: Master of Gothic Revival, Paul
Atterbury (ed.), exh. cat., The Bard Graduate
Centre for Studies in the Decorative Arts,
New York, 1995

New York, 1998
Edward Burne-Jones: Victorian Artist–Dreamer,
Stephen Wildman and John Christian (eds),
exh. cat., Metropolitan Museum of Art,
New York, 1998

Newall, 1990
Christopher Newall, The Art of Lord Leighton,
Oxford, 1990

Ormond, 1975
Leonée and Richard Ormond, Lord Leighton,
New Haven and London, 1975

Parry, 1983
Linda Parry, William Morris Textiles, London,
1983

Parry, 1996
Linda Parry (ed.), William Morris, London, 1996

Peterson, 1984
William S. Peterson, A Bibliography of the
Kelmscott Press, Oxford, 1984

Prettejohn, 2000
Elizabeth Prettejohn, The Art of the Pre-
Raphaelites, London, 2000

Proctor, 1997
Helen Proctor, The Holy Grail Tapestries,
Birmingham, 1997

Roberts, 1997
Leonard Roberts, Arthur Hughes: His Life and
Works, A Catalogue Raisonné, Woodbridge, 1997

Robertson, 1988
Alexander W. Robertson, Atkinson Grimshaw,
Oxford, 1988

Rossetti, 1965–67
The Letters of Dante Gabriel Rossetti, Oswald
Doughty and John Robert Wahl (eds), 4 vols,
Oxford, 1965–67

Ruskin, 1903–12
The Works of John Ruskin, E. T. Cook and
Alexander Wedderburn (eds), 39 vols,
London, 1903–12

Sewter, 1974–75
A. Charles Sewter, The Stained Glass of William
Morris and his Circle, 2 vols, London, 1974–75

Sketchley, 1909
R. E. D. Sketchley, The Art of J. W. Waterhouse
RA, London, 1909.

Smith, 1996
Alison Smith, The Victorian Nude: Sexuality,
Morality and Art, Manchester, 1996

Spielmann, 1898
M. H. Spielmann, Millais and His Works, London,
1898

Staley, 2001
Allen Staley, The Pre-Raphaelite Landscape,
2nd edn, London, 2001

Surtees, 1971
Virginia Surtees, The Paintings and Drawings of
Dante Gabriel Rossetti: A Catalogue Raisonné,
2 vols, Oxford, 1971

Swanson, 1990
Vern G. Swanson, The Biography and Catalogue
Raisonné of the Paintings of Sir Lawrence
Alma-Tadema, London, 1990

Trippi, 2002
Peter Trippi, J. W. Waterhouse, London, 2002

Vallance, 1894
Aymer Vallance, 'The Revival of Tapestry-
Weaving: An Interview with Mr. William Morris',
The Studio 3, July 1894, pp. 98–101

Vallance, 1897
Aymer Vallance, William Morris: His Art, His
Writings and His Public Life, London, 1897

Wentworth, 1978
Michael Wentworth, James Tissot: Catalogue
Raisonné of His Prints, Minneapolis, 1978

Wentworth, 1984
Michael Wentworth, James Tissot, Oxford, 1984

Wood, 1976
Christopher Wood, Victorian Panorama:
Paintings of Victorian Life, London, 1976

Wood, 1986
Christopher Wood, Tissot: The Life and Work of
Jacques Joseph Tissot, London, 1986

Photographic Acknowledgements

Index of Artists, Craftsmen and Manufacturers

Numerals in **bold** indicate pages with illustrations

The Marchioness of Dufferin and Ava
Mr Hani Farsi
Hirsh London
Ken and Dora Howard
The Lark Trust
Mrs Lore Lehmann
Mr John Martin
Claus and Susan Moehlmann
Miranda Page-Wood
N Peal Cashmere
The Worshipful Company of Painter-Stainers
Pickett
Peter Rice Esq
Mr Iain Henderson Russell
Mr and Mrs Anthony Salz
Mr and Mrs Robert Lee Sterling Jr
The Peter Storrs Trust
Mr and Mrs Denis Tinsley
and others who wish to remain anonymous

GENERAL BENEFACTORS
Mr and Mrs John Coombe
Miss Jayne Edwardes
P H Holt Charitable Trust
The Ingram Trust
The Catherine Lewis Foundation
Sally and Donal Main
and others who wish to remain anonymous

American Associates of the Royal Academy Trust

MAJOR BENEFACTORS
The Annenberg Foundation
Mr and Mrs Sid R Bass
The Brown Foundation Inc, Houston
Citigroup
Mr Edwin L Cox
Mr and Mrs Eugene V Fife
Mr Francis Finlay
Mrs Henry Ford II
The Drue Heinz Trust
The Horace W Goldsmith Foundation
Mr and Mrs Donald P Kahn
Mrs Katherine K Lawrence
The Henry Luce Foundation
Mr and Mrs John L Marion
Mr and Mrs Jack C Massey
Mr Hamish Maxwell
Mr and Mrs George McFadden
The Estate of Paul Mellon KBE
Ms Diane A Nixon
Leon B Polsky and Cynthia Hazen Polsky
Mrs Arthur M Sackler
Mrs Edmond J Safra
Mrs Louisa S Sarofim
Ms Kathleen D Smith
The Starr Foundation
Mr and Mrs Robert Lee Sterling Jr
Alfred Taubman
Mr and Mrs Vernon Taylor Jr
The Eugene and Clare Thaw Charitable Trust
The Honourable John C Whitehead
Mr and Mrs Frederick B Whittemore

BENEFACTORS
Mr and Mrs Herbert S Adler
The Blackstone Group
Mr and Mrs Roderick C Gow
Mrs Melville Wakeman Hall
Ms Frances S Hayward
Mrs Jeanne K Lawrence
Sony Corporation of America

SPONSORS
Mrs Deborah Brice
Mrs Jan Cowles
Mr and Mrs Marvin Davidson
Lady Fairfax
Mrs Katherine D W Findlay
Mrs Eva G de Garza Laguera
David Hockney, RA
Mr James M Kemper Jr
Mrs John P McGrath
Mr David McKee
Mr David Murdock
Mrs Milton Petrie
Mr and Mrs William Rayner
Mr and Mrs John R Robinson
Mr Richard Steinwurtzel
Arthur Ochs Sulzberger and Allison Stacey Cowles
Virgin Atlantic

PATRONS
Ms Helen Harting Abell
Mr and Mrs Steven Ausnit
Elizabeth and Stephen Bechtel Jr Foundation
Mr and Mrs Raphael Bernstein
Mr Donald A Best
Mr and Mrs Henry W Breyer III
Mrs Mildred C Brinn
Jane and Robert Carroll
Mr and Mrs Benjamin Coates
Ms Anne S Davidson
Ms Zita Davisson
Ambassador Enriquillo and Mrs Audrey Z del Rosario
Mrs Charles H Dyson
Mrs A Barlow Ferguson
Mrs Robert Ferst
Mr Richard E Ford
Mrs Raymond C Foster
The William Fox Jr Foundation
Mr and Mrs Lawrence S Friedland
Eleanor and Eugene Goldberg
Mrs Betty Gordon
Mrs David Granger
Mrs Rachel K Grody
Mr and Mrs Martin D Gruss
Mrs Richard L Harris
Gurnee and Marjorie Hart
Mr Edward H Harte
Mr and Mrs Gustave M Hauser
Dr Bruce C Horten
Mr Robert J A Irwin
The Honorable and Mrs W Eugene Johnston III
Mr William W Karatz
Mr and Mrs Stephen M Kellen
Mr and Mrs Gary A Kraut
Ambassador and Mrs Philip Lader
Mrs Kay Lawrence
Mr and Mrs William D Lese
William M and Sarah T Lese Family Fund
Mr Arthur L Loeb
Mrs Barbara T Missett
Mr Allen Model
Mr and Mrs Paul S Morgan
Mr Paul D Myers
Mr and Mrs Wilson Nolen
Mrs Richard D O'Connor
Mr and Mrs Jeffrey Pettit
Mr Robert S Pirie
Dr and Mrs James S Reibel
Mrs Frances G Scaife
Ms Jan Scholes
Mr and Mrs Stanley DeForest Scott
Ms Georgia Shreve
Mrs Frederick M Stafford
Mr and Mrs Stephen Stamas
Ms Brenda Neubauer Straus
Mrs Matilda Gray Stream
Elizabeth F Stribling
Mrs Royce Deane Tate
Mrs Britt Tidelius
Mrs Richard Barclay Tullis
Ms Sue Erpf Van de Bovenkamp
Mrs William M Weaver Jr
Ms Deborah White
Mr and Mrs George White
Mrs Sara E White
Dr and Mrs Robert D Wickham
Mr and Mrs Robert G Wilmers
Mr Robert W Wilson
Mr and Mrs Kenneth Woodcock
and others who wish to remain anonymous

Corporate Membership of the Royal Academy of Arts

Launched in 1988, the Royal Academy's Corporate Membership Scheme has proved highly successful. Corporate membership offers company benefits to staff and clients and access to the Academy's facilities and resources. Each member pays an annual subscription to be a Member (£7,000) or Patron (£20,000). Participating companies recognise the importance of promoting the visual arts. Their support is vital to the continuing success of the Academy.

Corporate Membership Scheme

CORPORATE PATRONS
Ashurst Morris Crisp
Bloomberg LP
BNP Paribas
B. P.
Debenhams Retail plc
Deutsche Bank AG
Ernst and Young
GlaxoSmithKline plc
Granada plc
John Lewis Partnership
Merrill Lynch
Radisson Edwardian Hotels
Standard Chartered Bank

CORPORATE MEMBERS
Apax Partners Holding Ltd
Atos KPMG Consulting
Bear, Stearns International Ltd
The Boston Consulting Group
Bovis Lend Lease Limited
The British Land Company PLC
Bunzl plc
Cantor Fitzgerald
CB Hillier Parker
Cedar Communications
Christie's
Chubb Insurance Company of Europe
Citigroup
CJA (Management Recruitment Consultants) Limited
Clifford Chance
Credit Agricole Indosuez
De Beers
Diageo plc
Dresdner Kleinwort Wasserstein
F&C Management plc
Fleming Family & Partners
GAM
Goldman Sachs International
Hay Group
Herdez Europa
Hewitt, Bacon and Woodrow
H J Heinz Company Limited
HSBC plc
King Sturge
KPMG
LECG
Man Group plc
Mizuho International
Morgan Stanley
MoMart Ltd
Pearson plc
The Peninsular and Oriental Steam Navigation Company
Pentland Group plc
Raytheon Systems Limited
Reed Elsevier Group plc
The Royal Bank of Scotland
Schroders & Co
Sea Containers Ltd.
SG
Six Continents PLC
Skanska Construction Group Limited
Slaughter and May
The Smith & Williamson Group
Travelex
Trowers & Hamlins
Unilever UK Limited
Veolia Water
Weil Gotschal & Manges
Zurich Financial Services

HONORARY CORPORATE PATRON
ABN AMRO

HONORARY CORPORATE MEMBERS
All Nippon Airways Co. Ltd
A.T. Kearney Limited
Derwent Valley Holdings plc
London First
Yakult UK Limited

Supporters of Past Exhibitions

The President and Council of the Royal Academy would like to thank the following sponsors and benefactors for their generous support of major exhibitions during the last ten years:

ABN AMRO
Masterpieces from Dresden, 2003
Allied Trust Bank
Africa: The Art of a Continent, 1995*
Anglo American Corporation of South Africa
Africa: The Art of a Continent, 1995*
A.T. Kearney
231st Summer Exhibition, 1999
232nd Summer Exhibition, 2000
233rd Summer Exhibition, 2001
234th Summer Exhibition, 2002
The Banque Indosuez Group
Pissarro: The Impressionist and the City, 1993
Barclays
Ingres to Matisse: Masterpieces of French Painting, 2001
BBC Radio 3
Paris: Capital of the Arts 1900–1968, 2001
BMW (GB) Limited
Georges Rouault: The Early Years, 1903–1920, 1993
David Hockney: A Drawing Retrospective, 1995*
British Airways Plc
Africa: The Art of a Continent, 1995
British American Tobacco
Aztecs, 2002
Cantor Fitzgerald
From Manet to Gauguin: Masterpieces from Swiss Private Collections, 1995
1900: Art at the Crossroads, 2000
The Capital Group Companies
Drawings from the J Paul Getty Museum, 1993
Chase Fleming Asset Management
The Scottish Colourists 1900–1930, 2000
Chilstone Garden Ornaments
The Palladian Revival: Lord Burlington and His House and Garden at Chiswick, 1995
Christie's
Frederic Leighton 1830–1896, 1996
Sensation: Young British Artists from The Saatchi Collection, 1997
Classic FM
Goya: Truth and Fantasy, The Small Paintings, 1994
The Glory of Venice: Art in the Eighteenth Century, 1994
Masters of Colour: Derain to Kandinsky. Masterpieces from The Merzbacher Collection, 2002
Masterpieces from Dresden, 2003
Corporation of London
Living Bridges, 1996
Country Life
John Soane, Architect: Master of Space and Light, 1999
Credit Suisse First Boston
The Genius of Rome 1592–1623, 2000
The Daily Telegraph
American Art in the 20th Century, 1993
1900: Art at the Crossroads, 2000
De Beers
Africa: The Art of a Continent, 1995
Debenhams Retail plc
Premiums and RA Schools Show, 1999
Premiums and RA Schools Show, 2000
Premiums and RA Schools Show, 2001
Premiums and RA Schools Show, 2002
Deutsche Morgan Grenfell
Africa: The Art of a Continent, 1995
Diageo plc
230th Summer Exhibition, 1998
The Drue Heinz Trust
The Palladian Revival: Lord Burlington and His House and Garden at Chiswick, 1995
Denys Lasdun, 1997
Tadao Ando: Master of Minimalism, 1998
The Dupont Company
American Art in the 20th Century, 1993
Ernst & Young
Monet in the 20th Century, 1999
Eyestorm
Apocalypse: Beauty and Horror in Contemporary Art, 2000
Fidelity Foundation
The Dawn of the Floating World (1650–1765). Early Ukiyo-e Treasures from the Museum of Fine Arts, Boston, 2001
Friends of the Royal Academy
Victorian Fairy Painting, 1997
Game International Limited
Forty Years in Print: The Curwen Studio and Royal Academicians, 2001
The Jacqueline and Michael Gee Charitable Trust
LIFE? or THEATRE? The Work of Charlotte Salomon, 1999
Générale des Eaux Group
Living Bridges, 1996
Glaxo Wellcome plc
The Unknown Modigliani, 1994
Goldman Sachs International
Alberto Giacometti, 1901–1966, 1996
Picasso: Painter and Sculptor in Clay, 1998
The Guardian
The Unknown Modigliani, 1994
Guinness PLC (see Diageo plc)
225th Summer Exhibition, 1993
226th Summer Exhibition, 1994
227th Summer Exhibition, 1995
228th Summer Exhibition, 1996
229th Summer Exhibition, 1997
Harpers & Queen
Georges Rouault: The Early Years, 1903–1920, 1993
Sandra Blow, 1994
David Hockney: A Drawing Retrospective, 1995*
Roger de Grey, 1996
The Headley Trust
Denys Lasdun, 1997
The Henry Moore Foundation
Africa: The Art of a Continent, 1995
Ibstock Building Products Ltd
John Soane, Architect: Master of Space and Light, 1999
The Independent
Living Bridges, 1996
Apocalypse: Beauty and Horror in Contemporary Art, 2000
International Asset Management
Frank Auerbach, Paintings and Drawings 1954–2001, 2001
Donald and Jeanne Kahn
John Hoyland, 1999
Land Securities PLC
Denys Lasdun, 1997
The Mail on Sunday
Royal Academy Summer Season, 1993
Marks & Spencer
Royal Academy Schools Premiums, 1994
Royal Academy Schools Final Year Show, 1994*
Martini & Rossi Ltd
The Great Age of British Watercolours, 1750–1880, 1993
Paul Mellon KBE
The Great Age of British Watercolours, 1750–1880, 1993
Merrill Lynch
American Art in the 20th Century, 1993*
Paris: Capital of the Arts 1900–1968, 2001
Mexico Tourism Board
Aztecs, 2002
Midland Bank plc
RA Outreach Programme, 1993–1996
Lessons in Life, 1994
Minorco
Africa: The Art of a Continent, 1995
Natwest Group
Nicolas Poussin 1594–1665, 1995
The Nippon Foundation
Hiroshige: Images of Mist, Rain, Moon and Snow, 1997
Peterborough United Football Club
Art Treasures of England: The Regional Collections, 1997
Pemex
Aztecs, 2002
Premiercare (National Westminster Insurance Services)
Roger de Grey, 1996*
RA Exhibition Patrons Group
Chagall: Love and the Stage, 1998
Kandinsky, 1999
Chardin 1699–1779, 2000
Botticelli's Dante: The Drawings for Dante's Divine Comedy, 2001
Return of the Buddha: The Qingzhou Discoveries, 2002
Reed Elsevier plc
Van Dyck 1599–1641, 1999
Rembrandt's Women, 2001
The Royal Bank of Scotland
Braque: The Late Works, 1997*
Premiums, 1997
Premiums, 1998
Premiums, 1999
Royal Academy Schools Final Year Show, 1996
Royal Academy Schools Final Year Show, 1997
Royal Academy Schools Final Year Show, 1998
Virginia and Simon Robertson
Aztecs, 2002
The Sara Lee Foundation
Odilon Redon: Dreams and Visions, 1995
Sea Containers Ltd
The Glory of Venice: Art in the Eighteenth Century, 1994
Silhouette Eyewear
Sandra Blow, 1994
Africa: The Art of a Continent, 1995
Société Générale, UK
Gustave Caillebotte: The Unknown Impressionist, 1996*
Société Générale de Belgique
Impressionism to Symbolism: The Belgian Avant-garde 1880–1900, 1994
Thames Water Plc
Thames Water Habitable Bridge Competition, 1996
The Times
Drawings from the J Paul Getty Museum, 1993
Goya: Truth and Fantasy, The Small Paintings, 1994
Africa: The Art of a Continent, 1995
Time Out
Sensation: Young British Artists from The Saatchi Collection, 1997
Apocalypse: Beauty and Horror in Contemporary Art, 2000
Tractabel
Impressionism to Symbolism: The Belgian Avant-garde 1880–1900, 1994
Union Minière
Impressionism to Symbolism: The Belgian Avant-garde 1880–1900, 1994
Walker Morris
Premiums, 2003
Royal Academy Schools Final Year Show, 2003
Yakult UK Ltd
RA Outreach Programme, 1997–2002*
alive: Life Drawings from the Royal Academy of Arts & Yakult Outreach Programme

*Recipients of a Pairing Scheme Award, managed by Arts + Business. Arts + Business is funded by the Arts Council of England and the Department for Culture, Media and Sport.

Other Sponsors

Sponsors of events, publications and other items in the past five years:

Carlisle Group plc
Country Life
Derwent Valley Holdings plc
Dresdner Kleinwort Wasserstein
Fidelity Foundation
Foster and Partners
Goldman Sachs International
Gome International
Gucci Group
Rob van Helden
IBJ International plc
John Doyle Construction
Marks & Spencer
Michael Hopkins & Partners
Morgan Stanley Dean Witter
Prada
Radisson Edwardian Hotels
Richard and Ruth Rogers
Strutt & Parker